D1596455

When Movies Mattered

Reviews from a Transformative Decade

DAVE KEHR

The University of Chicago Press CHICAGO AND LONDON

Dave Kehr moved to the *Chicago Tribune* after leaving the *Chicago Reader* in 1986, and he was its principal film critic until 1992, when he moved to New York. His work has appeared regularly in *Film Comment*, and he is a member of the National Society of Film Critics.

The University of Chicago Press, Chicago 60637
The University of Chicago Press, Ltd., London

Printed in the United States of America

20 19 18 17 16 15 14 13 12 11   1 2 3 4 5

ISBN-13: 978-0-226-42940-3 (cloth)
ISBN-13: 978-0-226-42941-0 (paper)
ISBN-10: 0-226-42940-7 (cloth)
ISBN-10: 0-226-42941-5 (paper)

Kehr, Dave.
When movies mattered : reviews from a transformative decade / Dave Kehr.
p. cm.
Includes index.
ISBN-13: 978-0-226-42940-3 (cloth : alk. paper)
ISBN-10: 0-226-42940-7 (cloth : alk. paper)
ISBN-13: 978-0-226-42941-0 (pbk. : alk. paper)
ISBN-10: 0-226-42941-5 (pbk. : alk. paper)
1. Motion pictures—Reviews. I. Title.
PN1995.K395 2011
791.43'75—dc22
2010029462

♾ The paper used in this publication meets the minimum requirements of the American National Standard for Information Sciences—Permanence of Paper for Printed Library Materials, ANSI Z39.48-1992.

CONTENTS

Acknowledgments · vii
Introduction · 1

Part 1: The Best

1974: *Le Petit théâtre de Jean Renoir* (Jean Renoir) · 13
1976: *Family Plot* (Alfred Hitchcock) · 16
1977: *F for Fake* (Orson Welles) · 19
1978: *Days of Heaven* (Terrence Malick) · 23
1979: *10* (Blake Edwards) · 28
1981: *Melvin and Howard* (Jonathan Demme) · 35
1982: *The Aviator's Wife* (Eric Rohmer) · 40
1983: *Francisca* (Manoel de Oliveira) · 44

Part 2: The End of Classical Hollywood

CLASSICAL HOLLYWOOD
The Man Who Would Be King (John Huston) · 52
Fedora (Billy Wilder) · 55
Escape From Alcatraz (Don Siegel) · 58
The Human Factor (Otto Preminger) · 61

NEW HOLLYWOOD
The Driver (Walter Hill) · 67
Halloween (John Carpenter) · 72
Reds (Warren Beatty) · 75
Sudden Impact (Clint Eastwood) · 79

NEW DIRECTIONS IN COMEDY
Victor/Victoria (Blake Edwards) · 85
Risky Business (Paul Brickman) · 91
Lost in America (Albert Brooks) · 95
After Hours (Martin Scorsese) · 100

MAVERICKS AND OUTSIDERS
Dawn of the Dead (George Romero) · 106
The Big Red One (Samuel Fuller) · 112
Love Streams (John Cassavetes) · 116
Trouble in Mind (Alan Rudolph) · 122

Part 3: Other Visions

OLD MASTERS

Blaise Pascal (Roberto Rossellini) · 130
A Piece of Pleasure (Claude Chabrol) · 132
That Obscure Object of Desire (Luis Buñuel) · 135
Perceval (Eric Rohmer) · 139

GODARD

Numéro deux · 144
Every Man for Himself · 149
Passion · 154
Detective · 158

NEW MASTERS

Jonah Who Will Be 25 in the Year 2000 (Alain Tanner) · 163
The Memory of Justice (Marcel Ophuls) · 167
Allegro non troppo (Bruno Bozzetto) · 171
The American Friend (Wim Wenders) · 174
Loulou (Maurice Pialat) · 178
Eijanaika (Shohei Imamura) · 182
Coup de torchon (Bertrand Tavernier) · 186
City of Pirates (Raul Ruiz) · 190

Part 4: Revivals and Retrospectives

The Story of the Last Chrysanthemums (Kenji Mizoguchi) · 197
The Flowers of St. Francis (Roberto Rossellini) · 201
Born in Germany, Raised in Hollywood: The Film Art of Fritz Lang · 204
Record of a Tenement Gentleman (Yasujiro Ozu) · 210
Peeping Tom (Michael Powell) · 214
Othello (Orson Welles) · 219
Crisis, Compulsion, and Creation: Raoul Walsh's Cinema of the Individual · 223
A Love That Caresses the Soul: Films by Carl Theodor Dreyer · 228
When a Woman Ascends the Stairs (Mikio Naruse) · 234
Le Silence de la mer and *Bob le Flambeur* (Jean-Pierre Melville) · 238
The Leopard (Luchino Visconti) · 242
Hitch's Riddle: On Five Rereleased Films · 247
Once Upon a Time in the West (Sergio Leone) · 264
French Cancan (Jean Renoir) · 269

Appendix: Top Ten Lists, 1974–86 · 275
Index of Names · 279
Index of Titles · 285

ACKNOWLEDGMENTS

This collection wouldn't have been possible without the patience and dedication of the many fine editors I worked with at the *Chicago Reader*. I owe a particular debt to Pat Clinton and Mike Lenehan. My editor at the University of Chicago Press, Rodney Powell, has been a constant source of encouragement. And I'll never be able to repay Martha Johnston for her efforts in excavating this material from the *Reader* archives. For that, and for the lifetime of friendship she has offered me, I gratefully dedicate this book to her.

Introduction

This book brings together a number of movie reviews written a long time ago and in a cultural context very different from the one we know today. If these pieces still have any interest, and I hope they do, it's in large part because they belong to a precious but transient moment in film criticism—before journalism and academia went their widely different ways and it was briefly possible to write about films with serious intent for a wide, popular audience.

The articles in this collection range from 1974 to 1986, a period that saw the emergence of both the so-called film generation—bred out of campus film societies and busy commercial art theaters—and the so-called alternative press, an extension of the underground newspapers of the flower power era into for-profit respectability. Publications like the *SoHo Weekly News*, the *Los Angeles Weekly*, the *San Francisco Bay Guardian*, and the paper where I was lucky enough to be hired as the first staff film critic, the *Chicago Reader*, discovered a formula that largely liberated them from the need to tailor editorial content to the narrow interests of a target audience.

By hooking readers on service features such as extensive event listings and free classified advertising, these publications could allow themselves a certain indulgence when it came to the topics (and lengths) of feature articles and reviews. The *Reader* could comfortably place a fifty thousand-word story about beekeeping on the front page, secure in the knowledge that readers would pick up the paper in any case in order to look for an apartment or learn what band was playing at their favorite club. Working on that principle, it was easy to slip in a two thousand-word review of a three-hour film by a forgotten Portuguese director (*Francisca*, 1981) or an experimental work by an exiled Chilean filmmaker (*City of Pirates*, 1985); if the readers weren't interested, they could always turn directly to the lonelyhearts ads in the back of the paper.

But the true stroke of genius for the alternative press lay in the decision to give its publications away for free—foregoing a thirty-five-cent cover price (most of which would be eaten up by the costs of collection and accounting) in favor of drawing a large circulation. In effect, the alternative publishers were no longer in the business of selling newspapers to readers, but of selling readers to advertisers.

This was a strategy that worked wonderfully well, at least until it was adopted by the new generation of Internet entrepreneurs that emerged in the 90s. Unburdened by the expense of printing and distribution (and eventually, it seems, of paying contributors a living wage), the Internet sites could deliver "eyeballs" to advertisers even more efficiently than the alternative weeklies. As I write this, most of the weeklies that prospered in the late twentieth century are barely hanging on in the early twenty-first. The luxury of printing long pieces without an obvious demographic appeal is something the weeklies can no longer afford—while, paradoxically, it is a privilege that the Web has actively refused. Although space would seem to be the Net's cheapest and most extensive resource, it's rare to find a critical piece that runs to more than a couple of hundred words, even on the sites specifically devoted to film reviews.

As a result, the long-form journalistic review has practically vanished from print publications. Even the *New Yorker*, the last redoubt for sustained critical essays in the popular press, has cut back drastically on the space devoted to film reviews: if Pauline Kael were writing for that publication today, she would barely be able to clear her throat without using up her allotment for the week.

The loss is a significant one, if only because, without the long form review, we'd be deprived not only of Kael's outpourings in the *New Yorker* (the secret model, with its judicious blend of service features and willfully esoteric journalism, for much of the alternative press), but also of the work of Sam Adams, David Ansen, Stuart Byron, Godfrey Cheshire, Richard Corliss, Manohla Dargis, David Denby, David Edelstein, Scott Foundas, Chris Fujiwara, Owen Gleiberman, Molly Haskell, J. Hoberman, Richard Jameson, Lisa Kennedy, Peter Keough, Stuart Klawans, Andy Klein, Dennis Lim, Janet Maslin, George Morris, Gerald Peary, John Powers, Peter Rainer, Ruby Rich, Carrie Rickey, Jonathan Rosenbaum, Lisa Schwarzbaum, Matt Zoller Seitz, Henry Sheehan, Michael Sragow, Amy Taubin, Charles Taylor, Ella Taylor, Stephanie Zacharek, and many other insightful critics whose careers began and passed through or prospered at the alternative weeklies.

But when a format disappears, sometimes a way of thinking disappears with it. At the moment, American movie criticism seems divided (with some exceptions) between two poles: quick-hit, consumerist sloganeering on Internet review sites and television shows, and full-bore academia, with its dense, uninviting thickets of theoretical jargon. The interested reader has few places to turn in hopes of getting a quick leg up on the work of Pedro Costa or Jia Zhang-ke, to name two working filmmakers whose celebrity would have been assured during the heyday of the alternative press, and consequently their films remain off the radar for most nonprofessional viewers, barely distributed in the United States either theatrically or on home video. Mainstream print publications no longer have the space to cover cultural subjects in depth; the Internet doesn't have the interest; and academia, at least along its postmodernist branch, has, in the name of overturning the Romantic notion of an all-powerful, autonomous creator, put the author to death. With the vanishing of that despised figure—so often and unfashionably white, male, and heterosexual—has gone perhaps the simplest, most empirically satisfying way of connecting an audience to a work of art: though a human figure. The author may be a fiction, but he or she remains a most useful one.

The pages that follow are full of authors, artists, and auteurs—as well as a whole range of concomitantly naive notions of self-expression, poetic transcendence, and form considered in hopeless isolation from ideology. In the early 70s, theory had just started to surface in the suddenly ascetic pages of *Cahiers du cinéma*—no more pictures!—and between the insistently stiff covers of the British publication *Screen*. I had been exposed to a few of the basic concepts of what was then still called "structuralism" through forward-looking professors in the English Department of the University of Chicago, and at a certain point word went out in cinephilic circles that it was now de rigueur to read Roland Barthes and Christian Metz. Attempts were duly made, but it soon became clear that any real progress in this direction would require mastery of Marx, Freud, and advanced linguistics, something clearly beyond my patience and mental powers. Forty years later, it still is. I'm sure my experience of the cinema has been shaped by theory in more ways than I am aware of. But I have always felt more comfortable talking about films than Film, a prejudice I acquired early on from the pages of a slim, white volume that appeared one day on a shelf in the suburban Chicago library near my home. Titled *The American Cinema*, it joined a dozen or so other books in the small film section. Among them were, most memorably, William K. Everson's *The Western*, Griffith and Mayer's *The Movies*, and Daniel Blum's *Pictorial History of the Silent Screen*, all of which I had checked out and pored over countless times in the first burst of my adolescent film buffery.

But this book was different. There were no illustrations in it, and it was largely concerned with a class of film artist of which I was just becoming aware. As a kid, I'd loved the silent comedians and had a particular fondness for Laurel and Hardy; as a teenager I had just discovered *Citizen Kane*, with its full stock of wonderful tricks and shifting moods. Orson Welles was my new hero, and I was gratified to find that the author of *The American Cinema* had included him in a category called "Pantheon Directors." But who were these other people?

I knew Keaton and Chaplin, of course, and Hitchcock was the funny fat man on TV who made movies (*Psycho, The Birds, Marnie*) I wasn't allowed to see. I knew Griffith's name from the other books, though apparently his movies could only be seen at a far-off place in New York City called the Museum of Modern Art. The others—Flaherty, Ford, Hawks, Lang, Lubitsch, Murnau, Ophuls, Renoir, Sternberg—were new to me, but the suggestion that they were peers of the great Orson was enough to fire my enthusiasm. I memorized their filmographies and read and reread the compact, epigrammatic essays that the author, one Andrew Sarris, had appended to them. To my fourteen-year-old self, these lists of titles were like posters in a travel office, representations of exotic places I hoped to visit some day but for the moment remained remote and inaccessible.

Mysteriously, the city fathers of my hometown, the bedroom suburb of Palatine, Illinois, had neglected to establish a local cinematheque. But we did have WGN, the locally owned (by the *Chicago Tribune*) television station, which had a Sunday late-night slot set aside for classic Hollywood films, as well as the erratic overnight programming on the network affiliates. Armed with the newspaper television listings, a well-thumbed copy of *The American Cinema*, and a functioning alarm clock, the dedicated teenage cinephile could see a range of movies that seems amazing by contemporary standards—albeit in the dead of night on a nine-inch black-and-white screen. This was probably not the best way to encounter, say, Sternberg's *The Devil Is a Woman* for the first time (which arrived courtesy of a classic movie series hosted on the *Sun-Times* station, WFLD, by Chicago's leading drama critic, Richard Christiansen). But I took as much pleasure seeing it then, my nose pressed up against the tiny screen in my bedroom, as I did when I finally saw it many years later in a fully restored 35-millimeter print.

By the time I made it to the University of Chicago in 1971, I was thoroughly obsessed with film. My choice of college had been dictated first by a vague plan to earn an advanced degree in English literature that might allow me to find a teaching job someday and second by the fact that the University of Chicago was home to a wonderful institution called the Documentary Film Group.

Doc Films, as it was affectionately and universally known, was (and continues to be) the oldest student-run film society in the United States, having been founded in 1932 by (as the vaguely Soviet name suggests) a coalition of left-leaning activists dedicated to the then-current notion that documentary films could be an agent of social change. By the early 1960s, however, it had become the first university film society to go whole hog for auteurism, thanks to a group member who had returned from a trip to Paris with suitcases stuffed full of back numbers of *Cahiers du cinéma* and *Positif*. At Doc Films, I met people who not only knew who John Ford and Howard Hawks were, but who could recite the filmographies of Edgar G. Ulmer and Joseph H. Lewis from memory, describe individual shots from forgotten B-movies in rapturous detail, and call up pages of complex dialogue at will.

Andrew Sarris, of course, was a god to us. Every Doc Films member carried a paperback copy of *The American Cinema*, invariably wrapped with rubber bands to compensate for the Dutton edition's flimsy binding. As you worked your way through each filmography, you would underline the titles you had seen. This dedication to a sacred text was something we shared with some of the other cultists then proliferating on the proudly radical campus—the humorless Maoists, with their Little Red Books.

But apart from envying the sleek plastic binding that the Chinese had wisely provided for the words of their helmsman, we had little to do with the political groups. Firm believers in Sarris's dedication to the trees rather than the forest, we were determined to rescue film culture from the sociologists and ideologues who then dominated the small amount of serious literature on the subject. For us, the best movies were those that reflected the sensibility of a single artist—namely, a director who could shepherd all of the various elements that constituted the cinematic product, both human (actors, technicians, screenwriters) and cultural (genre conventions and industrial economics), into a distinctive vision.

Today, that notion may seem both commonplace and quaint, but in the early 1970s it was enough to unleash passions on an epic scale. What riled people was not the idea that directors could conceivably be "authors" of films—a notion that dates back to D. W. Griffith—but that claims of artistic significance were being made for vulgar Hollywood product. Hollywood, as everyone knew, was the world capital of crassness and cheap commercialism, the place art went to die—and F. Scott Fitzgerald and Nathanael West were there to tell us all about it, in cruel detail.

And so, to suggest that films such as *Vertigo* and *The Searchers* were something other than obvious potboilers—as Sarris and the Sarrisites, following the example of the young French critics, had begun to do—was to challenge an entire ingrained belief system. Auteurism openly attacked the assumption that the European cinema was more emotionally mature and intellectually sophisticated than its adolescent Hollywood counterpart; that the East Coast literary establishment enjoyed an obvious moral and intellectual superiority over the West Coast movie crowd; and that a popular art form was inherently inferior to the elitist culture of the theater, museum, and concert hall.

When the discussion could be lured away from the safe, brightly lit terrain of A-list directors like Hitchcock and Ford and down the dark and dangerous back alleys of B-moviemakers like Edgar G. Ulmer and Joseph H. Lewis, it was generally enough for the anti-auteurist forces to cite a few titles—like Ulmer's *Babes in Bagdad* or Lewis's *Gun Crazy*—to carry the day. Nothing so lurid could possibly be taken seriously. But, as Sarris suggested in his introduction to *The American Cinema*, auteurism depends on a see-for-yourself curiosity rather than blanket dismissals of genres and styles. If, on close inspection, *Babes in Bagdad* turns out to be less momentous than *Ulysses* or *The Rite of Spring*, it remains a strange, sympathetic little film, poignantly illustrative of the lengths to which its doomed director would go in his determination to pursue his art against all odds. And if *Gun Crazy* turned out to be something like a masterpiece, new terms would have to be invented to account for it; the old literary standards just wouldn't do.

Looking back, it seems as if the auteurists lost a fair number of battles—particularly when the opponent was the wily Pauline Kael—but still resoundingly won the war. Hitchcock and Ford, and increasingly Ulmer and Lewis, are part of the syllabus of every Introduction to Film course, and even in postmodernist academia the pool of films under discussion continues largely to consist of the auteurist canon. In the end, even Kael seemed to come around, though her pantheon had its own distinctive population: not Hitchcock and Ford, but Brian de Palma and Philip Kaufman, as if she preferred the self-conscious imitation to the real thing.

Sarris, alas, was not all seeing. Published in 1968, which now seems so clearly a watershed year, *The American Cinema* offers few glimpses of the coming revolution. Arthur Penn, whose *Bonnie and Clyde* had in 1967 helped sound the death knell for classical Hollywood, appears only as a vague figure on the horizon; Sarris dismisses him in a few sentences for his early, not always successful attempts to merge Hollywood genres and East Coast theatrical aspirations. Francis Ford Coppola, whose 1972 *The Godfather* would open the studio gates to a new generation of university-trained directors, gets only a brief mention for his optimistically titled apprentice film, *You're a Big Boy Now*. Martin Scorsese, Robert Altman, Jerry Schatzberg, Steven Spielberg, and the rest of the founding figures of the "New American Cinema" of the 1970s make no appearance at all.

Perhaps Sarris suspected that the system he celebrated in *The American Cinema* had come to the end of its time; perhaps only at the moment of its passing could classical Hollywood be appreciated for the artistic marvels it had produced rather than dismissed for the commercial compromises and mountains of meretriciousness it had also yielded in abundance. In any case the American cinema would never be the same after the publication of *The American Cinema*: the richness and stability of the studio system, with its reliable formulas, balance of genres, and dependable audience, became a thing of the past.

If classical Hollywood operated like an assembly line, turning out product on a strict schedule to meet a largely predictable demand, the new Hollywood was more like a casino. Huge sums of money were bet on unknown filmmakers and unclassifiable screenplays, in the hope that one project out of twenty would hit the jackpot and turn a profit spectacular enough to make up for the losses on the others.

At first, the casino atmosphere was exhilarating. Anything seemed to be possible, much as it did in the similar period of chaos and uncertainty that accompanied the transition to talking films in 1927–30. A few young filmmakers, newly empowered by runaway hits, succeeded in imposing an exaggerated, European-flavored notion of authorship on American films. (Paradoxically, these young directors became known as "auteurs" in the popular press, appropriating a term of art originally intended to honor the humble studio craftsmen the new generation was determined to displace.)

But as the conspicuous commercial failures began to pile up—a category that included everything from deeply felt, personal films like Monte Hellman's *Two-Lane Blacktop* (1971) to seemingly surefire popular entertainments like Blake Edwards's *Darling Lili* (1970)—the inevitable reaction set in. In 1975, Steven Spielberg's *Jaws* pointed the way to a brutal new commercialism, based on saturation advertising on television and wide release patterns that bypassed the old downtown, first-run theaters in favor of suburban shopping malls. When George Lucas took the formula a step further with *Star Wars* (now and forever known as *Star Wars: Episode IV—A New Hope*) in 1977, the studios were happy and relieved to follow him. The wayward auteur was replaced with an almost fanatical adherence to the rules and regulations of juvenile genre filmmaking. Ancient Saturday morning formulas (horror, science-fiction, the action-adventure intrigues of the serials) were reproduced as simply as possible (though often with a new, protective edge of self-mocking knowingness) in the hope of providing visceral thrills for young filmgoers and nostalgic reveries for their parents. The adult dramas of the early 70s were banished from the multiplexes, as the Hollywood establishment concentrated on pleasing the taste of the average American fourteen-year-old boy.

That transformation, too, is part of the hidden storyline of this book. My tenure at the *Reader* (1974 to 1986) overlapped with the late stages of the transition from classical to postclassical Hollywood, which at the time felt more like a collapse into chaos than progress toward a new paradigm. A few lions of the old guard were still around, making their last films—Alfred Hitchcock (*Family Plot*), Billy Wilder (*Fedora*), Robert Aldrich (*Twilight's Last Gleaming*), Otto Preminger (*The Human Factor*)—to the general indifference of audiences and critics. Meanwhile, a new generation was rising that didn't seem to care for the classical virtues of a calibrated visual style and a carefully modulated narrative rhythm. Some of the newcomers seemed tremendously exciting—filmmakers such as John Cassavetes, Jonathan Demme, Martin Scorsese, Paul Schrader, and Albert Brooks—while others seemed to be flailing around, better at demolishing old models (Robert Altman, Brian De Palma, Bob Rafelson) than building new ones.

My fascination with the old way of doing things may well have blinded me to new developments. I never could muster much enthusiasm for the work of Woody Allen (*Annie Hall*), Bob Fosse (*All That Jazz*), Hal Ashby (*Coming Home*), Michael Mann (*Thief*), and the many other filmmakers of the period who seemed to be flying blind, with only a limited sense of the tradition that had produced them. I preferred filmmakers who built on the past, who seemed dedicated not to trampling on the classical model but trying to reconfigure it. The same year, 1976, in which Don Siegel and John Huston were creating elegiac genre films like *The Shootist* and *The Man Who Would Be King*, Walter Hill released his neonoir *The Driver* and Clint Eastwood delivered *The Outlaw Josey Wales*, both brilliant variations on old genre structures that opened established forms to new levels of stylization and moral insight. Thirty years later, Eastwood stands almost alone as a plausible candidate for the Last Classicist, perhaps the only working American filmmaker whose practical experience dates back to the 1950s.

My search for continuity led me to the work of John Carpenter, George Romero, and Joe Dante—all genre directors whose imaginations seemed liberated by the formal and thematic constraints imposed by the horror movie. In an important way, they seemed to enjoy more freedom than the big budget, mainstream moviemakers, like Spielberg, Lucas, Coppola, and Mike Nichols, whose work had to conform to an Oscar-friendly decorum. The new horror films were exempt from the unhealthy demands of good taste, and their examples were followed by a burgeoning field of low-budget, exploitation filmmakers. The 70s and early 80s would have been much less without the subversive genre pictures released by Roger Corman's New World Pictures (Paul Bartel's *Death Race 2000*, Stephanie Rothman's *The Velvet Vampire*, Michael Miller's *Jackson County Jail*), not to mention the even more obscure exploitation films that emerged from long-gone outfits like Crown International, Dimension Pictures, and Bryanston Distributing.

At the same time, the movie past was being rediscovered in a more systematic, better-funded way than ever before. It is during the 1980s that the film preservation movement got going in earnest, as institutions like the Museum of Modern Art, the Library of Congress, the British Film Institute, the Cinémathèque Française, the Deutsche Kinemathek, the Cineteca Bologna, George Eastman House, and the UCLA Film and Television Archive expanded their mission beyond the acquisition of vintage prints and into the brave new world of restorations. Cinephiles who had learned to be content with 16-millimeter collectors' prints and the battered inventories of the local studio exchanges could suddenly access the masterpieces of Sternberg and Griffith with something like their original visual qualities.

With these newly restored titles popping up at local museums, film societies, and even the occasional commercial theater (as was the case with Michael Powell's *Peeping Tom*, a disaster on its first release but an instant classic on its second), the past and the present commingled on the same repertory calendar. Old movies were never more with us, allowing scholarly filmmakers like Martin Scorsese, Peter Bogdanovich, and, in France, Bertrand Tavernier to build their work on firm foundations that would be immediately familiar to most filmgoers. This interest in the movie past was furthered by the explosive growth of home viewing in the wake of the VHS, and then DVD, revolution, which effectively all but destroyed repertory cinemas. But that's another story, played out after I left the *Reader* in 1986.

Some of the pieces in this book will seem naive or simply mistaken, and I have made no effort to cover up my errors of taste or fact, nor to smooth out my sometimes infelicitous prose. Still, I hope this volume will offer a sense of what it was like to live and work through a period of tumult and possibility, when movies were central to the cultural discourse, and we had the time and inclination to take them seriously.

A Note on the Selections

The introduction draws on my "An Auteurist Adolescence," originally published in *Citizen Sarris, American Film Critic*, edited by Emanuel Levy (Scarecrow Press, 2001).

The pieces selected for the first three parts of this book ("The Best," "The End of Classical Hollywood," and "Other Visions") are, with one exception, reviews of movies I included in my list of the top ten films of the year—in the case of "The Best," each film headed my list. The exception is the review of Godard's *Detective*, which I chose to include as a testament to his importance during this period. The selections within sections are arranged by date of publication.

Part 4 contains pieces on "Revivals and Retrospectives" that opened in Chicago during my years at the *Reader* and so allowed me to write about some of my favorite films and filmmakers. There's one "ringer" in this section: "Hitch's Riddle." Five of Hitchcock's films were rereleased in the fall of 1983, and "Hitch's Riddle," my revision and expansion of the reviews I wrote at that time, appeared in *Film Comment* in 1984.

The appendix contains my top ten list from each year of my *Reader* tenure; the list for 1986 was prepared for the *Chicago Tribune*, but I've included it since I was still at the *Reader* for much of the year.

A Final Note

I left the *Reader* to join the staff of the venerable *Chicago Tribune*, a daily newspaper with a long history and its own Gothic tower perched on Michigan Avenue. I recruited Jonathan Rosenbaum, an old friend from the festival circuit, to take my job at the *Reader*, where he continued to take full advantage of the freedoms of the alternative press to create an extraordinary body of original criticism, up to his (semi) retirement in 2008. The demands of the *Tribune* job were quite different from what I had been used to at the *Reader*: instead of writing extended reviews of one or two films a week, I was required to turn out shorter pieces on six or seven releases—whatever presented itself to the public each

Friday. What had been a nicely distanced, contemplative job turned into an adrenaline-fueled assignment on the front lines, where I had to contend with everything that came down the pike rather than picking and choosing my topics.

The *Tribune* gig afforded its own kind of pleasure and exhilaration—not so much that of doing a job well, but doing it on time—and I stayed with it for several years, eventually moving to New York to work for the tabloid *Daily News* in 1993. That experience, considerably less congenial, ended in 1999, and since then I have mostly been associated with the *New York Times*, where I have been writing reviews, Sunday think pieces, and (most gratifyingly) a weekly column on film history (lightly disguised as reviews of new DVDs). It's been a good run, and I wouldn't trade my daily newspaper experiences for anything. But the freedom I knew at the *Chicago Reader* is something I suspect I will never recover, mingled as it was with the energy of youth and the excitement of charging headlong into uncharted territory.

[PART 1]

The Best

These are pieces on my selections as the best film of each year. Because of the peculiarities of movie distribution in Chicago, I didn't always review my top choice in the Reader. *Curious readers can refer to the top ten lists collected in the appendix. List making may not be the most dignified or enduring of critical activities, but I find to my surprise that my regard for these choices hasn't changed substantially over the years.*

Le Petit théâtre de Jean Renoir

Directed by JEAN RENOIR {August 30, 1974}

The red plush curtain of the music hall stage rises with a classic solemnity as the pit orchestra begins the introduction to a song. Standing motionless in center stage, against a softly defined background of deep greens, warm yellows, subtle pinks, and elusive, almost ethereal blues, is the singer. It is Jeanne Moreau, dressed in a long white bustled gown of the 1890s, a vague suspicion of nervousness in the slight incline of her head, and in the way she holds a fan of white feathers spread across her shoulder. As Moreau begins to sing, her reservation disappears, her eyes glance downwards, the fan is gently closed, and her arm slides down to her side. In her low, familiar voice, she sings a sad, slow song, a song of love that has passed. The camera seems to answer the invitation in her look, and begins to approach the singer with a graceful restraint, until her face is finally held in a delicate close-up. Moreau does not look at us directly now. She holds her glance a little to our left, and only her lips seem to move, except for a barely perceptible tremor in her eyes as she sings a particularly personal line. This embrace can't last, it's too intimate, too intense to go on as we wish it could, and so the camera, after a few seconds, must leave her. She is perfectly still as the camera reluctantly glides away, finishing her song just as it crosses the footlights. The curtain descends, and then, the beautiful vision is gone.

This is Jean Renoir's brief evocation of "La Belle Epoque," a three-minute sequence from what will most likely be his last film, *Le Petit théâtre de Jean Renoir*. The film, which has only recently been acquired for American distribution, was made for French television in 1968. Today, six years later at the end of its three-month run in New York and the beginning of its Chicago engagement, *Le Petit théâtre* seems like a promise fulfilled. Now that all of the speculations have been cleared away, the film emerges as Renoir's last masterpiece. It is all that a final work should be: a reflection, an acceptance, and a conclusion. If Renoir's career has to end (he will be eighty this year), then let it end here. *Le Petit théâtre* is the proof that it is still possible to create beautiful films, even in a time that seems incapable of appreciating them.

"La Belle Epoque" is the third of four sketches which make up *Le Petit théâtre*. Unlike most compendium films, *Le Petit théâtre* is finally a unified whole, with all of the parts finding their places within a definite design. The first two sketches recall the two major subdivisions of Renoir's career, the third presents a summation and a synthesis, and the fourth an approval of the past and a look to the future. Renoir's last film becomes his aesthetic autobiography.

The first sketch finds its basis in an obscure Hans Christian Andersen story about a couple of elderly drifters who are treated to a banquet on Christmas Eve and then die in each other's arms on a snow-covered dock by the Seine. The theme and its treatment belong to Renoir's first, and still most popular, period, that of his pre-Hollywood realism. His apparently informal style, grounded in fluid camera movements, allows him to make a sudden turn in the middle of his narrative, executing that deft change in tone from Marxism to humanism characteristic of his early work. The second segment, about a middle class housewife's excessive devotion to her electric floor waxer, is a wild operatic farce recalling the style of Renoir's postwar work in its dismissal of conventional novelistic characterization in favor of the American use of archetypes and narrative compression. The contrast between the two sketches is central to Renoir's development as an artist. His obsession with realism waned during the years he spent in Hollywood as an exile (you can almost see the change taking place on screen in *This Land Is Mine*) as he discovered the greater thematic freedom allowed by greater stylization. And so, you have *La Grande illusion* on the one hand and *Elena et les hommes* on the other, two almost antithetical masterpieces.

The three minutes of "La Belle Epoque" have a nearly unbearable intensity on the screen. As he reminds us in his introduction, Renoir has always seen the nineties as a golden age of harmony and simplicity—the era reappears as his personal view of paradise in film after film. Against this background, Renoir sets the basic oppositions that have informed his filmmaking, the actor and the camera, the natural and the manufactured, the seen and the unseen, the realities of the theater and the illusions of life, and puts them into harmony as well. The movement of the camera conveys nothing less than the reconciliation of space and time directed towards the comprehension of the beautiful, adequately embodied here by Moreau.

Renoir returns to the pastoral genre for his concluding segment. An old, retired Navy man and his pretty young wife are living a life of blissful inactivity in a small village. The old man's estate is suffering a little from his benign neglect, but since he's clearly earned his indolence, his wife makes herself content with things the way they are. The couple comes to adopt a young doctor new to the village as their closest friend, and so, when the doctor (not surprisingly, but somehow, that's the point) turns out to enjoy nothing more than making himself useful around the house, life seems complete. Unfortunately, the doctor takes it upon himself to extend his duties to the care of the young wife as well. The gossip spreads fast in the town, and when the old man hears about the affair he seems totally destroyed. In a master stroke of common sense, though, he realizes that he loves both his wife and his friend too much to let something as small as this come between them. Just as he accepts the new dimension in his marriage, so do the people of the village, and a spontaneous celebration follows his public acknowledgment.

Renoir uses the conventions of the pastoral comedy to present a little parable on the birth of a new golden age, where all of the dictates of provincial tradition can be overruled by a sudden assertion of communal feeling. Underlying the irresistible sentiments of the parable, though, is a strongly implied allegory. The old man's physical and philosophical closeness to Renoir marks him clearly as the master himself, a man with the grace and intelligence to realize that the time has come when he must pass the love of his life, the cinema, on to younger hands. This last episode, which must be the most nearly perfect example of short film construction that we have to look to, shows with no room for doubt that Renoir can still please his old mistress. Jean Renoir's *Petit théâtre* is a play of moral, aesthetic, and metaphysical dimensions composed in the serenity of old age. And to experience that serenity, simply, is to experience the sublime.

Family Plot

Directed by ALFRED HITCHCOCK {April 9, 1976}

The only name on the opening credits of *Family Plot* is Alfred Hitchcock's—which, for once, is just as it should be. The mere actors, writers, and technicians have been banished to the end title. For most other directors, this might be unforgivable egotism, but for Hitchcock, his authorship is a simple fact. *Family Plot* belongs to Alfred Hitchcock no less than *Moby Dick* belongs to Herman Melville.

Not that *Family Plot* occupies the same level in Hitchcock's canon as *Moby Dick* does in Melville's. *Family Plot*, if you want to quibble, is second-rate Hitchcock; second-rate in the sense that it's not *Vertigo*, *Rear Window*, *Psycho*, or *The Birds*. But second-rate Hitchcock is still about ten times more interesting than first-rate Altman, Coppola, or Scorsese. There are things in *Family Plot* that we haven't seen in an American film in a long time; things like care, precision, and detail. *Family Plot* is probably the most beautifully crafted, thematically dense film that we're going to see this year.

In spite of its two-hour running time, *Family Plot* has the feel of a miniature. Bounded by its four main characters, the film doesn't have the epic sprawl of a *North by Northwest* or a *Topaz*. Instead, Hitchcock has concentrated on building an elaborate internal structure, playing off the permutations of the characters' relationships.

Continuing the dual narrative construction that began with *Shadow of a Doubt* (and reached one previous climax with the audacious midway break of *Psycho*), *Family Plot* follows two couples through two—at first—unrelated stories. Barbara Harris, a phony spiritualist, is trying to track down the lost heir to a family fortune with the help of her cabbie boyfriend, Bruce Dern. The missing heir, though, is now a professional kidnapper (William Devane), who heists millionaire industrialists and suchlike with the help of his respective lover, Karen Black. Following his custom, Hitchcock lets the audience in on the "mystery" early in the film (after 48 minutes, according to Joseph McBride's *Variety* count). The rest of *Family Plot* leads the two couples through an arabesque of coincidences and chance meetings, drawing them together only in the final reel.

Reinforcing the complicated narrative structure is a wonderfully detailed system of visual motifs. Hitchcock selects white as the key color for Dern and Harris, and black for Devane and Black—which is partly a joke on the melodramatic convention, but also a way of guiding the audience through the difficult thematic comparisons and contrasts Hitchcock wishes to make. Harris's character is named "Blanche," she drives a blindingly white Mustang, and, of course, she's a blonde. By underlining the identification of Harris with white, Hitchcock is able to bring off one of his best visual puns: late in the film, Dern is tipped that Harris has suffered some foul play not by the traditional trail of blood, but by a dribble of white paint running out from under a garage door. Compare the skill and subtlety with which Hitchcock realizes the color scheme in *Family Plot* with the coarseness of Ingmar Bergman's similar ploy in *Cries and Whispers*—the difference between a cinematic poet and a cinematic poseur.

Black and white, evil and good—this is how Hitchcock initially leads the audience to identify the characters. But that simple distinction, as it always does in Hitchcock's films, begins to break down. Through a series of strategic rhetorical moves, Hitchcock confuses the audience's positive identification, forcing us to share the guilt of the characters. Harris's crime—posing as a spiritualist—seems petty compared with Devane's abductions and murders. But guilt, for Hitchcock, is not a matter of degree. We're brought to see the "heroes" and the "villains" as two sides of the same psychological coin. The crystal ball associated with Harris is linked to the crystalline diamonds that Devane demands as ransom. When Hitchcock shows us the FBI hot on Devane's trail, our knee-jerk reaction is fear for his safety. Harris and Dern are lovable, bumbling children; Devane and Black are shrewd, sophisticated professionals. If we publicly empathize with one couple, we secretly admire the other—evil has an irresistible charm. We might like to think of ourselves more as the affable innocents that Harris and Dern embody, but lurking inside us all is Devane's criminal mastermind, fantasizing murders and robberies, fascinated with evil and its power. It's a part of ourselves that we've learned not to acknowledge, but it's just that barrier between ego and id that Hitchcock's films are dedicated to destroying.

Since *Family Plot* is, after all, a light comedy, we're not left with the horror of ourselves that many of Hitchcock's other films produce. Where *Frenzy* ends with a devastating glimpse into the heart of darkness—our "hero" commits a savage murder—*Family Plot* concludes with one small but comforting victory for the forces of "normality." It's the ending of *Family Plot*, I think, that most people are going to object to—it might seem too arbitrary and too easy. But the easiness may be deliberate, a way of emphasizing the tenuousness of the solution. The joking ambiguity of the final image—a wink addressed to the audience—is Hitchcock's way of acknowledging the game he's played with us, the perfect way for the Master to end what may well be his last film.

Family Plot is a movie filled with more incidental brilliancies than there's room to mention—the kidnapping of a bishop before a church filled with penitents, a slow chase through the Mondrian pattern formed by the paths of a graveyard, etc., etc. At once, it's a film of remarkable richness and remarkable economy. Not a single detail—a garden hose hung on a basement wall, for example—is placed without significance. I doubt that a dozen viewings would reduce its fascination one bit. *Family Plot* is made in a style that many will find anomalous or old fashioned. But if the exercise of care and craftsmanship is out of style—which it seems to be, judging from the reception that a mess like *Nashville* can get—then that's our loss, not Hitchcock's.

F for Fake

Directed by ORSON WELLES {October 14, 1977}

Orson Welles's long-awaited new film is a study in ambiguities, and Welles wastes no time getting down to business, offering three different possibilities for the film's title in its first few minutes. A title reading *F for Fake* has been spliced on before the action proper begins, looking suspiciously like a distributor's afterthought. A roll title, spinning a hundred printouts of the single word *Fake*, appears shortly after. And finally, there is a question mark, scrawled with a felt tipped pen over the face of an editing screen before the technical credits. Welles has compounded the problem by combining the last two choices, referring to the film as *Fake?* in some interviews. So what is the real title of *F for Fake*? *Fake*? *Fake??* Or *??* For the moment, I think I'll settle on *F for Fake*, just because it's the most obviously fake of the fake titles. The only way to get into Welles's wonderfully entertaining, half-playful and half-serious intellectual shell game (whatever it's called, it's playing Friday night, October 14, at the Midwest Film Center) is by seizing the paradox at the start.

F for Fake is a fake movie, assembled out of bits and pieces of new and old film stock—documentary footage, old newsreels (including some fake old newsreels), still photos, travel shots, paintings, television (including some fake television), radio (including some fake radio—Welles's *War of the Worlds* broadcast), and some special effects sequences from a 1950s science fiction film (tentatively identified as Fred F. Sears's immortal *Earth vs. the Flying Saucers*). Welles is credited as the director, but that might be a fake, too: most of the original footage was shot by the French documentarist François Reichenbach. Welles's personality completely dominates the material he has gathered from others; he is the "auteur" of the film in the most traditional 1950s *Cahiers du cinéma* sense. But Welles seems to be wondering, along with Pauline Kael in her introduction to *The Citizen Kane Book*, whether an auteur isn't just a fake author, putting his name on other people's work. We see an art forger signing Welles's name to a painting (and spelling it incorrectly)—an obvious fake, although ironically the painting is one that the forger has done in his "own" style. If he does a painting in Picasso's style, is it still his? If the painting is good enough to be a Picasso, is it a real Picasso or a fake? A work of art or a worthless forgery? Are the critics, who can't tell the difference, fakes too?

The relentless, inquisitory tone, discovering paradox behind paradox, sets the somewhat breathless pace of *F for Fake*, spinning a thousand related questions around a fundamental problem—what is the nature of the film? The days are long gone when Jean-Luc Godard could say that cinema was "truth 24 times a second." Under the influence of modernism, a movement that has belatedly seeped into film from literature, today's avant-garde would revise the slogan to "lies 24 times a second." Structuralist criticism has turned artistic interest from the content of the image to the image itself. No longer is photography naively presumed to capture "reality"—as Vladimir Nabokov once wrote, reality is the only word in the English language that means nothing unless it's surrounded by quotes. If we see the same object in a dozen different images, we see a dozen different objects—a dozen different points of view imposed by a dozen different observers. Does the object have any meaning divorced from a point of view? If it does, is that meaning its "reality"? And how do we find that "reality"? Certainly not through an image, because there is always more than one image, hence more than one "reality"—more than one truth, more than one lie.

These are the questions that seem to be occupying most of the time and energy of experimental filmmakers in the 70s. Some of the work that has been produced in this vein is empty sophistry—once you ask yourself what it is that film does to reality, you have to bring up the root questions: "what is film?" and the killer, "what is reality?," two problems that anyone who has ever had a taste of undergraduate philosophy can parlay into an evening of drunken conversation. Most of us have the courtesy not to bring the subject up in sober company, but a fair number of the narrow-gauge boys seem to have little else on their minds. The danger, of course, is that anyone can sound fairly profound by just learning to shuffle the terms: I'll see your non-diegetic insert and raise you one syntagma. Even when the issues are handled with intelligence and responsibility—as in Peter Wollen and Laura Mulvey's *Penthiselea*—the result is too often a sort of academic sterility, of interest only to a small coterie of those in the know. And that, perhaps, is the way it should be. Otherwise, the temptation is too great to promote structuralism and semiotics (as subjects, not as disciplines) to a privileged place in film, given the failure of the 70s to produce much else of interest in the wider sphere.

But in *F for Fake*, Orson Welles, as always, is functioning as the shock troops of the avant-garde. Welles is nothing if not a master showman (another kind of fakery, which he gladly embraces), and the taste for intellectual adventure—and even sheer boisterousness—that he brings to his exploration of illusion and reality lifts the film out of the specialists' camp. At the center of *F for Fake* is some footage that François Reichenbach shot for a documentary on Elmyr de Hory, the celebrated art forger and subject of a biography by Clifford Irving—the same Clifford Irving who later perpetrated the most spectacular fraud of the twentieth century, the fake "autobiography" of Howard Hughes. Reichenbach's camera captures de Hory and Irving in conversation, as Welles muses in voice-over that, even then, Irving must have been plotting his swindle, picking up a few tips from an old master. Welles himself is seen in some footage shot at a party in de Hory's home on the island of Ibiza—and this wonderful coincidence, the meeting of the world's three greatest confidence men (two actual, one self-styled) prompts Welles to his investigation, fakery becoming a metaphor for art, and finally—more specifically—for film.

An opening sequence presents a magisterial Welles performing coin tricks for a group of children in a train station, a setting that—with the help of a trick cut—metamorphoses into a film studio. Welles sits before an editing bench, manipulating strips of film with the same deceptive ease that he gave to his sleight-of-hand—only this time, instead of half-dollars, he will be making facts and fictions appear and disappear.

Sergei Eisenstein found truth in the joining of two strips of film, and his theory of montage remained the dominant film aesthetic until the French critic André Bazin—inspired in part by Orson Welles's deep focus work in *Citizen Kane* and *The Magnificent Ambersons*—proposed a counter-theory of mise-en-scène: truth was to be found in the unblinking eye of the camera, gazing upon a continuous scene. At first, Welles seems determined to defend his old champion Bazin, presenting a few minutes of conventionally edited documentary footage of Parisian men engaged in what Welles describes as "the ancient sport of girl watching." What could be more "real" than this footage, taken by a hidden camera, of men behaving unselfconsciously and instinctively? But, Welles points out, the woman is an actress—the scene is a set-up, a fake, and all of the "natural" men are nothing more than unknowing (and unpaid) actors.

As Welles segues into the de Hory–Irving story, the editing becomes faster and more jarring, cutting from Welles in the studio to Welles in Ibiza to Welles pondering the issues over lunch at a French restaurant. Welles stops the film to emphasize a revealing moment, or cuts two or more sequences together to point out contradictions and discontinuities. The mention of Howard Hughes introduces yet another level to the discourse—Welles's personal remembrances of Hughes as a young man in Hollywood, complicated by the fact that (he brings in Joseph Cotten to prove it) Hughes was the original subject of *Citizen Kane*. The mention of *Kane* brings in that film's famous fake newsreel, "News on the March," only this time, instead of telling the fake story of Charles Foster Kane, the fake newsreel tells the real story of Howard Hughes—which, as Welles points out, may be fake, too, since no one knows that much about Hughes anyway. The montage builds into a frenzy as the footage—which seemed so straightforward, so simple, so true in its raw state—becomes a rat maze of contradictions. *F for Fake* is an all-out assault on the notion of truth in the cinema: we're finally left to wonder if there's any difference at all between the stolid, objective documentary footage of de Hory and Irving and the obviously fraudulent special effects—flying saucers attacking the Washington Monument—that Welles has borrowed to illustrate the story of his own great fraud, the Martian invasion he staged on CBS. Contrary to Bazin, the image does lie; contrary to Eisenstein, two images, joined together, can tell a bigger lie.

The final sequence of *F for Fake* depends on a trick that didn't quite work for me, but I'm not going to spoil it. Suffice it to say that the last thirty minutes puts the ultimate banana peel under Eisenstein's sturdy Russian boots—this is montage, with a vengeance. Welles's greatest joke and crowning fraud is that, after a dazzling ninety minutes of virtuoso cinema, we're back to the starting point—Orson doing magic tricks, a subtle nudge in the ribs that says, after all the brouhaha has died down, that exploring the issue of illusion and reality in film may be just as trivial as making a man float in mid-air. It's a trick, but a tremendously entertaining one.

Days of Heaven

Directed by TERRENCE MALICK {October 13, 1978}

Thus far, even the most respectful reviews of Terrence Malick's *Days of Heaven* have made the film sound like the cinematic equivalent of a coffee table book, full of ravishing images but strangely devoid of immediate emotion or lasting substance. The consensus seems to be that Malick is not so much an artist as an illustrator, a purveyor of pretty pictures that may spark a momentary awe but leave the heart and mind untouched.

That was the film I was prepared to see—and, frankly, the film I was prepared to dislike. I have long since learned to blanch when I hear that a movie is "beautifully photographed." Translated, "beautifully photographed" generally turns out to mean that the film contains an unusually large number of mountain ranges and/or desert plains, preferably with the sun rising or setting somewhere in the immediate vicinity. Movies have a long tradition of aimless pictorialism—it's an easy way to make a film seem larger, more powerful, than it really is. By clipping a few postcards between the pages of the script, even the most mediocre director can make his film "look good," regardless of whether the imagery expands our understanding of the story or merely takes our minds off it. David Lean is a master at this sort of dodge: *Lawrence of Arabia* and *Dr. Zhivago* shamelessly milk Freddie Young's cinematography, inviting our eyes to linger over the landscape while the characters who have the temerity to intrude upon it gradually dissolve into the horizon line, unnoticed and unmourned.

There are more than a few sunrises and sunsets in *Days of Heaven*, and there are a large number of shots that seem calculated simply as aesthetic shock effects. An early image of a black, back-lit train snaking its silhouette across an iron bridge against an ice blue sky is literally breathtaking. At first, the beauty of the image seems out of proportion to its content. It's too pretty to present the reality: a freight train packed with migrant workers, being shipped from Chicago to an uncertain (but certainly oppressive) future in the wheat fields of Texas. Malick might even seem irresponsible in presenting the shot the way he does—aestheticizing, almost idealizing, one of the grimiest aspects of early 20th-century capitalism. Aimless pictorialism, pure and simple.

But is it? We hardly have time to enjoy the image before Malick snatches it away. Throughout the film, the director seems remarkably stingy with his visual creations. A brief glimpse is all we are given of a particular composition, and then Malick is off to something else, rarely granting us the leisure to contemplate and assimilate the images he puts before us. If this movie is a coffee table book, someone is turning the pages too fast. For all of the languor of the plot, *Days of Heaven* plays like a taut, driven film, relentless in its rhythm, hurrying the viewer along from image to image, scene to scene, tableau to tableau. The dialogue scenes, few and far between, are terse, clipped. Exchanges seldom last longer than three or four lines, as Malick insists on cutting away just as the characters seem ready to reveal themselves. The movie hovers slightly beyond our reach: we can't quite get a hold of it, can't quite connect with the characters or landscapes that flicker so briefly before our astonished eyes.

When people complain that *Days of Heaven* is beautiful but empty, it's this sense of distance, I think, that they're really objecting to. Apart from his elliptical story-telling, Malick also employs a long-ago time (1917, on the brink of the U.S. entry into World War I) and a far-away place (the Texas panhandle, although the film was actually shot in Alberta, Canada) to move us another step back from his subject. And there's the further complication of the narration, spoken by a teenage girl (Linda Manz) in a rough Brooklyn accent that seems to contradict the spirit of much of what we see. The sound of her voice is a constant intrusion, an urban reality impinging on a pastoral fantasy. She tells stories that have nothing to do with the action on the screen, although they often point to events that come later. As the *raisonneur*, her matter-of-fact interpretations of the action run straight against the cosmic thrust of the imagery. But just when we finally decide that she's there to bring the movie back to earth, she, too, becomes a mystic: "I talk to the wheat patches. When I was sleeping, they talk to me. They'd go in my dreams."

But while the editing, the setting, and the narration enforce an emotional distance from the drama, Malick's control of the sound and image give his film an uncanny physical presence. *Days of Heaven* is a uniquely palpable film: the breath of the wind, the texture of the grain, light snow melting on a woman's hair—we see, we hear, but somehow, we touch, too. Nestor Almendros's prickly-sharp cinematography (the film was made in 70mm, but, unfortunately, is playing in Chicago in only 35mm) finds its match in the crispness and subtlety of the Dolby sound. Crickets sing, a windmill hums, and the image is opened up. One of the most moving moments in the film occurs as the farmer (Sam Shepard) rolls a blade of wheat between his fingers, testing its ripeness. The chaff crinkles off, and the farmer blows it away with a light, delicate breath. In that second, the screen dissolves: not simply sound and image, the film becomes touch, taste, and smell.

Emotionally distant but physically present, the style and substance of *Days of Heaven* is spun out of tensions and contradictions. The visual style—lyrical, swooning, painterly—stands opposed to the editing, which is brusque, curt, precise. While the images create vast, harmonious wholes—man and landscape united under the sky—the editing is analytical, breaking the scenes down, almost scientifically, into their metaphorical components. Malick frequently inserts shots of animals—horses, dogs, particularly birds—that comment on the action in a direct evocation of Eisenstein's associative montage style. With a cut from a woman to a horse, Malick notes behavioral similarities in their ways of moving or reacting. But beyond that, the animal imagery links the human drama to a bigger story—a play of elemental emotions and instincts, the cycles of nature.

If, on the technical level, the film is a contest between montage and mise-en-scène, on the narrative level, it creates a tension between sociology and myth. A credit sequence, composed of still shots drawn from the work of Lewis Hine and other early 20th-century photojournalists, sets the film firmly in a milieu of urban squalor and exploited labor. Abby (Brooke Adams) is introduced picking through a slag heap, looking for usable metal scrap. Her lover, Bill (Richard Gere), works at the other end of the steel-making process, feeding a blast furnace. A fight breaks out (for reasons we never discover—the dialogue is totally obscured by the sound of crashing machinery) and Bill strikes his foreman. Perhaps he has killed him, for in the next sequence, Abby, Bill, and his teenage sister, Linda, are plainly on the lam, traveling south on the freight train that will deliver them, as harvest workers, to Sam Shepard's farm. In voice-over, Linda tells us that the unmarried Bill and Abby are posing as brother and sister—and in that moment, as the train crosses the bridge, the story shifts to the level of archetype. Specifically, it's the Genesis tale of Abraham and Sarah, entering Egypt as brother and sister. The king of Egypt takes Sarah as a wife, leaving Abraham to call upon his God for revenge, which arrives in the form of a plague of locusts. When the farmer (the character is never given a name) falls in love with Abby, Bill's reaction is a little less self-righteous. He'll go along with the marriage, since he's discovered that the wealthy farmer is dying of a slow, unnamed disease.

The title, too, belongs to the Old Testament, coming from the section of Deuteronomy that deals with the covenant between God and the Israelites. In return for the gift of "the land of milk and honey," the scriptures demand that the commandments be observed, "that your days be multiplied and the days of your children in the land which the lord swere unto your fathers to give them, as the days of heaven upon the earth." For a while, Bill enjoys his days of heaven: still posing as Abby's brother, he's free from work for the first time in his life, free to hunt in the fields, free to meet Abby for midnight swims. But the emotional balance begins to shift. Abby's love, while not lessened for Bill, begins to grow for the farmer.

The tensions are now dramatic, but they are developed less through the psychology of the characters (although that, too, can be read, through their actions and gestures if not through their words) than by means of a conflict of images. As Malick introduces his three main characters, they are each assigned an element from the classical trilogy of earth, fire, and water. We first see Bill standing next to his furnace, and throughout the film, he is associated with flames: the sparks of the blast furnace are echoed in the sparks that rise from a campfire, set to celebrate the completion of the harvest, and return again in the fire that sweeps the wheat field in the final apocalypse. Beyond fire, he is linked to the color red, a violent contrast to the greens and yellows that dominate the film. The wheels of the automobiles, the engines of the tractors, the airplane that takes Bill away, and the motorcycle that brings him back are all painted red. To Bill belongs the empire of machinery—specifically, the machinery of motion, of energy, of passion. To Bill belongs the 20th century.

The earth, of course, belongs to the farmer. The first time we see him he's eating an apple; the second time, drinking a glass of wine; the third time, tasting his wheat. His love for his land is physical, almost sexual: when Abby first meets him alone, he seems to rise up out of the earth, as he stands up from the cover of a patch of grass. He could almost be planted there. While Bill is associated with sweeping camera movements, as he strides up and down the hills and fields, the farmer is given static shots. He is rooted, permanent, a pre-industrial creature.

The water imagery is the film's most delicate, most ambiguous creation. It is Abby's property: even in the first shot of her, as she picks through the scrap heap, a stream of water pours from a drainpipe in the background. Water, at first, appears to be a sort of sanctuary, a place to clean off the grime of the world (as the field hands do, retiring to the farm's pond after a day's work), a place for human interaction (on the day after the wedding, the farmer takes his new family for a swim in a stream; later he takes Abby to see a waterfall on their honeymoon). Caressing, clear, refreshing, the water is Abby, her love and her sexuality. For the farmer, the water is calm and still: when Abby climbs the hill to his house to accept his proposal, we see the building reflected in a pond-sized puddle—the water cradled by the earth, and in the water, an image of the union. For the passionate Bill, the water is the rushing stream where he and Abby meet to make love at midnight. A passage in Deuteronomy describes water as "the rain of heaven." Through Abby, Bill and the farmer touch the divine.

But in the Bible, water is also the Flood, an image of destruction. The farmer discovers that Bill and Abby are lovers (ironically, at the moment when they are saying goodbye), and the days of heaven are over. The locusts come—not in the crude form of a special effects man's idea of the hand of God, but as fully individuated and sympathetic as the animals we've seen earlier in the film. See in microscopic close-up, one by one, as they devour the crop, they may be following a higher will, but they know no more of it than Bill and Abby. During an attempt to smoke the locusts out of the field, the farmer strikes Bill with a lantern—which breaks, and sends the dry wheat up in a torrent. It's the fulfillment of a prophecy, of sorts, that Linda makes during her opening narration, as she retells a child's story of the apocalypse that she heard, she says, from a fellow traveler named Ding-Dong: "The land will be in flames. Even the water will be in flames."

Bill kills the farmer in self-defense, stabbing him, significantly, with the screwdriver that belongs to his motorcycle. Running away again, just as he did at the start of the film, Bill takes Abby and Linda to a river, hoping to escape downstream in a steamboat. Sure enough, we find the water in flames—when Bill's boat passes a raft at night carrying a circle of river-rats gathered around a bonfire, the flames are reflected in the surface of the stream. By the time the police catch up with them, the water imagery has come full circle, from life to death. Bill dies in the water, shot in the back as he scrambles along a bank. Malick records his fall from beneath the surface: a splash into silence, and it is over.

If Malick has made an Old Testament movie, he's left out any sense of Old Testament sin. Bill is being punished, but for what? He has only followed his nature, his destiny, propelled by forces that are beyond his control or understanding. Of all of the tensions in the film—between the images and the editing, the social and the mystical, the 19th and 20th centuries—the most profound is the tension between man and God, between free will and fate. Great elemental forces—embodied in fire, water, the land, the locusts—swirl around the characters in *Days of Heaven*, as powerful and as invisible as the wind that whips the farmer's house. They are as arbitrary, mysterious, and beautiful in their rage as they are in their benevolence. *Days of Heaven* is a story of human lives touched by the cosmos, and then passed over—momentary intersections between the eternal and the immediate.

At the end of the film, we are back at the beginning—in a city, where Abby, who now seems to have some money (has she become a whore, as one image implies, or has she managed to inherit the farmer's fortune?) puts Linda in a boarding school. Abby leaves, boarding a train full of soldiers: America has entered the war. Linda escapes from the school, shinnying down a rope made of bed sheets to meet an old girlfriend from the farm. Together, they set off walking down the railroad tracks at dawn, with no place to go, nothing in mind. Like her brother Bill, Linda is on the lam now. One story ends, and another one begins: it's a perfect, open ending for the most graceful, most moving, and most original American film in recent memory.

10

Directed by BLAKE EDWARDS {October 12, 1979}

Forget *Manhattan*. The best romantic comedy of the year is photographed in bright, Los Angeles color instead of eastern-ascetic black-and-white; it makes jokes about hangovers and people falling in swimming pools instead of peddling sly references to Strindberg and Flaubert, and it stars Julie Andrews instead of Diane Keaton. For that matter, forget "best romantic comedy." Blake Edwards's *10*, generous, sharp, and perfectly assembled, is the best American film of 1979.

Manhattan had a surface truth: its people looked right, talked right, and dressed right. But, in a way, they also acted "right"—they were characters considered as fashions, this year's models, built in Bloomingdale's back room according to the strict specifications laid down by Woody Allen. Locked into their types—striking the right cultural attitudes, suffering from the right neuroses, and automatically following (or violating) the right moral precepts—they had no freedom of movement, no individuality. *Manhattan* was a movie about making choices—choices of partners, goals, and depth of commitment—but, for the people in the film, they weren't difficult choices. The rightness or wrongness of every decision was made obvious, and the emotional processes through which those decisions were made weren't fully dramatized. It looked easy, even when it wasn't meant to. There was something too pat about the movement of *Manhattan*—the three women, gliding in their firmly set orbits around Woody Allen—to give the film a sense of productive challenge, of a forward struggle instead of a smooth slide toward a foregone conclusion.

10 is also about making choices, but they're choices based on painful experience, the kind that comes from committing yourself to an ideal of a vision and following it through to its end—which, more often than not, means the end of the ideal. The title refers to the ancient and dishonorable male habit of rating women on a scale from one to ten, an enduring pastime in bars and locker rooms. Usually, the scale refers only to physical attractiveness, but for George Webber (Dudley Moore), the hero of *10*, the scale has a hidden spiritual quality as well. A ten is a perfect mate: innocent and sensual, emotionally pure and enveloping. Tens, of course, do not exist, so George, a successful Hollywood composer, has found comfort with a slightly downscale lady, a singer named Samantha (Julie Andrews), with whom he enjoys a distant, appreciative relationship. It's warm and casual, but still short of the mark—a disquieting compromise that comes to press harder as George enters his 43rd year. On the morning after his birthday—Sam has given him an unwelcome surprise party—George takes a drive through Beverly Hills. Pulled up at a corner, he glances into the car next to him, and there he sees Jennifer (Bo Derek). Jennifer is an 11.

Edwards's execution of this sequence is so exact, expressive, and im- · 29 ·
portant to the development of his film that it's worth a close look. It's shot as a silent film, with the appropriate musical accompaniment provided by a tape of Sam singing one of George's songs, which, ostensibly, George has punched into his car stereo. Edwards has always shown a particular affinity for silent comedy (as witnessed in his full-length homage, *The Great Race*, and the pantomime sequences in *The Party* and the Pink Panther films), but here the form is evoked as something more than a stylistic reference: by shutting out all exterior sounds, Edwards takes us directly into George's consciousness, his private reverie. The camera movements—sweeping pans, from left to right—also catch us up in George's state of mind; he floats down the city streets, smoothly and silently, as if in a dream. But the sweeping movements are interrupted, first by a shot of two bikinied girls walking to the beach, then by two female joggers pausing on a street corner. Cross-cut, in the traditional style of subjective montage, with close-ups of George's wondering, slightly ashamed glance, these shots describe the nature of his reverie—it's a distracted sexual daydream, of the sort everyone knows from solitary drives and long walks. Still, the brief flurries of cross-cutting are enough of an intrusion upon the surrealistic glide of George's journey to come as small shocks—flashes of disquiet that disturb the smooth course of the drive, which, with Sam's voice on the sound track (singing lyrics that clearly refer to him), has become an image of George's easy, tension-free relationship with her. Edwards has indicated the subject of George's fantasy, as well as the anxiety that feeds it, but the visuals do even more. We see both the guilt that George suffers in his mental betrayals of Sam, and the unformed, half-conscious yearnings that make those betrayals necessary. Like his affair with Sam, the ride has to be interrupted; it's too easy, too detached.

When Jennifer pulls up alongside George's car, Edwards uses the same cross-cutting as in the two earlier encounters. But the close-ups of Jennifer are taken with a longer lens, which has the effect of magnifying Jennifer's presence, as if through a telescope, making her larger and more luminous as she casts her perfect blue eyes into the depths of George's soul. The long lens, though, only appears to bring her closer: there is still a space between Jennifer and George (not to mention two car bodies), and by artificially manipulating that space, the long lens serves to emphasize it. Thus, with one shot, Edwards places Jennifer in the thematic complex he has already swiftly developed: she is more than the other women, but she is also more remote; her presence, both large and intangible, has the magic of a vision. She is there and not there, close and far away, the perfect fantasy of the perfect woman—flesh and fantasy, in fact, joined into one. Later, the long lens will be linked to a running gag involving a telescope, which George uses to spy on the spectacular sexual activities of his next-door neighbor. The connection makes the voyeuristic basis of George's fantasy explicit, but it also defines the dimension of the fantasy, of ideals both sexual and romantic: distant, tenuous, unreal. The long lens is equated with the dreamer's point of view, and what it reveals is an illusion.

The sequence continues as George, impulsively, decides to follow Jennifer's car. The long left-to-right pans resume as they snake through Beverly Hills. But as Jennifer's car rounds a corner and stops by the church where she is going to be married, the pan switches to right-to-left, a disruption of the flow. George's car pulls around her and straight into the bumper of the Beverly Hills police car that the sleek pan impassively reveals, hiding at the left-hand corner of the frame. And thus, the most carefully built lyrical sequence in any film of this year ends with an abrupt belly laugh—a laugh, moreover, that the languorous rhythms of the sequence have slyly set us up for. The shock of the collision is a return to brute reality—an appropriate dramatic statement as well as evidence of Edwards's full command of the psychological structures of physical comedy.

The hard smack of the wreck provides a vivid objective correlative to George's vision, and the rest of the film's physical comedy functions in much the same way—as a reminder of earthly limitations. As in Edwards's Pink Panther films, it is mainly a comedy of pain—of bee stings, dental extractions, and sudden tumbles down hillsides—but the sadism of the slapstick arises naturally from George's masochistic pursuit of Jennifer. She is the cause of his pain, its justification and its glory.

George is hopelessly smitten by his first sight of Jennifer. One glance is enough to trigger his obsession, as he automatically assumes that the face and figure of an 11 must imply a superior soul as well. It is an assumption that George shares with the art of cinema, which is often described as an art of surfaces: in the Hollywood star system, what you see is what you get, as directors are forced to define inner states by their outward appearances. Edwards has cast Bo Derek in the iconographical tradition of American film (as he has cast all of *10* with a perfect eye, down to the smallest character parts): it matters less that she is limited as an actress than that her angelic face and figure conform to George's special apprehension of the ideal woman. The surface becomes the substance.

But that assumption has always been a dangerous one in Edwards's films, from the elaborate levels of deception built into the Julie Andrews character of *Darling Lili* to the pitifully inadequate disguises adopted by Peter Sellers's Inspector Clouseau. Edwards's more serious critics have long been fascinated by the importance of "performance" in his films—

the need to keep up appearances, to fashion a pleasing public personality to hide the impassioned private being, as Craig Stevens does in Edwards's *Gunn*, exuding a glacial cool and tossing off one-liners as he goes about the wrenching task of clearing a friend charged with murder. Less frequently noted is Edwards's tendency to apply a similar outside/inside distinction to social groups and institutions: his films frequently feature an inner circle, an exclusive society—such as the country club in the early *Mr. Cory*, the ski resort in the first *Pink Panther*, or the Beverly Hills of *Gunn*—that puts up a façade of sophistication and glamour but that, when the hero finally penetrates it, is found to be empty or corrupt. Thus the Pink Panther films, apparently in the tradition of sophisticated "continental" comedy established by Lubitsch, are actually criticisms of it: the aristocratic worlds of high finance and international intrigue are invaded and shattered by Clouseau, the ultimate embodiment of the democrat as klutz.

Like Howard Hawks, Edwards has baffled several generations of critics by his refusal to remain faithful to a single genre: apart from his comedies, he has made thrillers (*Experiment in Terror*, *The Carey Treatment*), social dramas (*Mr. Cory*, *The Days of Wine and Roses*), romances (*Breakfast at Tiffany's*, *The Tamarind Seed*), a musical (*Darling Lili*), and even a Western (*Wild Rovers*, although it was one of his few artistic failures). But Edwards's thematic focus remains constant throughout, and the different genres serve to highlight different aspects of his central concern. *10* strikes me as a breakthrough for Edwards because it bridges the genre gap, uniting the very different structures of Edwards's comedies and romances and producing a coherent, definitive statement—a statement that cuts through the generic "personalities" that Edwards, like his characters, has adopted in the past. One has the feeling that Edwards is working here, for the first time, without a net—without the protection afforded by the impersonal pose of genre stylist. Edwards, at last, is speaking directly—and it should be noted in passing that Julie Andrews, in private life, is Mrs. Blake Edwards. There is no "performance" in *10*, on the part of either the director or his characters.

The action of Edwards's comedies is the exposure of a privileged circle—of an ideal life that turns out to be every bit as difficult and ambiguous as everyday existence. The agent of that exposure is either a comically inept hero like Clouseau, whose mere presence reduces the privileged world to chaos, or a smooth social climber, like the Tony Curtis character of Edwards's early Universal films (*Mr. Cory*, *The Perfect Furlough*, *Operation Petticoat*), who ambitiously hopes to infiltrate the privileged world but finally finds it disappointing and shallow. Both characters are presented as intruders; they shatter the inner circle because they are foreign to it. In *10*, significantly, the hero is already a member of the exclusive class—a famous composer, equipped with ranch house, swimming pool, and Rolls-Royce. His invasion will be emotional, his ambitions romantic rather than social.

Edwards's romances begin in the social world and move to a discovery of private individuals, their social roles cast aside. In the World War I musical *Darling Lili*, Edwards establishes a romance between a German spy (Andrews) and an American flyer (Rock Hudson); in *The Tamarind Seed*, a high melodrama with the spiritual commitment of Frank Borzage, the social conflict is raised to operatic proportions: Andrews and her lover (Omar Sharif) work for rival intelligence operations, she for the British, he for the Russians. The earlier and less personal *Breakfast at Tiffany's* pairs a party girl (Audrey Hepburn) and a gigolo (George Peppard); both must learn to see the person behind the profession. In the romances, the hero (or, more accurately, the heroine, since they generally take the point of view of the woman) must grow emotionally, learn to make a deeper commitment, in order to apprehend the full emotionality, the private dimensions, of the partner. It is a process of mutual transcendence, creating an intimate, emotional union that, once struck, can't be broken—even, as *The Tamarind Seed* says with its gloriously impossible happy ending, by death.

In *10*, Dudley Moore's extraordinary performance as George embraces both the comic and romantic Edwards heroes. Like Clouseau, he seems to attract disaster, but the privileged world that is being upset is his own. He has Clouseau's childishness: in the early scenes, Sam acts like a mother to him, throwing his birthday party, cooking his meals, and cleaning up after him. (A nice touch here: Sam has a son by a previous marriage, and his name, too, is George.) Still, for all his helplessness, George remains plausible as a romantic hero, his depth of feeling conveyed by the lushly romantic music he composes. His relationship with Sam is plainly inadequate in the terms Edwards develops in his romances: the partners are too far apart, their roles—as mother and child—too narrow, too artificial. Here, Edwards shrewdly plays off his wife's squeaky-clean, mother-protector screen image: for George, Sam has become Julie Andrews, sensible, strong, and somewhat remote. Not surprisingly, George has lost interest in sex with her.

Jennifer is sexually attractive, but she is something more. For George, she becomes an emblem of everything that is lacking in his relationship with Sam, an emblem of the privileged world of romance. She is the woman in white whom he pursues to a city of white—the Mexican resort of Las Hadas—and George identifies her with everything he reads in her face: purity, innocence, free emotionality. Jennifer is reminiscent of the white-gowned Claudia Cardinale figure in Fellini's *8½*, who keeps popping up to remind Marcello Mastroianni of the ideals he has just left behind, although Edwards avoids Fellini's obvious symbolism. She also has much in common with the Mariel Hemingway character in *Manhat-*

tan—youth considered as a pure, redemptive force. But here, Edwards picks up at the moment when Woody Allen leaves off: where *Manhattan* is content with its sentimental conclusion, Edwards presses further, looking for the person behind the image.

When George—through some complicated and very funny plot maneuvers—finally confronts Jennifer, Edwards discards the long lens, holding George and Jennifer together in the same frame, not as dreamer and dream but as two people. Invited to her hotel room, George has finally entered the privileged world, where, like the generations of Edwards heroes before him, he finds a disappointment. Jennifer is no heroine out of an Edwards romance. Beneath the surface, there is only more surface, as George discovers in the course of an interrupted seduction. The mixture of moods here is bold and meticulous: again, physical comedy serves to deflate the romantic image, as the real collides (almost literally) with the ideal, but Moore is also able to capture the pain of disillusionment, the anger as well as the agony. Jenny stands firm: there is no attempt to ridicule or dismiss her. She fails as a symbol for George because, in the end, she is not a symbol but a human being—a selfish, spoiled, superficial human being, but an individual with a rock-hard integrity of her own. She is perfectly guileless, and, in that sense, innocent, although her innocence extends only to her refusal to disguise her appetites and impulses. She lives for the surface—fleeting pleasures, casual encounters, whatever will make her "happy," if only for a moment. She does not redeem, she does not transcend. She simply enjoys. There is nothing deeper for George to discover. He has met his ideal, and she has turned out to be just that: a hollow concept.

George chooses to return to Sam, but he is a different George, his vision cleared. He is now able to see her, not as a mother or a sex partner, but as an emotional being. There is no ideal love, no ideal sex, but only people existing together. Edwards suggests that the real beauty of a relationship stems from a mutual ability to apprehend the thing itself, not what it might be, for to dream is to kill. There is a graceful, caressing camera movement as George and Sam sit together at the piano: George proposes, Sam refuses, and even the ideal of marriage is discarded. Edwards posits the ultimate romance in reality, a reality not social or intellectual, but emotional.

The long lens of idealism makes one last appearance in *10*, in a final shot that carries an extraordinary richness of meaning. George's Dionysian neighbor has a telescope, too: he points it at George's living room, and seeing only Sam and George sitting at the piano, he retreats in disgust. But then, the camera moves in on the abandoned telescope, assuming the neighbor's point of view through the long lens. And there we see, encircled by a romantic iris out of Griffith or Chaplin, George beginning to seduce Sam to the strains of Ravel's *Bolero*, a flourish he learned from

Jennifer. The embrace of the iris is supremely sentimental, almost Victorian in its implication: George and Sam have achieved an ideal romantic rapport. But the romance, again, is undercut by the joke of the *Bolero*, and the memories of Jenny that it conjures. It is a magnificent moment of integration: the culmination of George's experience, the evidence of his growth, and the consequence of his conscious choice, broadly funny and deeply moving. And finally, by putting the audience in the position of voyeur, the dreamer, Edwards gently reminds us that the happy ending we are witnessing is also a fantasy: the ideal of art, the dream of the movies.

Melvin and Howard

Directed by JONATHAN DEMME {February 13, 1981}

Tell someone that a movie is about America, and—if he has any sense—he'll head for the exit. But I don't know how else to condense the subject of Jonathan Demme's funny, stirring *Melvin and Howard*. The movie does so many things well, covers so much ground with such apparent ease, that it wriggles out of the usual categories—you have to reach for the big, transcendent ones. And yet, it isn't a big, sprawling film: it's short (a little over an hour and a half), and it restricts its focus to a handful of characters, digging in for small, precise observations. In its ideas and emotions, it's the largest American movie in a long time, but it's a modest, comfortable film, a movie that's a pleasure to spend time with. It leaves you like a good conversation with a friend. You've learned something, you're lifted up—but the conversation stays casual, unforced.

Melvin is Melvin Dummar (Paul Le Mat), the gas station attendant named as heir to 1/16th of Howard Hughes's fortune in the notorious "Mormon will." In most movies, the discovery of the will—with its promise of $156 million—would mark the point at which Melvin first becomes interesting, someone special. Another movie would start with the discovery and move on through the courthouse battle, with Melvin, the lucky, tenacious "little guy" of sentimental fiction fighting for his rights against the big, bad corporate attorneys—Mr. Average American taking on the bosses. Frank Capra might have made that movie, and it might have been passably, conventionally entertaining. But Demme's emphasis is different: the court battle is only the coda of *Melvin and Howard*, and it isn't fought with much determination. The will doesn't even come as a blessing—it's more of a burden to Melvin, one more false promise. He'll go through the motions, give it its due, but he'll never really believe in it—and *Melvin and Howard* is the story of how Melvin Dummar, dreamer, game-show addict, and perennial hatcher of get-rich-quick schemes, learned to shrug off a fortune.

Demme begins his film on a mythic note: we see a desert landscape in late afternoon, shot full with the special light of what cinematographers call the "golden hour"—bronzed, dimensional, pooling into long shadows. The extreme long shot shows a small figure on a motorcycle, shooting the gulleys and churning up the desert dust. The long shot respects his privacy—this is an intimate, personal pleasure, a one-man joyride—but it also shows us his isolation. The landscape, with its jagged hills, cradles him, but loosely. He could be a solitary child, abandoned to his toys, until Demme comes in for a close-up and we see the stained beard, the streaming gray hair, the empty glass eyes of a pair of antique aviator's goggles. It's a child with the face of death. The figure is romantic, mysterious, and incalculably aged. It's twilight, and he is the only remaining god.

Demme's Howard Hughes may bear no resemblance to the real one—whose madness seemed more sordid than majestic, more pathetic than tragic—but he is a magnificent metaphorical creation: the ancient child, lost in lonely joys. The motorcycle hits a dip, and the old man is thrown; he lies unconscious into the night, until the headlights of Melvin Dummar's pick-up truck pluck him out of the darkness.

This must have been the moment of Dummar's story, much more than the arrival of the will, that pricked Demme's imagination. The film flows from this quintessential American coincidence: the meeting of rich man and poor man, old man and young man, fabled and unknown, bound in the privileged camaraderie produced by the night road. Company, and the thin shelter of the truck's cab, are the only defenses against the aching emptiness of the desert sky and the scrub landscape; Demme understands how quickly the road creates friendships. And yet the scene begins in suspicion, distrust. The old man, who has hurt his ear, angrily refuses to see a doctor; he insists on being driven straight to Las Vegas. Hughes's flinty eccentricity jars Melvin—he had hoped to patronize the old man, the grizzled desert rat who, Demme suggests, is the first person Melvin has met in a long time who seems to be an even bigger loser than himself. Melvin, a little cruelly, goads Hughes into singing the chorus of a Christmas song he has written—his latest hope for fame and fortune—and the old man responds with a deep, dry croak. The voice has a surprising strength; it gives Hughes an unexpected toughness and tenacity (and with it, Jason Robards gives his subtlest, most considered screen performance in years). Hughes tells Melvin who he is, and the disbelief that comes back at him is expected, though disappointing—the gods don't reveal themselves every day, and they have a right to a better reception than this. An absurdly brief desert rain comes up, just after dawn, stirring the scent of the sage. The men inhale, solemnly, sharing the sudden sweetness of the landscape. "Sage," says Melvin. "Sage," says Howard.

I first saw *Melvin and Howard* nearly a year ago (it's been sitting on the shelf at Universal ever since, stumping the promotion department). What surprised me, seeing it again last week, was the film's concision: scenes that had expanded to epic length in my memory turned out to last only a few shots, a few lines. Demme has an amazing gift for actor's detail—the raised eyebrow, the downward glance that reveals a whole range of attitudes and emotions—and his screenwriter, Bo Goldman, has a similar gift for loading dialogue: his lines, simple and stripped, have an unforced density of expression, a poetry that never strikes our ears as "poetic." (There is Melvin's resigned observation that "Rome wasn't burned in a day," and in that unconscious demolishing of cliché, we see a life attuned to disaster, measured by it.) My mental *Melvin and Howard* is about 12 hours long: it would have to be, to get in all of that emotional texture, fullness of character, shape of experience. But the meeting with Hughes is finished in a few minutes; without effusion, we've seen the affection grow between the two men, and we can believe that Hughes would leave Melvin $156 million: Melvin has already given him something—an emotional connection that's more than charity, better than sympathy—in return; he's treated him like an equal.

A sense of sudden reversal is integral to Demme's presentation of Melvin's life, and to his grasp of the American experience. Melvin drops his passenger off in a hotel parking lot and returns to the battered, beached house trailer where he lives with wife Lynda (Mary Steenburgen). She wakes up as he slips into bed, and they make love. A little while later, she hears a noise outside: it's the men from the finance company, come to take Melvin's motorcycle away. The single event stands for dozens of similar ones, and in a minute Lynda has her daughter dressed, her bags packed, and a boyfriend waiting outside in a car. They're running off to Reno, to start a new life.

The new life lasts less than the length of a single establishing shot. Panning down from the Reno skyline, Demme catches the boyfriend storming angrily from a motel room, leaving Lynda and the child behind. The abruptness of the cut invites a laugh, but Demme makes it catch by quickly going inside to a bruised, sobbing Lynda, sitting amid the smoking ruins of this latest disaster. The brusque edit, going from one emotion to its opposite, is typical of Demme's technique. Feelings don't come out in bite-sized, sitcom chunks; the comic and the tragic, the satirical and the lyrical, are jumbled, and Demme almost never allows a simple, complacent response. Melvin's daughter returns home, and so, eventually, does a hugely pregnant Lynda.

Melvin can't divorce his wife without marrying her again, he can't earn money without spending it, he can't buy anything without having it repossessed. It's a metronome existence, ticking from one extreme to the other, and Melvin becomes accustomed to the rhythm. He doesn't give full credit to anything that happens to him—its opposite is sure to strike in a minute or two. He's used to sudden fortune, sudden disaster, and out of it comes a sense of unreality, a dreaminess. He has dreams and reality, hopes and facts, all mixed up. In one sense, he's the ultimate dupe of American culture, in that he believes that anything he wants will come to him, that wishing will make it so. In another sense, he's got a better grasp of American life than anyone around him: he knows that nothing lasts, and he enjoys what he has while he has it, not regretting it when it's gone. He puts Lynda on a game show, where she wins a $10,000 jackpot. Part of the money, at Lynda's insistence, goes toward a down payment on a modest—but real—new home, but Melvin takes the balance and puts it down on a speedboat and a luxury car.

Melvin blows the $10,000, just as he'd blow the Hughes jackpot if he ever got his hands on it. But Melvin's irresponsibility doesn't seem narrowly selfish, nor does it seem willfully self-destructive (in the way, say, of a habitual gambler). His dreams may be tawdry—to own a fast, red car, to win a television set—but there is something sublime in his motives: it's not the possession of the *thing* that counts, but the fulfillment of the dream, bringing it into being. Melvin has an idea, and it is a supremely American one: dreams are things to make come true.

Jonathan Demme's movies have always been about families—their growth, their preservation, the ties that bind them. In his early exploitation films *Crazy Mama* and *Fighting Mad*, they are families of blood ties, mother to daughter to granddaughter, father to son. In his first mature film, 1977's *Citizen's Band* (AKA *Handle With Care*), the family broadens into a community of feeling, metaphorically united by CB radio. The thriller *The Last Embrace* is about transgenerational guilt and transgenerational revenge, the family betrayed and perverted. With *Melvin and Howard*, Demme extends his family feeling to cover a culture. The scenes between parents and children have Demme's usual warmth and charm—there's a wonderful scene at a bus depot lunch counter, where Steenburgen hastily prepares a submarine sandwich for her departing daughter—but the warmth spills over now; it's as if everyone whom Melvin comes in contact with becomes part of his family. *Melvin and Howard* has a sense of social unity, of wholeness, perhaps because there are no impersonal characters in it—no sense of "us" and "them," of gradations of human value. Down to the most minor roles, Demme has cast his players with incomparable care; there is something distinctive, individuating, about everyone we see. Background characters emerge with an unusual degree of definition. Even the extras—a stripper at work with her arm in a cast, a stone-faced Indian in a game show audience—are people. Melvin, divorced for a second time from Lynda, marries again; his new wife Bonnie (Pamela Reed) has two children of her own, and Melvin's family continues to grow, literally as well as figuratively.

The motivating question of *Melvin and Howard* is, how can a man lose $156 million and not care? The answer the film gives draws on dozens of reasons, from personal psychology to imagined cultural attitudes, but ultimately it rests on the film's profound vision of democracy, its hopeful evocation of a genuine community of equals. The title, with its casual linkage of first names, finds the best embodiment of that vision in the midnight drive of Melvin and Howard. One is the archetypal American winner, the other the archetypal loser, but it makes no difference between them, not when the scent of sage is rising on the highway. Howard Hughes, too, is a member of Melvin Dummar's family, and that, Demme suggests, is the true fulfillment of the American dream. As he drives away from the courthouse at the end of the film, Melvin's mind drifts back to his meeting with the old man. In flashback, Melvin lets Howard drive for a stretch, and while the old man happily commands the wheel, singing a soft chorus of "Bye Bye Blackbird," Melvin falls asleep in the passenger seat. Even in his daydreams, he's dreaming.

The Aviator's Wife

Directed by ERIC ROHMER {July 16, 1982}

With *The Aviator's Wife*, Eric Rohmer begins a new series to set alongside his famous "Six Moral Tales," which he completed in 1972 with *Chloe in the Afternoon*. The title of the new series is "Comedies and Proverbs," though, as Rohmer explains in a prefatory statement, the episodes "will avoid conformity with the rules of the comedic genre; the proverb will not necessarily be stated. Even if it is stated, one will find several lessons within the same piece, as in the fables of La Fontaine." Judging from *The Aviator's Wife*, the arena will be the same as that of the Moral Tales: these will be small stories, set in parks, apartments, and city streets, of relations among a small number of characters; as Rohmer adds, "There will still be a lot of talking." What's changed isn't the subject, but the style. In *The Aviator's Wife*, Rohmer abandons the first-person, voice-over narration of the Moral Tales—the subjective overlay that gave those films their witty, trenchant doubleness, of acts observed and motives recalled—in favor of a fluid, shifting point of view—a subjectivity that moves from one character to another, giving them all a greater degree of freedom, more room to improvise, more contradictory and complex humanity. It's as if, having mastered one method of composition, Rohmer is ready to add new tones to his scale—new rhythms and new harmonies. The result, in *The Aviator's Wife*, is a surpassingly elegant, elaborate formal structure: the kind of movie Mozart might have made if he had had a camera. Not that the film, on the dangerous, far extreme, is simply an empty, abstract design. Narrative movies can't, and probably shouldn't, have the purity of music; they were born with dirty feet. And so Rohmer, the most rational and deliberate of filmmakers, has chosen as his perennial subject the limits of rationality and deliberation. *The Aviator's Wife* has its dissonances and unresolved chords, as if Rohmer were saying that the most sophisticated formal system imaginable must always break down in the face of human complexity; Rohmer is a formalist, but not a formalist of the Stanley Kubrick school of absolutism. There is always an awareness in his work that men made these designs—that the human hand precedes them. For Rohmer, form is the thing of beauty and a tool to understanding; it is never, as it often is in Kubrick's work, understanding itself.

It's easy to tease out the base pattern of *The Aviator's Wife*. François (Philippe Marlaud) is a 20-year-old law student who works nights at the post office to support his studies. He's in love with Anne (Marie Riviere), who, at 25, isn't sure if she wants to settle into a permanent relationship. Early one morning, François passes by Anne's apartment to drop off a note, and sees her leaving with her old flame Christian (Mathieu Carriere), a married, 30-ish airline pilot. What François doesn't know is that Christian has simply arrived a few minutes earlier than he—not to renew the old affair, but to break it off definitively. Upset and uncertain, François wanders the city, until by chance he sees Christian sitting in a train station café. There's a mysterious blond woman with him—his wife? another mistress?—and François, less out of curiosity than distracted agitation, decides to investigate. He follows the couple to a park, watching them so intently that he barely notices Lucie (Anne-Laure Meury), a pretty 15-year-old who has been walking the same path through the park. He turns suddenly and startles her; a conversation begins and, while he continues to spy, he's also begun to enjoy this girl's company.

The five-year spacing of the ages, and the discrete psychological stages the four main characters fall into—Lucie's open flirtatiousness, François' moody romanticism, Anne's uncertainty, and Christian's newfound domesticity—suggest a very rigid kind of schematization. But there's no trace of it in Rohmer's superbly languorous understated direction. When there's this much understanding of behavioral detail—the small, circuitous ways in which people move from point A to point B—the fixed, hard points of plot and structure no longer stand out; they're subsumed by character. There's probably no device more hoary than having a boy and girl meet by bumping into each other, but to watch Rohmer's revitalization of the cliché is pure pleasure—in the way Lucie's presence is planted, almost subconsciously, on the bus François takes to the park; in the way the camera movement and framing associate the two as they walk along independently, unmindful of each other; and, most important perhaps, in the way Rohmer so sharply conveys the state of each character's mind, Lucie's openness and François' obsessiveness, as they come together. Every moment is fresh and convincing, as if Rohmer had chosen the cliché deliberately, to show what he could do with it.

Rohmer needs to establish the age-spacing and the different outlooks distinctly; the contrast is necessary to put the play of points of view in motion. The Moral Tales used an internal/external contrast, pitting the first-person, past-tense narration of the sound track against the objective, present-tense flow of the images. We watched the characters acting, and heard, simultaneously, their own later recollections and explanation of those acts. The two tracks rarely ran parallel. In *The Aviator's Wife*, Rohmer makes a similar separation of visual and aural information, only here we listen to the characters' speech—which carries the attitudes and personalities they want to project to each other—and "observe" their thoughts. In the images, we read the visual clues Rohmer provides against the background of what we already know about the character: taken together, the gestures and the exposition give us a wonderfully clear picture of what's going on in the characters' minds; the old *Strange Interlude* device of speaking thoughts has here been cleaned up, made natural and expressive. Its absurdly reductive tendencies (no one ever thinks in discrete sentences, or only of one thing at once) have been eliminated, and it's played so lightly and smoothly that we may not even notice how decisively and deliberately Rohmer has inflected the usual rhetoric of movies. In order to make the effect possible, the structure plays a kind of leapfrog: one sequence will introduce us, explicitly, to the character's situation; the next will move him into a scene with a character who doesn't know what we know, which gives the scene two levels. There's one brilliant shot that encapsulates Rohmer's method: François and Lucie sit together talking, in a fairly tight two-shot, on a stone bench overlooking the park lagoon. François is in profile, Lucie in full face; in the space just between them, away in the background on the other side of the water, we see the pilot and the blonde sitting on a grassy slope. As François' glance shifts, from moment to moment, from the full presence of Lucie to the miniaturized remove of the couple, we can feel almost physically the indecision in François' mind: should he give in to this pleasant flirtation, or should he continue to be the wounded lover, looking off in the distance at his pain? Rohmer has the wisdom to realize that these two impulses are not incompatible; François enjoys and suffers at the same time. It's a beautiful, complex moment, giving in to neither masochism nor hedonism, but mixing these two very human motives into something honest and alive. Rohmer is not a moralist in any crude way that would simply condemn François' flirtation in the depths of his grief; his moralism is a higher one, finding something fine and optimistic in this eternal entanglement of agony and hope.

There's a fine spatial sense at work in this shot, too—as befits the man who wrote his doctor's thesis on "The Organization of Space in Murnau's *Faust*." Rohmer's visual abilities aren't always appreciated, perhaps because of the importance given to speech in his films (by the characters, if not always by the director) and perhaps because Rohmer—almost alone of the original New Wave directors—has continued to work in the apparently casual, open-air style the school pioneered. Rohmer doesn't call attention to his shots, either by moving the camera autonomously (he always moves with the characters' movement) or by forcing spatial contrasts between them (he prefers a gentle alternation of medium and medium-long shots, which gives his films a sense of even continuity). Rohmer whispers, the better to speak clearly when the time is right. There is, for example, a sharply poignant moment during a conversation between Anne and François—she is telling him that she doesn't feel capable of living with anyone, while he, still holding on to his dreams of marriage, picks up a souvenir glass paperweight from a table and looks at the artificial snow falling inside it. The force of the moment doesn't come from the originality of the metaphor (though it gains an extra edge from the probability that the paperweight is a gift from the pilot), but rather from the sudden impact of an insert close-up in a film that hasn't gone in that close before. The visual continuity has been broken, just as something in François has snapped. But Rohmer's effects are rarely even that aggressive: more often, you sense slow and gradual change in the visual design—a patient, earned movement into medium close-up and emotional intimacy, or the movement of characters together into harmonious two-shot. One of the loveliest motifs in *The Aviator's Wife* is the film's slow opening and closing of space. It begins in a crowded interior, moves to an empty, though narrow, street, then into a small apartment, and from there to the release of the park. At the end of the film, these same steps are repeated, but in reverse order.

When Lucie asks François why he's watching the mysterious couple, he tells her at first that he's a detective—and there is a sense in which *The Aviator's Wife* is a detective film, though the mystery isn't a whodunit, but what was done and why. When François begins to follow the pilot, his motives aren't clear (to him or to us), but he comes to focus on the unknown woman. If he can figure out who she is—if she's wife or mistress or what—then he'll be able to judge the seriousness of the pilot's involvement with Anne—or, perhaps, he can confront her with the evidence of her lover's infidelity. But finding out "who" someone is, concretely and definitively, is exactly what Rohmer's shifting points of view make impossible. To the extent that we can share the characters' thoughts, and to the extent that we know sometimes more and sometimes less than they do, we're privileged to see the deceptions and misunderstandings. We see the characters dissemble, deceive, and mislead; we see them behave differently in different situations and with different people. None of this is presented critically: for Rohmer, it's the natural state of things. We know ourselves only partially and seldom; therefore we can never know others, and spying, like love, is only a game that allows us to pretend, for a while, that we can. The mystery of the blond woman's identity is finally solved, but the solution means nothing. The only identity that really matters lies buried in motives and feelings, and that identity remains inaccessible—it's too personal, too changeable, and perhaps, too frightened. In the end, the open, extroverted Lucie proves no more comprehensible than the surly, secretive Anne. With his shifting points of view, Rohmer suggests that we can never escape our own self-involvement—that the Anne François sees is not the Anne she herself thinks she is—but the beauty of those shifting points of view is that they allow us, for once, to experience the illusion of having escaped. At the end of *The Aviator's Wife*, we know François and we know Anne—not completely, but in a depth few movies have achieved. That is, we know their contradictions.

Francisca

Directed by MANOEL DE OLIVEIRA {September 23, 1983}

I no longer try to reconcile my love for Hollywood with my taste for the structuralist-minimalist-materialist avant-garde, though for a long time it struck me as schizophrenic that I could be deeply moved by the high Hollywood illusionism of a Frank Borzage melodrama one evening and transported just as far the next night by Jean-Marie Straub's endless circular pans in *Too Early, Too Late*. There is a lot of aesthetic ground between Borzage's glowing, soft-focus close-ups of Margaret Sullavan and Straub's decision to mount his camera on the dashboard of a Citroën and drive around the Place de la Bastille for 20 minutes without a cut. Yet as time passes, those contradictions don't seem quite as contradictory. In the politicized atmosphere of film criticism in the 70s, it was too often a question of making a choice: you could be a modernist or a classicist, an innovator or a preservationist, a materialist or an idealist, but never both. In the exhausted 80s, however, the points of contact seem more visible, the battle much less heated. Straub, for example, is a great admirer of John Ford's *Donovan's Reef*, a film that stands stylistically, thematically, and ideologically at the other end of the spectrum from *Too Early, Too Late*. What we have been missing is a classically trained director who can admit his points of contact with the modern cinema. With the emergence of the 75-year-old Portuguese filmmaker Manoel de Oliveira we have one at last.

Oliveira has been making movies since 1931, though his international reputation is relatively recent, dating from the delayed release to the festival circuit of his 1976 *Doomed Love*—a 276-minute adaptation of a 19th-century novel. *Francisca*, Oliveira's latest film (it will be shown this weekend at the Art Institute's Film Center) is only his sixth feature in 50 years of activity, and certainly his undeserved obscurity is largely due to the very small number of films he has been able to make. Yet the suspicion remains that Oliveira could not possibly have matured as an artist until the last decade—that his was a sensibility that required a particular cultural moment to be activated. Even now, *Francisca* seems on the cutting edge of the avant-garde; it would have been both inconceivable and incomprehensible in 1942, the year Oliveira made his first full-length film. Without the context provided by Godard, Straub, and the other young filmmakers of the last 20 years, Oliveira could not exist. There is a strange sense in which Oliveira seems both a precursor of the modern cinema and one of its most glorious products.

There are two kinds of filmmakers in the world: those who believe that the image is an illusion, a made thing that has no necessary relation to the world, and those who believe that the image potentially contains an element of truth, which can be discovered once the veil of illusionism has been lifted. The first approach is the classical approach, and it lends itself to story telling—the creation, through the manipulation of the image and its ordering into patterns that emphasize symmetry and closure, of a world that seems whole, logical, and intelligible, that has a beginning, a middle, and an end. The second is the approach of modernism, which tries to tear through the illusory cohesion of classicism in search of an elusive authenticity, the ragged texture of life as it is lived. Modernism can't tell a story, because the logic imposed by story-structure is one of the chief illusions it is fighting against. Or so, at least, the saying goes.

In *Francisca*, Oliveira uses modernist techniques to tell a story—a story of great subtlety, density, and emotional impact. Instead of murdering the fiction, as many modernists do, Oliveira attempts to purify it, stripping away layer after layer of stylistic incrustation, finally leaving the fiction clean and glistening, like a tiny precious stone. And yet, for all of Oliveira's drive toward the elemental and unadorned, the film retains a curling sense of the baroque, which rests in the incessant, meticulously observed emotional fluctuations of the characters. It is as if Jean-Marie Straub has collaborated with Max Ophuls: the refined mechanism of the materialist cinema is brought to bear on the most delicate mysteries of human emotions, in what can be described as an attempt to photograph and measure a soul.

The film is based on a novel by the leading contemporary Portuguese writer, Agustina Bessa Luis, which was in turn based on a true story. It is 1850, and the country (so an introductory title tells us) has been dealt a strong blow by the loss of Brazil; in the aristocratic circles where the story is set, there is a pervasive sense of defeat and aimlessness—fertile ground, the title continues to tell us, for the cultivation of perverse passions. José Augustó (Diego Dória), a wealthy young nobleman with a dolorous mustache and weak, exhausted eyes, enters into a friendship with Camilo Castelo Branco (Mário Barroso), an aspiring writer from the middle classes (and the future author of the novel upon which Oliveira based *Doomed Love*). The friendship seems to be founded on an attraction of opposites: the aristocrat's feckless decadence finds its foil and conscience in the aggressively moralistic young novelist, who in turn envies his friend's position and power. Perhaps there is something sexual there, too—something that can never be acknowledged or acted upon, and so works gradually to turn the friendship to resentment and malice. When Camilo falls in love with Francisca (Fanny) Owen (Teresa Menezes), the virginal daughter of an English army officer, José Augustó resolves to court her for himself; he wishes both to spite Camilo and, by refusing to love Fanny himself, to indulge a Sadean impulse. His loveless marriage, he tells Camilo, will be an experiment in cruelty to refine and strengthen Fanny's soul—he will, he proclaims, "produce an angel in the plentitude of martyrdom." Fanny, apparently taken with the young aristocrat's romantic figure, declares her love for him and leaves Camilo, eloping to José Augustó's country estate. But Fanny isn't the innocent that José Augustó believes her to be: she has a plan of her own—to force José Augustó to love her—and she will accomplish it by waiting him out, turning her suffering into his pity and remorse, her pain into her triumph.

It is a dense plot, thick with paradoxical intrigues, complicated motivations, and emotions that oscillate continuously between extremes of love and hate. Many modernists would emphasize that density, exaggerating the complications of the plot to the point of tangled absurdity—the point where story telling breaks down under its own weight. But Oliveira takes tremendous pains to tell it clearly and fully, giving each sequence the time it needs to make the full range of its dramatic points (the film runs 166 minutes). Or, when the action is too complicated to dramatize adequately, modestly declining to depict it at all. (He offers instead written summaries of the course of events.) It is an approach to adapting a novel that retains, and even foregrounds, the novelistic dimensions: there is none of the compression of events, the concentration of locales, or the condensation of character that ordinarily define a "successful" filmed novel, but instead a lush proliferation of literary elements, as if Oliveira wanted us to feel the form of the novel straining against the form of the film, threatening to burst. You begin to feel that *Francisca* could run eight or ten hours and still not contain the wealth of detail possible in a 300-page book—Oliveira makes us aware of the film form as a barrier, a strict limit on what can be shown.

Francisca is full of barriers—divisions between characters, between formal levels, between different times and different places. As each barrier is crossed, something is left behind: the movie seems to be an ongoing process of filtration, at the far end of which stand the historical figures of Fanny, Camilo, and José Augustó. Augustina Bessa Luis based her novel on the writings of Camilo and the letters and diaries of Fanny and José Augustó; Oliveira based his screenplay on her novel, and his film on his screenplay. The only element that comes uncorrupted through all this adaptation is the spoken language, and Oliveira has accordingly made the words of the characters the focus of his film—its center of truth. The speeches, antique in their archness and formality, aren't performed by the actors but simply read, in a slow, uninflected, declamatory style. There is a great deal of talk in the film, but very little dialogue: the characters don't address their speeches to one another, but instead, look out to a point beyond the frame, into an emptiness that can't be identified with the dramatic situation, the director and his camera, or even with the audience in the theater. Oliveira can't use the traditional shot/countershot method of filming conversations between characters, because to do so would destroy the generalized, declamatory nature of the language—designating each statement for a too-specific listener, it would turn the speeches into false dramatic situations. Instead, he photographs virtually every scene in an uninterrupted master shot, usually placing his camera at a slightly higher level than the action so that it must look down into the set like a spectator looking down at a stage. This peculiar angle, which emphasizes the stylized, theatrical blocking of the characters as they move across the unusually prominent floorboards, proclaims the artificiality of the environment; it makes the world of the film seem small, flimsy, and claustrophobically self-contained. Combined with the absence of cross-cutting (and the whole mechanism of audience identification and involvement that cross-cutting brings into play), Oliveira's visual strategy works to separate the audience from the fiction, to establish the fictional world as something wholly artificial, arbitrary, and impenetrable. This is the end product of the process of filtration that began with the living figures of 1850: the artifice has been emphasized to the point where it is no longer possible to identify the actors with their characters or the stage they inhabit with any outer world. Oliveira doesn't film reality, but rather the only reality that is available on film—he films a representation, the artistic substitute for reality.

The images that Oliveira gives us are true—true to their own artificiality. Oliveira has stripped the illusion of its power by identifying it as illusion, a common enough modernist strategy. Yet something else happens over the course of *Francisca*'s two and three-quarters hours: the inadequacy of the illusion seems to bolster the strength of the underlying reality, as we begin to form an impression of the three-dimensional events that have cast this flat shadow on the screen. Oliveira wants to show us only what genuinely can be shown—the thoughts of the characters as recorded in their writing, the vague outline of their world as it has been transmitted in paintings and photographs. He does not pretend to make the characters come alive, and he will not permit us to enter their emotions. But with every fact that he is able to give us, our grasp of the essential truth of the situation increases. It no longer matters if the action is literally true—it is emotionally, internally true, possessed of a weight and sharpness assembled from a thousand different fragments. Oliveira divides his characters, divides his scenes, and divides his forms, using elements of film, theater, and literature to cancel each other out. Just as José Augustó promised to produce an angel from an excess of suffering, so does Oliveira produce a clear statement from an excess of conflicts, confusions, and falsehoods. A sense of the spirit emerges from his microscopic study of material evidence, something whole and transcendent from his accumulation of parts. *Francisca* leaves us with the fact of a passion—a dangerous, elusive passion that changes its sense and purpose as it moves among the three main characters. At the end of the film, you can feel its shape, you can hold it in your hand.

[PART 2]

The End of Classical Hollywood

As I explain in the introduction, my years at the Reader *coincided with the final breakup of the old studio system and the rise of an important new group of filmmakers. I had a great deal of sympathy for the hardy survivors who still worked in the classical tradition, and I gravitated toward the new directors who built on that tradition. This section gathers together some considerations of films that continued to honor the classical aesthetic in its twilight years or creatively diverted it in new directions.*

CLASSICAL HOLLYWOOD >>

The Man Who Would Be King

Directed by JOHN HUSTON {March 19, 1976}

Who knows what it is that makes a masterpiece? *The Man Who Would Be King* is the best and most valuable film that John Huston has ever made, but still, in its material, it seems little different from the Huston films I've spent the last few years of my life despising. Ever since I was first initiated into the mysteries of the *politique des auteurs*, Huston has been my subconscious symbol of everything an American filmmaker should not be. He has a gimmicky, artificial style, no sense of dramatic ebb and flow, an overriding obsession with his own philosophical profundity, and a puritanical conception of art as punishment. Huston's movies—even the best of them, *The Treasure of the Sierra Madre*, *The Asphalt Jungle*—are "message movies" in the worst sense, petty moral parables about greed, ambition, and the bitter fruits thereof. John Huston has never had much to say, and what little he has said has been garbled.

But here, now, is *The Man Who Would Be King*—a movie built of the same things I have always disliked in Huston, but a movie that struck me as something very close to great.

You can sum up the structure of a typical Huston movie in one (compound) sentence: man struggles for wealth and fails. For "wealth" you may occasionally substitute "women" or "power" or "fame." The goal itself seems to make little difference—*failure* is the most important element. Huston is an old line determinist, enjoying nothing so much as kicking his characters down in the last reel. But always in the moment of loss, as the goal slips through the protagonist's fingers, there is a suspicious note of regret in Huston's ironic chuckling. The gold dust blowing away at the end of *Sierra Madre* is photographed with more anguish than the deaths of the main characters. On one hand, judging simply from the number of times the image recurs in his films, Huston seems to have a fixation on the idea of a vast, unearned wealth (this may be the romantic in him, always looking for a means of escape). On the other hand, judging from the viciousness with which Huston draws the unholy ambition of his characters, he seems ashamed of his obsession—not that you could blame him. This may explain why Huston's most corrupt characters are usually his most interesting—Sydney Greenstreet in *The Maltese Falcon*, for example—and why his sternly moralistic resolutions seem forced.

Everything above is as true of *The Man Who Would Be King* as it is of Huston's other films, but (and this is a big but) where Huston's moralizing seems insipid in *The Asphalt Jungle*, it seems insightful in *The Man Who Would*. I'm not sure why. Perhaps it's because *The Man Who Would* is so archetypal—a "perfect" Huston film refined through thirty years, more or less, of working the same theme. It has a clarity that Huston never found before, uncomplicated by the fleeting social issues that always seemed to distract him in the past. And it doesn't hurt, either, that *The Man Who Would Be King* has a sense of humor about what it's doing. Rudyard Kipling, after all, isn't Melville, Freud, or the Bible—to tick off a few of Huston's more ambitious projects—and for once Huston seems to be able to keep his literary pretensions in check. From Kipling, Huston acquires a naive sense of grandeur and mystery, and for the man who is arguably the most cynical director the American cinema has produced, a little naivety goes a long way toward establishing a more open and approachable kind of art.

The Man Who Would Be King is made of two large movements. The first part of the film is a journey: two soldiers, Michael Caine and Sean Connery, cashiered from the British Indian Army for petty thievery, decide to head out for Kafiristan, a remote, isolated country north of Afghanistan, where they hope to use their military training to set themselves up as kings. Connery and Caine are victims of the same sort of mad ambition that characterizes Huston's other protagonists, but the actors are able to give a childishness to the roles that gives their quest an amiable Quixotic quality—they don't lust, they dream. The journey to Kafiristan has a plainly metaphorical quality. As the outer limits of civilization are gradually passed, Connery and Caine feel their individual powers growing and see the sphere of their effective action expand. Finally isolated in the blank of a snow-covered mountain range, the two soldiers seem to have reached the limits of their personal resources, and, with all the comforts and confines of civilization behind them, they must face a hostile nature. But where Huston's past protagonists have inevitably found their defeat in nature—think of Bogart trapped in the mountains at the end of the Huston-scripted *High Sierra*—Connery and Caine are allowed to survive, thanks to a timely avalanche that closes an impassable chasm.

Crossing the mountains into Kafiristan, Connery and Caine enter a new realm of experience—a world where everything seems to lie within their power. The natives are easily dominated, believing the two soldiers—the first Europeans to appear in the country in hundreds of years—to be the descendants of Kafiristan's last conqueror, Alexander the Great. Kipling's short story is, partly at least, a metaphor for the British colonial experience—imperialism predicated upon racism. Huston is able to expand (or reduce, depending on your ideological orientation) the political theme into a mad, Nietzschean fantasy. The conquerors become gods, with perfect freedom in action and command, and, not incidentally, with access to a treasure trove of unimaginable proportions. Caine, the cynic, wants to take the mundane, practical way out: pack up the loot and head back to civilization. But Connery has come to relish his role; he doesn't want to stop playing. Caine can go home, Connery will stay and be God. Kafiristan is the ultimate romantic fantasy of all of Huston's heroes, and Connery, for once, has been able to realize the dream.

When disaster comes—as it must to all men in John Huston movies—Connery is betrayed, not by his greed or guilt, but by his essential humanity. Huston allows us to forgive Connery for his hubris as we could never forgive Bogart for his more materialistic ambition. Greatness is the desire of all men, Huston says, just as greatness is finally beyond all men.

This is the stuff of pathos, not of tragedy; and it is a sign of Huston's new stature as an artist that *The Man Who Would Be King* ends not in a gasp of awe before a coldly ironic, malignant universe—as so many of Huston's films do—but descends instead on a note of quiet melancholy, made equally of a respect for man and a respect for man's limitations.

Fedora

Directed by BILLY WILDER {June 22, 1979}

Billy Wilder's *Fedora* seems destined to be a complete commercial failure, but that failure might be the surest sign of its artistic success. *Fedora* is Wilder's 25th film, the latest in a career that dates back to 1920s Berlin and includes a long period in which he was one of Hollywood's most consistently successful writer-directors. But in *Fedora*, Wilder almost seems to be working against his crowd-pleasing instincts: the film is a deliberate anachronism, a movie meant to seem out of its time. It's a personal summation, an emotional autobiography, addressed not to the filmgoing audience of the 70s but to some small coterie of friends and critics. In it, Wilder talks to his colleagues from the old days, sharing made-up memories of how things were or should have been. And he is also addressing some indefinite audience of the future, putting down some of his deepest thoughts and intuitions for a time when they might seem more meaningful and more important. *Fedora* is Billy Wilder's last will and testament (although there is no reason why it should be his last film). It doesn't belong in a movie theater, but in a bank vault.

It is no serene, autumnal reflection, though. It offers no rocking chair wisdom, no grandfatherly counsel. Instead, the film is full of anger, regret, self-pity, and flashes of terror; it's the work of an old man who won't lie down, who won't accept what has happened to him and his world. Sometimes, Wilder's anger and bitterness are communicated as sheer irascibility—he pushes the audience away, as if he were sure of being misunderstood. The film is heavy going, perhaps intentionally so. Wilder hasn't bothered to put his thoughts and observations into a cogent, apprehensible form—rather, he's loaded the plot with asides, piling on ideas, allusions, and privileged moments with an abandon that threatens to break the paper-thin story line.

It might have been better if the plot had collapsed, for, as the film stands, the story is more of a distraction than an organized principle. It comes from a chapter in Thomas Tryon's collection of Hollywood tales, *Crowned Heads*, and it depends on a series of annoying twists and tricks, all very "literary" and all carefully preserved by Wilder's screenplay (written with his old collaborator, I. A. L. Diamond). It's easy to see what attracted Wilder to the material—the book is practically a catalog of Wilder's twilight concerns, touching on age, romance, stardom, art, illusion, and memory. But these themes are *only* touched on, as the book blithely gathers them together for the purposes of a trivial *Twilight Zone* climax. Wilder is clearly using the novel as a sort of Rorschach test, a way of drawing out his own emotional associations. As fascinating as his responses are, though, he's still left with Tryon's plot machinery grinding away in the background. Tryon's construction is so pointlessly complicated that the characters are compelled, every two reels or so, to stand around and explain it to each other, armed with maps, charts, and Rube Goldberg diagrams. Without the exposition, the film would shed half of its running time.

The plot may be worthless in its details, but in its overall shape, Wilder has discovered an elegant and suggestive construction. It resurrects the flashback structure of his 1950 *Sunset Boulevard*, but it goes further, placing flashbacks within flashbacks and complicating the time scheme in a manner reminiscent of such demented 40s *films noirs* as Michael Curtiz's *Passage to Marseille* and John Brahm's *The Locket*. Wilder uses this firmly dated technique with a certain degree of self-consciousness; it's one of the ways in which *Fedora* can be lifted out of its proper time and place. But the jumble of tenses also clarifies the film's design as a subjective stream of consciousness. The images come floating up, appearing in the order of memory.

Again like *Sunset Boulevard*, *Fedora* is framed by death. William Holden narrated the 1950 film from the vantage point of a dead body floating in a swimming pool; in *Fedora*, Holden again narrates, but this time the funeral is not for him but Fedora (Marthe Keller), a legendary Hollywood star of the 30s who has suddenly died after a spectacular comeback. In the opening shot, we see her apparent suicide: in the dead of a blue and black night, she throws herself under the wheels of an onrushing train. The image, disconnected from the rest of the film, is presented as a puzzle—the puzzle the movie will attempt to solve. Holden, our agent, picks up the narration at Fedora's elaborate star funeral, where he has come, half to prove to himself that the legend is really dead, half to resolve his own responsibility in her death. As an independent producer who hoped to lure Fedora out of seclusion for one last project, Holden fears that he may have prompted her suicide by violating her sanctuary.

But the mystery that *Fedora* is addressed to is not the death of its star, but of its maker. By imagining himself in the place of his heroine, Wilder has executed a sublime, madly romantic explosion of ego, one of the most extreme in film history. Howard Hawks looked at his advancing age and declining skills in the serious comedy of *El Dorado* (and again, less effectively, in *Rio Lobo*), and Jean Renoir symbolically ceded his art to a younger generation in *Le Petit Théâtre*. But only Chaplin, as Andrew Sarris has pointed out, had the audacity to imagine his own death, in his great *Limelight* of 1952. Chaplin pictured himself passing as serenely as he did in real life, but Wilder's vision of his death is a violent one. He must be pushed out, just as he and his art have been pushed out of Hollywood.

The points of identification between Fedora and Wilder seem endless:

both are Germans, who come to America to practice their art. Both are phenomenally successful (Wilder has six Oscars), but both gradually fade from the public view. Fedora's late-life rebirth is revealed as an illusion: the artist can hold on to his audience only by creating a false version of his or her younger self (Fedora through plastic surgery, Wilder by returning to his roots in screwball comedy with his 1975 remake of *The Front Page*). Fedora's comeback is staged in England, where Wilder made his late masterpiece, *The Private Life of Sherlock Holmes*.

But Fedora, the artist and romantic, represents only half of Wilder's personality; the other, more cynical and self-interested, side is embodied by the William Holden character. Where Fedora is an extravagant European, Holden is a dourly practical American—Billy Wilder as brash show business entrepreneur, the persona that he has always presented in public, and a figure that recurs in many of his films. Holden tells himself, and us, that his mission is purely mercenary; only by snagging Fedora's star power can he salvage his shaky career as an independent producer. But as Holden pursues Fedora to her Greek island retreat, he betrays a deeper motive: to recapture the memory of the one night he spent with her, 40 years earlier, when he was a lowly assistant director, and she a leading lady. The link between the two characters and what they represent is, movingly, forged only in the shadowy past.

What to make of this film, as deeply flawed as it is deeply felt? The classical purity of the style is almost aggressive; by refusing close-ups, Wilder affirms his faith in a method that he knows to be hopelessly unfashionable. There are no jazzy zooms or hyped-up editing effects. Instead, the film has been conceived as a series of tableaux, careful long-shot compositions through which the characters move with a slow, deliberate grace. Some critics have called the film stiff and lifeless, but its eerie stillness seems to be part of Wilder's point. Ultimately, *Fedora*'s strengths are inseparable from its weaknesses; its stiffness is answered by its unearthly detachment, its romantic excesses are answered by the sincerity of their expression.

I admire *Fedora*, but it also frightens me. There's something intimidating in Wilder's ruthless self-exposure, something sad and awful in the way he hurls up his fears and fantasies—something, in the end, a little mad. In *Sunset Boulevard*, Wilder viewed the vain delusions of his aging film star, Norma Desmond, with his characteristic mixture of cynical contempt and romantic wonder. *Fedora* doesn't have that distance; it's *Sunset Boulevard* told from Norma's point of view.

Escape From Alcatraz

Directed by DON SIEGEL {June 29, 1979}

Coming at a different time, Don Siegel's *Escape From Alcatraz* might not seem as valuable as it does now, at the start of a summer season filled with drive-in retreads (*Alien*, *Prophecy*) and empty-headed comedies (*The Main Event*). Summer, when moviegoing is supposed to be a mindless, cooling experience, isn't the time for striking originality or heavy thinking, but the studios seem to have taken that commercial dictum to new lengths this year: a wrap-around movie like *Alien* practically defies us to think, marshalling its aggressive, gnawing effects like sensorial shock troops. *Alien* keeps you up against the wall, firing occasional bursts of Dolby stereo over your head—enough to keep you cowering and intimidated, if not pleasurably, cathartically frightened. If *Alien* lowered its barrage for one second, it would shrink into the crude, unmotivated, comic book fantasy it is at heart. It's all noise and clutter, standing in for tone and style. You *experience* it, all right, but you don't appreciate it. Shrewdly, it doesn't give you the time or freedom to.

The idea behind *Escape From Alcatraz* is no more fresh or imaginative than *Alien*'s: the plot is contained in the title. But in the filming, Siegel has given it a contour and polish, an elegance of form that is at once purely functional and a thing of beauty. It's a quiet, dark, insinuating movie—even the suspense sequences have an unnatural calm. The visuals are tight and claustrophobic, as they have to be in a prison picture, but even in the film's close spaces, Siegel's direction retains a distance—an aesthetic edge that lets us see and appreciate what he's doing. If a lesser director left a gap like that, it could be fatal. But Siegel, with the assurance of 30 years of filmmaking behind him, shows us how the tricks are done, and then captivates us anyway. His technique is a matter of pride to him, and he has confidence enough to set it off.

Escape From Alcatraz is one of those films—like Minnelli's *Yolanda and the Thief*, Hitchcock's *The Man Who Knew Too Much*, or, more recently, John Carpenter's *Halloween*—in which style is the ultimate subject: it's a movie about itself. Siegel, unquestionably, has done finer, more incisive work, including his own previous prison drama, *Riot in Cell Block 11* (1954). But style, in this stumbling, witless era for filmmaking, has become a subject of some nobility—it's almost a heroic act, in and of itself, to try to impose some shape and order, some grace of expression, on material that audiences have learned to accept in its crudest form. The skill and precision that Siegel has brought to bear on *Alcatraz* may, in commercial terms, be completely superfluous—or even detrimental, as audiences expecting the big zap of *Alien* walk away disappointed. If *Escape From Alcatraz* had been directed by, say, a Stuart Rosenberg or a Michael Winner, most moviegoers and critics would never notice the difference. Siegel's craftwork—the same steady job he's been doing, unheralded, since the 1950s—only becomes art when it is no longer the norm, no longer necessary. In the summer of 1979, it is art.

In 1968, Siegel, then a contract director at Universal, was assigned to *Coogan's Bluff*, a cops and robbers film designed to showcase a former TV actor returning from a successful sojourn in Italy. The actor, of course, was Clint Eastwood, and the rest was genre film history—in some ways, the only genre film history worth writing in the last decade. Siegel took the silent, menacing image that Eastwood had developed in his spaghetti westerns, and gradually—through a series of four films—whittled it down to human dimensions, adding humor and vulnerability (and, some said, a wide streak of masochism) to Eastwood's distant, calculating intelligence. As a result, Eastwood became one of the few iconographically complex performers to emerge in the 70s—one of the few actors who meant something, both as a character and a cultural force, to his audiences. (Charles Bronson had much the same potential, but he, unfortunately, never found a Siegel to shape his screen personality into meaningful terms.)

Escape From Alcatraz represents Eastwood and Siegel's first pairing since 1971, and a lot has happened in the last eight years: Eastwood has established himself as a director of talent and vision in his own right, and Siegel has begun to receive the critical approbations that once were his only in France. With their newfound reputations streaming behind them, neither star nor director can qualify as the humble artisan he was when they parted after *Dirty Harry*. Consequently, their reunion seems fraught with self-consciousness, and a slightly distracting air of artistic ambition hangs over the film. Siegel, uncharacteristically, has taken his credit as "Donald," an injection of formality that also affects the mise-en-scène. In its gravity and sparseness, *Escape From Alcatraz* owes less to *Riot in Cell Block 11* than to Robert Bresson's *A Man Escaped*.

Like Bresson's films, *Escape* subscribes to the theory that less is more. Plotting and character analysis are kept to a minimum, the color palette of Bruce Surtees's cinematography is restricted to greens, grays, and blacks, and the acting is confined to a narrow vocal range between low murmurs and whispers. The dramatic tension is generated entirely by the elemental conflict between Eastwood's restless inmate and Patrick McGoohan's repressive, vaguely Nixonian warden. Yet Siegel grants them only one real confrontation, and even that is brief and anticlimactic. We're a long way here from the popular notion of Eastwood as a bare-knuckled, mano-a-mano bruiser. Instead of pummeling his adversary, he chooses the deeper, more symbolic revenge of fatally undermining the warden's authority through his escape.

Nor is there ever any doubt that Eastwood will escape: that much is guaranteed by the title, and Siegel makes no real attempt to build up the tension. Once the decision to escape has been made, the action proceeds with a cool inevitability, as all of the blocks to Eastwood's success are swept away by a providential hand. The question is not, Will he make it?, but How will he make it?—and with that transformation, Siegel passes over the standard visceral pleasures of the escape film, and offers, instead, the more rarefied satisfaction of solving an intellectual puzzle. The action is not physical, but mental. During the escape itself, Siegel accentuates the danger of the situation only by departing from his restricted color scheme long enough to include a flashing red light (of unseen origin) that bathes Eastwood and his two partners in an eerie, disorienting glow as they climb down the walls of the compound. The effect, in its simplicity, has the sure, restrained touch of a master.

Some complaints have already been filed against the film's downbeat ending. Instead of bursting into downtown San Francisco and hoisting a few at Fisherman's Wharf, Eastwood and his companions simply fade away into the darkness that has been hanging over every frame. I think I can understand the objections—after so much constraint and repression, the audience might deserve a little release—but Siegel's choice strikes me as braver and more faithful to the ascetic spirit of the film. The disappearance is most magical—now you see them, now you don't—and the sudden emptiness and openness of the final images are liberating in a subtler, more resonant way.

Eastwood, too, has kept himself on a tight rein, bypassing the psychological complexity of his recent, self-directed characters in *The Gauntlet* and *The Outlaw Josey Wales* in favor of the towering, mythic enigma of his Italian films. For Sergio Leone, he was The Man With No Name; here, he's The Man With No Past—a phantom figure who emerges from the darkness in the opening images and is absorbed by it again in the end. Richard Tuggle's screenplay has supplied classically curt dialogue—someone asks Eastwood what kind of childhood he had, and his perfectly sufficient and expressive one-word reply is, "Short." Like John Wayne before him, Eastwood has the ability to invest the simplest speeches and phrases with a shuddering moral authority. I doubt that Lord Olivier himself could conjure the menace, contempt, and indomitability that Eastwood's soft, clenched voice gives to his pronunciation of "asshole."

The Human Factor

Directed by OTTO PREMINGER {April 18, 1980}

Style is often spoken of as a static thing: possessed by the director, displayed by the film, and devoured by the audience. Every director, by definition, has a style, be it elegant or clumsy, expressive or incoherent. But we sometimes forget that a director can have more than one style, be equally adept with a range of tones and technique. Such was certainly the case with John Ford: it is always a small shock to realize that the expressionist flights of *The Informer* and the direct, natural imagery of *Steamboat 'Round the Bend* both belong to the same year of 1935. More often, styles metamorphose over a period of time, as, for example, the neo-realist Renoir of *La Grande illusion* gave way to the wonderful artificialities of *Eléna et les hommes* and *Picnic on the Grass*. For many critics, the Renoir of *Grande illusion* is the only Renoir; everything else is decline and debasement, a betrayal of the lofty principles of realism. But this is a narrow, limiting point of view. An artist will naturally feel the need to say things differently at different times and the style that answers at one moment will not suffice at the next. Too often, we equate the style with the man, forgetting that it is, at best, a tool, and that the continuities that count are those that run deeper.

Over the years, Otto Preminger's style has changed as radically as Renoir's—perhaps even more so. The features of his 40s style—gliding camera movements, chiaroscuro lighting, and intense, long takes—find their blunt contradiction in the hard, flat images of Preminger's latest work, *The Human Factor*. The contrast is so striking that I'm afraid many viewers will take one look at the shallow, closed-in compositions of the new film, think back to the depth and complexity of *Laura*'s visual style, and conclude that Preminger has abruptly succumbed to senility. From its opening shot—a view of a small, sterile office, taken with a short lens that pounds out the perspective into a flat, uninviting space—*The Human Factor* is startling, abrasive, and dismaying. But as the film gathers force and detail, the relentlessly banal images take on a kind of beauty—a functional beauty, in that they continue to embody the precision and clarity that have always been the basis of Preminger's mise-en-scène, and also a beauty of brinksmanship, the thrill of an artist dancing on the edge, openly courting disaster.

The Human Factor represents the end point in a line of development that Preminger has been pursuing since the late 60s—a move away from well-rounded, emotionally shaded drama, into sparseness, severity, and logic. He has achieved a drama of pure surfaces (though it is anything but superficial), devoid of emotional appeals to the audience, free of directorial judgments of the characters, and purged of the seductive highs and lows of traditional narrative texture. *The Human Factor* plays out in an even, uninflected flow of events and images. No single episode is given a value over any other, as Preminger untwists the contortions of the plot into a clean, straight line. The film seems to consist entirely of exposition, of the careful gathering of information, unrelieved by confrontation or climax. And yet, when the climax does come, it cuts deeply and truly. Preminger has violated every commonsense rule of cinematic expressiveness and dramatic construction, and his risk has gained him a uniquely affecting work—unique, because I can't imagine the style ever working again for anyone else. Preminger has earned it with his intransigence and experimentation over the last two decades; in the hands of another director, lacking Preminger's commitment and assurance, it could only lead to debacle.

Based on Graham Greene's recent best-seller, *The Human Factor* is a spy story set in a shrunken world, where détente has turned the business of espionage from a life-and-death struggle into a petty war of annoyance between two malfunctioning bureaucracies. Already, the background is permeated with Preminger's characteristic ambiguity: although he is attracted to melodramatic situation, his films invariably work to soften and nullify the melodramatic contrasts. Preminger's battle of East and West is no titanic struggle of good and evil, but rather, a sordid, irrelevant squabble between two tired opponents, where the highest stakes are some slight loss of face in the eyes of a vaguely comprehended international community. But where a calm, balanced point of view—on issues political and personal—has always been a high value in Preminger's films, the same viewpoint seems to function here as weary disillusionment, an excuse for inaction and moral paralysis. Détente (it may only be a memory now, but it still works as a metaphor) becomes an image of blunted passions and abandoned ideals, spreading a spirit of debilitation and uselessness while it urges a healthy embrace of reality. For a rationalist like Preminger, the world of *The Human Factor* might be thought to be a kind of utopia—here, at last, is a life ruled by logic and dispassion, the two prime qualities of Preminger's directorial personality. But in this reduced, reasonable, supremely manageable world, morbid symptoms have begun to appear.

There is a leak—a small, trivial flow of information on economic matters—somewhere in the South African section of British intelligence. For the old boys who now listlessly preside over the network, word of the leak comes, perversely, as good news. Here, at last, is a chance to stir up some action and excitement, to get the cloak out of mothballs and shine up the dagger. Daintry (Richard Attenborough), a new security officer, is assigned to investigate the London end of the operation. His efforts are concentrated on the two-man office responsible for the collation and analysis of data—on Castle (Nicol Williamson), a veteran operative now comfortably in from the cold, and his junior partner Davis (Derek Jacobi), a pale, nervous young man, trying hard to live with the disappointing fact of his own mediocrity. Davis's disheveled life—he is unmarried, unhappy, and untidy about security procedures—naturally attracts suspicion, and the division's chief doctor (Robert Morley) eagerly launches the process of eliminating him, slipping Davis a slow-acting poison disguised as blood pressure pills.

Davis is, of course, the wrong man—guilty of nothing more than unfulfilled ambitions and romantic discontent. It is the colorless family man Castle who harbors the heart of a double agent, and it is the aim of *The Human Factor* to find that heart—no easy task, for it is buried deep, deep inside. Greene's novel is exquisitely structured, full of deft twists and turns. But while Preminger adheres to the outline of Greene's plotting, he takes the film in a different direction, using the carefully locked chain of events to move down into the soul of his protagonist—for Preminger, plot is character. *The Human Factor* moves through a series of revelations about Castle—from the fact that this narrow, conservative suburbanite has a black wife and child, along to the ultimate exposure of his double-agent status—but Preminger's presentation of the material is so unemphatic, so casual, that the word *revelation* hardly seems to apply.

This has long been Preminger's method: with the exception of Rossellini, Preminger is the least intrusive of filmmakers, the least inclined to pass judgments on his characters or offer the audience a rigid perspective on the action. Preminger demands an active, participatory viewer: to watch one of his films is to engage in a continual process of perception and evaluation, of the gathering of information and its interpretation (interesting to note that Preminger's fall from popularity occurred in the late 60s, coincident with the rise of the go-with-the-flow aesthetic spearheaded by *2001*). But in *The Human Factor*, the method reaches a new extreme; the viewer is asked not only to pass judgments for himself, but also to discern the emotions under scrutiny from the scantest of surface evidence—from looks, gestures, and actions that often go unexplained in dramatic terms. For example, there is the highly enigmatic business of Castle's repeated visits to a used book store, where he habitually buys two copies of the same novel; working on a deeper level, there is an apparently gratuitous nightclub scene, in which Preminger wordlessly presents three distinct sets of moral and political attitudes by cutting between the floor show—a striptease done up in African drag—and the reactions registered by Williamson, Jacobi, and Morley.

The Human Factor is a film about hidden feelings in which feelings are hidden from the camera. The images seem designed to express, wrenchingly, nothing more than their own inexpressiveness—blank faces against blank backgrounds. The film covers a wide range of settings—from an English country house to a cold-water flat in Moscow—but all of the interiors acquire an eerie sameness in their lack of detail: in the naked, evenly painted or blandly papered walls, in the sparse furnishings too neatly arranged. None of the rooms looks lived in—and none of them has been, not in any real sense. The characters move through them uncomfortably; they are cold, inhospitable, and belong to no one, decorated not to reflect a personality, but to confine it, deny it. For Castle, that denial provides a kind of security. He has long since ceased to live on the surface, in order to better protect the private world he shares with his wife and child.

Preminger was one of the first directors to discover the potential of the wide-screen image, using the greater freedom of the elongated frame to hold his players in balanced, complementary relationships, unseparated by the exigencies of cross cutting. He seldom used reaction shots, preferring to keep his characters united in a single emotional and physical context, a method that emphasizes interdependence and continuity over isolation and fragmentation. *The Human Factor* has been photographed in the standard narrow gauge, which, for Preminger, is not a casual choice—it is only the second of his films to use the standard ratio in the last 20 years. The visual style, once open and synthetic, becomes closed and divisive; the cross cutting (though still minimal) takes on an oppressively physical quality, cutting through conversations to isolate the characters in their individual frames—frames that imprison the actors, like clear plastic boxes. The two-shot remains the basis of Preminger's mise-en-scène, but with the constriction of space has come a strange loss of intimacy: the characters are forced closer together, but they have less to say to each other. The two-shots are unbalanced, tenuous; the relationships they create can't hold.

The characters strain to make contact—Daintry, with his sad fumblings toward friendship with Castle; Davis, with his unrequited crush on the secretary down the hall—but their overtures have no effect; their signals are too dim, too dispirited. Only two characters are able to evade loneliness: Morley's monstrous Dr. Percival, whose blind loyalty to his work leaves him without friends and wishing none, and Castle, who alone is able to override the debilitating requirements of his work and save something private for his family. In Castle, a spark of compassion and moral concern remains alive—the human factor of Greene's title. Castle guards it jealously, ferociously: it is the one thing that allows him to remain alive, the one warm corner in his cold world. But it will also destroy him.

Greene sets out Castle's dilemma as a moral paradox—he is torn between two loyalties, one to his wife and family, one less selfish, more abstract. Some information has come into his hands that could prevent a wholesale slaughter, but to pass the information along would mean exposure as a double agent. But Preminger, maintaining his distanced point of view, doesn't focus on the struggles of conscience that occupy Greene's protagonist—and that, for Greene, are also the climax of his Catholic fiction. Instead, Preminger handles Castle's decision to defect with the same matter-of-factness that has come before: it is less a choice than the logical consequence of the character's humanity, and it is reached without visible conflict. Given who he is, there is nothing else he can do. The qualities that bind him to his wife are the qualities that force him to leave her. Preminger presents his harsh conclusion as if it were the last step in a complicated theorem: he has logically proven the horror of logic.

Through its fierce repression of emotion, *The Human Factor* emerges as Preminger's most passionate film. When the characters' feelings are finally allowed to surface in the last sequence, the effect is devastating—it's like a flash into color at the end of a black-and-white film. Not that it is a simple effect or rhetorical flourish: Preminger has carefully hoarded his treasure, and to finally share in it is to have a glimpse of a rare and precious thing, an emotion sanctified by its scarcity. In *The Human Factor*, Preminger has followed his ingrained attitudes and stylistic preferences to their outermost extreme: it is a way of testing his most deeply held beliefs and a way of feeling their limitations most strongly.

NEW HOLLYWOOD >>

The Driver

Directed by WALTER HILL {July 28, 1978}

The Driver couldn't look less like a writer's film. There's no dialogue at all in the first reel, and the lead player (Ryan O'Neal) only manages to clear his throat in the middle of the second. Thereafter, the characters' speech is terse to the point of abstraction and beyond. No one says anything with a full sentence when one or two carefully chosen words will do, while the film's most meaningful passages—two long, meticulously choreographed car chases—take place with no literary accompaniment whatsoever. The writer and director, Walter Hill, makes his priorities perfectly clear when the most damning trait he gives to his heavy (Bruce Dern) is an unfortunate tendency to talk too much.

Nothing could be further removed from the traditional notion of the writer's film, as it's been elaborated in the work of Ben Hecht, Billy Wilder, Preston Sturges, and Joseph Mankiewicz (the classical grouping of writers turned directors). At its best, in the hands of Wilder and Mankiewicz, the writer's film aspired to the clear, crisp presentation of dialogue, expanded and inflected by the image track. The worst of the writer's films, Hecht's in particular, descended to a sort of illustrated radio, with disembodied dialogue whistling through unfocused compositions like wind through a cave. By rights, Hill ought to belong to the same school: *The Driver* is his sixth film as a screenwriter and only his second as a director. But Hill seems determined to rise above his dark past. *The Driver* is a writer's film only in the best sense: it was written as a film. Dialogue is relegated to its proper place, as only one tool among the range of expressive equipment at the director's disposal. Hill's camera placement, his cutting, his sense of décor, and his careful sequencing join his abstract dialogue as component parts of a single articulation. A flat phrase like "Go home," which is used twice in the film, carries two widely different meanings at two different times; not because of the eloquence of the line, nor the actor's inflection, but because of the different cinematic circumstances that surround it. Whatever its faults as a work of art—and it has several—*The Driver* stands as a work of cinema, making full and intelligent use of the resources of the medium. As such, it couldn't have come at a better time than this summer of discontent, when film after film, *Sgt. Pepper* after *Grease*, has failed to reach even a remedial level of visual literacy.

The Driver is classically plotted, which is to say it has practically no plot at all. Ryan O'Neal plays the title character, an underworlder who specializes in piloting getaway cars. For him it is more of an avocation than a job, more of a way of life than a living. O'Neal's identification with his work goes beyond mere pride in his skill; the act of driving is his entire existence. There is the almost symbiotic rapport with the vehicle, the tactical knowledge of the roads, byways, and back alleys of the city, the strategical sense of when to attack a pursuer and when to lie low, when to fly and when to crawl. When all else fails, there is raw nerve. O'Neal's last recourse is a blind, headlong rush at his opponent, determination raised to the level of moral force and incorporating chance, bravado, and an undeniable death wish.

O'Neal's opposite number is a police detective played by Bruce Dern, the only character to whom Hill is willing to grant a degree of psychological shading. In contrast to the enforced deadpans of the other performers, Dern plays his part with most of his manic Method style intact: he is all wild eyes and quick, jerky movements, as appalling and fascinating as ever. Dern's identification with his job is no less extreme than O'Neal's, but it takes a different direction. The satisfaction is not in the chase, but in the capture; he is a manipulator of ends where O'Neal is an artist of methods. Dern speaks continually in terms of "winners" and "losers." His job is a game (a metaphor that Hill slightly overextends) that he is obsessed with winning at whatever cost—moral, legal, social. For the moment, the challenger is O'Neal, whom Dern nicknames "Cowboy" in a bit of misapplied cultural analogy. The nickname implies a self-conscious romanticism that has nothing to do with O'Neal's motives; rather, the romantic zeal belongs to Dern, and he must bring O'Neal down to his level, from the existential to the obsessional, in order to effect the challenge.

The story is as linear as the structure of a Roadrunner cartoon—pure chase—and it is made even more so by Hill's careful paring of every social dimension. This is no story of cops and robbers, the defenders of society and its would-be attackers. Dern is as much of a maverick as O'Neal, and his motives have nothing to do with duty or responsibility, either to his superiors or to the public he is ostensibly assigned to protect. The challenge is made, in a beautifully conceived scene in which Dern wordlessly returns a burglar's tool that O'Neal has intentionally left in the wreck of a stolen car. Dern constructs his trap, and O'Neal walks into it wide-eyed, emerging one bank robbery, one gunfight, and one car chase later as the upholder of one half of a very delicate stalemate.

The structure is somewhat clouded by the introduction of a third main character: Isabelle Adjani, playing a gambler and part-time mistress who sees O'Neal at the scene of a crime, refuses to identify him for Dern, and eventually enters the game on O'Neal's side. Adjani is given the unfortunate responsibility of playing the love interest in a film that has no interest in love. Apparently written in more out of a sense of obligation than necessity, she has little to do, and Hill doesn't seem to know what to make of her. Stunningly attractive as Truffaut's Adele H., she is made almost plain here. Campily dressed in a black suit, her eyes hidden by the brim of a floppy 1940s hat, Adjani affects the classic pose of the femme fatale, but the temptations she offers mean nothing to the asocial and apparently asexual O'Neal. A love scene in O'Neal's hotel room was reportedly eliminated from the final cut—a shrewd decision on Hill's part, for the sudden intrusion of a recognizable human emotion (lust if not love) would throw the film fatally out of kilter. The moment of the cut remains one of *The Driver*'s most imaginative technical flourishes. Adjani, standing in O'Neal's room, makes a slight, almost imperceptible move toward him, and the shot is abruptly terminated, leaving nothing more than the subtlest possible hint of a relationship that goes beyond the purely professional. To show their dispassionate lovemaking would be merely sordid, but to imply it approaches the sublime, placing it in a half-world of dimly remembered feelings and unfulfilled impulses.

Given the linearity of its plot, its intentionally two-dimensional characters, and its highly stylized dialogue, nearly everything about *The Driver* seems simpler—not to say more superficial—than Hill's first directorial effort, *Hard Times*. A rich mix of atmosphere (New Orleans in the Depression) and allusions (everyone from Edgar Allan Poe to Robert Bresson), *Hard Times* forged its enigmas more carefully, more intriguingly. Alongside the Charles Bronson character in *Hard Times*—a drifter who is "filling in some in-betweens" by working as a street fighter with gambler James Coburn—Ryan O'Neal seems to exist wholly on the surface: no mystery is created about his past (the question never arises), and his motives seem almost straightforward. The thematic parallels are clear, and it's particularly interesting to see how the partnership between the silent Bronson and the verbal Coburn is transposed to the rivalry between the similar character types of O'Neal and Dern. At bottom, the subjects of both films are the same: professional skill is hypothesized as a way of confronting the vagaries and aimlessness of life; clear and unambiguous conflicts are created that answer restlessness through action. *The Driver*, though, lacks the implicit despair, the wider philosophical context of *Hard Times*. But Hill makes up for the loss of thematic resonance by turning to a different tactic. If the subject of *The Driver* is skill, Hill restates it on a technical level by displaying an extremely impressive skill of his own.

The car chases, which must make up nearly a third of the film's efficient 91-minute time, are virtuoso pieces, among the most accomplished montage sequences to be assembled in Hollywood in the last decade. The chases could almost stand as independent films—studies in motion through time—and the sequences do take on a plastic beauty quite apart from their function in the narrative. Hill uses an unusually large number of shots, taken from most of the available vantage points: the camera moving in front of, alongside, or behind the car, above or below it, moving back to the curb to capture the sweep of the chase, anticipating it, sometimes glimpsing the action off in the distance. Movement is conveyed primarily by the rhythm of the cutting, while the shots themselves develop a sense of contrasting spaces: the narrow confines of the vehicle, the sudden expansion from street to highway. The sound track montage is no less skillful. The cacophony of screaming tires, blaring horns, and wailing sirens (the latter among the most expressive voices to be heard in the film) is assembled with a musical sense reminiscent of Bernard Herrmann's electronic chirps and twitters in *The Birds*.

The nervous energy of the chase sequences carries over into the dialogue scenes. The cutting, of course, is slower, but Hill keeps up his compulsive shot-changing, providing more coverage of a simple two-character dialogue than most directors would give to a house afire. Even when the characters and camera are perfectly still, the relentlessness of Hill's montage keeps the scene on edge; a jitter creeps into even the most benign contexts. Overall, the rhythms of *The Driver* resemble the classic construction of a Howard Hawks film: dialogue alternated with action, the tensions created in a static scene exploding into movement in the next scene, to be either resolved or exaggerated.

The Driver takes place in a Los Angeles that will be unrecognizable to most of the city's natives—which is to say mainly downtown, which the vast majority of Angelinos seem to know only dimly and by reputation. Still, Hill's framing exaggerates the strangeness of the urban landscape: we see it only in its most elemental sections, bare walls and dim interiors, the shadows cast by buildings creating an artificial twilight even in the film's infrequent ventures out into the light of day. Large interior spaces—warehouses, parking garages, a train station—are contrasted to cramped rooms and dingy bars, but all of the settings have an unnatural nakedness, a lack of detail, in common. The Los Angeles that Hill conjures is spare, empty, anonymous, mysteriously compelling in its lifelessness.

The harsh neutrality of the setting immediately invokes the spirit of Robert Bresson, the great French filmmaker for whom all detail—architectural, psychological, or otherwise—is a sign of cinematic impurity. Hill, wisely, doesn't go to Bresson's extremes (only Bresson can get away with that), but a good deal of Bresson's method is also apparent in his direction of actors. Apart from Dern's performance, there is very little "acting" per se in the film. The players deliver their lines as flatly as possible, maintaining a perfect passivity of expression. It is this decision, more than any other of Hill's radical stylistic choices, that seems most clearly guaranteed to alienate the popular audience. But when it works, it works brilliantly: thoughts and feelings must be read by inference, and the viewer discovers them almost as the character does. It may be cruel to say that Ryan O'Neal gives his best performance in *The Driver*, where he isn't asked to perform at all, but it's true. In one purely static three-quarter shot near the end of the film, O'Neal stares inexpressively at a young driver who has come very close to outrunning him in a chase. Without moving a single facial muscle, O'Neal registers surprise, relief, and respect. With the barely exhaled line "Go home" comes a sudden surge of mercy.

The quality of his sources clearly marks Hill as a sophisticated student of film. Apart from the allusions to Bresson and Hawks (in the structure, but also in a perverse thematic variant on Hawks's code of professionalism), *The Driver* shows traces of Budd Boetticher's famous series of Randolph Scott Westerns, particularly in the way the plot is organized as a series of strategic moves and countermoves, like a game of psychological chess. Hill thus belongs to the scholarly enclave within the New Hollywood, a group that would include John Milius, George Lucas, Paul Schrader, Martin Scorsese, and Peter Bogdanovich (who was originally set to direct Hill's screenplay for *The Getaway*—a project that eventually went to Sam Peckinpah). Like the work of his fellow acolytes, Hill's films betray a reverent nostalgia for the days when genres were well-defined and American directors drew their art and inspiration from them, working from the outlines provided by the Western, the thriller, the romantic comedy. *The Driver* is an attempt to revive the *film noir*, the genre of dark thrillers that grew up in the 40s and 50s, just as *Star Wars* is a return to the fantasy of the 30s, and *New York, New York* a return to the big studio musical. All of these films seem to stand out of time, less old-fashioned than other-worldly in their insistence on playing by rules of structure and style that were revoked a decade ago. The *film noir* was not designed to bear the intellectual weight Hill places upon it—it was a genre of feelings, not ideas—and its structure seems to shake a little when Hill makes its philosophical assumptions explicit. Like the gangster films made by Jean-Pierre Melville in France (*Le Samourai*, *Le Doulos*), *The Driver* seems vaguely inauthentic, an intellectualized version of an instinctual form, out of touch with the feelings that inspired it and out of step with the time in which it was made.

Still, the stylistic achievements of *The Driver* are satisfaction enough. François Truffaut remarks somewhere that first films are made in a mad rush to pack everything one has ever thought and felt into 90 minutes; that second films are a time to stand back and try out technical skills; and, consequently, that the third film, with its balance of content and form, is the first one that's fair to judge. Walter Hill has had his mad rush (*Hard Times*) and his technical exercise (*The Driver*). The crucial third will be his next.

Halloween

Directed by JOHN CARPENTER {November 17, 1978}

While the 14th Chicago International Film Festival winds up this week at the Village, two films that the festival premiered—Claude Chabrol's *Violette* and John Carpenter's *Halloween*—will be moving into regular commercial runs. The two films came from opposite ends of the production scale and widely different cultural traditions. One is a thoroughly respectable, expensively mounted European import, the other a vaguely disreputable, low-budget American job. It's some small tribute to the festival's expanding interest that it managed to find room for both films on the same program. In the movies, the line between art and trash is very thin, and in the past, the festival has tended to draw it too firmly. *Halloween* comes from a long genre tradition, while *Violette* stands fairly sturdily on its own. But the Carpenter film has a dash and enthusiasm that makes its conventional tale seem fresh—fresher, in some ways, than *Violette*'s careful intellectual constructs. As André Bazin once said, all films are created equal. Whether they play at the Biograph (as will *Violette*) or the Chicago (as will *Halloween*), we owe them the same consideration, the same right to succeed or fail on their own terms.

Still, once the usual prejudices have been cleared away (would *Halloween* look more profound with subtitles?), the two films seem remarkably similar at heart. Both center on children who turn murderously on their families, both draw the same neurotic links between sex, death, and home sweet home. But where Chabrol seems to have abandoned his usual unrestrained stylistics in favor of a more detached, more temperate tone, Carpenter plays his melodramatic situation for all it's worth, and then some. The difference is one of temperament and emphasis, as Chabrol carefully goes about constructing his abstract ironies, and Carpenter lunges straight for the jugular.

Halloween is only John Carpenter's third film, but already his personality seems more firmly set than most of his New Hollywood contemporaries'. Eschewing the higher flights of self-expression encouraged by Altman and Company, Carpenter belongs to the oldest and, I think, finest tradition of American filmmaking, putting the audience first and letting his own quirks enter only later. As a director, he prefers invisibility over the stylistic intrusions favored by most junior auteurs: his camera placements are expressive without being obtrusive; his editing has the same subliminal smoothness developed by Ford and Hawks. In some ways, Carpenter looks like a more responsible version of Peter Bogdanovich. He's immersed in the classical tradition, but instead of mimicking and mourning it, as Bogdanovich does, Carpenter is able to make it alive again.

Invisibility, of course, does not mean anonymity, as Ford and Hawks knew. *Halloween* is a genuine tour-de-force, a film that would hardly exist apart from its directorial style. The story is almost absurdly thin: a homicidal maniac escapes from a mental hospital, fleeing back to the small Illinois town where, as a child, he knifed his sister when he saw her making love to her boyfriend. On his return visit, he seeks out three teenage girls who spark the distant memory and stalks them through a Halloween night.

There is a flurry of action in the first reel and another flurry at the end. For all practical purposes, nothing happens in between. Yet Carpenter is able to build a tempo that keeps audiences on the archetypal edges of their seats. Where the horror movie of the 70s has become largely a matter of stringing together a series of bloody set pieces (*The Fury* is probably the prime example), *Halloween* understands the value of careful exposition, devoting a good deal of footage to local color and character development. The size and shape of the town are scrupulously laid out: the characters (particularly the lead victim, played by Jamie Lee Curtis) become people worth caring about. This may seem like an obvious point, but it has been neglected too often of late to let Carpenter's considerable skill in the matter pass unnoticed. As his characters grow, so does the violence, beginning with a few devious shock effects inherited from the Val Lewton school and escalating from there to full-scale carnage. By the time the knife comes out, the threat means something—we've been drawn into the world of the film, with its evocative autumnal colors, its peculiar small-town customs, its full and well-sketched population.

After *Dark Star*, *Assault on Precinct 13*, and *Halloween*, it seems possible to make a few observations on Carpenter's standing as an auteur. All three films take place in lonely spots in the depths of the night: in *Dark Star*, it's a spaceship drifting through the outer galaxies; in *Assault*, it's an abandoned police station on the edge of Watts. Outside, strange and unknowable forces lurk: an empty cosmos punctuated by meteor showers, a street gang bent on revenge, a maniac on a homecoming trip. Carpenter's conception of evil is blackly primal; it enters the world of films without a face (the killer of *Halloween* always wears a mask) or motive, striking at whatever comes in its way.

Yet for all the implicit despair of the settings and situation, Carpenter's films retain a firm comic base. The humor, of course, is one way of drawing the audience into the improbabilities of the situation (a trick that Brian De Palma overworks in almost all of his films), but beyond that it works for Carpenter's characters as a cagey existential defense. The wit never degenerates into satire at the expense of the protagonists; rather, it's a weapon in their hands—the one barrier between them and utter devastation. Carpenter's heroes survive through a combination of pluck and self-irony—the character quirks that make them profoundly human in the face of the inhuman evil that waits outside. The structure is very close to the films of Howard Hawks—*Rio Bravo* (from which the plot of *Assault* was borrowed) and *Only Angels Have Wings*, in particular—but Hawks never took it to such extremes. Carpenter doesn't yet have the command of human detail that tied Hawks's films to the here and now: his movies drift off, occasionally, into excessive schematization—as at the end of *Halloween*, when a dialogue exchange between Jamie Lee Curtis and Donald Pleasence suddenly makes the thematic ideas that have been bubbling just beneath the surface disappointingly clear. Better that such matters should be left unverbalized, as Hawks did in the film that is the clearest inspiration for *Halloween*, his 1951 *The Thing*. It would be nice to say that Carpenter was a wholly original talent, but that, perhaps, will come with a few more years and a few more movies. In the meantime, though, there are many worse models than Hawks for a younger director to imitate.

[The additional discussion of *Violette* is not included.]

Reds

Directed by WARREN BEATTY {December 11, 1981}

Some movies are like plays, some movies are like short stories, some movies are like paintings. Yet very few movies are like novels—perhaps because very few filmmakers have the courage to pass up an immediate emotional effect (which is a theatrical aesthetic) and enter instead into the network of delayed effects, sustained motifs, developing characters, and echoing ideas that gives a great novel its power. And audiences, too, may lack the patience: at a time when almost everyone has been conditioned by television to respond to drama only in half-hour or one-hour chunks, even a two-hour film may be pushing the limits of retention and imaginative immersion, which are the qualities essential to the full grasp—and the full pleasure—of the novelistic effect.

Warren Beatty's *Reds* runs about three and a half hours (including an intermission). Near the end, there is a sequence in which Beatty, as the radical journalist John Reed, is seen returning from a propaganda mission on board a brightly painted Bolshevik train. In the wilds of the Russian steppes, the train is suddenly attacked by a force of White Army counterrevolutionaries. As the shells burst and the bullets whistle, Reed jumps from the train into a trackside ditch; peering over the top, he sees a squadron of Red soldiers bursting from a boxcar on horseback. Among them is a horse-drawn munitions cart, which takes off across the battlefield. When Reed sees the cart, he leaps from the ditch and takes off after it, running passionately, desperately, with every ounce of energy in his body. He can't catch it; it outdistances him, roaring into battle.

The sequence has struck some people as wholly mysterious, unmotivated, yet it is the climax of the film—a classic climax of self-realization, when the hero's past connects tragically with his present, and he sees with overpowering clarity what has happened to him and his world. What's missing for people who can't read the scene is the novelistic link—the memory of another image, placed some three hours earlier in the film, from another revolution of another continent: an image of John Reed running after a cart drawn by Mexican revolutionaries, a cart he was able to catch. Between those two carts lies the subject and method of *Reds*, a film that strikes me as belonging among the most accomplished, most rewarding applications of novelistic strategies in film history.

Movies and novels are in mortal conflict on most points—they do very different things, and do them in very different ways. But they do have one property in common, one they share with dance and music—the property of time. Time is what distinguishes a novel from a short story, and time is what distinguishes a movie from a photograph, turning static images into something changeable and fluid—images with a history. (Film time differs from stage time in its fluidity, its plasticity: time on the stage is much more literal, much less easily sculpted, than the imaginary time of books and movies.) In his direction of *Reds*, Warren Beatty seizes on that common property, bringing time forward as his subject, using it as the organizing principle of his style.

Reds deals with several different kinds of time—with historical time (the film is set in the late teens: the years of World War I, the attempted radicalization of the labor movement in America, the Russian revolution), with personal time (the private lives of its lead characters, John Reed and Diane Keaton's Louise Bryant), with novelistic time (the playing out of narrative patterns, motifs), and with cinematic time (time expanded and contracted through cutting). Beatty has found a wonderful device to double up the time sense of his film—both to put the past his film presents in an active, living present and to give the past a remembered quality, to make it something distant and lost. Testimony from what Beatty calls his "witnesses"—people who lived through the period of the film, some in direct contact with Reed, some removed from him—interrupts the action at carefully chosen points, sometimes to give a wider context to what we see, sometimes to undercut the ambitions and pretensions of the characters. The witnesses—among them are Roger Baldwin, Henry Miller, Adela Rogers St. Johns, Hamilton Fish, Rebecca West, Will Durant, and George Jessel, though none are identified on screen—are filmed sitting against a dead black backdrop, removed from time and the world of the movie. Yet Beatty and his cinematographer, Vittorio Storaro, establish their link to the period by shooting them with the same lighting scheme (a harsh side light that gives everyone a white luminosity on the edge of their figures) used for the main action. It's as if the witnesses still lived in the light of that time, as if they had been seared by it and still carried the light with them. There is a continuity after all, a link between time present and time past, between timelessness and history.

The usual tactic of historical epics is to play an intimate, personal story "against the backdrop of history"—to set two narrative trains running down parallel tracks. If the historical background ever impinges on the personal foreground, it's in the form of intervention: to bring the lovers together, to draw them apart, to reward the good and punish the wicked. History, in the traditional epic, is an independent force, something godlike and apart; it enters the action like a deus ex machina, to impel the intimate story or to resolve it. Beatty's great accomplishment in *Reds* is to erase the old distinction of foreground and background: he finds new points of intersection, new relationships between the individual and the historic event. In *Reds*, people make history, and not always for historic reasons (when Reed returns to Russia after the revolution, part of his motivation is to get away from his wife). And when history makes people, it does so ambiguously (Reed and Bryant are reborn as a couple in the excitement of the revolution, yet the revolution will draw them apart again).

Like Jean-Luc Godard in his late films and Milan Kundera in his novel *The Book of Laughter and Forgetting*, Beatty is concerned with the relationship of sex and politics—with the ways emotional issues turn into ideology and the ways in which ideology channels feeling. Are Louise Bryant and John Reed bound together by sexual attraction or shared politics? The question is ultimately impossible to answer; the two strands are bound too tightly to be separated. When Louise has a brief affair with Eugene O'Neill (Jack Nicholson, in a sharp, creative performance) while Reed is away covering a political convention, is she following the free-love principles she and her lover have agreed upon? Or is she using the affair with O'Neill to get back at Reed for abandoning her—and, ultimately, to provoke him into marriage? The film doesn't try to sort out her motives, to make her reasons clear—everything is present at once, as political ideals justify personal, sexual needs, as progressive concepts are used as cover to achieve traditional goals of security and possession.

Bryant's cloudy actions find their moral echo later in the film, when Reed, covering a workers' rally in Saint Petersburg, is brought to the podium to attest to the support of the American working class for the Russian revolutionaries. As Reed begins to speak, Beatty's camera abandons the detached, objective point of view it has held throughout and enters Reed's emotions: as he looks down at the cheering crowd, the reporter is transformed into a politician, the acclaim of the crowd carrying him up and away from his position as an observer and onto the main stage of history. (A similar shift into a subjective point of view comes in the attack on the train, linking Reed's response there to this speech as well as to his experience in Mexico.) Reed's motives in joining the revolution (he will return to America as a political organizer, not a journalist) are both questioned and exalted by the sequence: he is acting from the highest idealism, but also—inseparably—from the lowest egotism.

When an actor directs himself in a film, it's a safe bet that the results will be at least partly narcissistic, a contemplation of the self—obliquely in the case of Welles, lyrically in the case of Chaplin, compulsively in the case of Jerry Lewis. Beatty's self-scrutiny in *Reds* is remarkably sober and critical (though he has the vanity—and thank God for it—not to deny his natural charm and humor). It seems clear that what went wrong for John Reed in the teens is also what went wrong for Warren Beatty in the 70s: *Reds* traces the dissolution of political fervor, from a starting point of excitement and high expectation into a slough of division and disappointment, with honesty and understanding. Beatty's visual style is plain and classical—with simple images strongly put, it seems the embodiment of sureness, conviction, confidence. Yet the moral assurance of the images is constantly challenged by the cacophony of the sound track, with its rapid, overlapping dialogue, its bewildering assortment of different voices (it's a magnificent job of sound editing, executed by a team headed by Richard Cirincione). The din wears away certainty, limits action, and as the film progresses, the sound track envelops the images, taking the moral center away from them and absorbing it, dissolving it, into the hum of constant conflict. The ideological purity of the first, energetic impulse disappears for a time, and when it resurfaces, the purity has changed into something malignant, monstrous—the totalitarianism of Zinoviev (Jerzy Kosinski).

There is music on the sound track of *Reds*, too—the stirring martial strains of "The Internationale" alternate with tinkly American pop, notably a childish ditty called "I Don't Want to Play in Your Yard." Somehow, the entire thematic movement of *Reds* seems contained in the contrasts of the score—the movement between Russia and America, between political ideals and personal feelings, between group solidarity and action and individual isolation and petulance (I don't *want* to . . .). *Reds* radiates intelligence, sincerity, and creativity; it's the most complete, most mature epic I know.

Sudden Impact

Directed by CLINT EASTWOOD {January 12, 1984}

Clint Eastwood is hardly ever discussed as a serious filmmaker, but when he is, it's as a political filmmaker—a manufacturer of right-wing tracts in favor of harsh Nixonian notions of law and order. It is indeed difficult to shake the specter of Spiro Agnew from Dirty Harry, the renegade San Francisco cop who has become Eastwood's most enduring character. But just this once, let's grant Eastwood the favor we routinely grant to lefty filmmakers like Roger Spottiswoode (*Under Fire*) and Mike Nichols (*Silkwood*)—that of pretending that the artwork is innocent of all ideological intent. The evidence is, after all, much clearer in Eastwood's case than in Spottiswoode's that he is a maker of predominantly personal films: Eastwood has put his commercial standing on the line again and again with movies like *Bronco Billy* and *Honkytonk Man* (films that were, if anything, too personal), while Spottiswoode has the slashing industrial sexism of *Terror Train* to answer for. Eastwood's obstinacy over 12 years as a director (nine movies since his debut in 1971 with *Play Misty for Me*) is a strong tribute to his personal commitment; very few other contemporary filmmakers (Scorsese and Altman, perhaps) have shown such a willingness to buck the increasingly inflexible dictates of the American box office.

Sudden Impact is the fourth Dirty Harry film, but only the first that Eastwood has directed himself. I don't think Eastwood is comfortable with Harry Callahan, particularly with the bravura built into the character by director Don Siegel in the original *Dirty Harry* of 1971. When Eastwood acts under his own direction, his work is much more contained, even recessive; recession is, in fact, the subject of both *Firefox* (in which the star's presence is slowly diluted by a series of disguises and shrinks to a literal pinpoint in the film's final image) and *Honkytonk Man* (in which the dying singer gradually recedes behind the body of his music). What began as a laconic personality (in the spaghetti westerns of Sergio Leone) has by now become as minimal and mysterious as a figure out of Robert Bresson: Eastwood constantly pares away at his technique, to the point where his performance has become exclusively concentrated in his expressive brow. Only Buster Keaton could express himself with less facial mobility, and the spirit of Keaton does return, in surprising ways, to inform *Sudden Impact*.

Eastwood was trained as an actor in the male-dominated cinema of Leone and Siegel, and those two filmmakers have remained the strongest influences on his own directing style (Leone for the strong massing within a deep-focus Panavision frame, Siegel for the rhythmic sense of montage, or narrative lines that separate, build, and reconverge). But Eastwood has drawn away from them in content and emotional texture, notably by giving women an increasingly important place in his films. Perhaps the best, and certainly the strangest, of Eastwood's collaborations with Siegel was 1971's *The Beguiled*, a hothouse southern gothic with Eastwood as a wounded Union soldier recuperating under the ambiguous ministrations of the female staff of an isolated girls' boarding school. Siegel's film was a weirdly lyrical study of female hysteria and male masochism, themes Eastwood recast in thriller form for *Play Misty for Me*. With the advent of Sondra Locke (in 1976's *The Outlaw Josey Wales*), these themes became a permanent part of Eastwood's work. The brittle, angular Locke, with her eyes open in a perpetual deep, hard stare, crystallized these threatening notions of female emotionality; she was not only tougher than Eastwood, but also more passionate, more explosive. The cool, stoic, traditional male hero as incarnated by Eastwood for Siegel and Leone finally found its match: even with his monstrously phallic .45 clutched in his hand, the Eastwood character can't stand against the tide of nervous emotion the Locke character exudes. He recedes even further, disappears.

At this deeper level, Eastwood's films are much more psychological than political; in instances like *The Gauntlet* (1978) and now *Sudden Impact*, they approach something Jungian in their deployment of large, primal images. Eastwood's work is probably open to routine charges of sexism (Locke clearly belongs to the discredited tradition of the castrating femme fatale), but on the other hand, he can hardly be accused of pushing machismo. Eastwood's movies don't really work on a surface, social level at all; at their best, they operate in the realm of inner experience, emotional archetypes. They are mythic in the only meaningful modern sense.

The Gauntlet treated the Eastwood-Locke relationship as comedy; *Sudden Impact*—a more mature film, less occupied with formal effects—treats it as tragedy. Or, rather, *ultimately* as tragedy. Much of the force of the film comes from Eastwood's decision to play the male-centered Harry sections as comedy and the Sondra Locke passages as brooding, sinuous *film noir*. The contrast in tones is very effective and very well developed, from tempo (staccato for Eastwood's comedy, slow and solemn for Locke), to space (crowded interiors with lots of vertical lines versus deserted exteriors composed in sweeping horizontals), to color (browns and yellows for Eastwood, greens and blacks for Locke). As Eastwood cuts back and forth between the two stories, elegant parallels emerge: repeated images, gestures, or patterns of action. The intercut sequences comment on each other, accentuating actions and giving meaning to images, through the contrast of tones, that otherwise would have remained dormant. It soon becomes clear that a single story is being told through two different approaches, two different styles. As Locke and Eastwood draw nearer, their stories slowly merge: the cross cutting accelerates, until the two separate characters seem to be sharing the same instant in time; by the time they are allowed to share the same Panavision frame, they seem already firmly bound, inseparable. (It's a technique the great romancer Frank Borzage used in films like *I've Always Loved You.*) It is, of course, Eastwood who is slowly drawn into Locke's world, slowly absorbed by her stronger emotions and stronger expressiveness. The overall action of the film, though it comprises several weeks, is conceived as the course of a single day: The film opens with a predawn scene with Locke, moves into daylight for a long stretch with Eastwood, and gradually darkens into night as the two characters are brought together. It ends with the breaking of another dawn, the ambiguous half-light in which the newly formed couple exists.

Eastwood's minimalism makes him a perfect performer for the comedy of understatement and underreaction: no matter how extreme the situation is, his voice never rises above its breathy purr, and his gestures never lose their purely functional elegance. Like Keaton, he is a center of calm in a chaotic world, coping with every crisis that comes down the pike with perfect equanimity. Eastwood's calm, like Keaton's, is a powerful temptation to fate; disaster rains down upon him, as if the gods were desperately searching for something, anything, that might shatter his sangfroid. The opening sections of *Sudden Impact* suggest the cyclone finale of *Steamboat Bill Jr.*: wherever Buster goes, buildings collapse or race about him; wherever Dirty Harry goes, someone is pulling a stickup or tossing Molotov cocktails in the backseat of his car. These incidents pile up to the point of absurdity and considerably beyond, but while they're very funny in a very black way, they're also establishing something essential about the character. Eastwood's calm differs from Keaton's in that it isn't a natural attribute, but the product of a fierce self-control—a willful suppression of an emotional energy (chiefly anger) that still boils beneath the surface, pounding in the lightning-bolt vein that crosses Eastwood's left temple. For Harry, this suppression is synonymous with the law; he polices himself as strictly as he polices the streets, silencing every emotional insurrection. We all know what Harry's whopping Magnum means, but what's more significant is the tremendous control Harry exercises over the use of its phallic power. In one early scene (reminiscent of the end of *The Gauntlet*) a trio of hoods blast a salt box they believe Harry is hiding in with hundreds of rounds of machine gun ammunition; Harry, who of course isn't there, rises in the background and picks them off with three perfectly aimed bullets, a model of Apollonian restraint next to the Dionysiac incontinence of his enemies. Harry—or at least the Harry of *Sudden Impact*—isn't the exploding urban id he's usually characterized as, but a Spartan superego.

When Eastwood represses, Locke expresses. Her Jennifer Spenser is a painter of howling, expressionistic canvases, an outlet for the traumatic rage and pain caused when she was gang-raped by a group of teenage thugs. (Her younger sister, also a victim, has never recovered from the shock; she sits silently in a psychiatric hospital.) But the paintings are no longer enough. Jennifer has purchased a tiny, nickel-plated revolver and begun tracking down her violators, shooting them once in the groin and once in the head. The parallels between the Locke and Eastwood characters are elaborately drawn: both are hunters (Harry has been sent to the northern California resort town where Jennifer lives to investigate the rash of killings) who are also hunted (Harry has been followed by some syndicate hit men, who blame him for the death of their boss); both are victims (Jennifer by her rape, Harry by the continual assaults on his life) who are also criminals. Jennifer breaks the law for the same reason Harry bends the law: because she feels the court system cannot deliver justice.

But the differences between the two characters are just as important. The traditional male symbols that surround Harry give way in Jennifer's case to the equally archetypal female imagery of water—the ocean that roars just offscreen as she is raped and reappears as the background for each of her killings. Where Harry's skill and restraint with his gun come to represent his repressive faith in the law, the ocean embodies Locke's unrepressible, uncontainable anger—her equally fierce belief in personal vengeance.

The structure of *Sudden Impact*—and it is a beautifully filigreed, well-worked thing—hangs on the similarity between the classical romance plot and the classical detective plot: both are stories of pursuit and capture, and it is Eastwood's stroke of brilliance in *Sudden Impact* to realize that both plots can be played at the same time. As Harry tracks down his prey, he is also courting his ideal woman; as Jennifer attempts to escape him, she also leads him on. She sleeps with him to throw him off the track, but Harry rises in the middle of the night to check the license plate on her car, which confirms that she is the killer. The attraction between these two haunted outsiders is irresistible, but it must be resisted: for Harry to yield to Jennifer would mean the destruction of his faith in the law (and because his ethics are inseparable from his personality, it would mean an end to Harry as well); for Jennifer to yield to him would mean that her vengeance would be incomplete.

Various mediatory figures are written into the story, whose failures and grotesquerie suggest the impossibility of compromise between the male/female, law/emotion dichotomies represented by Eastwood and Locke: Audrie J. Neenan as the androgynous psychopath who organized the rape; Pat Hingle as the local police chief whose feelings for his son (one of the rapists and now, like Jennifer's sister, living in a trance of guilt) lead him to betray his duty. Eventually (inevitably), it is Harry who capitulates: knocked into the ocean during a fist-fight with one of the rapists, Harry emerges drenched with Jennifer's emotionality; he finds his assailant holding Jennifer hostage atop a boardwalk roller coaster, raises his Magnum, and fires. As the rapist falls, he crashes through the glass roof of a building that houses a carousel Jennifer has been hired to restore, landing straight on the horn of a wooden unicorn. The corpse, impaled on the phallic spike of an ancient symbol of virginity, becomes the seal of Jennifer and Harry's union; with this grotesquely sexual image, they make a love that is also death.

Eastwood's camera lingers briefly on the new couple as they emerge into the dawn light, and the shot—of an exhausted, hollow-eyed Eastwood and a still keyed-up Locke—is one of the most ambiguous and unsettling images I have ever encountered in the American cinema. The love story has ended happily (with the unification of the couple), the detective story tragically (with the annihilation of the detective and the escape of the guilty). Where can the couple possibly go from here? This isn't the didactic conclusion of a right-wing tract, but a moment of deep subversion. All the certainties have been erased, and the dawn rises on a frightening new world.

NEW DIRECTIONS IN COMEDY >>

Victor/Victoria

Directed by BLAKE EDWARDS {April 2, 1982}

Blake Edwards's art doesn't announce itself. He works so well and comfortably within established genres—the sex farce (*10*), the crazy comedy (*The Pink Panther*), the detective film (*Gunn*)—and gives the audience so much pleasure that it doesn't seem natural that he should also be among the most personal of American filmmakers—that, indeed, his work since 1955 amounts to one of the most unified and artistically rich formations in American movies. If the audience reaction at the previews I caught of *Victor/Victoria* is any indication, the film should be a big success; it creates a kind of rapport—a complicity, even—between audience and screen that is supremely satisfying and increasingly rare. Yet *Victor/Victoria* is as complex and mature as any film that has occupied the art houses since Maurice Pialat's *Loulou*, if not more so. It gathers themes and motifs from across Edwards's career and puts them into a fresh and exacting combination, marking what may be a new level in Edwards's art—a kind of acceptance and optimism new to him, a genuine coming-through.

Walking out of *Victor/Victoria*, a comparison occurred to me that I couldn't quite choke out—that *Victor/Victoria* stood to *10* in the way that Virginia Woolf's *The Waves* stood to *To the Lighthouse*, an acknowledgment and embrace of change, fluidity, and diffusion following the failure of a search for a single, frozen ideal. But somehow the link of high art and low, of austere experimental novels and popular sex comedies, struck me as ridiculous, and I could make the comparison only as a joke. I mention all this because it proves how deeply ingrained that old prejudice is—that some forms of expression are inherently more "serious" than others—even in someone who makes his living arguing against it. The artfulness of *Victor/Victoria* should be quite as evident as the artfulness of *The Waves*; it's our fault—and our loss—if we persist in believing that art has to hurt, has to make itself felt by hammering home its presence. Blake Edwards doesn't hammer: he seduces. And for that, I think, we should be more grateful than contemptuous.

Victor/Victoria does answer *10*, both thematically and stylistically. (*S.O.B.*, which came in between, is in many ways Edwards's most bitter and misanthropic work; its middle position now seems like a venting of the spleen, a harrowing.) The difference between the two films is registered in Edwards's choice of lenses. *10* was a long-lens movie, using a telescopic compression of space to express the essence of romantic fantasy: in Dudley Moore's subjective gaze, equated with the long lens, Bo Derek was always brought closer to him, made larger than life and isolated against a shallow, fuzzy background. The long lens emphasizes the authority of objects and individuals over their environment; it picks things out from a context, giving them an artificial size and an artificial independence. But the long lens is limited by its inability to grasp anything other than surfaces—it has no depth, no penetrating power, but only a worshipful abjection before the glittering face of things. It imposes a closeness that isn't there, closing gaps mechanically. But it can only bring surface close to surface; it can't describe the deeper attractions between characters, can't sound their harmonies.

Victor/Victoria is a short-lens movie; it uses the wide-angle viewpoint to place the characters in a physical setting, describing their precise spatial relations to the people and décor around them. The short lens makes connections where connections exist, photographing the ways people position themselves and react to each other. And where there aren't any connections, only the short lens can show the emptiness between characters, the psychological spaces that separate them. With a sensitive director, the composition in depth made possible by short lenses is a way of seeing in depth; spatial arrangements become emotional, moral, philosophical constellations. The first shot of *Victor/Victoria* is a pullback from a Paris street scene, with the camera moving in reverse through an open window, into the interior of an apartment. The frame lines of the window draw in from the frame lines of the image, carving off a separate frame-within-the-frame, dividing, parceling space. The mise-en-scène of *Victor/Victoria* hangs on similar divisions: deep-focus images interrupted by doorways and windows, the horizontal space of the Panavision frame masked off by foreground objects or jutting décor. Edwards takes the deep, continuous space the short lens gives him and chops it up: the film is a symphony of continuities and divisions, the most important of which is the proscenium arch—the invisible line that divides performers from their audiences, but also lays out the point of their meeting.

Victoria (Julie Andrews) is an out-of-work opera singer in the Paris of the early 30s (or rather, the Paris of movie imagination—the sets are forthrightly false). Toddy (Robert Preston) is a gay nightclub entertainer, freshly fired from his job in a fashionable bar. To get them both off the bread lines, Toddy has an idea: he'll pass Victoria off as his male lover, which will then allow her to perform as the world's greatest female impersonator, Count Victor. The fraud functions beautifully until the arrival of a Chicago gangster named King Marchand (James Garner); he's smitten immediately by the woman he sees on the stage (and he sees her through a long lens shot, just as Dudley Moore saw Bo Derek), and can't believe it when Victoria unmasks herself as a man. He keeps up his pursuit, and eventually Victoria falls in love with him—which is where the problems start.

Chaos has always been the primary condition of Edwards's fictional world, coursing through his comedies, melodramas, thrillers, and musicals alike. It is a profoundly unstable world, where living room floors are thinly laid over swimming pools (*The Party*), a floor rug conceals a two-story drop (*S.O.B.*), and a small Italian village has been so thoroughly undermined by underground passages that characters are randomly swallowed up by the earth (*What Did You Do in the War, Daddy?*). Three restaurants (and one twice) are destroyed by sudden fistfights in *Victoria/Victoria*, a repeated trope that transcends the realm of the running gag and becomes a cosmic principle: anarchy is only a blink away, the world is defined by its arbitrariness, treacherousness, and blind hostility. Edwards's comedies achieve a deep shade of black, not simply because they hinge on disaster, but because of the awareness of real pain, real tragedy, and real death that haunts their margins. *Victor/Victoria* opens on a low, agonizingly unsustained note of despair (Toddy's humiliation by a mercenary lover, the starving Victoria's attempts to peddle her virtue for a single meatball) that is as characteristic of Edwards as his slapstick exuberance. His comedy always grows from grim premises and never entirely vanquishes them; that those premises are stated more deliberately and sympathetically in *Victoria/Victoria* than ever before is a sign of the film's fundamental seriousness: it is a sex farce set in a world where the most pressing issues are those of survival.

The physical world of Edwards's films is one of calm surfaces lightly shellacked over chaos, and their emotional world is much the same: human relations can collapse as quickly as a bedroom floor. The prop knocked out in *Victor/Victoria* is one of sex roles—the superficial signs of maleness and femaleness that organize the social world at its most basic level. In their recent book on Edwards (published by the Ohio University Press), Peter Lehman and William Luhr trace the transvestite theme in Edwards's work back to his earliest film; it is one of his favorite metaphors for deceptive surfaces and wrenching realities, as embodied in Ross Martin's drag disguise in *Experiment in Terror*, the transvestite killer of *Gunn*, and even in Cato's karate attack, disguised as a geisha girl, on Inspector Clouseau in *The Return of the Pink Panther*. In a world where men so easily pass as women, the ground rules of the society are profoundly shaken: there is no believing your eyes, even over matters as forthright as gender. And when the gay theme is added (it has surfaced before in Edwards's films, but never as the centerpiece it is in *Victor/Victoria*), the chaos is increased: the binary pairs, one element chosen from each column, on which monogamous, heterosexual society rests suddenly become elusive, instable—an ordering principle, one of the strongest, has been removed.

In Edwards's other work, transvestism has been a hostile, aggressive force—in *Gunn*, it is the final blow dealt to the hero's sense of a stable, secure existence. But in *Victor/Victoria*, transvestism grows out of something more benign: we are in on the deception, parties to it rather than its victims. If Edwards before has used drag as a way of hiding identity, in *Victor/Victoria* it becomes a kind of liberation: an expansion of identity, its happy dissolution. *Victor/Victoria* begins with characters bound by their identities, identities imposed not only by maleness/femaleness, but by their jobs, arts, and social positions: Victoria is starving because she will not relinquish her sense of herself as an opera singer—she performs the classics or she performs nothing. And Toddy, too, is a victim of his role as an "old queen"; when his ex-lover shows up at Toddy's night-club as a gigolo to a wealthy hag, he can't resist shooting a few bitchy remarks—thus starting a fistfight, and thus losing his job. Ego-bound, both characters are crushed until they discover the magic of deception. Victoria hides a cockroach in her handbag and sits down, with Toddy, to a restaurant dinner, dropping the bug in the salad at the appropriate moment to avoid paying the bill. Another fistfight results, but this time chaos is on their side—they've stirred it up themselves—and they escape, well-fed and weirdly exhilarated. "Count Victor" is only a natural extension of the cockroach scam—a deception that taps a deeper vein of chaos, and produces more spectacular results.

Perhaps the chief formal beauty of *Victor/Victoria* is its elegant nesting of metaphors. Each image seems contained within another, and as the levels grow, the themes broaden. Deception is a way of making the chaos of the world work for you; it means dropping a fixed, static identity—which is always your most vulnerable point—and finding the freedom to adopt a series of superficial, provisional ones, all of which become incorporated into an ever-growing you. Chaos is no longer the enemy, but the essence; the characters learn to live with it and thrive on it. But the notion of deception suggests the notion of performance, another pet Edwards theme and one that *Victor/Victoria* also finds time to develop. Performance in *Victor/Victoria* is a kind of institutionalized deception (Count Victor, after all, does not exist), with the performer acting out a lie and the audience agreeing to be lied to; it is, following the spatial metaphors of *10*, a seductive but superficial apprehension of a surface. Yet Edwards, like Jean Renoir in *The Golden Coach* (and his development is hardly less complex or delightedly paradoxical), also finds an element of genuine communication between performer and audience—one that creeps around the edges of the material and doesn't always take polite forms. Victoria, for example, has a high C that can shatter glass; she uses it both as entertainment, rattling champagne glasses for the ringsiders, and as a weapon, bursting the brandy snifter of a nightclub owner when he turns her down for a job. Performance, here, is a violent, hostile act, a power held over the audience. But the same kind of power can also be exercised as seduction: there is an extraordinary shot-sequence in which Victoria, as Victor, sings a ballad onstage, the camera beginning with her face held in close-up against a black, neutral backdrop, gradually moving around to reveal the listening audience as she sings, and closing in a perfect circle back on her face as she looks out to the audience to receive her applause. The performer, alone and self-contained, seems to call the audience into being: the performance creates the audience, and the audience is reabsorbed into the personality of the performer. Performance is control, subtle or explicit, by means of art. And the performer, according to the rules, should never relinquish that control, even when the act appears to demand it. The climax of Victoria's act comes when she snatches the female wig from her head, revealing herself as a "man." The moment should mark the end of illusion, the relaxation of control, but of course it is exactly the opposite: in *Victor/Victoria*, exposure is the highest illusion of all.

In the cabaret sequences, Edwards keeps the stage and audience areas carefully divided: they are separate pockets of space in his deep-focus mise-en-scène, and no one is allowed to cross the proscenium line. One is either a viewer or a performer, a watcher or a doer. This same spatial plan is carried over into the other interiors, most notably in the hotel set that places King Marchand's room directly across an air shaft from Victoria and Toddy's: looking out his bay window, King sees Toddy and Victoria across the way as if they were performers on a stage. It's a static, standoff situation, and it exactly duplicates the circumstances of King and Victoria's first meeting, across the footlights of the cabaret stage. But on that first occasion, Victoria violated the rules of separation by tossing King a rose (a hostile act, in the context). Now, King, piqued by the attraction he can't understand, decides to cross over in turn: he sneaks into Victoria's room and hides there, hoping to settle the question of her gender once and for all.

With this scene, the theme of performers and audiences segues naturally into a theme of exhibitionists and voyeurs: King spies on Victoria as she undresses for a bath. What's happening here is a quick recap of *10*, in which eroticism is collapsed entirely into looking, and to see is somehow to possess. But where Dudley Moore was obsessed with a surface (and was disappointed when he penetrated beyond it) King seems attracted by Victoria's deeper ambiguity; simply seeing her isn't enough. But in order to penetrate beyond Victoria's surface identity, he'll have to leave his own behind—cast off his macho posturing and take up with Count Victor as his lover, for all the world to see. The exhibitionist/voyeur divisions of *10* break down, reappearing in parody form as two negative characters who bracket the main action: the Bo Derek figure as King's blowsy mistress Norma (Lesley Ann Warren), a platinum blond perpetually spilling out of her clothes, the Dudley Moore figure as an oddly Clouseau-like detective (Sherloque Tanney), whose attempts to uncover Victoria's true status are punished by collapsing chairs, bolts of lightning, and broken fingers. The characters of *Victor/Victoria* have the courage to cross the proscenium line, to act as well as watch—which is exactly what happens as Edwards completes his spatial metaphor by moving Victoria in with King, and King's bodyguard (Alex Karras) in with Toddy. In *Victor/Victoria*, as in *The Golden Coach*, it is ultimately impossible to say whether the theater is being used as a metaphor for life, or life as a metaphor for theater. Performance and reality, audience and actor, role and identity are gloriously intermingled; the chaos born here is a beautiful one.

Victor/Victoria ends in apparent frivolousness, with Toddy forced to assume the role of Count Victor for a final stage performance. His bull neck bursting through a borrowed dress, Toddy stomps his way through Victor's signature number, a mock operetta titled "The Shady Lady of Seville," tripping chorus boys, falling into fountains, and missing the high notes by half a dozen octaves. The sequence is wildly broad, very funny, and apparently wholly spontaneous, yet—and this is a radiant characteristic of Edwards's art—it also manages to recap the primary motifs, resolve the dramatic situation, put the themes into final alignment, and even suggest some further developments. By finally becoming Count Victor, an identity always partly his, Toddy frees something in himself—and as Robert Preston performs it, it's a tinglingly joyous moment, the only drag act in film history that is not humiliating, but genuinely expansive. And when Victoria, sitting in the audience, briefly mouths the words along with Toddy, it's an ineffably moving moment of closeness: she, Toddy, and Victor are suddenly united, identities dissolved in pleasure, performer and audience made one and the same. Toddy tosses a rose to Karras over the footlights, echoing Victoria's gesture to King and redeeming it. And finally, there is an impossibly deep, hearty laugh that abruptly booms out of Preston—an expression of pleasure so unmistakably honest that it clearly comes from the actor, not the character. Toddy's performance spills over the proscenium line, relinquishing control and reveling, pig-happy, in perfect disorder. And at the same moment, Preston seems to step out of character—step off the screen. He isn't acting anymore—he's living, and he's having one hell of a time.

Risky Business

Directed by PAUL BRICKMAN {August 26, 1983}

I put off seeing *Risky Business* for quite a while, mainly because I couldn't stand the idea of another teenage sex comedy so hot on the heels of Lewis John Carlino's *Class*. Carlino's film, with its story of a prep school kid seduced by his roommate's mother, seemed to be the last card this exhausted genre had to play: Carlino had made the buried incest theme as explicit as possible (it had been the genre's secret weapon since its inception with *Private Lessons*), which didn't leave any more moves to make. *Class* sounded the death knell for the teenage sex comedy (it had a run of about a year, which is pretty good for an exploitation cycle these days). But what I had forgotten was that the best films in a subgenre often appear at the last moment, when the squeezed-dry formula finally begins to admit some variations in a desperate effort to extend itself. With *Risky Business*, Paul Brickman takes advantage of that twilight freedom, introducing elements that haven't intruded on the genre before—elements like guilt, pressure, and anxiety. But the film is better than that—so good that it transcends its genre origins and stands on its own as a very personal, very original work. I'd be surprised if there were a better American movie this year.

Brickman has done something that most American filmmakers no longer seem willing or able to do: he's sat down with a narrow, codified genre structure and tried to figure out how to make it worthwhile, assessing what the genre can and can't do, developing its strengths into genuine expressiveness while looking for ways to redeem its weaknesses. It's an approach that has accounted for the vast majority of great American movies—allowing the filmmaker to negotiate a sure course between the demands of art and commerce—and it doesn't let Brickman down. *Risky Business* follows and revitalizes the formula so effectively that it looks to be one of this summer's sleeper hits, yet it also subverts the formula so thoroughly that it barely seems like a genre film at all. There's something clandestine, surreptitious, about Brickman's art, as if he had been forced to smuggle his talent past the front office; the qualities of his film are mainly qualities of direction, which won't be noticed by the mass audience or by most producers. It's too much to say that Brickman has written one film (a crass, unreflective fantasy of material fulfillment) and directed another (something dark and dreamlike), yet there is a tension between the material and the presentation—the visual style jars the script, and in jarring it, it deepens it. Perhaps this tension—the sense of a radically different point of view brought to bear on the action through the images—is the source of the film's strange and seductive mixture of tones: Brickman has made a lyrical, dreamlike satire, a harsh comedy of moral corruption that is also warm, enveloping, and deliriously, dangerously romantic.

Brickman has to face his biggest problem at the outset: how do you take a genre that, by definition, consists solely of grubby fantasy and make it admit complex, real-world feelings? Brickman's answer is to incorporate the fantasy element into his drama, to make it one of his subjects. The film opens with a voyeuristic scene that could be the genre's archetypal image: the teenage hero spying on a beautiful woman taking a shower. But where *Porky's* presents this image as reality (an alibi that allows the audience to participate in the fantasy), Brickman presents it as an image from a dream—the recurrent dream of the protagonist, 18-year-old Joel (Tom Cruise). In the dream, the girl invites Joel to join her in the shower, but as he steps through the curtain stream, he finds himself in his high school classroom, where all of his fellow students are hunched over their desks, filling in the fateful dots of the SAT. Joel is two hours late, and has only ten minutes to take the test that will determine his future.

Brickman's direction of the sequence veers from the blandly naturalistic (sunny suburban interiors) to the darkly expressionistic (high-contrast lighting, distorted sets, even the famous track forward–zoom back shot of Hitchcock's *Vertigo*, here actually used rather than simply quoted). Everyday life shades imperceptibly into a dream, just as Brickman shades his shots from coolly framed objectivity into the sinuous tracking shots of subjectivity. These graceful shifts in point of view are a technique that Brickman has borrowed from dreams; the film is haunted by the oneiric slide from first person to third, in which we first inhabit our own vantage point, and then find our perspective slipping away, to the point where we are watching ourselves from across the room, from the point of view of another person. This rolling perspective allows Brickman to have his subjective fantasy and to criticize it, too, to indulge the wish while analyzing its implications.

The locker-room fantasy of *Porky's* is a waking fantasy—an erotic daydream. The fantasy of *Risky Business* is the fantasy of night and sleep, and it obeys the dream laws. Joel's dream shifts from the erotic to the anxious, from indulgence to punishment (the examination dream is one of the "typical dreams" cited by Freud), and the link between the two sequences is guilt, the sudden assertion of a panicked superego. Sexual energy isn't simply sublimated here, but transformed into something else. The SAT will determine the kind of money he will make as an adult. Sex is transformed into cash, the erotic quest into the drive to succeed.

Brickman's stylistic choices lead him to his subject, and vice versa; *Risky Business* is a beautifully integrated piece of work. The subjective moving camera of the sex dream returns for an extended sequence in which Joel's parents brief him on his duties and responsibilities as they prepare to leave on a vacation; we share Joel's point of view as his father lectures him on using the stereo (don't turn up the bass) and driving his Porsche (strictly forbidden), and the camera wanders up for a look at the immense crystal egg Joel's mother keeps on the mantelpiece. It's a very elegant, unforced association of ideas, investing the egg with all the fragility of Joel's family situation: the egg becomes not only the symbol of the obligations Joel feels toward his parents (and the fierce self-control necessary to fulfill them), but also the image of the childhood he desperately needs to shatter and escape. The egg is a useless, precious thing, the embodiment of the material rewards Joel can expect for following the path his parents have laid out for him. Breaking it means breaking the family and the future, but it also means freedom.

The dream sequence establishes a rhythm of indulgence and punishment, surrealism and naturalism, sex and money. As *Risky Business* progresses, it follows that rhythm and elaborates it, to the point where the strict divisions of the dream begin to break down. Night falls over the film once Joel's parents leave, and under cover of the liberating darkness, Joel begins to enjoy himself, first breaking small rules (cranking up the stereo, cruising in the car), slowly building up to breaking the big one. He gets the phone number of a Chicago prostitute and asks her to come out to his parents' Highland Park home. When Lana (Rebecca De Mornay) arrives, Joel is dozing on the couch; young and blond and radiant, she lets herself in through an open porch door, unleashing a rush of night wind and leaves that wakes Joel (or does it?) from his reverie.

Brickman's filming of the sex scenes breaks the shot/countershot, voyeurism/exhibitionism pattern that has become the norm for the genre. Because voyeurism is the only sexual charge the movies can offer, most films treat sex as a voyeuristic experience—a game of peekaboo in which the audience is invited to share the privileged peeking-point of a single (invariably male) character. Brickman disrupts the process of easy identification, beginning the sequence with a classic voyeuristic image—Lana stands across the room, slowly pulling off her dress—and then allowing Joel to enter the shot himself, which turns a subjective image into a distanced, objective one. The balance of the sequence plays out at a perfectly pitched remove, largely in dark, symmetrical long shots that interpose a delicate formalism. The emphasis has been shifted from a voyeuristic gratification of the audience to a detached perspective on the character's emotions, from the display of sex to the portrayal of a sexual experience. Brickman describes the mystery, the fear, the sense of release and transformation of a first encounter: Joel has been changed, but not painlessly. The next day he finds that Lana has stolen his mother's egg.

Brickman's balance of the subjective and the objective, the dreamlike and the naturalistic, allows him to pursue his story on two distinct stylistic and thematic levels. Joel's sexual experience, by sweeping away his status as a child and the obligations that bind him to his parents, leaves his life in total disorder: as in a Hitchcock film, the first transgression opens the door to a swirl of surrealistic, disorienting events—an encounter with Lana's gun-waving pimp, a car chase down Lake Shore Drive, the eventual transformation of his parents' home into a bordello. As the dreamlike strain of the film follows these events (Brickman uses both montage and slow motion to expand and condense their sense of duration, giving them a dreamy apartness), the naturalistic strain pursues Joel's problems at school, focusing on the difficulties he's having with exams, an upcoming interview with a recruiter from Princeton, and his project for the business club. Much of the film's humor comes from the collision of the two levels and Joel's desperate attempts to keep them apart, but the real strength of *Risky Business* emerges when the two levels finally converge.

In a world where sexual energy competes with social pressure for success, one or the other must be sublimated, but for Joel it is an impossible choice: he's too much in the grip of early passion to renounce romance (he feels he's falling in love with Lana) and too much the dutiful Highland Park son to renounce the values of his family and friends. But perhaps he doesn't have to choose: with Lana, he has before him an example of sexuality made socially compatible, made to conform to the rules and values and ethics he has been taught. As De Mornay interprets her, Lana is a richly ambiguous figure, neither sentimentalized (as were the hookers of *Night Shift*), nor coarsened into castrating cynicism (as were the whores in *Porky's*); the broad planes of her Slavic face are suspended between affection and indifference, and her look can flash from teenage coquetry to cold calculation. De Mornay's talent is in the way she allows Lana a full measure of magnetism and vivacity, while still letting us see that some small part of her is dead. When she makes her offer to Joel—let her use his parents' house as a pay-as-you-go party and "I'll be your girl friend"—it's impossible to judge her sincerity: the sentiment is cold, but the saying seems innocent, even wistful. By accepting the offer—agreeing, in effect, to pimp for Lana and her friends—Joel is making the only move he can make, trading his innocence for success (the party will gross $8,000, putting him at the head of the Young Enterprisers club). Something dies in Joel, too, at this moment, and Brickman mourns it: the dark glasses Joel slips on make him a permanent resident of the night world, but they also make him old. Joel has grown up.

Lost in America

Directed by ALBERT BROOKS {March 15, 1985}

On the short list of today's formally inventive American filmmakers, Albert Brooks belongs right at the top. There really isn't anyone else in the Hollywood end of the art who's conducting the same kinds of experiments with visual presentation and narrative structure, who's analyzing the received formulas with so much acuity and intelligence, and who's set for himself the goal of creating a genuinely new kind of comic rhetoric. Indeed, if Brooks could arrange to have *Lost in America* dubbed into German it would fit effortlessly into a retrospective of the most formally aggressive works of Jean-Marie Straub and Danielle Huillet—it's that radical. Watching *Lost in America*, I was reminded more than once of Straub-Huillet's last feature, an adaptation of Kafka's *Amerika* retitled *Class Relations* (because of a quarrel over the rights, the film hasn't yet been released in the U.S.). Not only is there a kinship of title and subject (both films are about uprooted naifs trying to make their way across an alien landscape), but also a striking similarity in the design of the brutally stripped-down images and a shared taste for impossibly protracted long takes. It isn't likely that Brooks has ever seen a Straub-Huillet film—or an Akerman, Bresson, or a Godard. Yet, working on his own (and from a very different set of premises), Brooks has arrived at much the same point they have: he's one of the leading modernist filmmakers.

Because Brooks is a comedian—and a very funny one—he'll never have the same kind of cultural cachet as the unmistakably "serious" Straub and Huillet. He belongs to another, almost antiart tradition, that of the comic filmmaker who, in pursuit of his particular vision, gradually leaves his audience behind as his obsessive explorations take him into ever more dangerous territory. The movies seem to produce one obsessive comic genius every 20 or 30 years: Buster Keaton in the 20s, Frank Tashlin in the 50s, Jacques Tati in the 60s. In the 80s, Brooks is well on his way to becoming the kind of vitally marginal figure that they were in their times: he doesn't draw the crowds, or acclaim, of a Woody Allen (just as Keaton was always overshadowed by Chaplin), yet, because he hasn't been crowned the official comic spokesman for his generation, he's free to explore darker, more personal themes in more formally sophisticated ways. Keaton needed Chaplin, just as Brooks needs Allen: the consensus comic draws off the audience's need for identification and reassurance, leaving the marginal comic free to follow his own lights.

The paradox is that Brooks has identified himself with his intended audience more closely than any other comic in the medium's history.

The great comedians of the past have all been eccentrics, in one way or another; Brooks, on the other hand, strives for a perfect normalcy, a seamless unexceptionalness, tracking the progress of the baby-boom audience and presenting himself, with each succeeding film, as their exact statistical image at each film's point in time. In *Real Life* (1979), he was a young idealist, committed to improving the world through his creative efforts. In *Modern Romance* (1981), he was a big city single, feeling the approach of the marriage deadline but unable to make the final commitment that would propel him into the world of his parents. In *Lost in America* he is, of course, a yuppie: a successful creative director with a large advertising agency confidently looking forward to a fat promotion and a new Mercedes. His wife, Julie Hagerty, is a personnel director for a major department store; by pooling their resources, they've managed to buy a $400,000 Los Angeles home. As the movie opens, they're ready for the move: under the opening credits, the camera snakes around the midnight house, inspecting the mountains of packing boxes waiting for the moving men. But a light is burning in the bedroom: haunted by some vague dread, Albert can't sleep.

Brooks's comic persona is brazenly average. Unlike other comics, he doesn't present himself as especially witty, charming, or graceful; with the way he exposes his cowardice, anxiety, and insensitivity, he shouldn't even be very likable. (And he's a big guy, too, with the bulk and square jaw of a football player—nothing could be further removed from the sympathetic frailty of the Chaplin-Allen "little fellow.") His line delivery is so dryly uninflected, so free of the comic's "punchy" rhythms, that when he makes one of his potboiling appearances in a more traditional comedy (in something like Howard Zeiff's *Unfaithfully Yours*, for example) he's almost invisible—he doesn't seem to be doing anything at all when he's placed alongside a laugh-beggar like Dudley Moore. Brooks's overwhelming averageness means that we identify with him easily, yet at the same time his averageness pushes us away—he's too much like what we fear ourselves to be. Helped along by Brooks's distinctive editing patterns (he resists both close-ups and cross-cutting, the two time-honored ways of binding up an identification between character and spectator), it is this strange rhythm of identification and alienation, of attraction and repulsion, that defines the peculiar transactions between spectator and screen at an Albert Brooks movie. We find ourselves sympathizing with Brooks's all-too-recognizable (and always realistically rendered) anxieties and frustrations, yet at the same time the coolness and the distance of visual style is forcing us back, to a point of view outside the situation. There is a constant circulation between identification and alienation and objectivity, and it is in this circulation, this instability, that Brooks's humor is born. To suddenly see objectively what we have been experiencing subjectively is to open a gap between two equally valid but hopelessly incompatible worlds: what seems of immense importance in one sphere seems vain and trivial in the other, courage becomes foolhardiness, idealism becomes self-deception. The gap is huge, absurd, and Brooks's comedy leaps from it.

Like Keaton, Brooks is fundamentally a realist, a filmmaker with a profound respect for the physical world. It's an aesthetic that shouldn't be confused with naturalism, that timid concern for plausibility, continuity, and motivation: an important part of respecting the real world is knowing that it isn't always believable, or even comprehensible. The plot line of *Lost in America* is propelled by unlikelihoods. The expected promotion turns out to be a cross-country transfer to a more subservient position, and Albert angrily quits. (The scene in the boss's office, with Brooks's manic shifts from smiling servility to eye-popping outrage and back again, is some of the most impressive acting I've seen this year.) Albert decides to take advantage of the situation by cashing in the family savings (some $200,000) and, inspired by *Easy Rider*, setting out on a journey across America to "find himself." ("We have to touch Indians," he tells Hagerty, shortly before hitting the highway in his shiny new Winnebago motor home as the chords of Steppenwolf's "Born to Be Wild" thunder on the sound track.) The couple makes it as far as Las Vegas, where Hagerty, finally self-destructing after years of enforced conformity, blows their entire nest egg on an all-night roulette game.

The loss of the money arrives like an A-bomb from a clear blue sky, and it's particularly astonishing because, in both of Brooks's other films, women have provided the one element of stability and rationality in Albert's up-and-down existence. The stroke is wholly arbitrary, yet Brooks is careful to follow its ramifications down to the tiniest emotional detail, a process that turns a screenwriter's trick into something horribly, inescapably real. Brooks does not broaden or falsify his characters' feelings: Albert must move through a complexly rendered chain of shock, anger, resentment, and resignation before he can forgive his wife, and Hagerty must cross a similarly authentic terrain before she can forgive her husband for his lack of understanding and compassion. Brooks is able to portray psychological nuances that go well beyond the range of most contemporary Hollywood dramas; his accuracy of observation seems all the more striking in a comedy, where depth of characterization has long been rendered out of place.

Brooks renders his characters' feelings with a remarkable clarity and precision: every fleeting emotion is clearly presented and immediately legible. This same clarity of regard extends to his rendering of people, objects, and landscapes: Brooks purges every trace of aestheticism or editorial comment from his frames, leaving the object to stand on its own, as something sharp, hard, and absolutely immediate. (In this, he goes straight against the grain of such fashionable filmmakers as De Palma and

Coppola, who clot their images with so many overtones that the objects lose all their integrity, turning into wispy metaphors.) Brooks's long takes reinforce this feeling of solidity: by resisting the temptation to cut (to enforce a rhythm, to punch up a joke, or simply to vary the visual field), Brooks gives his actors and settings the time they need to exist on the screen, to occupy a place in the film with a weight that goes beyond the immediate demands of the screenplay.

It is this extra sense of weight, of solidity, that makes Brooks a modernist filmmaker. He doesn't simply think up gags and then run out and trick up a setting that can contain them. The humor emerges from the setting, from the physicality of the place and the actors that inhabit it. This is the same shift in emphasis that Rossellini made when he invented the modern cinema with *Voyage to Italy*: the filmmaker no longer seeks to stage a pre-scripted "truth," but to find the truth of the situation as it emerges from the interaction of these particular performers in this particular space. For Rossellini, it was above all an aesthetic of drama; in adapting it to comedy, Brooks alters the ends but not the means. He lets reality determine the humor, and in the process, reality becomes the joke. When Albert and his wife have their first violent fight as they pause for a look at Hoover Dam, the joke isn't in the dialogue (which is quite realistic), but in the juxtaposition of the dialogue and the place. The domestic squabble is played against the immensity, the overwhelming physicality, of the dam: the sheer size and scope of the spectacle make their argument seem absurd; at the same time, the importance of the argument to the characters makes the dam itself seem like a ridiculous intrusion. The wild leaps in scale, the preposterous disproportionateness of the two different frames of reference (physical and emotional) that Brooks offers simultaneously, are what make the scene hilariously funny; in any other setting, or filmed in a way that gave the dam less of an immediate presence, the scene would be merely pathetic or banal.

Brooks doesn't need the spectacle of the Hoover Dam to produce this effect: it goes the same with the small desert town where he and Hagerty try to set up house after they've lost their money, and it goes the same with the minor characters Brooks comes in contact with—his treacherous boss, a sympathetic casino manager, an unemployment counselor. Brooks doesn't treat these minor characters as straight men he can bounce jokes off of: no matter how little time they have on the screen, he allows them to establish complete personalities and presences of their own—you feel they'll still be there after the movie crew moves away. It's easy for a filmmaker to mock supporting characters of this kind (particularly if they're small-town or suburban types, as many of the characters in Brooks's film are), and Brooks himself wasn't above taking this kind of cheap shot in his first feature, *Real Life*. But in *Lost in America*, the minor figures are presented without a trace of caricature—they're just as smart and assured as the stars, more so in some cases—and the humor produced by Brooks's uncondescending attitude is at once more mature and more complex. They are authentic enough to impose their own point of view, their own reality, on the action, and again the humor comes from the gap the competing realities produce.

Brooks's comedy is above all a comedy of disappointment. His characters set out in a haze of lofty ideals (a belief in the drama of day-to-day existence in *Real Life*, a quest for an all-consuming, romantic love in *Modern Romance*, a search for authentic, grassroots experience in *Lost in America*), yet always find themselves bumping up against the same old banality and boredom, the inescapable unsatisfactoriness of the real, stubbornly untranscendent world. Because most of those ideals are movie-induced (the filmmaker-hero of *Real Life* was inspired by *An American Family*; in *Lost in America*, Albert wants to turn his life into a road movie), it is necessary to invent a different kind of movie in order to strike them down. Which is exactly what Albert Brooks has done: the formal system he has found for his films is, almost literally, a system of disillusionment—a way of stripping the cinematic image of its gauziness and dreaminess, of tearing aside the layers of abstraction and self-containment it has acquired over the years, and returning to the material world, to the thing itself in all its lumpy prosaicness. For many filmmakers, this return would be a tragic one; that Brooks finds in it a source of humor and optimism (the hero of *Real Life* goes mad at the end, but Brooks's characters in *Modern Romance* and *Lost in America* are allowed to begin again, with healthily diminished expectations) is the mark of an honest, thoughtful, and unsentimental personality—of a truly modern comedian.

After Hours

Directed by MARTIN SCORSESE {October 11, 1985}

Martin Scorsese's new film, *After Hours*, unfolds like a calculated inversion of *Raging Bull*, his 1980 biography of prizefighter Jake La Motta. The protagonist of *After Hours*, Paul Hackett (Griffin Dunne), is a tiny, almost toylike man, with fragile features and a body that barely seems able to support the weight of his clothes; the hulking La Motta could probably have used him as a toothpick. Where *Raging Bull* covered a period of some 20 years with its narrative wanderings up and down the east coast, from New York to Florida and back again, the new film takes place in the small hours of a single night, with the action largely confined to the few square blocks that constitute Manhattan's SoHo district. Where La Motta's turbulent life was shaped by his ferocious attachment to his young blond wife, Paul's night on the town is dominated by four blondes: Marcy (Rosanna Arquette), a mysterious, jittery woman who lures Paul from the safety of the Upper East Side with a vague promise of unbridled sex; Julie (Teri Garr), a spacy 60s refugee who takes Paul in when his liaison with Marcy turns unexpectedly sinister; Gail (Catherine O'Hara), the paranoid proprietor of a Mr. Softee ice cream truck who, believing Paul responsible for a wave of neighborhood burglaries, leads a shrieking vigilante mob against him; and June (Verna Bloom), a gentle, earth-motherly sculptress who offers him shelter from persecution, only to entangle him in the stickiest web of all. And finally, where *Raging Bull* was a tragedy presented in harsh, naturalistic terms, *After Hours* is a black, wincingly funny farce, filmed in a wild mix of antirealist styles that ranges from Kafkaesque understatement to a delirious expressionism, with a side trip through the sketch comedy of *Saturday Night Live*.

And yet, Paul Hackett and Jake La Motta have a great deal in common: both *Raging Bull* and *After Hours* are centered on characters who feel profoundly uncomfortable in the world, who have somehow slipped out of sync with the rhythms of daily life. Painfully isolated individuals, they have lost the secret of easy, casual human relations that seems to be possessed by everyone around them. Unable to reach out emotionally or intellectually, Paul and Jake can connect only in physical ways—through sexuality or through violence—yet these encounters leave them guilty and ashamed. As much as they may yearn for something higher—for a spiritual connection, though the words would never occur to them—they find themselves trapped by physicality, prisoners in their own bodies. When this conflict is played out internally, as in *Raging Bull*, it becomes the stuff of self-lacerating drama; when it's projected outward, onto a world that becomes a nightmarish reflection of the central character's own conflicts, it becomes the comedy of *After Hours*. Unlike La Motta, Paul has the chance to confront his demons—the film is comedy not simply because it uses humor, but also in the classical sense of allowing the protagonist to overcome his opposition and achieve his goals. In a hilariously metaphorical final sequence, Paul is admitted to paradise, and he finds it just as light and airy as he'd always dreamed.

Scorsese keeps his distance from La Motta, approaching him externally through an objective camera technique and a narrative structure that imposes more normal, more accessible characters—Jake's wife and brother—between the audience and the eccentric hero. But in *After Hours*, Scorsese plunges us straight into Paul's consciousness with a stylistic flourish borrowed from the master of subjective filmmaking, Alfred Hitchcock. As Paul, the chief of word processing for an anonymous midtown firm, sits in his office half-listening to the whining of a new employee, Scorsese inserts a series of random, uncentered shots—desk tops, bulletin boards, passersby. These images, which represent Paul's distracted glances, interrupt what has been up until this point a perfectly traditional shot/countershot cutting pattern (the alternation of close-ups, timed to lines of dialogue, that serves to keep the focus on and involved with the interaction of the characters). Suddenly, we are sharing Paul's point of view, his very personal reactions (boredom, irritation, disengagement) to the conversation he is ostensibly taking part in. With this abrupt, strongly marked departure from realist technique, Scorsese is setting us up to accept the film's other stylistic distortions (which include speeded-up motion and unmotivated camera movements) as projections of Paul's inner state.

But it is also this sequence that, through a few quick, simple strokes, gives us the key to Paul's character. Because the random images cut off the naturalistic flow of the shot/countershot cutting, they seem to stand in some space outside the story line. Yet, because the employee's drone continues uninterrupted on the sound track, there is something in the sequence that seems to be tugging us back to the narrative, to the "real world" established by the shot/countershot technique. Hitchcock uses this stylistic figure in *To Catch a Thief*, when Cary Grant, a reformed cat burglar, is momentarily tempted by a dazzling diamond necklace worn by Grace Kelly, and Scorsese's reworking of it retains its odd pang of guilt and shame—the embarrassment of being caught in a daydream. Scorsese lets this sense of guilty dislocation simmer for a moment, suggesting that the relationship between these nonnarrative images and the narration is also the relationship between Paul and Paul's life. Paul feels cut off from his own existence (and, from what we see of it—a sterile apartment and an impersonal office—we can understand why he'd want to be), yet he's ashamed of his noninvolvement; he wants to get back. There aren't more than a handful of filmmakers at work today who can establish an emotional condition as complex as this through purely cinematic terms; again and again in *After Hours*, Scorsese reminds us of the real power of the movies.

When Marcy comes on to Paul (he's sitting in a nearly deserted coffee shop reading a copy of *Tropic of Cancer*, when she blurts out from a nearby table that it's her favorite book too), he sees his chance to make some kind of a connection. The fact that Marcy's invitation seems to be purely sexual automatically raises him from his torpor: his reaction is involuntary, instinctual; the encounter seems safe and easy. But from the moment Marcy enters the frame, the film experiences another stylistic convulsion. Scorsese films the coffee shop conversation through a bewildering variety of lenses (again, it's a moment that would normally demand a simple shot/countershot treatment). Sometimes he uses a telephoto to isolate Paul's face in tight close-up against a blurred, indistinct background; at other moments he'll shift to a wide-angle lens that registers the background with perfect focus and clarity. The space around Paul and Marcy seems to be pulsating, changing its contours with every shot. It's as if the image track were constantly contradicting itself, and Scorsese picks up this rhythm of spiraling self-negation in the dialogue. Every statement Marcy makes is followed by another that undermines it: she likes him, she doesn't; she's coming on, she's running away. She leaves Paul her phone number, and when he calls her a couple of nights later, she invites him down to the SoHo loft she shares with an artist-friend. But by the time Paul arrives, the contradictions have escalated to the level of behavior. Though she's just told him to come over, Marcy is gone when Paul gets there. The artist, Kiki (Linda Fiorentino), a sultry package in a black bra and slip specked with papier-mâché, lets him in; the phone rings and it's Marcy, telling Kiki to get rid of the visitor. Kiki, though, tells him to stay, and a little while later Marcy walks in, greets him warmly, and invites him to her bedroom. Scorsese doesn't try to account for these abrupt reversals. He simply presents Marcy's actions as they appear to Paul—opaque and imponderable. Just as Paul has begun to reach out to the world, he finds the world withdrawing from him, turning into something remote and mysterious. Now that he wants to, he can't get through.

Barriers provide the film's main visual motif—the armored doors of artists' lofts, the steel security shutters that descend over bars and shop fronts, the metal gratings that cover the apartment windows through which Paul glimpses flashing scenes of sex and violence. There is even a punk bar named Berlin, where the décor consists of chain-link fencing and the bouncer who bars the door is only slightly more accommodating than an East German border guard. Paul manages to pass through several of these barriers—it's the blond women who let him in—though once he's crossed them he can't go back: the doors open only one way. Every time

Paul believes he's escaped—as when he flees from Marcy's apartment to a friendly-looking saloon (though the sign over the door does say "Terminal Bar")—he finds that he's only fallen in deeper (the bartender turns out to be Marcy's boyfriend). The only characters who can pass freely through this Chinese box environment are the two burglars played by Cheech and Chong: merrily (and obliviously) cleaning out the neighborhood while the mob pursues Paul, they appear as sprightly, almost supernatural figures; eventually, they will prove to be the agents of Paul's salvation.

If *After Hours* seems to be reaching the kind of wide audience that eluded Scorsese on his last two films, *Raging Bull* and *King of Comedy*, it's probably because Scorsese has been able to tap into what has become the dominant strain in 80s comedy—the comedy of underreaction, defined by an unflappably cool protagonist (Bill Murray, ideally) who steadfastly refuses to be provoked by the outrageous, surreal, often threatening goings-on around him. Paul's sense of detachment isn't unlike Murray's in a film like *Ghostbusters*, but Scorsese takes the idea one step further, humanizing it: he identifies its psychological roots, and then lets us see the increasing amount of effort Paul must expend on maintaining it. Paul wants to withdraw from the nightmare that's happening to him, to make himself small and inconspicuous (his most frequent lines of dialogue are "I didn't know" and "I'm sorry"), but the anger is building up inside. He's ready to turn into a raging bull himself, or at least a raging heifer. Paul's desperate detachment, his strangely hysterical reasonableness, represents another kind of barrier: you begin to feel that if only he could explode, take command of the situation, his nightmare would be over. But every time Paul lets his anger show—his violence is verbal, sarcastic, rather than physical—as he does with the first three blondes, the results are catastrophic: if he strikes out at the world, the world strikes back twice as hard at him. It was an instinctive, physical response—good old lust—that got him into this situation. Another instinctive response—violence—isn't going to get him out.

Paul is as much a victim of his physical urges as Jake La Motta; as much as he may try to repress them, he can't entirely snuff them out—they keep getting him into trouble. This is, of course, the classic Catholic boy conundrum—why has God built these things into me if he only wants to punish me for them?—as Scorsese makes explicit when he has Paul, a Job in the SoHo wilderness, stagger down a deserted street and cry to an unseen auditor, "I just wanted to get out of my apartment, meet a nice girl . . . and now I've gotta *die* for it?" But if Catholic doctrine—the resentment of the body—is the blueprint for Scorsese's fiction, he's equally concerned with cultural doctrine, with what this resentment has done to the relations between men and women. If men must be made to bear the exclusive burden of sexual aggression, they must all become monsters; if women must somehow be placed beyond sexuality, they must all become harpies. Scorsese's four blondes—their hair color is flaunted as the traditional emblem of innocence and purity—become the objects of a mingled fear and desire, sought after because they promise some relief from the sexual burden, flown from in horror because they seem to want to appropriate the sexual prerogative for themselves. The barrier between the sexes is the ultimate line of demarcation in *After Hours*; there is only one way to cross it—the body must be cast off.

The film's concluding section consists of a riotous, virtuoso shuffling of satirical birth and death images. June, Verna Bloom's motherly sculptress, takes the by now exhausted Paul down to her dark, damp basement studio; he curls up in her lap, clutching her like a baby. When the vigilante mob arrives at her door, June decides to hide Paul by disguising him as a sculpture: covered with rapidly stiffening papier-mâché strips, his eyes peering out from a tiny hole, this thickened, immobile Paul suddenly comes to resemble the overweight La Motta at the end of *Raging Bull*, trapped inside his own physical bulk. June goes off with the mob, leaving Paul alone until Cheech and Chong arrive. Thinking he's an art object, they steal him, pulling his rigid form up into the street through a manhole cover. With Paul loaded in their van, they take off uptown, but a strategically placed pothole bumps Paul out the back door and into the street directly in front of his office building. It is dawn, and the barrier in front of the building—a magnificent golden gate—swings open magisterially to admit the new arrival. The fall having broken his plaster shell, Paul staggers to an elevator and ascends to his celestial office, where his computer, like a friendly disembodied deity, blinks him a message of greeting—"Good morning, Paul." It is here in this lifeless land, where all sexuality has been sublimated in work and there are only words, not bodies, to deal with, that Paul finally finds freedom and peace. As if in celebration, Scorsese's camera flies off for a rushing, swooping dance around the room—a flight of angels rejoicing in the salvation of a sinner.

MAVERICKS AND OUTSIDERS >>

Dawn of the Dead

Directed and written by GEORGE ROMERO {May 18, 1979}

When George Romero's scurrilous, humbly budgeted horror movie arrived in Chicago two weeks ago, it carried some high hopes and dreams with it. Many people in the film business—exhibitors, distributors, and critics—felt that Romero's nonunion, made-in-Pittsburgh film would pick up where John Carpenter's *Halloween* left off last fall; that here, at last, was the independent production that would finally promote America's beyond-the-fringe filmmakers from the drive-ins, their traditional domain, into the plush suburban shopping center theaters long exclusively held by the Hollywood majors. *Dawn of the Dead*, it was thought, had the potential to break the west coast big studio monopoly once and for all and open the way to the legions of regional filmmakers who cowered beyond Hollywood's door. It was an infinitely admirable goal, and one that involved, not incidentally, making a lot of money for the people who supported it.

But when *Dawn of the Dead* accordingly opened in some of Chicago's most prestigious outlying theaters, it withered and almost died. The film was outgrossed, ironically, by another horror movie from the hinterlands (Oregon, this time), Don Coscarelli's moderately interesting *Phantasm*. The distributors of *Phantasm* had the conservative wisdom to open their film in the conventional way: in a large number of theaters, mainly urban, backed by an intense exploitation campaign on television. *Phantasm* took away Romero's hard-core audience and left *Dawn of the Dead* to flounder in its own ambitions. It did do well where tradition might dictate—in the Loop and on the near north side—which suggests that the horror film audience simply feels a natural reluctance to drive ten miles and pay four dollars for a sensation that is available more cheaply and conveniently elsewhere. But despite the very enthusiastic reviews in the daily papers, the wider middle-class audience that *Dawn* aspired to rejected the film out of hand—almost immediately, as if by instinct. Perhaps its distributors had not fully reckoned with the film's aggressiveness and antisocial stance. As an independent film, *Dawn of the Dead* might be *too* independent—too fierce and original and threatening. Whatever else might be said about it, *Dawn of the Dead* is not a safe film, and safety (or, at least, a threat presented in safe terms, like *Jaws*) is what the suburban audience apparently requires.

But it would be a sad waste if the film were left to die, unmourned, in the action houses around town. Romero's movie—a sequel to his 1966 shoestring thriller *Night of the Living Dead*—has more dash and vigor than 90 percent of this year's Hollywood films. For a change, it looks like a movie that somebody wanted to make, or even had to; it bears no trace of the rote work that marks so many of today's commissioned projects. One has the feeling that Romero is genuinely enjoying his art, testing the limits of his skill and exploring the possibilities of his form. And even if that form may seem hopelessly corrupt, or irretrievably lowbrow, the film has much to offer to a discriminating audience.

If, that is, said discriminating audience can get past the gallons of blood and gore that Romero has lavished on his movie. *Dawn of the Dead* must set a new record for on-screen mayhem: the corpses pile up beyond count and beyond imagining. Any attempt to keep score would be defeated by the end of the first reel—the bodies multiply like gory jackrabbits. And the violence is kept squarely in the center of the screen, rendered in close-ups too gruesome to describe. Heads are blown off, limbs ripped from sockets, and stomachs torn open with an abandon that borders on the truly savage. Borders on, I should say, but does not enter, for there is a firm moral intelligence at work in the film, popping up in the strangest and most effective places. Few of the deaths are "real," even in the film's terms. Most of the victims are, in the premise Romero puts forward, already dead—and that is a distinction that the film makes much ironic and knowing use of.

Violence becomes something of an artistic end in itself in Romero's movie. It's not as stylized as the balletic gang fights of *The Warriors*, but it acquires the same kind of interest. The violence is *elegant*, in some odd way that has nothing to do with beauty or taste or discretion. It makes its own aesthetic out of excess and repetition. Going to movies for a living, I've found, has given me a skewed perspective on film violence. After seeing three or four on-screen throat slashings in the space of a week, you become strangely inured to the experience; time passes, and the regular shooting and gouging become just one more example of movie magic, special effects that you learn to appreciate with a distanced eye. It took me at least five years to become as numb as I have; *Dawn of the Dead* could do it for my grandmother in five minutes. Romero's shock effects pour down so heavily that they soon cease to shock; they become part of the rhythm and structure of the film. At the start, you begin to expect them; by the end, you've come to assume them—the blood is one of the movie's basic postulations, a rule of style that the audience is brought to accept as abstractly as the invisible orchestra in a musical.

With great deliberation, Romero makes bloodshed the norm. As the movie continues through its two-hour course, the gore gradually loses its impact. Fright and revulsion are slowly subsumed by a growing fascination; from a horror movie, it turns into a kind of magic show, and you find yourself not shrinking under your seat, but sitting with rapt attention and wondering how the trick was done. When the movie launches one of its mass attacks, with bodies lunging and dropping in all directions, Romero's controlled staging gives the spectacle a demented Busby Berkeley effect: the action flows along sweeping, abstract lines, and Romero selects his shots to keep it swirling, around and around. The emphasis, in the production numbers as elsewhere, is on speed for its own sake (the exposition is completely dispatched under the opening titles), and Romero's editing—breathtakingly fast and painfully accurate—keeps the pace pounding through a multiplicity of viewpoints, cutting down low for a subjective shot or rocketing the camera to the rafters to catch the grand design. I knew I had had it when the bloodstains on the walls began to remind me of Jackson Pollock. Andrew Sarris once wrote that the pie fight in Blake Edwards's *The Great Race* was "the last spasm of action painting in the Western world." He was, unfortunately, wrong.

Dawn of the Dead hangs on a beautifully simple idea. Four survivors of the first film's zombie plague—two cops and a man and a woman who work in the news department of a Pittsburgh television station—escape the besieged city in a commandeered helicopter. In flight, they discover a huge suburban shopping mall, abandoned except for a few gaggles of zombies, who wander aimlessly among the glowing storefronts, potted plants, and display fountains of the two-level covered complex. There being no better place to weather the storm, the four settle down to scouring out the remaining pests, raiding the stores for supplies, and setting up luxury living quarters in a remote and carefully barricaded corner of the maintenance tower. But peace, alas, does not hold for long.

The setting suggests an elaborate variation on Cary Grant's adventure with a sinister crop-dusting plane in the open fields of Alfred Hitchcock's *North by Northwest*. This is the horror of the everyday—horror taken from the crumbling, shadow-laden castles of the Universal shockers and set down amid the brightest and most familiar surroundings imaginable. Nowhere in *Dawn of the Dead* is there the slightest intimation of the supernatural. The original *Night of the Living Dead* contained an offhand "explanation" to the effect that the unburied dead had been brought back to life (as oblivious, flesh-eating zombies) by that 50s favorite (and comeback of the year) radioactive fallout. *Dawn of the Dead* does make a prophetic reference to Harrisburg, but that one inadvertent remark is as close as the new film comes to justifying its premise. But explanations, of course, have always been redundant in horror movies. What counts is the primal effectiveness of the menace: the more evocative the monster, the less rationalization it requires. And Romero's Living Dead, in their great, dumb ordinariness, are among the most evocative monsters ever to step out of the subconscious.

In his excellent *Village Voice* profile of Romero, Tom Allen objects to the zombies as a tired horror film device: they're plainly gimmicks, but they're not gimmicky enough to be interesting or unique. But the banality, the plainness of the conception, is, I think, what gives it its power. The Living Dead are disturbingly unexotic, even familiar: no one has ever met a vampire, but almost everyone has seen a corpse; most often, the body of a friend or a relative. Death is the one process of mystical transformation that enters our daily lives. Dead bodies seem magically changed, qualitatively different: what once was a person is suddenly a thing, an object of a vague and barely acknowledged fear and revulsion. And when the body belonged to someone we loved, our feelings of horror are mixed up, unbearably, with grief and loss. The Living Dead step straight out of that complex of feelings; somehow, we know them, we've met them already. And because we know them, they're horrible—something out of our lives has turned against us, something we once loved has now become strange and awful. Romero's two movies draw their most harrowing moments from that mixture of love and horror. *Night of the Living Dead* has one particularly crushing sequence—in which the revived body of a little girl goes after her parents—that is so vivid in its associations that audiences immediately fall silent, even at the campiest of midnight shows.

Another key component of the Living Dead's insidious ordinariness is their slowness and stupidity—they have no special powers or abilities, just a dumb dogged determination, a stick-to-itiveness that eventually helps them muddle through. Individually, they're no real threat. A good punch in the head, or even a casual shove, sends them reeling off in blank confusion. Standing alone, they seem helpless, even pathetic; the problem is, there's so damn many of them.

Romero sets the most prosaic of monsters down in the most prosaic of settings—a shopping center. As they wander the corridors—heads bloodied, eyes glazed, but still dressed in the uniforms of their everyday lives—they look like they're out for a weekend spree. One character theorizes that the zombies return to the mall because "it was a very important place in their lives." Creatures of consumer society to the very end, they shop compulsively, instinctively. Elements of social satire begin to creep into Romero's film during these sequences: the jokes may be obvious, but they're not forced, and many of them are very funny—as when the two cops, dazzled by the freebies that await them in the abandoned stores, launch their attack with a battle cry of "Let's *go SHOPPING!*" As they hack their way through the crowd, their guerrilla tactics wouldn't seem all that out of place on a sale day at Wieboldt's. They fill a wheelbarrow with radios and TV sets, although there is little to listen to and nothing to watch.

Some critics have read the entire film as a satire on materialism, trotting out the few moments of parody as evidence of *Dawn of the Dead*'s redeeming social value, just like the gynecological lectures that used to be inserted into sex films. The humor is there, but it's not really at the heart of the film. Somehow, it seems like those critics were ashamed to admit that they enjoyed the film for what it is—a violent, tasteless fantasy—and so they should be. The redeeming social value of *Dawn of the Dead* lies in the fact that it redeems nothing and damns everything, including the audience's own enjoyment. The film opens a Pandora's box of forbidden pleasures, linking a marginally acceptable guilty fantasy—running wild in a department store—to a much darker and more sinister one, that of having a license to kill. *Dawn of the Dead* is violent, shocking, and repulsive, but its dirtiest secret is that it's *fun*, too—fun to pick off all of those stumbling zombies, dressed in the clothes of people we love to hate: cops and nuns and Hare Krishnas. If the film first seduces us by playing to our lowest consumer instincts, it soon captivates us by playing to instincts that are even lower. Romero invites us to enjoy the spectacle of mass slaughter, and we do, feeling no guilt or shame because he has provided us with a special kind of killing—killing things that are already "dead." The zombies may look like humans, and sometimes act like humans, but they're not humans, right? And so it's OK to enjoy the vicarious pleasure of killing them, right? *Right?*

Well . . . maybe not. Just as the film careens between satire and suspense, low comedy and horror, so does Romero constantly redefine our loyalties and levels of identification with the characters. And as our sympathies shift, so do our moral judgments—subconsciously, perhaps, but tellingly.

The two cops, for example, first meet and become friends during a brutal first-reel shootout in a tenement building—the residents of which are suspected of sentimentally harboring their unburied dead (thus creating more zombies) instead of turning the bodies over to the public incinerator. The police raid on the building is genuinely savage: a hog-faced sergeant blows down the tenants as soon as they open their doors. Our heroes become our heroes because they are deeply appalled at what they see—as are we, at this point, since these are *people* who are being slaughtered. But by the end of their adventure in the shopping center—after they've become accustomed to using zombies for casual target practice—our heroes don't think twice about treating the members of an invading motorcycle gang in the same way they once deplored; they shoot them down as they retreat. The killing has become detached, automatic—second nature both for the protagonists and for us.

But if the heroes lose their humanity, the zombies regain some of theirs. Through the first half of the film, they're alternately threatening and funny—monsters or jokes—and we don't feel any attachment to them either way. But once they've been safely put down, corralled, they acquire a certain pathos: they're so dumb, slow, and helpless that we start to feel protective toward them, particularly when the motorcycle gang begins to tease them—pushing them around and even hitting a few of them with pies lifted from a bakery shop. Things have gone too far, we think: it's like watching someone mistreat a pet. And when that pet turns again in the last reel, it's the cruelest reversal of all: we've been betrayed.

Like Paul Bartel's grisly and intelligent exploitation film of a few years back, *Death Race 2000*, *Dawn of the Dead* takes the antisocial assumptions of the action film—our willing suspension of human feeling—and twists them around, eventually throwing them back in our faces. The harmless fantasy of violence—what we think of when we say, "It's only a movie," or here, "It's only a zombie"—is revealed as very harmful indeed. We might not even notice how much our attitudes have been changed, how thoroughly our sympathies have been transformed and displaced, until we leave the theater. Like the satire of Jonathan Swift, Romero's film works by making the outrageous seem reasonable—and beyond that, even entertaining. It's not until that delayed moment of reflection, of sudden self-consciousness, that we realize how ruthlessly and skillfully we've been had, how happily we've abandoned our most basic moral principles.

Beneath Romero's Swiftian method lies a hint of Swiftian misanthropy. *Dawn of the Dead* presents its people in the worst of all possible lights—as grasping, selfish, unthinking, and brutal. There's some measure of the universal contempt that Romero feels in the blithe way he sets out to manipulate his audience's most fundamental responses. That he succeeds in manipulating them is some proof that his contempt is not misplaced. His film is a jeremiad, directed not simply against the "consumer society" but also—more deeply and more urgently—against a general cheapening of humanity, the same sort of cheapening, one can't help but think, that our soldiers were encouraged to practice in Vietnam. From zombie to "gook," and the same intimation of guiltless slaughter, is not a very long step. *Dawn of the Dead* would be totally bleak were it not for its striking last scene, in which one of the heroes makes a sudden, ineffable rediscovery of his own humanity in turning away from suicide. The moment is arbitrary and almost unbelievable, but it throws the issues of the film into sharp relief—it's the touch of grace that arrives, without need of reason, at the end of a hell-raising sermon.

The Big Red One

Directed by SAMUEL FULLER {August 22, 1980}

The Big Red One marks Sam Fuller's return to mainstream American filmmaking, and that alone would be enough to place it among the most important movie events of 1980. Fuller hasn't completed a Hollywood production since 1963: the intervening time has been a wasteland of unproduced scripts, compromised foreign projects (*Shark* and *Dead Pigeon on Beethoven Street*), and abrupt firings (among them, *The Klansman* and *The Deadly Trackers*). But Fuller, back in the big leagues at last, seems as limber as ever, still pitching his spitballs with speed and accuracy. The style and substance of American filmmaking has changed drastically since Fuller last directed, but *The Big Red One* seldom seems anachronistic: Fuller has faced, head-on, the issues of filmmaking in the 80s, adjusting his style to accommodate the new demands of surface realism, color photography, and psychologically acceptable characters. The zoom has replaced the tracking shot as the basic unit of Fuller's vocabulary, just as the zoom has conquered in the cinema as a whole, but, even with this fundamental alteration, the visual style is unmistakably Fuller's, and unbendingly personal. *The Big Red One* is as much a Fuller film as was *The Naked Kiss*, his last Hollywood effort of 17 years ago, but it's also a film of its time—unlike, say, Billy Wilder's *Fedora*, a film by another veteran director that wrapped itself self-consciously, hermetically, in the classical style of its creator's ascendancy. *Fedora* is a film of reflection where *The Big Red One* is a film of action; though its creator recently turned 69, it's in no sense an old man's movie. Fuller is still investigating his art, redefining his positions. His attitude toward the past is best summed up by the death chant of *Fixed Bayonets* (1951), intoned every time a soldier dies: "Strip him of everything we can use, and bury him." Fuller, likewise, takes what he can use from his past work, and buries the rest.

If Fuller can accept the new rules and regulations more readily than Wilder, it may be because Fuller was never much of a classicist, even in his classic period. Like many instinctive, untrained artists, Fuller makes an end run around the classical virtues of balance, moderation, and proportion, heading straight for the wide-open ground of modernism. With their willingness to shift the levels of discourse, from drama to documentary and back again, their foregrounding of ideas and feelings over naturalistic detail, their fascination with the written word in banners, slogans, headlines, Fuller's films constantly violate the conventions of the well-made movie. It was this aspect of Fuller's work that attracted Godard (and the above could be a description of *Masculine Feminine* as much as any Fuller film), but where Godard's intent is intellectual, Fuller's is frankly emotive. In the urgency of his emotions, Fuller has no patience with the niceties of form and presentation; his work is never elegant, though it is often beautiful in its naked strength. His films aren't plausible as drama—never in the sense that we can recognize and enter their worlds—but they're always believable, as projections of a particularly rich and conflicted personality. Fuller's sincerity is never in doubt: no matter how extreme his emotions are, they all carry the guarantee of having been felt, of their truth to the artist. Often, it's this sense of conviction that we respond to in a Fuller film, above the actual quality of the ideas, beyond the frequent triteness of conception.

In the past, Fuller's plotting has been so dense and convoluted as to be nearly illegible. I doubt if anyone could recall the precise story lines of *Forty Guns* and *House of Bamboo* without consulting a reference book. Fuller, unwittingly perhaps, achieves a kind of abstraction with this approach: impossible to keep track of, the plot twists and motivations drop out of consciousness, leaving an open field of vivid, elemental emotions. Fuller isn't interested in the terms of conflict: it's the experience of conflict, the crash and splatter of loyalties, beliefs, and allegiances, that is the object of his obsessive fascination. In Fuller's last Hollywood films—*Merrill's Marauders, Shock Corridor, The Naked Kiss*—plot begins to disappear; the conflicts are no longer between characters, but between a character and his surroundings. The surroundings, often, are highly metaphorical: a jungle, an asylum, a small American town. The films break down into vignettes of confrontation, waves of environmental assault. *The Big Red One* follows that line of development: it's a history of Fuller's own division in World War II, and its only plot line is a progression of battle, from a beachhead in North Africa to a concentration camp in Czechoslovakia. But even that description makes the film sound too linear: there is none of the overview of the typical war picture, with the animated maps and charts marking progression toward a strategic goal; in fact, there is hardly any sense of physical progression at all. The transitions between battles are marked only by shock cuts and expository subtitles ("Sicily," "Normandy," etc.). No one seems to go anywhere; they are simply there (this is the exact inverse of *Merrill's Marauders*, in which the battle sequences were elided in favor of the march). In *The Big Red One*, "war" is not a place—it's a condition; the landscape changes but the environment remains constant.

With his usual bluntness, Fuller states his theme in a black-and-white prologue: On a deserted World War I battlefield, an American soldier (Lee Marvin) meets a German and kills him. Back at his base, the American learns that the armistice was signed four hours earlier—that he is, in fact, a murderer. *The Big Red One* is about shades of killing: when it is noble, when it is not, and when it is simply a squalid, meaningless fact. It is not about dying: Fuller finds no value there, and he attaches no sentiment to death. Death is a constant, it *is* the environment: in the opening sequence, a gigantic, grotesque crucifix looms over the battlefield; the empty, shadowed eye sockets of the Christ's head give it the appearance of a skull—and that's the reigning deity of these parts, holding no promise of redemption or release. A dead man is a man who has lost; for the others, the struggle goes on.

That crucifix, of course, isn't what anyone would call a subtle, discreet touch: as a symbol, it weighs about ten tons. But the point, for Fuller, isn't subtlety—the symbol may be monstrously heavy, but it falls with an equal force; it's the impact that counts. The crucifix turns up again in the film's full-color present tense: Marvin, now a sergeant, finds himself back at the same battlefield with his new squad. A war memorial now stands at the spot where he killed the German soldier; the base of the crucifix is ringed with fresh bodies, the crew of a bombed, burned-out German tank. Fuller lets the irony swell, to the breaking point and beyond: an American reads the list of the dead inscribed on the memorial and recognizes names from his own division—the same men are dying again, 30 years later. Another twist arrives, as Marvin discovers that not all the Germans are dead: an infantry squad has mingled with the corpses, waiting in ambush. In the shadow of the crucifix, Fuller stages a grotesque parody of resurrection: the dead men rise and attack. But no sooner has Fuller finished exploiting the irony of this image—in Fuller's cosmology, there is only death after death, as the revivified soldiers are killed one by one—than he is ready to swoop down with yet another. The surviving Americans discover a French woman, heaving in labor. They take her to the burned-out tank, and there, amid the bodies and spent bullets, deliver her baby. And so, this riot of debased religious imagery ends with a sincerely evoked, gruffly hopeful nativity. It's never easy to pinpoint the exact moment when Fuller's imagery rises from the ridiculous to the sublime. (For more refined souls, that moment never comes; perhaps a sign should be hung over the theater door—"Abandon all taste, ye who enter here.") Largely, it's a process of accretion: Fuller multiplies his images, piling one atop another, until the structure is too imposing to be resisted. And there is always the threat of imminent collapse, as if Fuller's manic energy were about to explode—a force that could annihilate everything in a 40-mile radius. At a time when entire films are sustained by one or two ideas, the prolificacy of Fuller's imagination seems almost dangerous—too rich, too full, too dense. The viewer feels swamped—there's no time to digest, no time to recover. And yet, Fuller never works very far from cliché—even his most startling images, such as the crucifix, have an air of familiarity, though it is seldom possible to identify exact sources. Perhaps Fuller's work is best thought of as collage: he selects his material from the body of images that float free through our culture—churned up by movies, television, pulp fiction—and clips what he wants from its context. The act of creation lies in the arrangement of Fuller's found images, as the juxtaposition of clichés creates new impressions, new meanings—establishing links where none existed before. A Fuller film is something like a Cornell box, though it won't stand still long enough for a thorough inspection. Late in *The Big Red One*, there's a sequence that outdoes the crucifix: Marvin and his squad come across a French monastery, which is serving as a wartime asylum for the local insane. It's also serving as a German observation post, and Marvin is determined to take it, helped by a French resistance fighter (Stéphane Audran) disguised as an inmate. While the squad waits outside, Audran pirouettes around the inner courtyard, silently slashing the throats of German guards with the straight razor she hides behind a baby doll. As the squad attacks, an inmate grabs a machine gun; firing on a group of monks and patients at dinner, he chatters, "I'm sane! I'm sane!" while Fuller drops in portentous close-ups of the reproduction of *The Last Supper* that hangs on the wall behind. If you shook that sequence down into its literary components, you'd have little more than a collection of platitudes: war is crazy, appearances are deceptive, God is dead. But as it jumps across the screen, Fuller throws out his associative connections—monk-Nazi-madman, woman-baby doll-razor, peace-violence-God—and something in that visual cacophony strikes a loud, clear chord. The rain of images creates a twisting, rushing line of emotion—horror, exhilaration, triumph, despair, horniness, revulsion—that words can't encapsulate. There are those who would say that effects like that are the definition of pure cinema; I've never been sure that such a thing exists, but as long as *The Big Red One* holds the screen, I'm willing to believe it. Pure or not, Sam Fuller's movie is brilliant cinema; there hasn't been anything like it in a long, long time.

Love Streams

Directed by JOHN CASSAVETES {September 28, 1984}

The history of film is in some ways also a history of the repression of emotion. The actors in silent films used the whole of the body as an expression of feeling: gestures were large, movements broad and rhythmic, the eyes and mouth were exaggerated by makeup and by the orthochromatic photography into emotional signs of a startling directness. Sound films diminished the importance of the body, focusing expressiveness on the voice. And when, after the war, the first modernist films appeared—those of Bresson, Tati, Antonioni—the voice lost its primacy, too: emotion eluded words; it became concentrated in the actor's regard, in the silent exchange of looks. The refinement and repressiveness of modernism continues to define the dominant film styles—it's our generation's index of realism, just as extravagance was "real" for the filmgoers of the teens and early 20s. Pop melodramas like *Kramer vs. Kramer* fake the placid surfaces of *L'avventura*; comedies—notably *Ghostbusters*—are built on a hip detachment carried to an absurd degree.

John Cassavetes stands outside this history. His actors are full-bodied, demonstrative, and his camera doesn't back off from them: there is an emotional intensity in his films, a readiness always to go too far, that can be embarrassing, intimidating, for some audiences. And because Cassavetes couches his emotional extravagance within the traditional signs of realism—location shooting, long takes, a grainy documentary quality to the image—many audiences feel betrayed by his films: they present themselves as "real," but this isn't the reality of other movies. Cassavetes is compelled to expose, expand, to apotheosize emotion; it is no wonder then that he is consistently drawn to themes of breakdown and madness—the only way the contemporary cinema can assimilate emotions of Cassavetes's size is to characterize them as insanity.

Love Streams renews those habitual themes; it takes the essence of his 1974 *A Woman Under the Influence*—Gena Rowlands as a woman who drives her family away because she loves them too intently—and marries it to the essence of his 1970 *Husbands*—Cassavetes himself as a man who looks for emotional refuge in brief affairs. The synthesis produces a masterwork, a film that brings together the insights and innovations of an entire career and allows them to crossbreed and flower. *Love Streams* is by far the best American film of 1984; as the culmination of Cassavetes's personal aesthetic, it will probably prove to be one of the best American films, period.

One of the hallmarks of Cassavetes's style is his complete disdain for exposition. There's no setting up of the story, no introduction to the characters: typically, the film begins full blast in the middle of an already extreme situation, and several minutes pass before we can begin to decipher the action and identify the players. I used to think that Cassavetes's neglect of the narrative niceties was the sign of a far-reaching contempt for the artificial smoothness and symmetry of the classical style—a rejection of classicism in the name of ragged naturalism. But *Love Streams* makes it clear that Cassavetes's deepest concerns have nothing to do with realism: at the innermost level, the film is as classically constructed as could be imagined, bound together by a tight system of thematic contrasts and echoing imagery. It is only the narrative surface that seems chaotic, and if the story is sometimes confusing, it is only because Cassavetes is unwilling to distance himself from his characters even for the few minutes required to introduce the expository information. Cassavetes's commitment to his two principal characters is complete: his camera never once abandons them—never goes behind their backs to offer an editorial judgment—and we must experience the events of the film as they experience them, as integral blocks of time.

Love Streams opens with Cassavetes in a violent argument with a woman; as he strides up and down, he keeps a little girl slung over his shoulder. Eventually we learn that this is Robert Harmon, a celebrated novelist, and that he is fighting over alimony with one of his ex-wives, using the girl, his daughter, as an emotional buffer. Mother and daughter leave, and Robert goes back to his current companions—half a dozen young prostitutes whom he pays, apparently, to live with him in his Los Angeles canyon home. There is a jump cut to a scene in a darkened gay bar, where Robert watches a parade of transvestites and listens to a young black singer, Susan (Diahnne Abbott), perform; intrigued, he asks after her. Another jump cut takes us to a hearing room in Chicago, where Sarah Lawson (Gena Rowlands) is settling the terms of her divorce from her husband Jack (Seymour Cassel). Sarah strains to be reasonable, to present herself as a calm, compassionate woman, resigned to the death of her marriage. But suddenly she cracks: her mouth stretched into a desperately charming smile, her eyes burning, she demands that Jack not be allowed to see their daughter, though she had previously granted him visiting rights. The negotiations in ruins, she storms from the room. Another cut takes us back to the nightclub, where Robert has taken up a position near the bar. Susan is still performing, and we assume that the scene is picking up from before. But the dialogue tells us that four months have passed: Robert has become a regular at the club, and Susan is his new obsession—the latest in a line of women he has looked to for salvation.

These opening scenes, apparently so arbitrary and disconnected, establish Cassavetes's rhythm and method. Much of *Love Streams* is constructed around the ambiguity of the editing. Because Cassavetes refuses to mark his transitions, we have no way of knowing that what seems to be a simple case of parallel montage (the return to the transvestite bar) is actually a radical flash-forward: the unmarked edit covers a huge elision of narrative time. In a similar way, Cassavetes later takes Sarah to Europe with a single cut—suddenly, she's in a train station in Paris, struggling with a mountain of luggage, without the slightest allusion to how she got there. Space, as well as time, disappears in the black hole between two shots. And the editing even devours different levels of reality: Sarah's hallucinations are also introduced with a simple cut; there are none of the traditional codings of subjectivity—no dissolves or camera movements in to the subject's face—that allow us to sort things out. When Sarah imagines her husband and daughter killed in a car wreck, the sequence is "real" for all the time it's on the screen. It's only with the cut back to Sarah's face that we find it has all been a fantasy.

The unmarked editing creates a profound instability in the film. Time, space, and reality are no longer constants; they don't exist independently, but are instead subsumed by character—by the perceptions of Robert and Sarah. But if the editing is subjective—tied to the specific experiences of the two leads—Cassavetes's visual presentation is studiously objective. Though he keeps his camera close to Robert and Sarah, he doesn't privilege their point of view over that of any of the other characters in the scene; in fact, he often introduces moderating figures—minor characters who react more or less normally to the goings-on—who function as bridges between the audience and the eccentric behavior of Sarah and Robert. What Cassavetes creates with this objective/subjective friction is the sense of a terrible disparity between the world of emotions and a world of facts. Both worlds are equally real: the tragedy of Robert and Sarah, and also their glory, lies in their inability to reconcile the two realms. Their feelings—their love and their pain—are too large to be contained by the literal world, and yet they are not large enough to break it.

One hour of *Love Streams* passes before Sarah and Robert meet; another 45 minutes go by before we learn that they are brother and sister. Movies haven't often treated sibling relationships, perhaps because—short of taking them into incest—there's something fundamentally antidramatic about them: there's no real possibility for a strong resolution. But Cassavetes's indirect treatment of the subject lifts it above a literal level. The cross-cutting of the film's first section (between Sarah's failed attempts to escape her pain on a trip to Europe and Robert's boozily incompetent seduction of the wary Susan) build a mysterious bond between the two characters; we feel that they are strongly linked—through a shared temperament, sensitivity, desperation—even though the script refuses to specify their relationship (Sarah even denies, in one of the early scenes, that she has any family). We are invited to believe that they are lovers who are fated to meet (the high romantic option) or former lovers who have separated (the grimly naturalistic solution); the revelation that they are brother and sister is at once a shock (though Cassavetes characteristically underplays its climactic value) and a deep disappointment—we have begun to feel that their only real hope lies in each other, yet this is the one relationship that can never be consummated. But disappointment soon gives way to a strange sense of awe. There is an almost mythological dimension to the relationship, as if Robert and Sarah were the last survivors of an ancient race: they must be related; the world could not have produced two people of such unworldly intensity otherwise. There is no one else in the world who could understand them, love them, or even put up with them for long. Robert and Sarah do attract other people to them (one of the film's motifs, a witty one, involves the number of service personnel—taxi drivers, porters, doctors—they seem to require, and the good grace with which these people respond to Sarah's and Robert's excessive demands), but they are ultimately alone. During the brief time Sarah spends as a guest in Robert's home, he learns to focus his free-floating, always hopeful affection on her; only she, it seems, is sufficiently constant and uncompromising in her affection to genuinely forgive him. But she, divorced from her family, rejected by her husband and daughter, is beginning to learn an opposite truth: that a too-exclusive focus of affection is a terrible risk. At the end of the film, after a long, stormy night during which Sarah collapses from nervous exhaustion and Robert cares for her as if she were a child, they seem to have traded roles. Sarah packs her bags and goes off with a man she barely knows, leaving Robert alone in the house to face its sudden, and apparently permanent, emptiness.

Cassavetes's direction of dialogue is so fresh and sensitive that it's a shock to discover that *Love Streams* was fully scripted (it was cowritten by Cassavetes and Ted Allan, and actually began as a play). The dialogue throughout has the authenticity and slightly loopy spontaneity of inspired improvisation, though in fact only one scene—Sarah's fantasy of winning back her family by making them laugh—was improvised. It's only in retrospect that the superb literary qualities of the piece begin to emerge. Robert has a line—"Whenever I meet a beautiful woman, I ask her to give me her secret"—which he repeats several times in the film; it begins as the show-offy pronouncement of a professional writer trying to impress with his poetic nature (it could be the opening line of the novel Robert is planning to write), becomes a clumsy pickup line when he tries it out on Susan, and ends up as a cry for help addressed to the unconscious Sarah—the variation is elegant, accomplished, and deeply moving. And Cassavetes is just as attentive to his use of objects. The house in which much of the action takes place is Rowlands and Cassavetes's own home in Los Angeles; it seems alive in a way movie settings almost never do: everything in the house, from the pictures on the wall to the jukebox in the den to the box of kitchen matches on the stove seems to have been chosen and set out by the characters. Cassavetes gets more expressive mileage out of cigarettes than any director since Howard Hawks in *To Have and Have Not*: the inch-long ash that hangs precariously from Robert's perpetual smoke is the perfect index of his manic recklessness; when he hugs Sarah to him at the end, his cigarette still in his mouth, its smoldering tip comes close to brushing her cheek, and the image is a sublime embodiment of both Robert's needfulness and his obliviousness, his need for constant succor and his inability to see very far beyond himself. In the fury of his tenderness, he threatens pain.

But the actors, of course, are Cassavetes's primary medium. In Rowlands's work and his own, you can see Method acting brought to a new level, extended to the point where it becomes something else: it's no longer the externalization of interior feelings, but the complete possession of the body by those feelings; the actor is almost inseparable from his expression. Which isn't to say that the performances are consistently tense and emphatic: one of the richest moments in the film—Robert's reaction to Sarah, when he finds that she's brought home a whole menagerie of pets (birds, a dog, a pair of miniature horses)—is played entirely in Cassavetes's gaze, which shifts from comic double take to a serious concern for his sister's sanity and finally (as he too slips into her madness) to an ecstatic acceptance. It should be pointed out, though, that the scene—or any other scene in the film—would not be nearly as effective if Cassavetes were not also an accomplished visual stylist. The framing he gives to the reaction—a slightly distanced, full-figure shot, rather than the expected close-up—transforms it from an isolated show of technique into an expressive stroke fully integrated with the dramatic context.

Late in the film, Robert is sitting alone in a darkened room when he hears a noise. He looks over and sees a heavyset, bearded man—a total stranger—sitting in one of the armchairs. There is a cut back to Robert, and a cut back to the chair, which we now see to be occupied by the dog Sarah brought home. It's an astounding sequence (the more so because it's executed so simply, as a standard shot/countershot cut), not so much for its narrative purpose (to show that Robert is now sharing Sarah's hallucinations) or for its thematic suggestion (that Robert's womanizing might have something to do with a repressed homosexuality) as its sheer, startling originality. Is there another filmmaker in the world who would even think, in the context of a straight dramatic narrative, of turning a dog into its human personification? As Cassavetes's work progresses, it becomes more and more unaccountable. He no longer seems to be working in any identifiable tradition, and his films share no concerns—either thematic or stylistic—with those of any other filmmaker I know of. He is genuinely out there on his own, making his own way in uncharted territory. At a time when American films have become almost obsessively standardized, Cassavetes is an invaluable resource—the last American individualist.

Trouble in Mind

Directed by ALAN RUDOLPH {March 21, 1986}

It seems impossible to dream an old dream again, but that's what Alan Rudolph does, and brilliantly well, in *Trouble in Mind*. It's a late 40s dream, from the high romantic period of *film noir* most memorably embodied by Charles Vidor's *Gilda*. Its world is one of late nights and early mornings, of cafes, hotel rooms, and smoky clubs; its drama, of innocence threatened by evil and redemption through love, seems less a story line than a ritual, a pattern of action that satisfies precisely because it is so familiar. Yet Rudolph hasn't tried to imitate an old style—films from Dick Richards's *Farewell, My Lovely* to Lawrence Kasdan's *Body Heat* have made it more than clear that direct imitation of another era's forms leads only to a lifeless academicism. Instead, Rudolph has extracted the essence of the genre and applied it to a contemporary structure; the film feels very modern and spontaneous, with its rhythms that veer from extravagant absurdist farce to moments of a discreetly observed, deftly underplayed psychological realism. Rudolph doesn't pretend that film history stopped with the era he wants to invoke. He makes full use of the discoveries of the last 40 years—tonal mixes, narrative discontinuities, stylized colors, Dolby stereo—to create a film that belongs equally to now and then. In *Trouble in Mind*, he doesn't revive a dead genre as much as he establishes an illusion of continuity. Watching it, you feel sure that this is the point where the *film noir* would be today had it survived in the 60s.

Just about everyone in the film has a nickname (even Seattle, where the movie was shot, appears as "Rain City"). Hawk (Kris Kristofferson) is an ex-cop just emerging from a long prison term (he was convicted for the killing of a sadistic gangland chief); his first stop when he returns to the city is Wanda's Café, a clean, well-lighted place poised on the edge of a desolate industrial neighborhood, where the proprietor (Geneviève Bujold) is an old flame. The same morning brings two other new arrivals: Coop (Keith Carradine), a drifter driven back to the city by his failure to find work in the countryside, and Georgia (Lori Singer), a beautiful, child-like teenager who is the mother of his baby son. Wanda takes Georgia under her wing, while Coop falls under the influence of Solo (Joe Morton), a black Vietnam veteran who composes poetry and plots stickups. Hawk watches, falling more in love with Georgia as Coop becomes more dangerous and debauched (his transformation is physical—he trades his blue jeans for an iridescent new wave suit and mousses his hair into diabolical waves). When Coop's activities bring him into conflict with the local mob boss, Hilly Blue (Divine, in his first male role, reinventing the creepy softness of *Gilda*'s George Macready), Hawk hesitates—should he let Coop be killed, which would allow him to claim the woman he loves, or should he save him and let him go back to Georgia and the baby?

Many of these themes are familiar from other Rudolph movies: imprisonment as a metaphor for a deep and aching loneliness (*Remember My Name*); the restaurant or bar, presided over by a single woman, as a warm, safe refuge from a hostile world (*Choose Me*); and above all, the sense of the city as a gridwork of potential relationships, where people come to seduce or be seduced and hope is inseparable from distrust and fear (*Welcome to L.A.*). But the stylistic assurance of *Trouble in Mind* is new. Rudolph has always been a formally ambitious filmmaker, but his innovations have been largely confined to the level of narration—the odd, ingenious plotting that informs *Welcome to L.A.*, *Remember My Name*, and *Choose Me* hasn't always found its equivalent on the visual level. But in *Choose Me*, most memorably in the opening sequence, Rudolph began to flirt with a choreographic sense of movement. The scene, which showed a number of patrons leaving a bar, some of them lingering a moment in the street before moving on, matched the movement of the actors in a way that seemed to suggest that an actual dance number was coming on; that the pattern of movement never coalesced into anything as definite as a dance, but remained suspended in isolated gestures, suggested a great deal about Rudolph's world. The dance that never quite materializes becomes the perfect correlative to the relationships that never quite settle down as Rudolph's characters drift through his crisscross cutting.

As much as I like *Choose Me*, I was disappointed that the film didn't manage to sustain the grace of its opening all the way through (though a bit of it does come back at the end). *Trouble in Mind*, though, disappoints not at all: Rudolph has not only extended the effect of *Choose Me*'s opening, but refined and improved it; the whole film seems to exist as a potential musical, posed on some microscopically thin line between realism and fantasy, between the world as it is and the world as it might be. Hawk's hobby in prison was the construction of detailed scale models of his old stomping grounds. He's brought one of them—a perfect reproduction of the building that houses Wanda's Café—back with him to the room he rents above Wanda's Café. Periodically, Rudolph drops shots of the model into the story line, and because they're so realistically lit (and placed at the points where we'd expect a conventional establishing shot), for a fraction of a second we take them for the genuine article. And if Rudolph often treats the models as if they were real, he also treats the real as if it were a model—all of Seattle becomes a vast studio set, and its landmarks—the monorails, the Space Needle, even the local art museum (which becomes Hilly Blue's mansion)—are absorbed into the narration as if they were pure products of Rudolph's imagination, built expressly for the film. There's a constant exchange in *Trouble in Mind* (suggested by the title) between interior and exterior realities. The world exists both as a projection of the characters' desires (Georgia arrives just when Hank needs her, as if he'd willed her into being) and as the material block of those desires (Georgia arrives with a lover in tow). Hawk's crisis at the end of the film—should he save Coop or allow him to be killed?—stems from exactly this conflict: are we allowed to remake the world to give us what we want, or should we leave the world as we found it? As he films Seattle, transforming it into "Rain City," Rudolph is faced with the same decision: is he a realist or an expressionist, inventing the world or recording it? The moral and the aesthetic questions merge, as they must on the higher levels of art.

For the most part, Rudolph doesn't interfere physically with the world before his camera (though he has added a few touches, such as the subtle profusion of nagging signs—those red circles with a line through them, banning a mad range of objects and activities). Instead, the transformation takes place in the filming, through the eccentric camera angles he chooses or, more imaginatively, through the patterns of movement he sets up from shot to shot. A strong horizontal movement to the left—by camera or actors—will be answered in the next shot by a perfectly matched strong movement to the right; a movement will be continued through a cut into a closer perspective; or a movement within the frame (by an actor) will be answered by a movement of the frame (by panning the camera). These patterns represent some very close, meticulous work by Rudolph and his editor, Sally Coryn Allen, and they do so much to establish the film's atmosphere of dreaminess: we sense a dancelike coherence of movement where there is no dance to be seen, and there is something mesmerizing in the continual to-and-fro, a bit like keeping your eyes on the hypnotist's watch.

The term "postmodernism" gets thrown around a lot these days; it seems to be popular mainly because it can mean whatever you want it to mean. But if we take postmodernism to be an aesthetic built on an understanding and acceptance of the basic principle of modernism—that is, a consciousness of the artwork as an artwork, rather than as a slice of reality—coupled with a willingness to go beyond the principle, then *Trouble in Mind* is one of the few films that genuinely merits the label. Rudolph has created an elaborate, self-conscious formal structure that nevertheless serves to tell a story and through that story produce a strong emotion. *Trouble in Mind* is story telling taken to the second degree. It acknowledges the fact that we have heard the story before (and even suggests that the characters have heard it, too—"I never met him," says Coop when he first sees Solo, his tempter, sitting in Wanda's Café, "but I know him"); it omits the naturalistic details and narrative connections that pre-modernist art used to make the story seem "realistic," "plausible"; and yet, through this collection of fragments, recycled bits, and deliberate absurdities, it discovers all the pleasures of story telling. *Trouble in Mind* is the newest film in town.

[PART 3]

Other Visions

Outside the United States, a wondrous group of new talents emerged, while venerated figures from the 40s, 50s, and 60s continued to produce important works. Like many observers I was particularly interested during this transitional period in the work of Jean-Luc Godard, a critically minded filmmaker who continued to explore fundamental problems of cinematic form and meaning in movies (four of which are considered here) that eluded traditional classifications.

OLD MASTERS >>

Blaise Pascal

Directed by ROBERTO ROSSELLINI {January 30, 1976}

Roberto Rossellini made his last fiction film in 1962, a short satirical sketch ("Chastity") for the compilation film *Rogopag*. The director of *Open City*, *Paisan*, and *Voyage to Italy* then announced that, after twenty-five years as a director, he was giving up the cinema.

Rossellini, of course, has continued to make films, but films so radically different from what we know as "cinema" that his promise has been more than fulfilled. With *The Iron Age*, a series of five films made for Italian television in 1964, Rossellini took his first step toward a complete redefinition of the form of narrative film. He has rejected plot, dramatic structure, psychological characterization, point of view, and even the traditional cinematic language of cutting and framing. And in doing this, he has undertaken what now appears to be by far the most ambitious artistic effort in the history of film, if not of the twentieth-century art entire—a complete documentation of the history of man.

Blaise Pascal (1972), which is to be shown tonight (Friday, January 30) at the Art Institute, can't be reviewed, or understood, as a single, self-sufficient feature. It's only one part, a chapter, of the one unified work that began with *The Iron Age* in 1964, and continues through *The Rise of Louis XIV* (1966), *La lotta del l'uomo per la sua sopravvivenza* ("Man's Struggle for Survival," twelve 60-minute episodes, 1967), *La rivoluzione industrial* (unfinished series, begun in 1967), *The Acts of the Apostles* (five episodes, 1968), *Socrates* (1970), *Augustine of Hippo* (1972), *The Age of the Medici* (three episodes, 1973), and *The Messiah* (American release scheduled for Easter, 1976). This master work has no formal beginning apart from its chronology, and at this point there is no conclusion in sight. The scope of Rossellini's undertaking is astounding. The fact that it has also been successful, brilliantly so, seems almost unbelievable.

The technique of this work is not one of narration, but of reportage. For each episode, the selection of a representative individual or group of individuals (Pascal, Augustine, Cosimo de Medici, Leon Battista Alberti) becomes a way of getting at, in Rossellini's words, "the customs, fears, aspirations, ideas, and agonies of an epoch and a place." Even though the films make use of these "key" figures, the history is not an idealistic one of great men, great events, and great ideas. For Rossellini, history lies in the observation of people and their surroundings, in how the individual confronts, modifies, or advances the forces of society and culture. Rossellini's Pascal is not an overbearing genius, making Great Discovery after Great Discovery in the manner of traditional film biographies, but a confused, vulnerable man, trying to reconcile, in his own mind, the two contrary forces of reason and religion that ruled the seventeenth century. Some people have complained that nothing "happens" in the films, and in one sense this is perfectly true. Rossellini's films do not build to great climaxes, but move along, from episode to episode, in the even, quiet rhythm of everyday life. The director weights no one thing more than another—Pascal's discovery of the vacuum is just as significant as his invention of public transportation. The idea of *duration* is more important than the idea of *event*.

Duration is also the key to Rossellini's mise-en-scène. The primary unit of expression in his historical films is the long take, the scenes developing without the use of conventional analytic montage. Tracks and zooms take the place of cross-cutting within the scene, giving a unique sense of total spatial and temporal integrity. This, of course, is the ultimate extension of the Neo-Realist style that Rossellini helped to introduce in the forties. The director never uses the camera to make editorial judgments—the emphasis is on the accurate portrayal of real events. The films strive to observe rather than create, presenting people and things in their own immediate beauty and truth. Rossellini gives us the freedom to see for ourselves.

Rossellini's realism is not the banal sort of a Bergman (*Scenes from a Marriage*), a Coppola (*The Rain People*), or an Altman (*Nashville*)—directors who use the realist mode to cloak their personal ideas and feelings in a false and inappropriate sense of legitimacy. Rossellini puts himself at the service of facts. He is a synthesizer, an artist who tries to give us facts in all their proper complexity and precision, but in such a way that we may understand them better, respect them, and most importantly, *use* them. Jean-Luc Godard said of one of Rossellini's early documentaries, "*India* is the creation of the world." And so, no less, is the historical re-creation *Blaise Pascal*.

A Piece of Pleasure

Directed by CLAUDE CHABROL {April 8, 1977}

Claude Chabrol's *A Piece of Pleasure* covers much the same ground as Ingmar Bergman's *Scenes from a Marriage*: the decline and fall of a relationship. The difference between Chabrol's film and Bergman's is the difference between life portrayed and life photographed. Where Bergman is obsessed with a superficial realism, Chabrol takes advantage of film's capacity to remake reality. Stylized, illogical, and almost absurd, *A Piece of Pleasure* is a more complex, more disturbing, and finally more satisfying film than Bergman's psychologically impeccable study.

By rights, *A Piece of Pleasure* should be even more "realistic" than *Scenes from a Marriage*. Bergman was dealing with a fiction, but Chabrol, in one of the most baroque epistemological maneuvers in memory, has cast Paul Gegauff and his wife Danielle in a rerun of their own marital breakdown, with a script by Gegauff himself (a longtime Chabrol collaborator). Watching the Gegauffs re-enact their personal crises is a discomfiting experience: it's impossible to tell how much of the tension between the two is genuine, how much is performance. Are the arguments real because they happened once, or are they real because we're seeing them now, on the screen? Or is it all exaggeration, memory's rewrite? As a critic, Chabrol was one of the first writers to discover the depth of Alfred Hitchcock's art, and Hichcock's concern with the voyeuristic overtones of filmgoing is, no doubt, the inspiration for the similar moral problems that *A Piece of Pleasure* presents to the viewer: are we all Peeping Toms for taking such an unhealthy interest in the private problems of these two evidently quite real people, or does the distance of art take us off the hook?

Gegauff's self-portrait is hardly a flattering one. He presents himself as an icy intellectual, self-possessed and self-sufficient, blissfully isolated from the common run of humanity in the country house where he lives with his common-law wife and small daughter. Paul and Danielle (or Philippe and Esther, as they've been renamed for the film) enjoy a completely dependent relationship. As he never tires of telling her, Philippe "made" Esther, taking her out of her lower-class background and giving her the full advantage of his taste and discretion in intellectual and material matters. She's not much more than a reflection of Philippe, a point Chabrol makes (with, admittedly, something less than breathtaking originality) by occasionally catching her image in a mirror. With no real spirit of her own, Esther has dedicated herself to the care and feeding of her husband (although he persists in giving her cooking lessons), while Philippe would clearly prefer that she blend with the wallpaper when she's not needed for his immediate gratification.

But Philippe's carefully constructed narcissistic marriage carries the germ of its own destruction: boredom. Esther fulfills his romantic fantasies (satirized by a shot that captures a love scene through a sickeningly pink haze of out-of-focus cherry blossoms), but his sexual ambitions are uncheckable. Esther has been conquered; Philippe is looking for new frontiers. He makes a very convincing argument, drawn from the New Morality, that a little mutual infidelity might be a way of strengthening their marriage. Esther, at first apprehensive, later takes him at his word, spending the night with one of their weekend guests, Habib—a man who works for a music company and plays the guitar, embodying everything that the rationalist Philippe despises.

When Philippe confronts Esther the next day, he begins by feigning nonchalance, asking her, as coolly and academically as he can, about Habib's technical proficiency. But soon the shell starts to crack: Philippe deplores Esther's bad taste in lovers, just as he'd criticize her for selecting the wrong wine. He makes a stab at revenge, taking to bed another one of the omnipresent weekend guests, a studiously liberated redhead, but he discovers, to his infinite horror, that he's impotent with her.

Once Esther has broken the bond, there's no turning back. She begins to form a personality of her own, as if for the first time in her life; she insists that they leave the country house for Paris, where she will get a job in Habib's office. As Esther's independence grows, so does Philippe's obsession with his power over her. Their life turns into a ritual of dominance, culminating in a horrible moment when Philippe forces his wife to lick his foot. If he can't control her intellectually, he'll dominate her physically. She leaves him.

The central paradox of *A Piece of Pleasure* lies in Philippe's discovery that the alternative to ennui is madness. But even in his growing insanity, as masochistically satisfying as it may be, Philippe is doomed to play the same scenes again and again. Repetition becomes a motif: Philippe's daughter practices her counting as a way of marking time; a metronome ticks away on a piano; a party guest plays the same section of a record over and over again. Philippe moves in with another woman, finding that she's Habib's ex-wife.

By choosing melodrama over realism, Chabrol is able to make use of the genre's outrageous coincidences, extreme emotions, and sudden psychological reversals, giving his film the texture of a distorted, subjective experience—the only kind of experience that a megalomaniac like Philippe could know. Events take on far more (or far less) importance than they would in a normal order of things: it's less disturbing to Philippe, for example, that he has to put his daughter in a home after Esther leaves him, than it is that his new wife isn't afraid to bait her own hook, as Esther was, when he takes her fishing.

In a naturalistic film, the ending would seem hopelessly excessive (you'd better skip this if you like surprises): Esther, after a long silence, calls Philippe to ask him to go with her when she visits her aunt's grave. Philippe takes the opportunity to beg her, once more, to return to him, but she won't. Suddenly, he beats her to the ground, crushing her head with the heel of his shoe against the dirt of the freshly covered grave, while members of a passing funeral party try to pull him away. Chabrol shoots the scene as a series of detailed close-ups, much like the shower murder in *Psycho*, but the strangely slow rhythm of the cutting anesthetizes the shock of the violence: shots go on too long, the compositions seem too formal. Giving in to his madness, Philippe seems to have found something like tranquility. The impact of the action is balanced by the alienating artifice of the style; and the brutality of the attack (or murder; Chabrol is deliberately unclear on this point) is seen both as pure horror and as the logical, almost therapeutic, outcome of Philippe's obsession.

Asked why his films weren't generally understood in the United States, Douglas Sirk once blamed the American audience's underdeveloped sense of irony. That's likely to be a problem with *A Piece of Pleasure*, too: most of the reviews I've read equate Philippe's point of view with Chabrol's, and nothing could be further from the truth. Philippe may be the protagonist, but the moral center of the film is Esther, whose slow blossoming into selfhood seems almost heroic. Chabrol takes a chance with his audience when he manipulates our natural tendency to identify with the people we see on the screen; like Hitchcock, he wants us to share some of the guilt. If we sometimes sympathize with Philippe over Esther, we learn something about ourselves, something, perhaps, that we'd rather not know.

That Obscure Object of Desire

Directed by LUIS BUÑUEL {March 31, 1978}

Luis Buñuel, the young Turk of the Surrealist cinema, will be 78 this year. It's been half a century since he slit a woman's eyeball in *Un chien andalou*, the film he codirected with Salvador Dali, and sent fashionable Paris into paroxysms. We may be harder to shock now—and Buñuel seems less interested in direct assaults on his audience—but he's still on the attack, making films that eat away at the small complacencies, the convenient assumptions, the thin illusions that we adopt to make our lives seem more orderly, more rational, more simply livable.

With 50 years of filmmaking behind him, Buñuel no longer needs the flashy effects of his early films. There are no dead donkeys, no priests in bondage in *That Obscure Object of Desire*—but there is death, there is religion, and there is bondage, of a less literal sort. The themes have outgrown their symbols now, and Buñuel's imagery has become simpler, less shocking and more insidious. Throughout *Obscure Object*, Buñuel cuts repeatedly to a shot of a train rushing through the countryside, an image that seems, at first, perfectly explainable in terms of the story. Mathieu, a rich old gentleman (Fernando Rey), is regaling his traveling companions in the first-class coach of the Seville-to-Madrid express with the story of his strange love affair with Conchita, his maid—what could be more natural, more conventional, than punctuating the flashbacks with a shot of the moving train? But we know, as Mathieu does not, that Conchita is on the train, too—the woman he's running away from in a desperate fury remains a few fixed yards behind him. The train is moving, but it's not taking Mathieu anywhere. The image takes on other associations—with the endless walk through the countryside of the dinner party guests in *The Discreet Charm of the Bourgeoisie* (1972); with the constantly interrupted journey of *La Fantôme de la liberté* (1974); with the pilgrimage of *The Milky Way* (1968); and even further back, in time and evolution, with the incessantly buzzing insects of Buñuel's 1952 *Robinson Crusoe*. Notice how the image—of meaningless movement, misplaced energy—is constantly refined, simplified from the obtrusive "symbol" of the insects to the elegant understatement of the train. That's one of the marks of a great film artist, I think—the ability to compress, condense, to find resonance in the simplest of images, and to never waste an image, making it work on a number of levels.

The train, with its raging phallic overtones, also belongs to the stable of

Freudian clichés. *That Obscure Object of Desire* is a film about an unconsummated affair—Conchita continually puts Mathieu off, with excuses that range from the vaguely reasonable to the thoroughly perverse. So the train evokes Mathieu's frustrated lust, too—it never does go into a tunnel. But at the same time he's using a cliché, Buñuel makes a joke of it, installing a professor of psychology (who gives, he says ominously, "private lessons") among Mathieu's companions. Played by a four-foot dwarf sporting a beard in impeccable imitation of Herr Doktor, the professor supplies stunningly banal "insights" at appropriate moments in Mathieu's narrative—a less than subtle warning against facile psychological interpretations of the film.

Buñuel is the poet of paradox. An anti-Freudian, he uses Freudian images—but that's only the surface. Buñuel's basic narrative strategy is the contradiction: a character displays one attitude in one scene, its complete opposite in the next. Where most films are devoted to creating consistent, convincing characters, Buñuel delights in abrupt changes and unaccountable shifts. In *Obscure Object*, he goes so far as to have the central character of Conchita played by two different actresses and dubbed by a third. Conchita, the guardian of the obscure object of Mathieu's desire, is both more and less than a conventional film character. With her dual nature—the cold, slightly calculating schoolgirl played by French actress Carole Bouquet and the warm, ripe woman played by the Spanish Angela Molina—Conchita has a more complex reality than we're used to seeing in filmed fiction. In the movies, we tend to read character mainly from faces. It's Eisenstein's concept of *typage*: people behave as they look. But Buñuel frustrates that convenient lie by granting Conchita two faces, two characters, and then shuffling them up as the film continues, so that Conchita I is capable of behaving like Conchita II, and vice versa. There is no simple virgin/whore dichotomy: Conchita is never laid out, never "explained," and to that extent we perceive her more as an authentic human being than as a shadow on a screen—she's an enigma, retaining something unknowable, unreachable.

But still, since Conchita is denied the flesh and blood reality of an actress of her own, she drifts into a generalization: more than a woman, she is a sort of eternal erotic principle. She is the love object, the perpetually sought-after but never attained prize of mad, romantic passion. At first, when Conchita denies Mathieu's advances, he's angry, frustrated. But as he keeps coming back, continues his supplications, it gradually becomes clear (to us, if not to him) that the frustration is the consummation, that desire is more satisfying than satisfaction. Rejected, rebuffed, humiliated, he constantly returns. Consummation would be an anti-climax—in the midst of his rage and agony, Mathieu is sublimely, supremely happy. He and Conchita are the perfect couple.

The name Conchita, as we learn in the film, is the Spanish diminutive of "Concepción"—and this Conchita is immaculate with a vengeance. That's about as close as Buñuel comes here to overtly stating the religious theme that always hovers behind his work. Mathieu is a kind of priest, worshipping at the shrine of his virgin, praying for the reward that never comes. For Buñuel, the great lie of the Catholic Church is hope, a lie he has answered by turning hope into a reward in itself. If our actions are always frustrated, if our desires are never fulfilled, what is left to get through the world but hope, in and of itself? Mathieu, as Buñuel draws him, is an immensely wealthy man—everything is within his grasp. But the one thing he wants, as Conchita tells him, is the one thing he can't have. And that's what keeps him going, makes him happy, at last.

Obscure Object, like many of Buñuel's films, is built on a rhythm of repetitions and interruptions, the predictable and the unpredictable. The story, as Buñuel develops it, seems perfectly rational: Mathieu always has good reasons for leaving Conchita, as he always has good reasons for coming back to her. The madness emerges later, as the action is repeated, again and again, with infinitely subtle sadomasochistic variations. For Mathieu, this predictability is a kind of freedom, a freedom from the chaos and irrationality of the world that lies beyond his control. No Buñuel film is complete without a band of revolutionaries; Mathieu has to cope with a terrorist gang (named, with irony as magnificent as Buñuel has ever conceived, "The Revolutionary Army of the Infant Jesus") that assassinates one of his fellow fat cats at the beginning of the film, and returns to dispatch him at the end. Buñuel, back to his roots in Spain, is a genuine anarchist, and he never questions the need to destroy the old order of politics, religion, and culture. But at the same time—a paradoxist to the end—he finds a certain grace and beauty in Mathieu's artificially ordered existence: as a member of the bourgeoisie, Mathieu has his discreet charm as well.

That Obscure Object of Desire is the work of a man in complete control of his medium. After 50 years in the cinema, Buñuel has achieved a level of formal virtuosity that he shares, perhaps, with only two other directors working today—Alfred Hitchcock and Robert Bresson. From the subtle stylization of his settings—too evenly lit and too bright for "real life"—to the balletic sensibility he displays in choreographing his actors and his camera, Buñuel seems genuinely incapable of taking a false or inessential step. With his camera usually placed at a discreet distance from the action, Buñuel creates images that seem perfectly open and accessible, and yet they remain fraught with hidden dangers and uncertainties—a bed that cuts too closely through the angle of a room, a table that sits too stolidly between the characters.

That Obscure Object of Desire is a great film, the first we've seen in Chicago for longer than I'd care to think about. If it doesn't have quite the edge of Buñuel's two masterpieces, *Tristana* and *Discreet Charm*, it's nonetheless a brilliant achievement, a film that will be discussed and debated for years after the momentary sensations of 1978—*Close Encounters, An Unmarried Woman*—are gone and forgotten.

Perceval

Directed by ERIC ROHMER {June 15, 1979}

Eric Rohmer's *Perceval* is a musical comedy costume epic full of swordplay, romance, and Christian allegory, which draws equally on the work of Buster Keaton, Bertolt Brecht, and the anonymous icon painters of the Middle Ages. The film eludes any simple classifications of genre or style, yet it is based, virtually word for word, on a 12th-century Arthurian romance by the French poet Chrétien de Troyes. In his almost complete fidelity to his source (the director has provided his own contemporary translation from the middle French), Rohmer has created a completely personal film—personal to the point of eccentricity. It doesn't look or play like any other movie in recent memory, nor does it resemble Rohmer's own past work: where his "Six Moral Tales" are models of modern naturalism, *Perceval* runs off into the most remote regions of stylization. There isn't a single blade of real grass nor a patch of genuine sky to be glimpsed in the entire project. *Perceval* is a self-contained, hermetic film, but within its tiny, determinedly abstract world, Rohmer discovers a fable of universal significance—the same fable of personal growth, acceptance, and actualization that courses through the Moral Tales. *Perceval* is unique, but nothing in it is original.

Visually, *Perceval* resembles a television production of limited resources. Most of the action is contained within a single, cramped sound stage, where a forest of half a dozen stainless steel trees grows from a lawn of Astroturf. In the background, a wooden castle towers to a height of perhaps eight or nine feet against a sky-blue backdrop. The same props—a table, a bed—turn up in every interior scene, repainted to match the color codes that are Rohmer's only differentiation among the various settings. The supporting characters are all drawn from a pool of 11 actors, who also provide the choral and orchestral accompaniment to the action. The TV effect is further compounded by the flat, even lighting that Rohmer applies to almost every sequence, as well as the impossibly bright, vibrant hues that Nestor Almendros's exquisite cinematography draws from stenciled backgrounds. All in all, the mise-en-scène might seem more hospitable to the Muppets than King Arthur.

But somehow Rohmer brings it off. The combined effect of his visual strategies is to drain the images of all perspective: everything is impacted on the surface of the screen. As the film progresses, with its largely static compositions and formal camera movements (across the scene, and seldom into it), the flatness acquires its own expressiveness. We are seeing the characters as they might see themselves, according to the rules of visual perception expressed in medieval painting. Without the fatal distractions of depth, the seductive byways and blind alleys of deep focus photography and chiaroscuro lighting, the images attain a remarkable harmony, an unnatural wholeness and ease. They are images of sureness and profound complacency, of a world that doesn't doubt its perception of itself. The style is the exact opposite of the epistemological confusions propounded by Expressionism—the style, not only of medieval painting, but of the first master of the cinema, D. W. Griffith.

That it is also the style that technological limitations impose on television is a point *Perceval* doesn't lose. In fact, much of the film seems dedicated to the proposition that the most modern of techniques—visual and narrative—can be found in the oldest of sources; that the antiquarian is the true avant-gardist. In transcribing de Troyes' text, Rohmer has preserved its quirks and digressions—the narrative convolutions that might seem anomalous to the modern eye, accustomed to "well-made" fictions, but which were the stock-in-trade of the earliest storytellers. The plot lurches from episode to episode, and there is no guarantee that the narrative threads left dangling in any given segment will ever be tied up. (Interestingly, time, no less than space, is flattened in Rohmer's presentation—the action could comprise several days or several years; there's nothing in the text to cue us.) *Perceval*'s most radical departure takes place when the film suddenly abandons its hero entirely and launches into a lengthy account of the adventures of a rival knight, Sir Gawain. But just as the digression is building to a climax, Rohmer cuts away, doubling the narrative interruption. All of that, it seems, is contained in de Troyes' poem, but when Rohmer re-creates the naive maneuver of the 12th-century text in the structurally self-conscious 70s, he reinvents it. No longer is it simply a matter of wandering off the narrative track, but of placing story elements in formal opposition. The Gawain episode illuminates Perceval's story through thematic contrast (setting Gawain's graciousness and humility up against Perceval's general bumptiousness) and through a variation in the narrative rhythm (Gawain's segment is more leisurely and psychologically nuanced). Its abrupt termination foreshadows the spectacular anticlimax of Perceval's tale, which gives way, without warning, to a full-scale Passion Play. None of these techniques would seem out of place in the most passionately modernist of experimental films (or, for that matter, in contemporary best sellers, as witness *The World According to Garp*). Yet Rohmer has discovered them, whole and pristine, in one of the oldest texts in his language.

The most significant variation that Rohmer has worked on the original text lies in his decision to do away with its narrator. Some of the exposition is given to the chorus, but for the most part, the characters themselves speak the descriptive passages, commenting on their actions as they perform them, or introducing their dialogue with a "he said" or "she said." With this decision, Rohmer propels his research project into the forefront of Brechtian epic theater. The text is not so much acted as read, generally in a firm, even tone, and only occasionally inflected by facial expression. But for all of the irony and distance built into the conception, the characters retain their emotional expressiveness. Even as their speeches fluctuate between first person and third—sometimes in the same breath—the actors never seem to step away from their roles, perhaps because they never fully inhabited them. As in Brecht, the effect of the acting style is to lend a life and legitimacy to flatly archetypal characters—it's a style that denies psychology on its way to discovering a different kind of emotional truth.

Still, there's a sense in which Rohmer's characters have always stood independent of their speech. His screenplays, even as rendered in subtitles, are among the most literate and happily wordy in modern cinema, yet the characters' lengthy discourses on fine moral and intellectual points are validated only to the degree that they reveal what remains unspoken—the intimate, circuitous, and highly instinctual process of reaching a decision to act. All of the words in the universe will not cure Jean-Claude Brialy of his obsession with Claire's knee, nor will Pascal prevent Jean-Louis Trintignant from spending his night at Maud's. Everyone in Rohmer's world ultimately acts from impulse, but they act (or choose not to) only after a painstaking examination of all the possible consequences. That is the use of words and reason: to act with responsibility. (The most profoundly passive of Rohmer's characters, the Marquise of O, eerily keeps her peace.) To learn to accept responsibility is the moral of the Moral Tales; it is also the moral—and it is foregrounded as such—of *Perceval.*

Rohmer has cited Buster Keaton as the primary inspiration for his hero. As played by Fabrice Luchini, Rohmer's country-bred knight certainly has Keaton's impassivity of expression, but, more importantly, he has Keaton's implacability—his sublime straight-line energy. Just as Keaton propels himself forward through every conceivable disaster, drawing his determination from some unspeakable center of will, so does Perceval push his way through his endless encounters with damsels in distress and glowering seneschals. Like Keaton, Perceval has a natural nobility: a god-given way with people and things that ensures his eventual triumph. In his blessed naivety, he relies only on himself, and somehow that seems to be enough.

But Perceval's naivety has a pointed, malignant side that Keaton's does not. In his blind rush toward knighthood, he abandons his mother, abuses a damsel, and loses his faith, committing all of his sins in perfect obliviousness. Perceval may be unwise in the ways of the world, but he is not entirely innocent: there is a drive and ambition in his character that bespeaks something hard and selfish behind his limpid, puppy-dog eyes.

As the film moves through its frankly didactic stages, Perceval gradually learns to look beyond himself—first by learning to honor his opponents in combat, secondly by discovering commitment in love, and thirdly by regaining his religious piety. This final lesson takes the form of a Passion Play, which Rohmer has extrapolated from de Troyes' last line, "Thus Perceval learned how God was crucified and died on a Friday, and on Easter Day he received the Communion." Appended as a coda, the sequence stunningly illuminates the Christian, and specifically Catholic, basis of Rohmer's moral investigations. When Perceval steps into the role of Christ (a transformation effected with a simple shock cut), he assumes the responsibility not only for his own actions, but for all of mankind.

According to Rohmer, his highest aim in making *Perceval* was to present, not the theme, but the text of de Troyes' poem to a new audience. Unfortunately, the subtitles don't support the director's claim that the work is "one of the most beautiful in French literature." For non-francophones like myself, *Perceval* necessarily remains an incomplete experience. But even without the words, there is more than enough grace and freshness in Rohmer's mise-en-scène to communicate the serene simplicity that he must have found in the original. With every passing year, Rohmer's art seems more and more valuable. Dedicated to balance, discretion, and the clean, clear line of thought, his films do more than preserve the classical virtues that have faded from much of world cinema—they make them live.

GODARD >>

Numéro deux

Directed by JEAN-LUC GODARD {July 1, 1977}

May 1968 was a crucial month for film as well as politics. The Paris student revolts of the spring completed the politicization of Jean-Luc Godard. Already a committed Marxist, Godard found in the riots—apparently as he was filming them for his documentary short *Cinétracts*—the motivation to make the final transition from a socially concerned artist to a dedicated revolutionary.

In the years since, Godard has been working toward a new film language, one capable of expressing the ideas and the urgency he discovered in that month of upheaval. The old language—that of the classical "realist" cinema—wouldn't work. For Godard, and the other filmmakers who followed him into radicalization, the classical cinema of storytelling was a barrier to class consciousness, a way of repressing revolutionary rage by selling the idea that problems and plots could be solved within the existing system. To tell a story, to seduce the audience with appealing characters, was a betrayal by emotion: a new cinema had to be found, one that would prod the audience to think and act instead of reinforcing illusions of prosperity and supporting the old ideologies of capitalism and individual achievement.

Godard's radicalization alienated most of his early supporters. He was no longer the intellectual comedian and reluctant romantic of *Breathless* but a determined, stone-faced ideologue. It was as if Woody Allen had abandoned *Annie Hall* in favor of a 16mm documentary on the Palestine Liberation Front. No one knew what to make of this new Godard, whose films, suddenly, were no fun anymore. The few popular critics who continued to pay attention to him seemed to find the films produced by Godard and his Dziga Vertov Group to be the products of a monster, a man who had completely abandoned human feeling and human decency and become a political savage. *Le Gai savoir*, *Une film comme les autres*, *One Plus One*, *British Sounds*, *Pravda*, *Wind From the East*, *Struggle in Italy*, and *Vladimir and Rosa* came and went almost unnoticed, receiving little more than a perfunctory distribution in the United States if they received any at all. Only with *Tout va bien*, Godard's self-styled return to "popular" filmmaking—it actually had stars in it, Jane Fonda and Yves Montand—did his stock seem to rise, and then only slightly. The pacesetter of 60s cinema had become the pariah of the 70s.

I'm a long way from making up my mind about Godard's post-'68 work. Much of it is cold, forbidding, obtuse, and plain dull. But much of it is also stimulating and genuinely insightful. It's hard to argue with a filmmaker who says his work is designed *not* to be enjoyable—to say that *Pravda*, a painful theoretical analysis of failed communism in Czechoslovakia, is boring, is to say nothing at all. Of course it's boring—it was meant to be. Godard went out of his way to make it dull, clearing away all the diversions and distractions of life as it is lived to make way for *le gai savoir*—"the joy of learning"—pure theory, solid facts, and sober politics. There's a streak of Puritanism in Godard's late work: if it hurts, it must be good for you.

But if Godard sometimes seems to be out to stupefy the audience, he's also capable of sustained stylistic experiments that open doors to entire new ranges of cinematic expression. *British Sounds* (a.k.a. *See You at Mao*), released the same year as *Pravda*, seems to break new ground with every frame. It opens with a long lateral track, several minutes in length, down the assembly line of a British auto plant. The shot is a formal device that puts a necessary screen of intellectual detachment in front of what we see: the dehumanized, machine-like workers, each trapped in his own section of the assembly line, each endlessly performing his own trivial task, none of them realizing the satisfaction of the completed job or the value of their labor. We're trapped in the tracking movement as much as the workers are trapped in their jobs. We want to break free, get out—if five minutes of this is unbearable, imagine nine hours a day, five days a week, for a lifetime.

This is what Godard means by a "materialist" cinema—a kind of filmmaking that deals in particulars, doing away with the identification (the traditional approach would be to follow one worker—played, no doubt, by William Bendix—as he comes home from a frustrating day at the factory and beats up his wife). It's also a kind of filmmaking that insists on the mechanics of the process. We're always aware of the shot; it's artificial, something imposed on reality, and we can't mistake what we see on the screen—as we supposedly do in classical films—with unmediated "real life."

Those are the two basic ideas that have informed Godard's filmmaking since 1968. They take different forms in different films, as Godard continues his experiments and hones his technique. It's important to remember that the films *are* experiments: the new language is far from perfect. The tentative nature of the work is something that Godard himself seems to forget from time to time. Each film seems perfectly secure in its structure. "This time," he seems to be saying, "it's the real thing"—there's a smugness and sense of finality to each of the films, a sense that's destroyed, of course, by the next film that comes down the line, taking a completely different tack. Godard's refusal to admit uncertainty, to share his evident doubt about his technique or his ideology, is perhaps the most off-putting aspect of his recent work. He seems closed off, locked away in his own world of absolute control and absolute intellectual order.

Numéro deux, the most recent Godard film to reach the U.S., goes a long way toward correcting that fault. It may even go too far in the other direction: Godard seems so confused, demoralized, and defeated in *Numéro deux* that the film becomes a profoundly depressing experience. It seems to be born of the same late-career revisionism that makes John Ford's bleak *7 Women* come as such an affecting surprise at the end of his generally optimistic body of work. Godard is still looking for answers, but he's looking deeper inside himself, and he doesn't seem to like what he finds there.

Numéro deux begins with Godard standing in the shadows of a darkened editing room. Behind him, two projectors churn slowly and noisily. His face is almost completely obscured, but we can see his expression more clearly on a video monitor in the foreground, which carries a simultaneous shot of the director taken from another angle. The scene is strikingly reminiscent of the climax of Fritz Lang's late masterpiece, *The Thousand Eyes of Dr. Mabuse*, with Godard standing in for the mad doctor, struggling with his bank of tape machines and video terminals. Lang's Mabuse tried to control the world by watching it; Godard's voyeurism is scientific: he watches the world to learn. What dominance there was, he tells us in a long and rambling monologue, has begun to break down. His friends are leaving him, his politics are muddled, his health is failing. He doesn't understand what's going on outside, but here in the editing room, "it's simple because there's only machines left"—machines that give him some control over words and images. But as *Numéro deux* continues, even the last vestige of control—control of language, the tool that puts the world in order—begins to slip from his grasp.

In the second section of the film, Godard sits at an editing table, running tapes through two monitors. One screen shows trailers from commercial films, including scenes from Claude Sautet's recent triumph of empty bourgeois realism, *Vincent, Paul, Francois, and the Others*. The screen below it carries images of a political demonstration. Here are Godard's two cinemas: the classical and the committed, the illusory and the real. As the two soundtracks blare, a woman's voice—presumably belonging to Anne-Marie Miéville, Godard's current partner—explains the significance of the two images and the title of the film: for every number one, there is a number two, a contradiction. Out of this contradiction, the dialectic, comes change. But the contradiction we see on the screen tends more toward empty chaos than fruitful dialectic, and the narrator's voice only adds to the confusion, fighting with the two soundtracks for our attention. Three soundtracks, three images: the channels of communication are overloaded. Messages struggle with each other, none quite getting through.

The third and longest passage of *Numéro deux* continues the rush of sound and image in the guise of a sociological investigation of a suburban family. Here, too, there is breakdown, contradiction. The screen sometimes contains one image, sometimes two or three. The split screen continues the dialectic as the images reinforce or undermine each other, occasionally in ways that go unexplained. Sometimes the images separate or compartmentalize the members of the family: parents are divorced from children, grandparents are divorced from grandchildren, brother from sister, husband from wife. The cause of the separation is seen as political: the ideology of capitalism draws the members of the family apart. The husband must leave his wife to go to work, the children leave for school. Even when they're together, they seem to seek isolation, staring at the television, listening to music through headphones.

The most interesting development in *Numéro deux* may be its use of explicit sex scenes. Advanced French criticism has recently taken a Freudian bent, studying the repression of sexuality in the classical cinema. Godard's own work in the 60s offers an example of that repression: most of the sexual relationships in his early films are marked by a strange fascination with child-like women, a fetish that turns sex into defilement. In *Numéro deux*, Godard has achieved something of a personal liberation, sex becoming the only genuine means of communication between the characters. But more importantly, Godard has found an effective way of challenging the traditional narrative codes by restoring sex to its normal role in life. We never saw Mr. and Mrs. Cleaver in the sack, a fact that accounts for most of the sterility of the television world. Sexual feeling, one of life's fundamental emotions, is displaced, its energy channeled into other pursuits: money, success, power.

Still, sexual communication is open to only two of the characters in *Numéro deux*. The grandparents seem to have lost their desire, the children, naturally, are children (although their parents encourage their sexual development). But even so, Godard finds this line breaking down as well. Shots of the husband leaving work are juxtaposed with an image of his wife vainly trying to arouse him orally. His life as a worker apparently sapped his passion, reducing his wife to masturbation, a succinct image of solitude.

The image of impotence carries over into *Numéro deux*'s final section. We're back in the editing room with Godard, who seems to have collapsed over his desk. As he lies there, head buried in his arms, outtakes from the family section play on the machines behind him. His effort to control the world, to reduce human nature to strips of film and tape, has apparently failed. The manipulator is now being manipulated. The images play on and on, seemingly of their own volition. The artist has been beaten.

Numéro deux is a wrenching experience for anyone familiar with Godard's work—both as an art and as a personal manifesto. Never before has he dared to put himself on film. He's always been the off-screen interviewer, guiding—and sometimes bullying—his actors into self-relevation.

But now that he's turned to look at himself, he seems to have reached a null point: where can he possibly go from here?

Godard has, of course, continued to work. He has completed two films, *Comment ça va?* (on the ideologies of journalism) and *Ici et ailleurs* (on Palestine), as well as a ten-part television series, *Sur et sous la communication*. To judge from the titles, he seems to be continuing his investigation of the breakdown, here, more specifically, of language. It might be a while before we know for sure: Godard's films have been preposterously slow in reaching the U.S. Without them, we're missing the work of one of the most important and audacious filmmakers of the 70s.

Every Man for Himself

Directed by JEAN-LUC GODARD {August 28, 1981}

Jean-Luc Godard's *Every Man for Himself* is one of the most important movies of the last few years, yet it isn't a "masterpiece"—Godard himself would probably choke on the word. For that matter, "important" would probably be too much for him to swallow. Any words of high praise carry a connotation of being above the crowd, above the everyday: they set the work on some rarefied spiritual plane, placing it apart from the time and culture that produced it. Godard has always insisted on the context of his films: he has a unique talent for fixing the present moment, or rather, for making himself permeable to it. His movies absorb the circumstances of their making; they seem to carry, not only what Godard is thinking, but what everyone is thinking around the movie, from the actors in front of the camera to the technicians beside it, and even perhaps to the passersby who wander through the background of the shot. When Godard abandoned the studio to make *Breathless* in 1959, he did more than take movies into the street (in search of "natural" lighting, "natural" locations, as most directors after him have understood his innovation). He took movies into life, opening them up to chance, to accident, to random observation and spontaneous meaning. His method denies masterpieces: he refuses to labor over his work, giving it the completeness and smoothness and fullness of perfection. He prefers to let his art find him, and if it enters as something ragged and contradictory, so much the better. It is, unmistakably, still breathing.

Godard himself apparently regards his old films as disposable: he never refers to them except when he's trying to raise money (his 1978 *Numéro Deux* was rather shamelessly promoted as a "sequel" to *Breathless*). They were made in and for a particular moment and for him, they died when their moments passed. It isn't true, of course—almost all of Godard's work retains its interest and vitality today. But there is a special excitement that comes from seeing a Godard film *in* its moment: you feel bound to the screen in unique ways, because Godard has put your world up there. The clothes are right, the décor is right, the omnipresent advertisements are always right, but more important, the casts of mind, the attitudes displayed and the concerns expressed, always seem supernaturally correct, of the second. Unfortunately, the excitement of seeing Godard in his moment is an excitement American audiences have largely missed for the last decade. Godard's films have been so badly distributed for the past ten years that there is a widespread assumption he is no longer at work. Actually, Godard had directed more than a dozen feature-length films since 1968 (the exact number depends on how you assess his various uncompleted projects and television programs), of which only two or three have been shown theatrically in Chicago. With *Every Man for Himself*, Godard has come back to the commercial mainstream (or at least, he's dipped his feet in the water). The excitement is back, too—as vivid as ever—yet this is a different Godard from the man most of us left in the late 60s. He is still immersed in the moment, but the moment, perhaps, has betrayed him. A sadness now underlies the excitement of his work, as Godard struggles to rebuild his values in the face of the disappointments of the 70s.

Every Man for Himself (the French title is the somewhat more cryptic and elegant *Sauve qui peut (la vie)*; the English title Godard originally wanted was *Slow Motion*) has been hailed in some circles as a return to common sense and in others as a reactionary repudiation of his radical work in the 60s and 70s. But I personally don't see a serious break with the ideas and methods Godard has been developing for the last decade, and the central dilemma of *Every Man* is not much different from the dilemmas of the political films. What Godard has returned to is narrative: to plot (it's abstract and inconclusive, but it's there) and to psychologically realistic characters (well, to a degree—they do tend to wobble toward allegory). Godard has simply exchanged one form of rhetoric (the essay) for another (the story), which shouldn't be such a momentous decision—many of the great figures in literature (particularly in French literature) felt the same freedom to move between means of address. But in the movies—and surely this is part of Godard's point—to change forms is to address audiences. Stories are much more acceptable to film distributors than essays: a story will receive more bookings, be seen by more people, make more money. By choosing again to film a plot, Godard is really making an economic decision as much as an artistic one. Making a story returns him to visibility, to the single form of movie that is allowed to make an impact on our culture. In a sense, the simple existence of *Every Man for Himself* makes one of its main thematic points: that business always determines art, and there is no free choice of expression within our society, that the systems of finance invariably determine what is said and how.

Godard now seems willing to accept those limitations, though his motives aren't quite clear. It's possible that he's come back to narrative out of some romantic impulse to subvert the system by working within it, to attack the dominant culture on its own terms. But Godard's apparent dissatisfaction with *Tout va bien*, his Maoist film "starring" Jane Fonda and Yves Montand, seems to stem from the realization that such an approach is impossible: to think that one man or one movie can affect the established order is naive and sentimental, and then there's the more abstract and troublesome sense in which accepting the terms of the dominant culture is already a guarantee of defeat. My own feeling, judging from the overall temper of *Every Man*, is that Godard's return is fiercely anti-romantic, anti-sentimental: he wants to hug reality as hard as he can, to destroy his illusions of independence once and for all. Like the political essays, *Every Man* is an attempt to understand things as they really are, but it is also an attempt to make a film as *they* really are, to engage the form of movies that most of us know and accept, for better or for worse, as the right, the real form.

There are no overt political discussions in *Every Man*, yet the film is wholly political. "As for me, I've become aware, after 15 years of cinema, that the real 'political' film that I'd like to end up with would be a film about me which would show to my wife and daughter what I am, in other words a home movie—home movies represent the popular base of the cinema." This is Godard speaking several years ago to an interviewer from the French magazine *Cinéma pratique*, and *Every Man for Himself* is that home movie. The main male character, played by Jacques Dutronc, has been given the name of the director's father, Paul Godard. This Godard is a famous filmmaker; he has an estranged wife and daughter (Paule Muret and Cécile Tanner), and he is breaking up with his current lover, Denise (Nathalie Baye), who has a video production company in a small Swiss city.

Every Man is a highly autobiographical, intensely (and sometimes excruciatingly) personal film, yet it is not a self-centered confessional in the manner of Woody Allen or Bob Fosse. Godard establishes his extreme subjectivity in order to be more objective; there is a push-pull of inside and outside views that is very characteristic of Godard's long-established dialectical method. Paul Godard is not at the middle of *Every Man*; his attitudes and experiences don't influence the shape of the film. Instead, there is a fairly rigorous, four-part formal structure (plus a short introduction) that establishes the presence of a cool, analytical consciousness somewhere outside the perceptions of the characters. This is the double vision, at once swooningly personal and icily removed, that transforms Godard's home movie into a "real political film." For Godard, politics is the art of living in the material world; it begins with the smallest, most trivial gesture a person can make toward the people around him. Something of Godard's old Maoism remains here, in the insistence on politics as an everyday presence, but he is approaching the routine of his life not from the Maoist, idealist perspective of trying to purify it, "radicalize" it, but from the practical, analytical perspective of trying to understand what it is that he does and why he does it—how his life works.

Godard's focus is microscopic: at times, he will slow down the frames of his film, in order to dissolve gestures into their constituent, cinematic parts (the "slow motion" of the original English title). He is looking for meaning in the smallest places imaginable: if it isn't hiding within the frozen frame, perhaps it exists in the blank spaces between the frames, too minute for a movie to capture. The film has a feeling of desperate search, as if Godard were looking under the furniture, under the carpets, for something lost, something immensely important.

What has he lost? The film's opening section, subtitled "*La vie*," tells us: As Paul is leaving the luxury hotel he lives in, he is accosted by a busboy in the parking lot. "I love you!" he tells Paul, who, embarrassed, confidently corrects him: "You mean you love my spirit." "No," the busboy responds, "I love your body"—and launches into a hilariously obscene homosexual proposition. The sequence has the rough, improvised feel of sketch comedy, but it's here that Godard lays down the opposition that governs his film and his search: the opposition of love and sex, of spirit and flesh, of ideals and reality.

The subject of *Every Man* is the lie of transcendence—the search for abstract spiritual, emotional, and intellectual values, and its inevitable failure in the face of rough reality. Part one, "The Imaginary," follows Denise's search for redemption in the natural, physical world; she visits farms and rides her bicycle through the countryside. Part two, "Fear," looks at Paul's relations with women—Denise, his ex-wife, his daughter—and what he really wants from them. The third section, "Commerce," introduces a third character, a prostitute (Isabelle Huppert), who seems a conscious extension and rethinking of the prostitute figures who appear in many of Godard's 60s films. He is no longer interested in the romantic image of the woman who sells her body but retains her soul, but in a new metaphor—of the prostitute as the ultimate realist, seizing and exploiting the two true forces in the world, sex and capital. The final section, "Music," brings the characters together (the prostitute wishes to sublet Denise's apartment) for a haunting, witty finale.

Godard has chosen to film his investigation of the "real" in a style that systematically subverts the main component of cinematic realism—the synchronization of sound and image. The most impressive montage in *Every Man* takes place on the soundtrack—a dense weave of music (several different themes, ranging from classical to jazz to disco, composed by Gabriel Yared), dialogue, natural and industrial sounds, and, most fatally, silence. The soundtrack attacks the image, questioning its primacy, undermining its authority, telling us things the image can't. The "reality" the movies give us doesn't seem very real after all; Godard makes us realize how much it hides. And the image, too, gains a new freedom: no longer dependent on the soundtrack for support, the camera can leave the drama, wandering out into the streets or the countryside, while the dialogue it has left behind continues to be heard. Music, which occupies a curious half-world in conventional films—heard by the audience but not by the characters—is suddenly allowed to commute across the screen. "Do you hear that music?" someone in the film will ask, apparently receiving an intimation of the ideal through the soundtrack they shouldn't be able to hear. Sometimes we in the audience hear it, sometimes it is reserved for the privileged characters alone.

Music runs through the film as a motif independent of the drama, as do some visual symbols—trucks (an image taken from *Le Camion*, by French novelist and filmmaker Marguerite Duras, who also makes a funny nonappearance in the movie), cows, musicians, and another, more mysterious, prostitute. This is good old-fashioned surrealism, possibly contributed by coscenarist Jean-Claude Carrière, who has worked on many of Buñuel's late films. But the most disturbing motif in the film is obscenity, both verbal (Paul's incest fantasies) and visual (the elaborate sex games demanded by Huppert's customers). Godard is going for several effects here, not the least of which is shock: he will show us the unshowable, the reality the movies are socially forbidden to represent. And he is also making an abstract, general point: just as Marxism structures Godard's idea of social reality, so does Freudianism govern his idea of interpersonal reality (several very different characters are tied together by common sex fantasies, just as everyone is tied together by business relations). But perhaps his most profound intention is personal: he is showing himself as he really is, the strange evasions of his 60s films (which marked Godard as the most paradoxically puritanical of all French directors) finally lifted to reveal a deeply troubled sexuality, confused by misogyny, sadism, homophobia.

In the end, Godard suggests that there might not be much more to Paul than his sex problems: if they eventually destroy him, sealing him off from the women in his life, they have also helped to define him and his art. The film's profound mistrust of the transcendent all seems founded on a single, sexual confusion: how can I love you if I want to rape you? Godard seems genuinely to have touched bottom here, exposing himself with an almost appalling frankness, yet he retains enough distance to enlarge the confessional point into a general insight: in finding his limits, he has found his reality, his ground zero. In its wholesale trashing of treasured illusions, of hopes and dreams and higher impulses, *Every Man for Himself* can be a bleak, dispiriting film: it reveals a society of isolated individuals, bound together only by money and neurotic need. Yet there is always an opposite term in Godard's habitual dialectic, and the despair of *Every Man* is answered by faint hope. If we can at least recognize the real, have the courage to admit it exists, perhaps we can now really begin to work with it. Someone once remarked that "real" is a word that means nothing without quotation marks; *Every Man for Himself* is Jean-Luc Godard's last-ditch attempt to knock them off.

Passion

Directed by JEAN-LUC GODARD {March 23, 1984}

Jean-Luc Godard is at once the most confiding of filmmakers and the most elusive. I don't know of another director who seems so anxious to speak directly to the audience, who seems so desperate to communicate. And yet communication is always the central problem in a Godard film. In *Passion*, a 1982 feature that will have its delayed Chicago premiere at the Parkway this week, Godard has cast Jerzy Radziwilowicz, the Polish star of Andrzej Wajda's *Man of Iron*, as a filmmaker much like himself (he wears Godard's glasses, as Jacques Dutronc did in 1980's *Every Man for Himself*). Jerzy's French isn't so great, but it's at least as good as his co-star's: playing opposite him is Hanna Schygulla, Rainer Werner Fassbinder's icon of feminine cunning, as the wife of a factory owner. For the native French speakers in the cast, Godard has imposed equivalent handicaps: a monumental stutter for Isabelle Huppert, who plays a factory worker, and a ferocious hacking cough for Michel Piccoli, who appears as Huppert's boss and Schygulla's husband. Radziwilowicz has also been given an Italian producer and a Hungarian assistant, but the theme finds its poetic culmination in the figure of a beautiful deaf-mute girl, a niece of Piccoli's who is working as a nude model in the movie Radziwilowicz is making.

It's Godard's anxiousness to speak that stops him. Like Huppert with her stutter, he's never able to finish a sentence, never able to bring a scene to dramatic completion. Huppert stumbles because she can't find the right words; Godard stumbles—as Radziwilowicz says—because he can't find the right light. *Passion* proceeds in fits and starts, through scenes that seem to begin too quickly (before we've had a chance to recognize the characters or the situation) or end too soon (before the rhythm of the sequence has been fully played out, or before the dramatic payoff has been delivered). The Italian producer wanders through the chaos of Radziwilowicz's set, demanding to know what the story is (is this Godard's tribute to Carlo Ponti, who produced his *Contempt* in 1963?). It's a question that Godard's audiences have always asked, yet the fact is that this time there is a story, and even a fairly classic one: a romantic triangle that isolates Jerzy (the actor's own names are used for the characters) between Hanna of the calculating ruling classes and Isabelle of the virginal proletariat. It's just that we never seem to encounter the story at its key moments: Godard has left out the climaxes—the conflicts felt and the decisions made—that give the story its tension and shape. *Passion* is a movie that always feels "in between"—moving away from some crucial point we haven't seen and toward another we never will. The film is composed of these moments that most directors strive to minimize: the moments of transition, of modulation between one emotion and another, of dramatic suspension. Of course, it is exactly these moments that are the most realistic—the closest to the ambiguity and uneventfulness of lived experience—in a conventional film. They seem strange because we aren't used to seeing them on a screen, because they aren't satisfying in the way movies are supposed to be. By showing these moments, Godard makes every other movie seem false. But at the same time he makes his own movie seem foreign and mute. Godard wants to tell the truth, but this truth isn't easy to tell. It emerges in fragments, hesitations, confusions. He stutters because he can't find the right word, but also because he suspects the right word doesn't exist—that no word is sufficient to express the complexity of the world.

And yet the right word, the right light, did once exist. It can be seen in the art of the past, to which Godard, the modernist artist par excellence, now longingly looks. The movie that Jerzy is working on appears to be an elaborate attempt to reconstruct a series of classic paintings—beginning with Rembrandt's *Night Watch*—in three dimensions; as his camera floats through his complicated compositions, the studio playback system blares snatches from Mozart, Beethoven, and Fauré, which don't quite drown out the clangor of Jerzy's extras moving into place. These sequences are of a lush, classical beauty, lighted in a ravishing chiaroscuro by cinematographer Raoul Coutard. (It's a pity that, as usual, the dupe prints made for American distribution betray the color values of the European original.) It's startling to see them in a film by Jean-Luc Godard (and the same Coutard) who in 1959 shocked the world with the rough-edged, all-natural lighting of *Breathless*. With its battle cry of "Out of the studios and into the streets," *Breathless* touched off a stylistic revolution that isn't over yet; by returning to the elegant, abstract, carefully manufactured images of the studio, Godard might seem to be recanting. But I think that what Godard is expressing here is a temptation rather than a capitulation—a sweet nostalgia for the clarity and confidence of life and art before the revolution. The impossibility of a complete return is suggested by the modernist imperfections that remain embedded in the studio sequences: by the ambient noise that threatens to stifle Beethoven (when Godard brings on a troupe of knights on horseback, the clatter of hooves is a reference to the modernist use of sound in Bresson's *Lancelot du Lac*), and by the network of wires and lighting rigs that descends over Rembrandt. Godard isn't filming the living paintings: he's filming Jerzy filming them, with Jerzy and his camera visible in almost every shot (at moments, Jerzy's camera crane and Godard's seem to perform a duet, answering each other's gliding movements in a silent, weightless ballet). There is, of course, something naive and almost kitschy about Jerzy's project, an impression pointed up by the fact that Jerzy is shooting with a video camera, which can't possibly capture the range of tone and detail we see in Godard's filmed images. Jerzy's movie, if he ever manages to finish it, will almost certainly be an artistic failure. It isn't the movie that matters to Godard, but the urge behind it—the urge to escape from modernism to return to a time when art was unselfconscious and whole. Jerzy is pursuing an ideal of unity, clarity, and completion, yet he must be aware that his search is hopeless. That's why the light is never right for him, why he can't bring himself to shoot. Rembrandt's light was right for Rembrandt; it isn't right for 1982. Jerzy is suspended between two artistic moments—between classicism and modernism—just as the story always seems suspended between two climaxes we never see.

Godard begins *Passion* with a lovely, ethereal image: a jet plane tracing a long white line high in a brilliant blue sky. The flight of the plane is interrupted by close-ups of each of the three main characters—a sequence of classic, Eisensteinian montage that sets up an opposition between the near and the far, the human and the ideal, the real and the abstract. Crucially for Godard, it is also an opposition of two kinds of filming: the cinema of the image (the plane in the sky as a visual metaphor, perfectly expressive in itself) and the cinema of the actor (the human face as a vehicle for meaning, with its potential for spontaneous, ambiguous, generalized expression). Godard has always been more of an image director than an actor's director; he chooses his performers more for their iconographic value than for their acting skills. In *Passion*, Jerzy Radziwilowicz is present as a symbol of Eastern Europe, the Solidarity crisis, and the agitprop cinema of Andrzej Wajda. Schygulla is there to invoke the economic strength of West Germany, but also the theatricality and self-consciousness of Fassbinder's melodramas. Huppert represents the realism of contemporary French films—antiartifice, antiglamour, and, in some sense, antiacting (she never seems to rouse herself for the camera). The relationships between the characters all seem established in the casting; Godard doesn't have to direct his performers but merely stand there and watch their contradictory styles and meanings bristle up against each other. But in *Passion*, Godard shows a new interest in faces; he lingers over them looking for qualities that go beyond the narrowly symbolic, the simply expressive—looking, that is, for their beauty. There is a remarkable sequence in which Schygulla watches herself performing on videotape: she sees the theatrical tricks she uses (the pursing of her mouth, the hooding of her eyes) and she laughs at her own artificiality. The laugh is genuine and surprising—it could be the first time we've really seen Schygulla in a film. There are several extended close-ups of Huppert doing what she does best: sitting in silence and radiating unknowability (Godard seems fascinated by the quality most of her directors don't even perceive—her blankness). But above all there are the faces of the models in the living paintings, the faces that, with their uniqueness and aliveness, spoil the illusion that Jerzy is trying to create. In a painting, faces can be compositional elements, planes of light and darkness. But on film, every face is specific: we can't forget that it belongs to a human being, and we can't help wondering who these people are. The elements of chance, of ambiguity, of aliveness that Jerzy has tried to banish from his work return through the faces, bringing the beauty and complexity of the modern cinema back with them.

Passion seems to divide almost evenly between scenes with Jerzy in the studio and scenes outside with the two women (we never see people entering the studio—the set and the street are two different worlds). The opposition here is a conventional one—of work and love, art and life. Yet Godard is in between these poles, too. Every Godard film has a slogan; this one has two: "It is necessary to live stories before inventing them" and "To love to work; to work to love." Jerzy does not carry his experiences with the two women directly over to his art, but he does carry over their essence: his inability to shoot is his inability to choose between his two lovers. During his Marxist phase, Godard was the most cerebral of filmmakers; now, he is returning to an experiential, emotional base for art, backing away from the theoretical ideal he once found in politics. He wants to return to the passion of his title—"to love to work" and, through his art, through his discovery of those faces, "to work to love." The passion of *Passion* is both emotional and aesthetic, visible both in the close-ups of Hanna and the long shots of the living paintings. Passion is what unifies the fragmented world of the film—the "right light" that Jerzy has been searching for. Yet, at the end of the movie, Jerzy is considering an offer from Hollywood while the two women, believing themselves abandoned, take off together on a car trip to Poland. The characters are still en route, still in between; the ultimate resolution, the cementing passion, has not been found. But it is a beautiful day for a drive.

Detective

Directed by JEAN-LUC GODARD {July 25, 1986}

It's all been said, it's all been done: artists don't do anything but circulate received meanings and exhausted metaphors in forms that, for a moment, might appear to be fresh, but turn out on closer inspection to be as old as Aeschylus. That's the attitude assumed by most of the art that today is called "postmodernist," but since the late 1950s at least, it's also been the attitude of Jean-Luc Godard.

Godard's first feature, *Breathless*, was built out of bits and pieces of old American gangster movies; it depicted a world where the natural and spontaneous was being replaced by the artificial and secondhand—even revolution could only be conceived in terms of borrowed images, as Jean-Paul Belmondo copied Humphrey Bogart's mannerisms in a foredoomed search for personal freedom. *Detective*, Godard's latest film, returns to the *film noir* archetypes that haunted *Breathless*, but this time, 26 years later, the received formulas and patterns seem to have driven out any trace of the real world. *Detective*, which takes place almost entirely within the rooms, corridors, and restaurants of a huge Parisian hotel, is set inside an impenetrable media environment—an environment that has become a prison and where there is no escape from archetypal situations, archetypal actions, and archetypal characters. Occasionally, someone will rattle the bars, but the only way out is through originality, and there is no originality left.

Detective isn't even a project that originated with Godard. It was made on a commission from a French producer, Alain Sarde, who had a star (Nathalie Baye) and a vague idea for a thriller plot; Godard accepted the project because he needed the money to finish his own film, *Hail Mary*. Godard doesn't try to disguise the impersonal nature of *Detective*: with typical perversity, he makes the project's impersonality the subject of the film, thus making it personal. He uses the credits, which are spaced out over several minutes of the action in the opening reel, to spell out the conditions of production. Sarde's name comes first, followed by a group of performers identified as "actors" (Jean-Pierre Léaud, Laurent Terzieff, Alain Cuny), and then by another cluster identified as "stars" (Baye, Johnny Hallyday, Claude Brasseur). It's the stars—human archetypes in their perfect state—who dictate the line of the action and the shape of the film. Baye, much beloved in France for her portrayal of the simple, virtuous, long-suffering average Frenchwoman, will play a simple, virtuous, long-suffering average Frenchwoman. Hallyday, a pop star who became wildly popular in the 60s by imitating American rockers, will play another pseudo-American, a cynical, growly-voiced flight promoter straight out of 1940s Hollywood. And because Baye and Hallyday had just gone through a front-page romance and marriage at the time of the filming (they've since split up), the film will have to feature them falling in love. Brasseur, a puppy-faced supporting man in approximately 400,000 French films made since the 1950s (mostly of the glossy, commercial variety that never make it to these shores), will be the supporting man once again: he's Baye's husband, the owner and chief pilot of a small airline, whose business concerns keep him much too much away from home.

The stars have the plot, but the actors have the subplot. Léaud, who often appeared as one of Godard's "Children of Marx and Coca-Cola" in the funky 60s films that made Godard's reputation, returns to Godardland for the first time in over a decade, and he brings a whiff of that old New Wave with him. Giving a stylized, bizarrely comic performance, full of elaborate, dandyish gestures and weird vocal inflections, he's some sort of police inspector who's moved into the hotel in a last-ditch attempt to help his uncle (Laurent Terzieff, a grave, skeletal figure from the French avant-garde theater) finally find a solution to the unsolved murder that, three years ago, cost his uncle his job as house detective. Along for the ride is Léaud's fiancée, Aurele Doazan, a willowy brunette who immediately recalls Anna Karina, Godard's star (and wife) through most of the New Wave years. Settled into a cramped double room, the jolly trio pass the time observing the comings and goings of the hotel's other guests through an elaborate video setup and swapping philosophical paradoxes. Rather than achieve characters, they seem to be the representatives of the audience within the film, not so much participating in the plot as observing it, trying to coax out its increasingly obscure significance. There's another passive character, too—an elderly Mafia chieftain played with weary authority by the classical stage actor Alain Cuny. Inexplicably accompanied by a little girl, just like the archangel Gabriel in *Hail Mary*, Cuny seems to possess a complete knowledge of all the other characters' actions and motivations; he is either God or—more likely, given the film's lay orientation—the producer, from whom all wisdom and authority (i.e., the money) flow.

The two halves of the film are joined through a typical Godardian pun: the solution (of a murder) is intercut with the dissolution (of a marriage). But what Godard has arrived at here is a parodic distillation of the two most prominent French commercial genres: the middle-class melodrama (as represented in the work of Lelouche, Sautet, and Kurys) and the high-tech thriller (Beineix, Besson, Behat). What really unites these two plots is their crushing banality, their deliberate predictability—qualities that have everything to do with their commercial viability, their cash value. For, as always in Godard, the real structuring principle is economic, and the relationships between the characters are most firmly defined by the cash-flow chart: Brasseur has borrowed money from Cuny, Baye has borrowed money from Brasseur, and Hallyday has borrowed money from Baye. Love, such as it is, is something lived furtively in the shadow of this system. Indeed, the film's most haunting scene finds Baye and Hallyday lying in bed in total darkness; when they want to declare their love for each other, they do so by the flickering light of a disposable cigarette lighter, as if these words could not be pronounced under the glare of the klieg lights—which represent the industrial weight of the film production, which represents money.

The detective, in the classic murder mystery formula, is someone who discovers a story—he takes all the clues and conflicting testimonies and puts them together, producing, out of apparent chaos, a plot line: who did what to whom and why. *Detective* follows the old formula, yet the stories it discovers—through the detecting trio of Léaud, Terzieff, and Doazan—are meaningless, empty things. "There are so many stories here," Léaud observes at one point, "our own and the others', that I'm sure something is going to happen." He seems to be speaking for Godard, who, having put all these characters and situations in place, is sitting back to see what will come of them. But nothing does. When Baye leaves Brasseur for Hallyday, the emotion is simply thrown away, lost in the haze of conventional images and the din of tired dialogue; when Léaud discovers the solution to the murder, it's banal and unilluminating (and it's been tipped off, as well, by a shot early in the film). There are stories everywhere, but nothing happens—nothing authentic, anyway. This is our world, Godard suggests—a world so choked by fiction, by formula narration and exhausted tales, that things can no longer be felt firsthand, that people can no longer act without falling into ancient patterns, the already done and the already said.

Godard's last few films have been concerned with breaking through this media-poisoned world, with breaking through to something clear, clean, and transcendent—be it classical art (*Passion*), erotic intensity (*First Name: Carmen*), or God (*Hail Mary*). *Detective* is the first of this new series of films that remains earthbound—bottled up within the hotel, within the house of fiction. Hallyday's repeated instruction to his boxer is "Break! Break! You've got to learn to break!" but he doesn't learn—nobody does—and that might be why *Detective* ultimately seems less rich, less inspired, than what we've seen from Godard lately. In spite of its surface wit (Léaud is consistently hilarious), it's the most depressive, the most pessimistic of Godard's recent efforts, which is why it's doubly unfortunate that the film is playing in Chicago shorn of its dazzling Dolby stereo sound track: it's in the sound experiments—the overlappings, the reversal of foreground dialogue and background music—that most of the film's creative exhilaration lies. But even in a world as bleak as that of *Detective*, Godard's faith in his chosen medium remains unshakable, a bright beam of hope. "Where is the truth?" wonders Doazan, as people usually do in Godard films when, like her, they're staring out a hotel window into the Parisian night. "*Entre apparaître et disparaître* [between appearing and disappearing]," responds Terzieff, to which she answers, "*Alors, ç'est transparaître* [so, it's transparent]." The passage is a typical Godardian riddle, and the answer, which he doesn't provide, can only be "film"—the transparent image that appears and disappears 24 times a second. Movies, which have done so much to clog the world with fictions, remain, for Godard, the surest way out.

NEW MASTERS >>

Jonah Who Will Be 25 in the Year 2000

Directed by ALAIN TANNER {March 4, 1977}

Chicago will be lucky if it sees another film this year that's as warm, open, and downright friendly as Alain Tanner's *Jonah Who Will Be 25 in the Year 2000*. And it seems a fairly safe bet that we won't see another with nearly as much intelligence, rigor, or responsibility.

From the Midwestern perspective, it sometimes seems that the European film has whittled itself down to two extremes. On one side there's the easy sentimentalism of *Small Change* and *Cousin, Cousine*; on the other, the forbidding intellectualism of *The Chronicle of Anna Magdalena Bach* or of late Godard. Most of the energy (and much of the interest) of western European filmmaking lies in the latter category, where contemporary film theory and film practice have met to create the dictum that the only kind of film worth making is a structurally revolutionary, highly political one. But what Godard, Straub, Kluge, and the others have gained in understanding the ideological operation of film, they seem to have lost in base appeal. Today's film theorists, armed with the semiology of Christina Metz and the psychology of Jacques Lacan, have gone beyond the point of declaring pleasure a bourgeois perversion, a sop to the audience's collective anal and Oedipal complexes. What began as an important and valid investigation of how movies "mean" has turned into a New Puritanism, and the films produced under the philosophy go largely unseen.

But where does it say that the free play of ideas can't be, shouldn't be, an enjoyable thing? Alain Tanner's contribution to the cinema of the 70s seems to lie in his answer to that question: "nowhere." With *Jonah* and his four previous feature-length films, Tanner has given a sense of adventure and enthusiasm back to the political cinema. By bringing thinking and caring together again, Tanner is doing more than offering a Mary Poppins spoonful of sugar to help the medicine go down; he is making a fundamental structural change, creating a new dialectic of emotion and intellect.

Tanner's films use most of the criticisms that Godard's work has leveled against the traditional narrative form. Godard and the other radical theorists have eschewed the standard narrative as a device that deceives the audience, that creates an illusion—by using a story with a precise beginning, middle, and end—of an order that doesn't exist in life. The gaps, contradictions, and confusions of living in a capitalist society are smoothed over when the audience is made to identify with a protagonist who suffers not from the unnamable alienations of economics, but from concrete, personal, and most importantly, solvable problems. For Godard, the problem was to create films that would be open-ended and provocative, rather than closed and misleadingly affirmative of the old ideological order. Most of the answers were taken from the plays of Bertolt Brecht, where the famous "alienation effects"—declamatory instead of naturalistic acting; short, choppy scenes in place of the standard flowing narrative; the use of placards, projections, and songs to draw the "moral" of the story; and so on—served to break the audience's psychological identification with the story and the characters and ideally, to prod the audience into thinking about what it saw.

Alienation effects have become an end in themselves, treasured by Marxist directors as warmly as a writer hugs his metaphors. Some radical films, like Alexander Kluge's *The Part Time Work of a Domestic Slave*, seem to be so obsessed with the alienation effects that they finally alienate themselves into oblivion. But against the Brecht-Godard axis, Tanner has erected a line of humanism, based (as he has said) mainly on the work of Jean Renoir. Ever since Eisenstein postulated the "explosion of thought" that results from the collision of two contradictory shots spliced together, montage has been the rhetoric of the radical film. At the other extreme, Renoir's long takes, deep focus, and freely moving camera have been the hallmarks of cinematic naturalism, a style that tries to preserve the continuities of time and space. *Jonah* is conceived almost entirely in terms of long takes—characters face each other across tables and walk together down paths, their conversations seldom interrupted by cross-cutting. When two characters who will become lovers meet for the first time, Tanner pans from one face to the other and then back, a shot that Frank Borzage put to brilliant use in his Hollywood romances of the 30s. The pan creates a magic, magnetic link between the characters, in place of the conflict that would be generated by a cut from one close-up to another. In a later scene—which is, in fact, the dramatic climax of the film—Tanner uses an extraordinary long and graceful take to capture the flow of conversation as the eight members of *Jonah*'s community (one present in spirit only) sit together at a dinner table, the camera gliding around them, tracking in for closer looks and moving back to examine the whole. All the while, the camera movements draw the characters together in a unique kind of spatial and personal unity that testifies to a commonality of purpose, but one that also—through the shifting perspectives of the tracking shot—preserves a multiplicity of points of view.

Where Tanner's mise-en-scène emphasizes continuity, his narrative is based on the episodic structure of Brecht's plays. *Jonah* has no plot per se; instead, a dramatic rhythm—of coming together and drifting apart—determines the shape of the film. Mathieu, a printer who has been fired for trying to organize his shop, answers an ad for a farmhand placed by Marcel and Marguerite, who grow organic vegetables on the outskirts of Geneva and worry about the extinction of the whale. Mathieu accepts the job and brings his earth-mother wife, Mathilde, and his children to live in the apartment that goes with the post. Marco is a high-school history teacher who lives nearby; he falls in love with Marie, a supermarket cashier who gives food away to elderly parishioners. Max, a former radical journalist, learns of a plot to buy up Marcel and Marguerite's farmland from his (eventual) lover, Madeleine, a bank secretary who dreams of saving the world through Tantric sex.

The eight characters of *Jonah*, along with the leads of most of Tanner's other films, share a post-'68 bond of political disillusionment. They are the people in the middle, burdened by the knowledge that their romantic revolution has failed, and they make an uneasy peace with society by taking jobs that mean nothing to them, by pursuing arcane philosophies, or by finding a quiet place in the country to hide. Each of the eight characters represents a different response to the dilemma of the revolutionary in non-revolutionary times; they are, as Tanner said in an interview, "metaphors on two legs." Maintaining his careful balance of naturalism and stylization, Tanner never lets the audience forget that the people in his films are, after all, fictional creations. (Giving all the characters first names that begin with "Ma" is an alienation effect that Brecht himself would doubtless have admired: subtle but insistent.)

But Tanner has drawn his ambulatory allegories with such a sense of compassion and wit that their philosophies become as appealing as their personalities—the two, in fact, are inseparable. Marco, the high school teacher, tries to radicalize his class by delivering funny and imponderable Marxist-mystic lectures on the nature of time and space. Like Godard, Marco sometimes gets carried away by his rhetoric, pursuing his metaphors (a sausage becomes the line of history) to the null point, but his intellectual enthusiasm is exhilarating in itself. All of the characters are permitted their moments of private fantasy (Marco's dream is going to bed with two women), as Tanner shifts to black-and-white to capture the contrast between the real and the hoped-for. But if the characters have their secret hopes, they also harbor private fears: newsreel visions of storm troops, police riots, military parades.

Mathieu, the printer-turned-farmhand, is the visionary of the group. When the eight members first come together, entirely by coincidence, on a Sunday afternoon at the farm, Mathieu's children are busily defacing a garden wall with chalk drawings of their parents. Mathieu imagines the completed mural: he and his seven friends in a permanent embrace. But nothing is permanent—time passes, and Mathieu loses his job at the farm, taking work at a factory in the city. Still, something had come out of that commingling of spirit. Mathieu's wife, Mathilde, gives birth to a son—Jonah, who will be 25 in the year 2000, and who carries with him the vision and hope of the entire group.

The Middle of the World, Tanner's last film, was also built on the unification of opposites (a middle-class Swiss politician falls in love with an Italian working girl), but *Jonah* comes closer to being a genuine dialectic. Out of the opposition of two cinematic forms, those of Godard and Renoir, and out of the opposition of two artistic motives, to educate and to entertain (not such an evil world after all), comes a film that holds as much aesthetic promise as its final image—the smiling face of Jonah, age five—holds hope for the future.

The Memory of Justice

Directed by MARCEL OPHULS {March 25, 1977}

It seems inadequate to describe Marcel Ophuls as a man who makes documentaries. With the scale and the scope he brought to *The Sorrow and the Pity*, and now to his new film, *The Memory of Justice*, Ophuls has established himself as one of the few filmmakers to master the epic mode. His films show the organizational skill of a Griffith or a Ford in the way they approach their monumental subjects, every theme and subtheme finding its precise place in the large design. Like Ford, Ophuls brings a double perspective to his work: an event is shown in all of its immediate complexity, but also in its historical context. Past actions affect the present. This sense of continuity is the mark of a director who thinks in terms of epochs instead of moments, a sensibility that is seldom apparent in today's movies. In fact, with a few rare exceptions (like Richard Attenborough's forthcoming *A Bridge Too Far*), budgetary restrictions seem to have made the epic extinct among fiction films—only the documentary permits the kind of scale that Ophuls needs in his work. Even so, the money ran out on *Memory and Justice* before Ophuls completed it. The film was rescued at the last minute by New York hip capitalist Max Palevsky, and it will have its Chicago premiere this week at the Art Institute's Film Center, in all of its 278 minutes.

The Memory of Justice studies the postwar Nuremberg Trials, in which the Allied powers put to judgment the 22 surviving leaders of Nazi Germany for war crimes against humanity. Merely documenting the trial would be a mammoth undertaking in itself: the proceedings were filmed, but while Ophuls makes extensive use of the available footage, he supplements the newsreels with his own interviews. The surviving defendants explain their side of things: Admiral Karl Doenitz, head of Hitler's navy, still insists that he was "only following orders" and that he knew nothing of the death camps. Albert Speer takes a more sophisticated tack, weaving between the assertion that he knew little of what was going on and the willingness to accept responsibility for it anyway. A Spandau prison psychologist describes Hermann Goering's behavior during the trial—accused of unimaginable brutalities, he maintained his swagger throughout the hearings, laughing and joking: "Why not? They will hang me anyway." The British, French, and American prosecutors recall their overzealousness, their failure of tactics, the judges' impatience as the trial wore on and on, the evidence mounting to the point where death statistics became meaningless. Telford Taylor, one of the American prosecutors and currently a law professor at Columbia University, speaks about the idealism that he and his colleagues brought to the trial: here, for once, was a chance to hold a government responsible for its actions—a unique event, in some ways, with a strident morality. At Nuremberg, institutionalized evil was to be wiped out, the ethical basis of man governing man was to be restored.

Ophuls continues his investigation. Nuremberg, with all its faults and internal contradictions (no Allied general was to be tried for the bombing of Dresden) clearly accomplished something. But what?

Ophuls interviews Marie-Claude Vaillany Couturier, a survivor of Auschwitz who testified at the trial. Couturier recalls the moment when she left the witness stand and turned to look at those who were responsible for what had happened in the camps. As Ophuls cuts to the newsreel footage of her second confrontation, she describes what she felt—nothing. Could these 22 gray men and women, made slightly ridiculous by the earphones they wore to hear the German translation of the proceedings, contain among them all the evil that had created such a horror? Can these few, sad people bear all the guilt?

Another sequence: Ophuls and his cameraman drive through the German countryside, looking for the home of a woman doctor who had been sentenced at Nuremberg for, among other things, giving gasoline injections to camp inmates. They find the village: the woman has moved away, but the townspeople are still willing to protect her. She was a good doctor, they trusted their children to her. Ophuls tracks the woman to another village; they find her house, the cameraman remaining outside while Ophuls goes to the door with a tape recorder. The bell is answered, Ophuls introduces himself and asks if she will give an interview. From the shadows of the doorway, a pathetic voice comes back: "I am sorry. I am not well."

Whether or not the Nuremberg defendants were "only following orders" or only dimly aware of the consequences of their actions, they seem to make disappointing scapegoats. Jailing them or executing them doesn't wipe out the enormity of the crime, doesn't eradicate the guilt. Nuremberg was morally necessary; it may also have been morally futile.

The circle of complicity widens. Hitler took power legally, resistance was isolated—surely, the German people must share in the responsibility. Ophuls examines the way in which postwar German culture dealt with the Nazi past: censorship during the period of occupation, sublimation afterwards. A sequence filmed at a co-ed sauna in Berlin contrasts the slightly absurd innocence of a group of young skinny-dipping Germans with the confusion they feel about their country's past. Their tax money goes toward paying reparations to Israel—should they feel responsible for what happened before they were born? Some do, some don't.

The first half of *Memory of Justice* is subtitled "Nuremberg and the Germans." The second part, "Nuremberg and Other Places," broadens the issues that Ophuls's investigation of the trial has raised, looking at the American involvement in Vietnam and the French experience in Algeria. Telford Taylor provides the narrative link—the former Nuremberg prosecutor visited Hanoi as an observer and saw the bombed-out hospitals, the attacks concentrated on population centers instead of the industrial outskirts. Taylor describes, in calm, reasoned tones, his realization that the principles of justice established at Nuremberg had been betrayed by his own country, that crimes against humanity were going unpunished and even unreported. Anthony Herbert, a career Army officer cashiered for talking about Vietnam atrocities, testifies that the American soldier had as little choice as the German in "following orders." The parents of a GI killed in action recount how they came to understand that their son had died for nothing, for even worse than nothing.

Should all Americans who didn't resist Vietnam share in the guilt of the Germans who didn't resist the Nazis? If everyone is guilty, then everyone is innocent, and there is no justice in that. Ophuls explains the title of his film with a few printed words at the beginning—"the memory of justice" is a reference to Plato's idea that ideal justice exists in an ideal world, but that in our imperfect world, all we have for guidance is the memory of the ideal. The memory of justice, the memory of Nuremberg, can't deal with an evil that remains beyond the individual—an evil of the twentieth century.

None of the reviews I read quite prepared me for the experience of this film; I doubt that this one will do for you. Running over four and a half hours (the Film Center is thoughtfully providing an intermission), *The Memory of Justice* is demanding and exhausting. Information accumulates and ideas are produced at a dizzying pace; Ophuls expects the viewer to do his own work in evaluating the material. Conclusions are reached only to be undermined, ideas that seem sound in one context are taken out and examined in another. The film is, in a sense, deliberately confusing—Ophuls has abandoned the customary voice-of-God tone of the documentarist; he is no more possessed of the "truth" than anyone else. There's no false objectivity or intellectual detachment in his method; the film is a personal quest for understanding, a point that Ophuls clarifies by including scenes that reveal his private reasons for undertaking the project (his wife was born and raised in Nazi Germany, while his father, the great director Max Ophuls, was the victim of Nazi persecution).

If *The Memory of Justice* were merely a mass of contradictions, it would be a dull, frustrating film. But Ophuls has organized the material with such skill that the momentum is never lost, not even in the depths of his most obscure digressions. The montage reminded me of nothing more than D. W. Griffith's *Intolerance*: where Griffith rhythmically joins and separates his four narrative strands, Ophuls orchestrates ideas on a similar level. Sequences develop to independent climaxes, interviews play in counterpoint to other interviews and newsreel footage, everything finally spinning together for the conclusion—which is, notably enough, that there is no conclusion. The film opens and closes with the music of Yehudi Menuhin, a man who was, as a gypsy, a target of Nazi genocide. Yet he and his art endure, a sign of hope in the face of the horror the film has presented. *The Memory of Justice* is as full of compassion as it is of outrage; that a film like this can be made is a testament, like Menuhin's music, to the possibility of twentieth-century man's essential humanity.

Allegro non troppo

Directed by BRUNO BOZZETTO {July 29, 1977}

A year ago, who would have thought that the animated film would be making such a spectacular comeback in 1977? For all practical purposes, animation is a lost art, too expensive to survive the shrunken film market of the 70s. But first we had Richard William's engagingly ambitious *Raggedy Ann and Andy*, and then Ralph Bakshi's self-defeatingly ambitious *Wizards*. Walt Disney bounced back after a serious slump with the lovingly crafted *Rescuers*, the richest and best designed film to come from that studio in more than a decade. Later this year, we're promised Bakshi's long-delayed *Hey, Good Lookin'*, and (incidentally) another of Bill Melendez's discount *Peanuts* projects, *Race for Your Life, Charlie Brown*. This week, the Biograph Theater is showing a film that may be the best of the lot: Bruno Bozzetto's *Allegro non troppo*, an Italian production that combines the impeccable craftsmanship of a Disney film with a freedom of imagination that surpasses even Bakshi's highest flights. This is a dying art?

Disney's finest product, *Fantasia*, is currently enshrined at the Carnegie, where it is being shown in its original aspect ratio (without the top and bottom of the image cut off, as so often happens when an older film is carelessly projected onto today's wider screens) and with the stereo soundtrack prepared for its initial 1940 engagements restored. A trip from Carnegie to the Biograph tells the story of animation over the last 30 years. *Allegro* is both a parody of and a *homage* to *Fantasia*, following Disney's classical music format through six animated segments linked by live-action footage. Instead of Leopold Stokowski and the Philadelphia Symphony Orchestra, Bozzetto provides a band of little old ladies in the grips of senile dementia led by a blimpish Italian maestro (don't worry, the actual recordings were provided by Deutsche Grammophon). In the prologue, the Artist, a freakish Bozzetto look-alike, is led in chains from his dungeon cell and deposited in front of a drawing board, where he's ordered to draw as the musicians play. All of this is a sly reference to the actual working conditions at the Disney studios in the 40s, the days when Walt financed his spectacular leaps of imagination by ruthlessly exploiting his staff. A bitter strike broke out during the filming of *Pinocchio*; fatherly Walt responded to his employees' demands for a living wage by firing everyone and closing down production for months. But Disney's unscrupulous labor practices were responsible for making *Fantasia* the masterpiece it is—the film could never have been made if every animator and assistant had been getting his fair share; costs would have gone through the roof.

The naturalistic style that Disney brought to its apotheosis in *Fantasia* required painstaking detail work. Every figure was rounded and shaded, every movement was drawn to the slightest nuance. When a group of disgruntled Disney employees broke off to form their own company, UPA, they had to discover a new style to suit the restricted budget of independent production. Through a series of shorts—the fondly remembered Gerald McBoing-Boings and early Mr. Magoos—the UPA artists evolved a technique of "limited animation": figures were reduced to simple line drawings, depth was taken out of the backgrounds, and the "in-betweens"—the individual drawings that carried a character from pose to pose—were cut back, creating a rougher, more stylized kind of movement. Essentially, this is the style that prevails today—it's economical, and, in the right hands, it can be just as impressive as Disney's full-bodied technique.

Allegro is done in limited animation, although in this case "limited" seems like a completely inappropriate word. Unburdened by Disney's naturalistic bias, Bozzetto exploits the unreality of his animation: figures and backgrounds are in constant flux, changing shapes and colors with happy abandon. Bozzetto's most direct challenge to Disney is his "creation" sequence danced to Ravel's "Bolero," a parallel to *Fantasia*'s "Rite of Spring." Disney begins with a narrator solemnly promising a "scientifically accurate" reconstruction of the earth's first few million years, and, sure enough, the sequence starts with a few fireballs lifted from Genesis and gradually assembles a parade of molecules, amoebas, lizards, birds, and dinosaurs, all struggling through a series of natural catastrophes. "The Rite of Spring" is relentlessly realistic—you can almost see the animators paging through the illustrations in the *Encyclopaedia Britannica* as they draft every detail of the tyrannosaur. It remains earthbound, banal, and—apart from a few impressive rhythmic effects—utterly unmoving. Admittedly, "The Rite of Spring" (along with the cloying "Symphonie Pastorale") is one of *Fantasia*'s weakest sequences, but Bozzetto's version is superior on every count. His "re-creation" begins with the fermenting slime in the bottom of a Coke bottle left behind by a fleeing space ship. A bubbling, amorphous creature climbs out of the bottle neck, tentatively extending an eye, a leg, scurrying across rock formations, reproducing and evolving itself, becoming first one reptilian creature, then two, then a predator, then a victim, eventually multiplying into a parade of eccentric dinosaurs stumbling through the ages of the earth. The march of time ends when the dinosaurs encounter a superhighway stretching across the desert. Crossing it, they enter a city that quickly snuffs them out, a city ruled by an ape.

"Bolero" is Bozzetto at his finest, covering the screen with shifting, brilliant colors given depth and fluid form by his constantly metamorphosing characters. The cold note of satire at its ending is characteristic of Bozzetto's tone—most of the sequences in *Allegro* begin with a lyrical innocence and build to the inevitable destruction of that innocence by an unwelcome intrusion of the modern world. Like Disney, Bozzetto is occasionally prone to whimsy for its own sake, but his animation carries an undercurrent of intelligence that prevents it from ever becoming merely "cute."

Which is not to say, either, that *Allegro* contains a moment of unjustified pretension. Bozzetto seems afraid of taking himself too seriously. A sequence built around Sibelius's "Valse Triste"—a starving cat wanders through the ruins of an abandoned building, remembering it as it was when he lived there—comes as close to genuine pathos as anything I've seen in a cartoon, but as soon as it's over, Bozzetto self-mockingly cuts to the old ladies of the orchestra, sobbing obscenely and tossing their handkerchiefs to the artist's feet in tribute to his "sensitivity."

Bozzetto is the author of two other animated features, neither of which has been shown in the U.S., and is at work on a fourth. But even if the rest of Bozzetto's work never reaches this country, *Allegro* alone can provide the best evidence that animation is still a vital and important factor in film. *Allegro* is articulate, intelligent, moving, and funny—qualities rare enough in the cinema of fresh blood.

The American Friend

Directed by WIM WENDERS {April 14, 1978}

When Wim Wenders's *The American Friend* opens tonight at the Cinema, it will be the first film of the German New Wave to be given the honor of a commercial premiere in Chicago. That's a rather sad fact, since the German New Wave, through the films of Wenders, Werner Herzog, and Rainer Werner Fassbinder, has been pounding on the breakers for nearly ten years now. Still, for those who frequent only commercial movie theaters, the movement remains an unknown quantity. The fault lies less with the relative difficulty of the films than it does with the arch-conservatism of Chicago's "art" audience, which, it seems, will always prefer a second-rate Bergman or a predictable French sex farce to taking a chance on something new, different, and challenging. But now that *Time* magazine, in an article on the German cinema that appeared a few weeks back, has officially certified the movement as legitimate, the time might be right to open the floodgates. I can't think of a better movie to introduce the pleasures of the new German film than *The American Friend*: it's as enjoyable as a thriller as it is moving and accomplished as a work of art.

Wenders scripted *The American Friend* from a novel by Patricia Highsmith, whose first book, *Strangers on a Train*, became the basis of one of Alfred Hitchcock's most famous films. Like *Strangers*, this story concerns two men who meet by chance and end by sharing a murder. But the resemblance to Hitchcock—apart from a stunning evocation of his style in a train-board killing—ends there. *The American Friend* is no idle imitation of Hitchcock, in the manner of a Brian De Palma, but a film that uses the materials of a Hitchcock thriller—and beyond it, the American film—to create a vision that belongs entirely to its director.

The American Friend carries a dedication to Henri Langlois, the late director of the Cinémathèque Française, where, as an art student in Paris, Wenders discovered the American cinema. In a sense, American movies are "the American friend"—they brought Wenders something, as he said recently, that he couldn't find in the moribund cinema of his own country. As practiced by two directors who make cameo appearances in *The American Friend*, Samuel Fuller and Nicholas Ray, the American movie has a power and directness that European films rarely found—a sense of pushing life to its physical and emotional limits, a sense of danger and its fatal attractiveness. But Wenders remains very much a man caught between two cultures, unwilling to abandon the security and tradition of the Old World, unable to resist the risk and violence of the new. A character in his *Kings of the Road* observes glumly, "The Americans are colonizing our subconscious," but Wenders's films continue to display a delight in the by-products of that colonization: rock music, pinball, pool tables, Polaroid cameras, the toys of a destructive but alluring society.

Wenders's characters, consequently, are at home neither in America nor Europe. Genuinely rootless, they're always on the road—journeys provide the structure of *The Goalie's Anxiety at the Penalty Kick* (1971), *Alice in the Cities* (1974), *False Movement* (1975), *Kings of the Road* (1976), and, in a different, more elliptical sense, *The American Friend*. The films show a fascination with means of transportation—cars, boats, subways, trains. But significantly, airplanes hold no magic for Wenders: an integral part of the journey is the movement through a landscape, the brief contact with people, places, and things. Destinations are unimportant and largely arbitrary. The eternal trip becomes a search for someplace to belong. In *Alice in the Cities*, it's a search for a literal home, as a reporter criss-crosses Europe trying to find the grandparents of a little girl he unwillingly has been entrusted with. But for the heroes of *False Movement* and *Kings of the Road*, the goal remains vague and undefined, a sense of self, perhaps, or of a simple, constant value. A bitter, poignant sense of moral nostalgia pervades Wenders's work: the films begin with the premise that something important has gone out of the world, that some fundamental principle or quality that once made life livable has been lost, to be replaced only by the bonds of commercialism that are the darkest aspect of American culture. The feelings of loss are all the more disturbing for never being defined; Wenders can only offer metaphors, the most telling of which may be the "death of cinema" theme that runs through *Kings of the Road*. The search, of course, never ends: the films build to anti-climaxes, as the characters run out of time, space, or faith. The one note of optimism that Wenders permits is sounded in the tenuous emotional connections his searchers make along the way. Two people become friends, then part.

The two people of *The American Friend* are Tom Ripley (Dennis Hopper), an American involved in a black market in art, and Jonathan Zimmermann (Bruno Ganz), a Hamburg frame-maker who is slowly dying from a blood disease. Ripley learns of Zimmermann's illness accidentally, and—perhaps maliciously, for Zimmermann has insulted him at their first meeting—suggests him as a possible hit man to a French gangster (Gérard Blain) who is looking to eliminate some of his competition. At first outraged by the suggestion, Zimmermann is convinced, by means of a false medical report, that this will be his last chance to earn some money to pass on to his wife and child. Persuaded, he nervously executes his anonymous victim in a Paris Métro station—an impressive set piece rousingly directed in the style of Fritz Lang, as Zimmermann hesitatingly tracks his prey through a maze of spatially abstracted staircases and open platforms. But his employer demands another job, and Zimmermann, more fearful but somehow seduced by his experience, travels to Munich to meet his target on a train. This time, the killing goes badly—death is slow and clumsy, and Zimmermann is saved only by the unexpected appearance of Ripley, who has become his friend, and now, his accomplice.

The plot, laid out baldly, gives only a thin impression of the film itself. For one thing, Wenders has systematically eliminated most of the purely expository scenes (purposefully, after shooting them). The story moves murkily, and by inference. We never learn how deeply Ripley is involved with the French gangster, never learn how the rival gangs are connected. Even though things tend to be confusing on the first viewing, Wenders's decision to cut the plot mechanics seems defensible—a lesson in how unimportant narrative details can be in the context of a thriller. The atmosphere and the emotions count more. We already know the story, having seen its variations in a hundred films. Wenders is interested instead in the edges of the plot, in its digressions and undertones.

The American Friend takes place in a crumbling nightmare city, New York, Hamburg, and Paris coming together in the montage to form a single metropolis of the mind. In its first few minutes, the film jumps from New York to Hamburg in the blink of a single cut—we find out that an ocean has been bridged only after the fact. Gradually, a key emerges in the color scheme: blue for America, red for Germany. The clash and blending of colors, of cities, of cultures underlies the relationship between Ripley and Zimmermann: two contrasting personalities, from two different worlds, momentarily merge and then separate.

In each other's lives, Ripley and Zimmermann see answers to the anxiety of their own. Ripley, the wanderer, envies Zimmermann's security—his home, his family, his craft, his life, summed up in the image of his workshop, a place of order, quiet, and comfort. But his fatal disease has made Zimmermann acutely aware of the limits of his life, limits that Ripley will destroy by introducing him to an underworld of strange new sensations, of violence, adventure, and freedom.

Ripley and Zimmermann maintain their precarious balance of values for only a brief while before the friendship ends—significantly, amid the vast, empty space of a seashore. They've gone as far as they can, left the world of the cities behind them, and now there's no more room, no more time, and the balance is destroyed. A final cut brings us back across the ocean, to New York, where another man looks out over the water. He is Derwatt (Nicholas Ray), the painter who has been supplying Ripley with canvases to sell in Europe. Derwatt almost seems to hear the distant explosion of the friendship: he watches, and then walks back to the city—a delicately ambiguous image that projects home and resignation.

The Wenders retrospective at the Art Institute's Midwest Film Center, by the way, continues tonight with his 1972 *The Scarlet Letter* and ends next Friday with his first feature film, the 1970 *Summer in the City* (originally subtitled “Dedicated to the Kinks”). I haven’t seen either of them, but I’d recommend them both. Wenders is a more traditional filmmaker than either Herzog or Fassbinder, but with the passing of time and the fading of fads, his work is beginning to seem more solid, more responsible than theirs. Wenders’s is the quietest talent of the group; it may also be the most promising.

Loulou

Directed by MAURICE PIALAT {August 7, 1981}

Content doesn't shock us much anymore: it's hard to think of an atrocity that hasn't appeared in one movie or another, and even a mass-market blockbuster like *Raiders of the Lost Ark* contains enough explicit sadism to have ensured its consignment to men's smokers a decade or two ago. But there's one frontier we still refuse to violate—the frontier of a coherent, "readable" form. When a filmmaker like Jean-Luc Godard or Jean-Marie Straub starts fooling with the logical, temporal progression of the narrative—giving us scenes out of order, or scenes unconnected by the presence of consistent, accessible characters—we're still capable of reacting like a nation of Mrs. Grundys. We feel outraged, irritated, or—in what may be a deeper and even more angry reaction—we feel bored and confused. We feel the film hasn't been made for us, and we reject it out of hand—as much as if it were a novel written in Arabic.

We can accept shock in conventionally structured films because the form—closed, serene, and symmetrical—is always there to reassure us. A movie with a beginning, a middle, and an end tells us that every action has its consequence, that *B* still follows *A*. The ordered form tells us that the world still makes sense, no matter what outrages we've seen within it. One of the most intriguing insights of the French structuralist critics is their contention that all narrative is based on a logical fallacy: the assumption that, because we see event *A* followed by event *B*, *A* has caused *B* to occur. We confuse temporal progression with logical succession, and we do it willingly, naturally, because it offers such a warm, comforting illusion: the illusion of order. The structuralists go on to postulate that our enjoyment of narrative relies on continually putting that order at risk—by threatening chaos, disaster, dissymmetry—and continually pulling it out. We get a giddy thrill from seeing our sense of order in danger, and a profound pleasure from seeing it restored. In the structuralist view, narrative becomes a kind of continuative reassurance: the form itself pulls order, law, out of chaos and anarchy.

In their "open" films, both Godard and Straub retain a sense of intellectual order: their narrative may be full of gaps, contradictions, and dislocations, but the ideas are strong and consistent—the gaps, in some ways, even help to produce them. Maurice Pialat's *Loulou* is an open film in a different, perhaps more dangerous sense: though Pialat, too, has good, strong ideas, they aren't foregrounded. The intellectual order of *Loulou* hangs in a very risky suspension above a disruptive, wide-open narrative, a narrative that takes pains to suppress and even deny the logical links between scenes, and compacts and distorts the time sequence so that even the illusion of temporal causality is threatened. The force behind the disruption of the narrative is a very old and powerful one—sex—and it also attacks most of the other notions of order contained within the world of the film: social (the sense of a lover as "private property"), and interpersonal (in the division of the sexes). Seeing *Loulou* gave me my first clear sense of what the structuralists mean by the untranslatable term *jouissance*—that pleasure beyond pleasure that lies, not in the testing and affirmation of order, but in its ultimate breakdown. *Jouissance* occupies the place where language fails, where words and the ordered thought they make possible cease to apply. For the structuralists, *jouissance* is analogous to the obliteration of death and sexual climax, and you can see their point: where language ends, so do you.

To summarize *Loulou* is already, in a sense, to betray it. Pialat's film moves in rocky, palpable segments; everything in the narrative design conspires against the illusion of smooth, continuous action that a plot summary conjures. Still, the lines of "what happens" are perfectly clear—on a second, if not the first viewing. It's rather as if Pialat had begun with a traditional story—model bourgeois Nelly (Isabelle Huppert) leaves her husband André (Guy Marchand) for thuggish Loulou (Gérard Depardieu)—and then expanded some segments at the expense (often fatal) of others. *Loulou* is a film of moments extracted from a story, rather than the story itself. The moments are presented without transitions and sometimes ordered with deliberate logic: A scene in which Nelly refuses to return to work for André is followed by a scene in which she is shown back in her husband's office, working away. The jump cut between the sequences carries such blunt contradiction that I was sure, for a second, that the projectionist had mixed up the reels—the cut is "shocking" in a very real, very suggestive sense. Pialat forces us to invent the missing "story"—of how Nelly changed her mind, because she needs the money or, perhaps, because she is still attracted to her husband and the kind of life he represents. He takes away the character's explicit motivations—the clear "reasons" that make her comprehensible, readable—and puts an enigma in their place. Nelly's act somehow continues to "make sense" (if only because we see it, and hence believe in it), but her motivations remain mysterious, as if they were too complex, too personal, to be contained in the dramatic structure. Again and again, Pialat reminds the audience of the limitations of film and language; there is a level of complexity and contradictoriness that they cannot represent without imposing a false orderliness upon it.

The incidents of *Loulou* are built around patterns of possession: a husband possesses his wife, a woman possesses her (economically dependent) lover, a boss possesses his employees, the bourgeois possess the underclass, a mother possesses her son, a man possesses a woman's pregnancy. Possession, of course, is also a sexual metaphor (to make love is to "possess sexually"), and Pialat casts all of the possessions in his film in a sexual light (as in the image of the wife as the husband's "employee"). What Nelly discovers with Loulou is, if not quite a sexuality untainted by possession, at least a possessiveness that works both ways: for the first time, she is allowed to "own" a man, both sexually and, to the extent she supports him, economically. This break in the chain of possession itself echoes throughout the film: Nelly is a traitor to her class; she has deliberately violated its structures, its law. New alternatives, previously unthinkable, present themselves: she accompanies Loulou on a warehouse robbery, and her smile of excitement has something sexual in it, too.

Pialat doesn't forget the sense of possession that exists between an author and his characters; he tries to break that down as well. The layout of his narrative, with its gaps and confusions, abandons the omniscience of the traditional narrator—the godlike storyteller who, because he created his characters, knows exactly what's going on in their minds at every minute. Pialat shows something like humility before his characters: he doesn't presume to control them, or even to understand them all the time. And his visual style, which depends on long takes captured with a highly mobile hand-held camera, works to break down the strict divisions of the frame line. The surface of the image, its formal composition, is no longer a barrier between the director and the characters: so strong is the physical force of Pialat's camera as it moves toward, away from, and around his actors that it seems an active participant in the scene, with even some powers of intervention. By using a hand-held camera so extensively and so obtrusively, Pialat suggests that he is on the same level as his characters, that he is observing them, not from above and apart, but from their midst. The author seems almost to share a single physical space with his creations.

And if the author is no longer allowed to possess his characters, neither is the audience. The scenes aren't shaped for our convenience: the actors are working for each other, not for us, and we have to work to understand them. The language of *Loulou* is an informal, highly idiomatic French, and it comes from all directions with the kind of "realistic" density that can only be the product of an elaborate sound mix. The subtitles, which make the most muffled speeches comprehensible, are an interference, though the raggedness of the sound makes Pialat's point: this isn't rhetorical dialogue, addressed to the audience to make dramatic and character points, but speech considered as a sound effect, part of the natural content of the image. And the images can contain anything: even in those scenes that have a single, clear point to make, Pialat's camera is loose enough—fluid enough in its attention—to admit all kinds of apparently extraneous detail, nudges into other stories (such as the couple who keep their garbage piled behind an elegant screen in their living room) that threaten to overwhelm the narrative in front of us.

Near the end of *Loulou*, there is a more or less traditional climax: Nelly has to make a choice (though, characteristically, Pialat presents the choice only after the fact) that will determine her future, and in the results of her decision we can see a final breakthrough—a firm denial of the ordered society she's from, and a movement into a freedom that seems even larger, more dangerous, than Loulou's. But a closed ending here, a firm choice, would mean putting an artificial end on this open movie; Nelly's choice, if it is to be meaningful within the categories the movie has established, must mean that she has escaped order entirely—that she has, in a way, escaped from the movie itself. And so, we last see a drunken Loulou and a supportive Nelly walking down an alley, and Pialat's camera, for once, doesn't follow—it can't. At what seems to be the moment of highest imbalance in the shot—against the rhythm of the scene—Pialat cuts to a black screen. *Loulou* ends where it absolutely has to—when it has reached the limit of what it can show.

Eijanaika

Directed by SHOHEI IMAMURA {February 12, 1982}

Mountainous women wrestle in the nude; a "mountain girl" bites off the head of a snake and, after chewing its fat, spits a stream of fire over an open flame; a pretty girl in a kimono suddenly extends her neck to a height of six to seven feet, the camera rushing upward with her smiling face to catch her tiny giggle of satisfaction when she reaches full length. Welcome to the sideshow of cultural change and ambiguous revolution, as presented by Shohei Imamura in his witty, grotesque, brightly spinning epic of Japan's Edo era, *Eijanaika*.

Though Imamura has been making films since the late 1950s, his reputation wasn't secured in the West until the release of *Vengeance Is Mine* two years ago; with *Eijanaika* following so quickly, Imamura seems clearly established as the most creative filmmaker in Japan today. Next to the willful stasis and curious, cold resignation of Kurosawa's *Kagemusha*, *Eijanaika* places a swirl of action and color; there may not be another director in the world today who can manage so many elements—of design, of theme, of character, of rolling plot structure—on such a large scale, and with such consummate control. Imamura is a political filmmaker—he is interested in the lowest classes of society, in the way they maintain their buzzing vitality despite the weights piled atop them—but he is never a pedant. His imagination glitters, brews; there are enough ideas in *Eijanaika* for half a dozen films, and each is given a full, commanding development.

The title comes from the rallying cry of an 1867 mass movement—which may or may not have been a genuine revolution. The translators render *eijanaika* as "why not?" or, more satisfyingly, as "What the hell?" It is a cry of a dangerous, rock-bottom freedom, of the abrupt realization that traditions are dead, laws arbitrary, society an empty convention. Such was the pass in which the lower classes of Edo (present-day Tokyo) found themselves in the middle of the 19th century, when the local Shogun clans were battling the emperor for control of the country, inflation was spinning out of sight (a running gag in *Eijanaika* is the price of rice—if a character goes away for a day or two, it's tripled by the time he gets back), and the entire culture was reeling under the opening of the country to the West after 200 years of enforced isolation. For the poor, there is nothing left—a condition that makes everything possible. Why not wear costumes, dance in the streets, loot stores, tear down buildings? What the hell?

Though *Eijanaika* is based on historical incident, Imamura doesn't have much interest in historical detail (apparently, he even flaunts his indifference—the film is said to be full of unsettling anachronisms that Japanese audiences perceive immediately). The causes of the conflict between the Shogun clans and the emperor are never given (though we assume they are economic) and there's no real attempt made to keep the two sides politically (or even morally) distinct. Instead, Imamura is interested in the *eijanaika* state of mind, which he clearly believes holds clues to modern Japanese life.

The subject is approached from two directions, in two different narrative styles. From above, Imamura looks at the political machinations—the briberies, broken alliances, and murders that lead to the breakdown of order—in the style of an action-adventure film (the paranoid drive of these passages, with their insanely complicated plotting, suggests the highly stylized samurai films of Hideo Gosha). And from below, Imamura looks at individual experiences—the gradual erosion of certainty in ordinary lives—in a style of richly ironic character comedy. The two styles blend into something quite original: it's as if Buster Keaton were starring in one of Fritz Lang's Dr. Mabuse films.

The carnival of the opening scene becomes Imamura's ruling metaphor and main stage area. It's actually an entire district, spread out along the riverbank near the Ryogoku bridge (which was rebuilt by the Tokyo government especially for Imamura's film). The area is home to Edo's pickpockets, beggars, prostitutes, and slave dealers—a Times Square with everything but the neon—and the head man is Kinzo (Shigeru Tsuyuguchi), who runs crime and the carnival as two branches of the same business. Kinzo, a practical man if ever there was one, is on the payroll of both the shogunate and the emperor's forces; when the two sides simultaneously order him to start a riot at a silk warehouse and protect it from the mob, he gives both orders to his men without a glimmer of contradiction (and they successfully carry out their mission).

The life-as-a-carnival metaphor isn't a new one—Fellini pretty much holds the patent for movies—but Imamura manages some fresh effects. This carnival isn't the whimsical playground of illusions of the Fellini films: it's a malignant illusion, an institutionalized fraud, recognized by both the people who run it and the people who pay for admission. Yet the need to believe in something is so strong that the carnival has a positive social function: these dreams may be manufactured and ruthlessly peddled, but they are dreams after all—everybody needs something and not even the show people are exempt. When paper charms begin to float down mysteriously over the carnival—a sign from the sun goddess that she approves of the *eijanaika*—the carnival people pitch in and start distributing their own counterfeits, telling themselves they're helping the gods. The fraud (which was probably started by some showman in the next district anyway) has a divine origin; the gods can be served and money made simultaneously.

Kinzo's mistress is a country girl named Ine (Kaori Momoi), sold to the carnival by her impoverished parents after her husband disappeared in a shipwreck. She's now the star of an attraction titled "Tickle the Goddess," in which members of the audience take turns trying to blow a paper streamer between her flashing legs; she thinks of herself, unshakably, as an artist. But when Genji (Shigeru Izumiya), her missing husband, suddenly pops up (he'd been rescued by an American ship, and spent six years in the U.S.), she isn't sure what to do—return to the U.S. with Genji and start the farm they'd always dreamed of, or stick it out in Edo, where things are getting pretty interesting. Ine is the pivot point between Kinzo's ruthless pragmatism and Genji's moony idealism, and pivot she does, betraying both in turn and in increasingly rapid succession. If there's a crisis in the culture, she's living it, unable to choose among the options suddenly and dizzyingly open to her. And, like the *eijanaika*, she's enjoying the crisis, dancing through it with a smile of calculating naivety.

Ine is also the link between the film's two styles, acting as a willing pawn in Kinzo's political plots and playing a comic heroine in Genji's misadventures. Genji burns with his new knowledge of America and wants to share the dream of freedom with Ine; it won't be complete without her. But every time the dream is within reach, Ine lets him down, turning back within sight of the ship that will take them to America, getting herself kidnapped (and not objecting too much) from the farm Genji has managed to secure in the countryside. Is Genji's freedom—abstract, idealized, and pretty hard work—really preferable to the freedom Kinzo offers in his way, the freedom of money and power? Genji sticks with his plan, with a sober determination that is truly Keatonesque, brushing himself off and grimly starting over every time something explodes. But Genji's adversaries aren't Keaton's inanimate objects and natural forces—they're people, and much less predictable.

The unpredictability that dogs Genji is also the principle of Imamura's narrative line—episodes fire off one another with a lightning crackle, as Imamura puts several plot strands in motion at once and leaps between them, jamming them together and yanking them apart. Kinzo plots schemes involving Genji; the political factions plot schemes involving Kinzo; soon it's impossible to say who is controlling whom. Causes and effects are carefully, exuberantly muddled: the complicated plot soon seems to be roaring along on its own, impelled by some internal energy none of the characters can grasp. Meanwhile, Imamura is multiplying the focal points in his images—bright colors compete with sudden movement, individual faces compete with compelling group compositions for our attention. Imamura seems to be shooting lines of energy across the screen: sometimes he'll exploit the hard, sharp lines of Japanese architecture to give the frame an internal, geometric tension; at other times, he'll create a rhythmic tension between foreground and background actions, a contrast that seems to pull the image apart.

Over the course of its two and a half hours, *Eijanaika* has been gathering energy, storing it up. When the *eijanaika* riots finally arrive, the stored energy bursts forth: it's an interestingly giddy, rushing moment. (And it's a tribute to Imamura's intelligent, offbeat timing that, even though we've expected the riots to serve as the climax of his film, they still arrive unexpectedly, spontaneously.) As the dancing, shouting hordes stream out of the riverside carnival, threatening to cross the Ryogoku bridge into forbidden territory, Imamura allows us to feel the crowd's excitement, its sense of mad freedom—yet, by photographing the river-crossing through space-compacting telephoto lenses, he also traps it, pinning it down in a two-dimensional space where the energy of the crowd loses its thrust, its purpose. Though Kinzo has encouraged the riots for practical, political reasons, they are more than political now. The energy created, exploited, and barely contained by the carnival has slipped out, leveling everything before it. It is an energy without cause and without control, fed equally by greed and ideals, dreams and frauds. The politicians can play with it, but they can't keep it down. The cry of "*Eijanaika!*" is innately human. Vital and monstrous, it sounds through every culture.

Coup de torchon

Directed by BERTRAND TAVERNIER {April 8, 1983}

"Black comedy" is a badly abused term these days—it can mean anything from Mel Brooks's Nazi jokes to the campy horror of the *Texas Chainsaw Massacre* and generally settles on anything that combines slapstick and dead bodies. But black humor in its more elevated sense, as practiced by Swift, Kafka, Waugh, is very rare in the movies; there is Howard Hawks's *Scarface*, Jacques Becker's *Goupi mains rouges*, George Romero's *Dawn of the Dead*, and not much else (though I think I'd add an obscure British film I'm fond of, Dick Clement's *A Severed Head*). Death, violence, and moral corruption aren't just slapstick props in these films, but agonizingly real presences, and their comedy isn't a release from horror but a confrontation with it. Laughter can often be a defense, a way of shunting aside disturbing emotions, of reducing horror to triviality. But in these films, humor and horror exist side by side; they play on the very thin line that separates a laugh from a scream, touching the hysteria common to both. To laugh is to give yourself up to the irrational as much as to scream; it is an irrational, emotional, convulsive response to an irrational situation. The best black humor makes us feel the horror, and if we laugh instead of shudder, it's only because the artist has nudged us that way. The slighter and subtler the nudge the better, and in Bertrand Tavernier's *Coup de torchon*, the nudge is so slight that it's almost imperceptible. Tavernier has placed his film exactly on the dividing line; it demands a deep complexity of response, with its ambiguity filtered from levels of theme to character to style to audience reaction. It's a black comedy of the richest kind: a film that teeters on the edge.

The film is dark and sometimes despairing, yet it's a surprisingly warm movie. If there's one characteristic that runs through the stylistic diversity of Tavernier's work, it's his closeness to his characters; he takes an evident delight in observing the patterns and quirks of their behavior from up close, never allowing his visual ideas (which range from the high baroque of *The Judge and the Assassin* and *Death Watch* to the classic simplicity of *Spoiled Children*) to come between them and the audience. And Tavernier prefers a certain kind of actor—best represented by Philippe Noiret, who has appeared in five of his films—that hasn't been seen much lately: a classical, open-faced kind of actor, who declines the Method priorities of "being" in favor of a more theatrical "showing," a concentration on an absolute clarity of gesture and diction, more directly addressed to the audience. In *Coup de torchon*, Noiret is Lucien Cordier, the cowardly, corrupt, hopelessly ineffectual police chief of Bourkassa, a small village in the colonial French West Africa of 1938. Huguette, Cordier's wife (Stéphane Audran), is carrying on a barely concealed affair with her live-in boyfriend, Nono (French pop singer Eddy Mitchell); she tells Cordier he's her brother, and she might be telling the truth. Cordier has a mistress, Rose (Isabelle Huppert, in a very lively, funny performance), but when he hears her husband beating her in the street, he can hardly stir himself to have a look. But his real problem is Le Peron, the local pimp (Jean-Pierre Marielle), who has bribed Cordier so many times that he has a line of credit; Le Peron insults Cordier constantly and shoves him around, while Cordier meekly puts each new offense on the tab. But when Cordier finds Le Peron and his sidekick engaged in a new kind of sport—taking target practice on the bodies of plague victims cast into the river—it is, finally, too much. He takes the bribe but travels to district headquarters to ask his superior, Chavasson (Guy Marchand), what to do. Chavasson's advice is to kick them back twice as hard as they kicked him. It's good advice: Cordier returns to town and murders both men in cold blood.

Tavernier doesn't signal any obvious change in Cordier's character: he's still the same affable, easygoing loser after the murders as before (which is why, in part, he's able to get away with it). But something has changed deep inside: Cordier's sense of right and wrong, dormant for so long in this sun-baked climate, has been revived. Suddenly, he feels the need to act morally—to do something decisive to redeem the debased world around him—yet if the need is clear the methods are not. Most of Tavernier's films are built around one of two basic situations—passive, observant characters who are brought to realize the need for action (*The Clockmaker*, *Death Watch*, *Spoiled Children*), or characters who are already in a position of power but are struck by the suspicion that their actions are useless, their methods immoral, or their goals unclear (*Let Joy Reign Supreme*, *The Judge and the Assassin*, *A Week's Vacation*). *Coup de torchon* combines these two plots: Cordier's moral awakening is followed by a moral paralysis, the crippling generalization that doing right entails a great deal of doing wrong. Cordier's first killing has a social justification behind its personal motivation—he has murdered two men who have humiliated him, but he has also rid the town of two thugs. The second killing—the execution of his mistress's brutish husband—has a greater element of personal satisfaction; by the end, he is killing only to cover his own tracks.

Throughout the film, Noiret's performance is so rumpled, relaxed, and witty—there aren't many actors as instantly likeable as he is—that it becomes harder and harder to reconcile the character with his acts. A kind of shadow character emerges behind Noiret, a different Cordier who is haunted by black thoughts and deep despair, and who may have been driven mad by those thoughts. This other Cordier, as morbidly romantic as a figure out of Poe, appears only rarely; it's a tribute to Tavernier's skills as a rhetorician that he emerges as clearly as he does, defined only by the implications of fleeting acts and fleeting expressions. It's as if the film had two fully developed protagonists, both inhabiting the same body, and it's impossible to tell from moment to moment which Cordier is on the screen. By splitting his protagonist, Tavernier deliberately knocks his film off-kilter. There's no moral center (either positive or negative) for the audience to focus on, no reliable point of view that the audience can simply share. Even the images fail to provide stability and certainty: instead of using balanced, formal compositions and the traditional logic of angle, reverse-angle editing, Tavernier covers many of his scenes in single long takes filmed with a hand-held camera. This isn't the jittery, ragged hand-held familiar from documentaries and the old Warhol films, but an eerily elegant, free-floating effect made possible by the new gyroscopic Steadicam mounts. It's unusual to see a filmmaker so readily turning new technology to personal, expressive ends, rather than simply using it to punch up his style; the Steadicam here is used to describe a world in constant flux, in which the always evolving, unbordered image is no easier to pin down than the moral certainties of the plot. The Steadicam does provide a point of view, but it is a profoundly fluid, slippery one. Nothing in this world is anchored, not even the camera.

Coup de torchon is based on *Pop. 1280*, a novel of the neglected American writer Jim Thompson (the book, unfortunately, has long been out of print). Thompson's novel was set in the deep south, but Tavernier's transfer of the action to colonial Africa preserves the setting in its essentials, and possibly adds some new themes (the setting is further unsettled by the approaching war with Germany). The fundamental division in this world is, of course, the division of race; once the majority of the population has been defined as nonhuman (Cordier and his police superior have a long argument over the differences between blacks and cows), morality no longer exists—you can't commit a crime against an animal. Bourkassa, as designed by veteran set decorator Alexandre Trauner (his career goes back to *The Children of Paradise* and beyond) and photographed by Pierre William Glenn, is a village of glaring primary colors, madly jumbled together. The only visual constant is the yellow heat of the sun, which blends with the dry, yellowed earth. Everything seems to run backward here—the river isn't a source of life, but a cemetery—and many of the gags hang on this scene of reversal. In a movie seen from behind a bed-sheet screen, an officer crisply salutes with his left hand; a priest, replacing a termite-worn cross, enthusiastically recrucifies a statue of Jesus by nailing him to a new mount. When the twin brother of the murdered pimp shows up in town, no one seems very surprised: dead men are regular visitors in this neighborhood. Is Cordier really reacting against this upside-down world, or is he just another product of it? In this inverted context, it seems only natural that the town coward is also the local hero—that cravenness is courage and spinelessness is strength.

Tavernier is often attracted to didactic formats (sometimes literally—the heroine of *A Week's Vacation* is a schoolteacher, and teachers appear in both *Spoiled Children* and *Coup de torchon*), yet he always ends by subverting them: teachers and pupils exchange roles, or the lesson turns out to be that there isn't any lesson. Didacticism is a closed form, but Tavernier's content is open—he's the enemy of pat conclusions, final judgments. When he applies a closed form to an open thematic, the form inevitably snaps, and that snap—the spillover of unresolvable problems, unanswerable questions—is nowhere more satisfying in his work than in *Coup de torchon*. During the film's last half hour, the violence contained in Cordier breaks out, infecting the other characters, and the narrative breaks down, fragmenting into shorter scenes and harsher transitions. The sanitizing operation implied by the title (it translates literally as "stroke of the towel"—wiping up) has left more grime than before. Yet it is still too simple to say that violence inevitably fails and that nothing can be done about the evil in the world. Cordier has unquestionably accomplished some good through his actions, and in a way they have purified him. He is a better man at the end of the film, more aware, more compassionate, more involved. He's a monster with a lofty soul.

City of Pirates

Directed by RAUL RUIZ {January 25, 1985}

I read in the papers that we're living in a great period of fantasy films, made possible by the tremendous breakthroughs in special effects technology and the soaring imaginations of a new generation of American filmmakers. But scratch a *Star Wars* or a *Close Encounters* and what you find is the same old realism: a linear, cause-and-effect story line, characters defined by perfectly conventional psychologies, a visual style still based on the Renaissance norms of "natural" perspective. In their story-telling techniques, these films couldn't be more naturalistic; the fantastic intrudes only at the level of content, in the more or less standardized form of slobbering monsters, super-powered heroes, and sleek spaceships. If this is fantasy, it looks awfully familiar.

The only real maker of fantasy films I know of is the Chilean-born director Raul Ruiz, who now lives in France as a political exile and makes his movies in a bewildering number of countries and languages. He makes them quickly, too—an average of two or three features a year, plus half a dozen short films and documentaries. Though Ruiz's films are full of ghosts and mysterious happenings (all executed, charmingly and effectively, through essentially the same range of camera tricks that Georges Méliès invented at the turn of the century), what makes them fantastic isn't their content, but their style. His fantasies take off from the narrative conventions that most filmmakers (and audiences) accept instinctively. Where a Spielberg will ask, "What would happen if a spacemen came to earth?" Ruiz's "what ifs" are predicated on forms; they are at once more bold, more fundamental to the medium, and more elusive. There is a moment in *City of Pirates*, a 1983 Ruiz feature that will have its American premiere this weekend at the Film Center, when a character complains of a toothache. As he points out the afflicted area, the camera moves to a position inside his mouth, shooting out from between his open jaws. The shot is a joke on the Hollywood convention of impossible camera angles, the archetypal example being the camera that peers out at a pair of lovers from within the depths of a fireplace. This kind of shot is disturbing, even in its cliché form, because of the attention it draws to the bulk—the physical fact—of the camera. In a conventional realist style, the fact of the camera is always hidden; we are not supposed to feel it there, but to identify its point of view with a sort of free-floating omnipotence—a mysterious, unseen, almost godlike presence. The fireplace shot violates a taboo: it points to the profane physicality of the sacred object that is the camera by denying it too ostentatiously. Obviously, the camera could not be where it is if this were a real fireplace and the actors were real people. The shot comes dangerously close to overturning the naturalistic code of narration that the Hollywood cinema is built on, but for some reason we accept it—perhaps because the space the camera is violating is only a physical space. Ruiz's shot is shocking—and shockingly funny—because it violates a spiritual, psychological space: the space of the human head, where the mind and the soul are supposed to reside. *The Exorcist* notwithstanding, Ruiz's shot is the most vivid image of possession I've ever encountered. A foreign presence is, very literally, occupying a human body, and in the act of penetrating the flesh, the camera is transformed from benign, invisible sprite to rampaging demon. The shot is a throwaway, over in a second. But as the story unfolds, we encounter other possessed characters: two policemen who can swap spirits (and voices) by kissing each other on the cheek, a man living alone on a rocky island who is occupied by the half dozen different personalities of his mysteriously missing family.

A whole series of transformations is involved here, and the way in which it progresses is a vivid illustration of the workings of Ruiz's imagination. A narrative event (the toothache) produces a formal event (the shot). The shot is then analyzed for the story elements it might contain, producing the idea of possession. Finally, the theme of possession is incorporated into the overall narrative, producing a plot—a plot of which the toothache is a part. This interpenetration of form and content—this endless circulation, really, of form into story into form into story—is the basis of Ruiz's cinema. As nonlinear as his narratives are, they unfold smoothly and continuously—and, in a sense, coherently—because they are bound together by this underlying network of transformations and associations. One constant image of Ruiz's films is the sea, and *City of Pirates* begins with the image of an ocean that at once seems to be rolling out and rolling in. Ruiz's work intimates the shape of the sea: always shifting, always changing, yet restricted to definite boundaries. The boundaries give the work its finesse, its definition: it isn't just a flow of images, but a directed flow. The challenge in Ruiz is finding where those boundaries lie; his films are games we play by trying to discover the rules.

What is *City of Pirates* about? It's easier, and perhaps more to the point, to define the range of its references. Where *The Hypothesis of the Stolen Painting* drew on art history, television documentary, and Rosicrucianism, and where *The Three Crowns of the Sailor* confounded sea tales, Orson Welles, and Jorge Luis Borges, *City of Pirates* alludes to the avant-garde of the 20s, Victorian children's stories, and Hammer horror movies. The heroine (dark, deep-voiced Anna Alvaro) is named Isidore, in homage to Isadora Duncan; she lives by the side of the sea with her adoptive mother and father, exiles from some unnamed Latin country who spend their time on the high 20s pursuit of spiritualism, trying to contact their dead son. Their beach house evokes the chateau of Dulac's *The Seashell and the Clergyman*, and the rocky coast of the pirate island recalls the prologue of Buñuel's *L'Age d'or*.

The surrealist background requires a surrealist heroine, and Ruiz summons the ultimate exemplar, turning Isidore into a slightly overgrown Alice in Wonderland who confronts the astonishing events around her with girlish aplomb. But a streak of dawning adolescent seriousness in Isidore also evokes the Wendy of Barrie's *Peter Pan*—and so Ruiz produces pirates (who are never seen, but fight their battles in the form of flowers in an allegorical garden) and a boy who can never grow up. The boy, Malo (Melvil Poupaud), appears in Isidore's bedroom after a séance. He may be the ghost of the dead son, but he claims to have no parents; Isidore later reads an account in a yellowing newspaper of an entire family that was raped and massacred and concludes that Malo is the family's missing son—and apparently, the perpetrator of the crime.

Malo slits the throat of Isidore's father while he is sleeping and takes the girl off to Pirate Island. Malo mysteriously vanishes, and Isidore is taken prisoner by Tobi (Hugues Quester), a well-mannered young man who lives alone in a castle and speaks in the voices of his unseen family. Tobi might be a grown-up Malo (has he murdered his family and taken on their personalities like Norman Bates in *Psycho*?), he may be a ghost or a vampire waiting for victims in his crumbling castle, or he may be the romantically haunted hero of a gothic novel—Heathcliff of *Wuthering Heights* or Maximilian De Winter of *Rebecca*. Isidore eventually escapes and is reunited with Malo, who urges her to return to kill her captor. Malo vanishes again, and Isidore finds that she is pregnant.

What does it all mean? For French critic Alain Masson, the plot is a progressive pun on the words *mère-mer-mort-mords*: "mother-sea-death-bites." It's possible to decode some political implications (the theme of exile, common to all Ruiz films, plus a portrait of dictatorship in the film's many domineering males), and there's also a psychological level—the film is about the individual's need to define himself through his family, and the conflicting need to escape it. But I think that what matters for Ruiz is the beautiful blurrings of sense that his story creates. Each image is the product of so many different associations and connections that it becomes, in a way, unmoored. The overburdened images overwhelm their referents and float free. Losing their centeredness, their core of meaning, the images are liberated from the system of language; they no longer occupy fixed positions in a hierarchy of meaning, but are free to signify everything and nothing. This, too, is a surrealist project (more than once in *City of Pirates* I was reminded of the stream of false symbols—a giraffe, a priest, a burning Christmas tree—that are thrown from a window in *L'Age d'or*), but Ruiz doesn't share the surrealists' taste for the purely arbitrary. It is almost always possible to retrace the routes through which Ruiz arrives at his images (and maps, too, are a visual constant of his films). His work is not just a system—of narration, of language—reduced to chaos, but the spectacle of one system (Ruiz's system of imagining) devouring another (language's system of signifying). One order replaces another: it is revolution, not anarchy.

Ruiz's visual style, strongly influenced by Orson Welles, continues the process of decentering on another level—literally, because Ruiz's compositions, with their multiple, conflicting points of interest, have no center. Plays of mirrors and shadows make an actor occupy two or three different positions within a single shot; an exaggerated depth of field (a pair of feet loom monstrously in the foreground, while the actor's face appears, seemingly a football field away, in the distant background) forces our attention from the spatial center of a shot to the extremes of the far and near. The shallow, centered compositions favored by television and most of today's movies make the viewer feel at ease, at home; they tell us just where we stand in an ordered, stable world. Ruiz's images shake our security. It is impossible to extrapolate a single, definite point of view from them: they seem to demand that we look everywhere at once, be everywhere at once.

Ruiz's morbid themes and his destabilizing style ought to add up to some profoundly dispiriting work. That they don't—and that his films are, in fact, entertaining and often exhilarating—is due to the spirit of playfulness, of fantasy and invention, he always keeps in the foreground. The pastiche Hollywood scores provided by his regular composer, Jorge Arriagada, are full of soaring sentiments and galloping melodrama. They promise extravagant climaxes and tumultuous passions—it's music that wouldn't seem out of place in a Republic serial. But even if those passions and climaxes never quite materialize, there is something in the quality of Ruiz's imagination that summons up those primal Hollywood pleasures, something that connects to our first film-going experiences, when we weren't old enough to follow the plots and still too young to care. Lucas and Spielberg pursue these same memories in their films, but they're too literal minded, too committed to realism, to really revive them. Ruiz, the real fantasist, flushes them out.

[PART 4]

Revivals and Retrospectives

I relished the opportunities my years at the Reader *gave me to cover revivals of older films and retrospectives devoted to individual directors. This was a moment when the first major restorations of classic films were emerging from the archives, allowing us to see familiar titles with their original visual qualities intact and often with missing footage returned, and new subtitling initiatives made many important works from Europe and Asia available to English-speaking audiences for the first time.*

The Story of the Last Chrysanthemums

Directed by KENJI MIZOGUCHI {September 23, 1977}

Learning to watch a Kenji Mizoguchi film is hard work. The cards are stacked against you from the start: his movies are often tightly bound to areas of Japanese culture—the geisha, the Kabuki, the samurai—that Western audiences know little about. Superficially, his films seem stately to the point of stasis. For the filmgoer who's used to the constant climaxes of American movies, very little seems to be happening as Mizoguchi leads his characters through the long and difficult emotional journeys that constitute his plots. The narration is restrained, understated. Often enough, a two-and-a-half-hour film will build to a single, brief moment of release, a sudden burst of insight and power that is over in the length of a shot. The language, too, is always a problem—there is something sweetly soporific about the Japanese tongue, and the subtleties of the dialogue are inevitably lost in the subtitles, which a Japanese friend once assured me were hopelessly and consistently inadequate.

It's hard work, but learning to watch a Kenji Mizoguchi film affords one of the great pleasures of the cinema. Like Robert Bresson, Roberto Rossellini, and his countryman Yasujiro Ozu, Mizoguchi is a director who resists casual interest. He has a language of his own, a language that is often initially difficult to understand. I remember seeing my first Mizoguchi—I was a callow teenager at the time, and *Citizen Kane* had just introduced me to the wonderful world of mise-en-scène. There, in the midst of the standard Truffaut and Godard features that formed the film program at the local junior college, was an enigmatically titled movie by a Japanese director I had never heard of. I went, I saw, and it conquered me. I fought to stay awake (not quite successfully) for the better part of two hours, and I didn't see another Mizoguchi until I was well into college. The film, of course, was *Ugetsu*—the 1953 ghost story that most Western critics regard as Mizoguchi's masterpiece and one of the finest films of all time. After all these years, it's an opinion that I'm finally able to share (although I don't think *Ugetsu* is necessarily his best work). But one part of that original experience has stayed with me. Before a Mizoguchi film, I always try to sneak a cup of coffee. It may not be a substitute for a degree in Japanese Studies, but it helps.

The Story of the Last Chrysanthemums is a 1939 film that will have its Chicago premiere this Thursday (September 29) as part of the Midwest Film Center's ongoing series, "Women in Japanese Cinema." A director with a strong sense of the social boundaries that have always imprisoned Japanese women, and a man with an almost mystical awe for women's emotional resilience, Mizoguchi is a natural choice for the program. But *Last Chrysanthemums* is one of his least explicit "women's films"—although a woman, as always, plays a central part. Set in the late nineteenth/early twentieth century, the film uses the tradition-bound power structure of the Kabuki theater as an image for the greater, more insidious pressures of Japanese society. Mizoguchi, though, isn't manufacturing a simpleminded social tract. An oppressive society is only one manifestation of a greater problem that confronts all of Mizoguchi's characters—an emotional oppression, a spiritual tension that is the product of living in the material world. Society erects a network of confusions, contradictions, and compromises, a barrier to life that Mizoguchi's protagonists try to penetrate by capturing a hint of the eternal through art, duty, or love.

Last Chrysanthemums is the story of Kikunosuke, the spoiled son of a theatrical family and the next in line to inherit his father's name and reputation as a Kabuki actor. But Kikunosuke's acting is undisciplined and unskillful, as he and all around him recognize. No one will criticize the heir apparent to his face; only the family nursemaid, Otoku, has the courage to confront him with the truth.

Taken by her frankness and her faith in him, Kikunosuke falls in love with Otoku—but the strict laws of Japanese society prevent the marriage of an artist/aristocrat to a mere household worker. The family sends her away, but Kikunosuke searches for and finds her. Cut off by his family, Kikunosuke tours the countryside with a traveling, third-rate Kabuki troupe, still struggling to perfect his art, his impatience and frustration soothed by his lover.

The theme of hierarchy is established visually in a breathtaking opening sequence. After an establishing shot of the Kabuki theater, the curtain goes up on a new production, Kikunosuke playing a sadly inadequate second lead to his father. Behind the stage, Mizoguchi's camera explores the multi-level architecture of the playing space and dressing rooms, the tracking shots revealing unexpected drops and open areas between stairwells and rooms. Backstage becomes an image of the patriarchal society's idea of itself—the small, neatly ordered rooms speak of a compartmentalized society, a place for everything and everything in its place, graduating from the dank shadows of the offstage area, where the extras prepare, to the brightly lit and decorated dressing room of the star. Kikunosuke is literally called from the depths to confront his father when the performance is over. In the elevated, shimmering dressing room, he feels grotesquely out of place; he nearly runs down the stairs, the camera panning with him, the moment he is dismissed.

The harsh angularity of Japanese architecture has always been an integral part of Mizoguchi's mise-en-scène. The bare, simple spaces that often seem so secure and comforting in Ozu's films become cells that contain and threaten the characters. The hard, black lines that form the frames of the walls seem to attack the actors, drawing them apart from one another. Large, apparently insignificant objects fill the foreground of many shots, silent but intimidating physical masses that almost challenge a character's right to share a room with them. Mizoguchi often places a doorway in the background of his compositions, but the promise of escape is usually a false one: the restricted space of one room leads off only to more, equally confined areas. Kikunosuke's family mansion becomes a labyrinth of twisting corridors, sudden pockets of darkness, and unexpected partitions.

If the characters are placed in a constant tension with the setting, Mizoguchi's camera does little to ease their pain. Faced with a long dialogue sequence, Mizoguchi will select a single, often oblique angle and place his camera well back from the actors. The scene is played out in a continuous take, with no cross cutting between speakers. The film "space," unviolated by changing camera angles, binds the characters to the décor and to each other. Sometimes the effect is oppressive: the actors seem trapped, unable to break through the emotional reserve of the standoffish camera. They move slowly, if at all, like swimmers in an underwater ballet. At other times, as in the love scenes between Otoku and Kikunosuke, the long take is liberating: we don't feel the frame that steadfastly encloses them as a restriction; it becomes an emblem of unity, emotional bonds. But always, the distant camera remains morally neutral. Without close-ups, no character is given a privileged place in the narrative. Each must be evaluated by his actions, which are always seen in the social context provided by the long shot. The actor's emotional appeal to the audience is consistently denied—we *observe* the characters, we don't identify with them.

Generally, the movement of a Mizoguchi film takes the form of one character's revolt against the social, moral, and spiritual oppression embodied by the mise-en-scène. For Mizoguchi, Japanese life is defined by a set of limits—day-to-day life is a matter of fulfilling prescribed forms, carrying out the dictates of custom and tradition. Only a few have the power to transgress those limits—they become the great soldiers (*Tales of the Taira Clan*), the great artists (*Utamaro and His Five Women*), and the great lovers (*Chikamatsu Monogatari*).

The moment of revolt is also reflected in the mise-en-scène. For Kikunosuke's first serious conversation with Otoku, Mizoguchi chooses his characteristic long shot and long take—but, for once, the camera follows the movement of the characters; it is they who determine the image, not the image that determines them. As they meet on the street and begin to talk, the camera, placed in a ravine below street level, follows them down the road. It's a supremely moving sequence, not because of the expressiveness of the actors (we can hardly make out their faces), but because of the expressive position of Mizoguchi's camera. For the first time, we see Kikunosuke in a low-angle shot: he has gained a certain stature. For the first time, Kikunosuke is allowed to lead the camera: in a sense, he has broken out of the frame, out of the world, and is pursuing his own destiny. The camera movement, a long lateral track, is repeated two more times in the film, when Kikunosuke, separated from Otoku, goes to look for her. The unexpected camera movements, always operating against the context of the static shots that constitute most of the film, are moments of genuine physical release.

Kikunosuke violates social traditions by falling in love with Otoku: he will violate artistic traditions, with her help, by training himself as a Kabuki actor. Otoku is, at once, the source of his inspiration and of his strength. First presented as a nursemaid, with a baby in her arms, she becomes, in a way, Kikunosuke's mother, calming his fears and encouraging his hopes, responsible for his artistic birth.

But Kikunosuke's popular success ultimately depends on regaining the family name; this is one rule of custom that even he cannot violate. Returning to his family, and to the Tokyo stage, means giving up Otoku. At his first comeback performance, Otoku, in a return to the backstage-hierarchy metaphor of the opening sequence, hides *beneath* the stage, where she prays for his success.

A return to the family also means a return to the static camera setups that characterize the restrictions of family life. At a celebration, Kikunosuke sees a relative carving a watermelon, sitting in the same spot in the kitchen, and using the same knife that he had used to cut a melon for Otoku on the night of their first meeting. Kikunosuke says nothing—the meaning of the event is as clear to us as it is to him because Mizoguchi chooses the same camera angle and same lighting used in the first sequence. Kikunosuke's success has cost him everything. Otoku, meanwhile, lies dying in her sister's house in another city.

The emotional climax of *Last Chrysanthemums* comes when Kikunosuke, finally granted grudging permission by his father, rushes to Otoku's bedside. It is his last chance to redeem himself. Climbing out of a carriage, he runs to the door of the house. The shot is an extreme close-up, the tightest in the film, and Kikunosuke seems to be shoving the camera before him in the violence of his haste. The enervating mise-en-scène is broken for one last time, but only for a moment. He can stay with Otoku for only a few minutes; he must return to a boat parade in which he is to be honored. As the ceremonial boat slides past the impassive camera, Kikunosuke standing in the bow and gesturing to his admirers, we know that Otoku has died. He has gained his art, but he has lost his life.

The Flowers of St. Francis

Directed by ROBERTO ROSSELLINI {September 8, 1978}

Masterpieces are supposed to be grim, weighty things, objects of infinite suffering and painful self-denial both for the artist and for the audience. But Roberto Rossellini's *The Flowers of St. Francis*, which will be playing at the Art Institute's Film Center this Friday after a long period of unavailability, is a buoyant, almost airborne masterpiece. It's so simple and so graceful that we seem to discover it almost as the director does, wandering through the hills of Assisi and coming across a group of monks practicing a strange, new religion that apparently consists of scampering across the countryside. There is no anguish, no suffering, no obvious effort in Rossellini's 1950 film: things simply happen, and the camera is there to record them, as openly, as generously, as possible. It's over in 75 minutes, but Rossellini is able to create such a deep sense of continuity, in either side of the narrative, that it seems to go on forever. We glimpse a few privileged moments of a world in process.

The Flowers of St. Francis has been out of distribution in the United States for several years, thanks to the usual haze of copyright and contractual problems. Like many long lost films—Orson Welles's *Othello*, Chaplin's *A Woman of Paris*—*St. Francis* has taken on the aura of a legend, spoken of in hushed, reverent tones as the pinnacle of Rossellini's early career. I don't think it is—I still prefer *Voyage to Italy*—but neither do I think that Rossellini was ever capable of producing anything that was less than genuinely and profoundly fresh (if he ever did, I haven't seen it). Of all the great filmmakers—and he belongs with Ford, Renoir, Hitchcock, Mizoguchi, and Hawks—Rossellini is the most consistently surprising. More than a mere innovator, he is one of the few authentic revolutionaries, never capable of making the same film twice, and never content to leave the art in quite the same state in which he found it. *St. Francis* is no exception: I had been expecting something spare, spiritual, and deeply serious, more on the model of Robert Bresson. *St. Francis* is spare and spiritual, but it owes more to Mack Sennett than anyone else. It describes a religion in which a slip in the mud is as meaningful as a prayer in the woods—it is all experience, a matter of making contact with a God who lives in the earth and the rain as much as he is in the heavens. Francis's followers resemble a spiritual brand of Keystone Cops, attacking everything they do with more enthusiasm than competence, as disarmingly foolish as they are inspired. The most sublimely unbalanced of the monks, Brother Ginepro, never quite gets it through his head that giving away his clothes to every beggar who passes isn't the best way to further his mission. After he returns to camp naked, Francis orders him never to give up his cloak again. But the next night, Ginepro comes back in the buff once more. He met a beggar, he explains, and when he asked for his clothes, he told him he couldn't give them away—but if the beggar accepted his offer to steal them, well, there wasn't much he could do about it.

Brother Ginepro, bouncing through the film with a smile pitched halfway between the idiotic and the celestial, is a far cry from the stone-faced, unsung martyrs scrutinized by Bresson, and, for that matter, from the compulsive rhetoricians invariably sanctified by the Hollywood religious spectaculars. Francis tells Ginepro that he must open all of his sermons with the jingle, "Bo, bo, bo, much I say but little do"—it will be good for his humility—but Ginepro can hardly get that much out. His big apostolic moment comes when he spots a group of farmers working in a field and climbs a wall to deliver his address to the masses. As he begins to speak, he discovers that a nearby waterfall is drowning out his words. No matter. With a nod toward the rushing stream that acknowledges the water's superior spiritual articulation, Ginepro jumps down from his perch to join a group of children playing on a seesaw. Francis tells his flock that actions are more persuasive than words, and his followers are never more expressive than when they run to their work and come home singing, or simply stand in the midst of a mystical union that Rossellini's camera creates between the earth and the sky.

There are no De Mille miracles, or even Bressonian moments of transfiguration. Francis's God is nowhere to be seen, but yet he's everywhere, palpable in the harmony that Rossellini's gliding camera poses between man and the landscape. In Rossellini's hands, Francis's religion comes closer to animism than Catholicism: there is a divine presence behind every rock and tree. As José Luis Guarner points out in his excellent book on Rossellini, *St. Francis* is in part a reaction to the malignant, overpowering landscape of Rossellini's immediately previous film, *Stromboli*. Francis and his followers have struck a mystical, privileged truce with nature; it supports and nurtures them. When Ginepro sets out to find a pig's foot that a sick brother has requested for his cure, he stumbles straight into a family of hogs as if by divine revelation. The pig squeals as he cuts off his foot, but for Ginepro, the screams of pain are the pig's way of praising God—it's happy to be able to serve. Sometimes, the sense of harmony seems almost hallucinatory, the product of a glorious mass delusion. The closest *St. Francis* comes to offering a genuine miracle is when Ginepro trundles off to borrow a large pot from a neighboring group of shepherds. Ginepro returns, running down the hillside, with the gigantic pot bouncing along at his heels like a faithful puppy. The sequence becomes fantastic only through Rossellini's choice of camera angles: it's the point of view that makes a miracle out of a simple physics, and somehow, that implicit observation becomes the key to the entire film. Spirituality is a matter of perspective, of seeing things in the right way—a subject that the movies are uniquely qualified to treat.

Rossellini was the cinema's first great modernist filmmaker to fully break away from the classical narrative pattern of exposition, development, and climax. *The Flowers of St. Francis* begins with the monks' arrival at Assisi and ends with their departure. In between there is no story, but only a series of scenes, each given equal weight in the structure. Partway through the film, the narrative focus switches from Francis to Ginepro, subverting the traditional idea of a single, central hero. Rossellini even interrupts the visual flow with a long sequence, set in the camp of a traveling warlord, that is shot in an entirely different style, emphasizing the close vertical lines of trees and battle towers rather than the wide, rolling curves of Francis's retreat. Through these interruptions, reversals, and deletions, Rossellini opens up an independent world in front of the camera. No design is imposed upon it, no distortions are made for the sake of developing ideas. With no particular thesis to work from, Rossellini is content to stand back and observe, but to observe in an active way, coaxing meanings out of the most trivial of actions. Building a fire is as important as convincing an army to lift a siege—Ginepro does both, but both actions are given the same patient attention, the same narrative value. As Guarner observes, *St. Francis* thus becomes the first historical film to take place in the present tense. There are no abstract historical forces, viewed with the determinism of hindsight, but simply a group of people living their lives according to a rhythm that is true and free.

Born in Germany, Raised in Hollywood: The Film Art of Fritz Lang

{September 1, 1978}

The great body of film literature seems to contain two very different directors named Fritz Lang. In the standard histories, we find Lang riding at the head of the German Expressionist movement, present for the creation of the seminal *The Cabinet of Dr. Caligari* in 1919, and thereafter standing as F. W. Murnau's only serious rival during the German film's richest and most radical decade, the 20s. In a series of crime melodramas (*Dr. Mabuse the Gambler*), Teutonic fantasies (*Die Nibelungen*), and science fiction films (*Metropolis*), Lang documents Expressionist Man's struggle with fate, inventing much of the Expressionist vocabulary of harsh dramatic lighting and highly stylized sets. Then, as it invariably does, sound steps in and destroys the art of the silent film just as it is reaching its peak. Lang is destroyed, along with the Golden Age of cinema, although he is able to realize two sound films of some artistic merit, *M* and *The Testament of Dr. Mabuse*. Thereafter, all is darkness. Forced to leave Germany in 1932, Lang settles at the teat of the bitch goddess Hollywood. He makes one film that shows some signs of his personality, *Fury* (1934), but soon succumbs to the blandishments of crass commercialism, turning out a string of unspeakably vulgar Westerns and thrillers. He is never seen, or heard from, again.

But in the revisionist version, we find Fritz Lang, director of some interesting if rather studied German films, arriving in America and picking up roughly where he left off. Lang embraces the superior technical facilities of the Hollywood studios, finding that the American advances in cinematography and set design allow him to adopt a more naturalistic camera style. Effects that once required bizarrely distorted sets and exotic camera angles can now be produced in subtler ways: through a carefully placed shadow or a discreet camera movement. The faster tempo of American films leads him to streamline the design of his narratives: the ponderousness of many of his German projects is replaced by an unerring sense of what is and what is not essential to the telling of the story, and Lang becomes a master of taut, intense plot construction. As for the vulgar thrillers and Westerns, Lang seems to embrace them, too. After all, what is the myth of *Die Nibelungen* if not the Germanic equivalent of the Frank and Jesse James legend, equipped, perhaps, with slightly more impressive academic credentials? The first *Dr. Mabuse*, on the other hand, indulges in material that many would have thought too pulpy for a Republic serial. Lang's concerns and techniques fit smoothly into the American genres; they even gain something in shape and resonance. And so, far from sandbagging Lang's creative development, Hollywood nurtures his talent, giving it the means to grow in new, more dynamic ways. There are the usual number of commissioned projects and outright failures, but Lang's American films finally amount to one of the most mature, most accomplished, and most valuable bodies of work in the history of the movies.

And also, it should be said, one of the most seriously neglected. As you might have guessed, I prefer the second interpretation of Lang's career to the first: *You Only Live Once*, *Man Hunt*, *Scarlet Street*, *The Big Heat*, and *While the City Sleeps* seem to me superior on every level to the official classics of Lang's German period. They aren't simply slicker films—better acted and better photographed; they are also more thoughtful, more rigorous, and more vivid. Lang himself felt that *While the City Sleeps*, a bitter newspaper drama released to no perceivable critical reaction in 1955, was one of his best efforts, while the perennially revived *Metropolis* was one of his worst. This is one case in which the teller should be trusted above the old tale of commercial corruption and artistic decline. Still, I've encountered more than one film enthusiast who seemed surprised to learn that Lang had ever set foot in Hollywood, much less that he had remained there for more than 20 years. Even today, when the work of Hitchcock, Hawks, and Ford has ceased to be the property of a small group of cultists and has begun to enter the public domain, Lang's American films go unseen and unknown. This Friday (September 1), Facets Multimedia begins an 18-film retrospective of Lang's work, the first of such series to be presented in Chicago in nearly nine years.

Part of the problem may be that Lang's filmography lacks the single, overriding popular success that might give audiences a foothold on his work—as *Psycho* does for Hitchcock, or as *Bringing Up Baby*, in its revivals, does for Hawks. The credits of Lang's films also betray a singular lack of charismatic star power: no John Waynes, no Cary Grants, no James Stewarts. Lang may have begun his American career by bringing Spencer Tracy (*Fury*) and Henry Fonda (*You Only Live Once*) to two of their most memorable performances, but thereafter he was more likely to be saddled with the conspicuous deficiencies of Glenn Ford and Walter Pidgeon. Even so, Lang was able to prod Ford (*The Big Heat*, *Human Desire*) and Pidgeon (*Man Hunt*) to higher flights of expression than they ever achieved elsewhere.

In retrospect, Lang's avoidance of such personalities looks at least partly like a matter of choice. His work doesn't invite the heroic identification engendered by traditional romantic leads—his one film with an unambiguous action hero, *American Guerrilla in the Philippines* with Tyrone Power, is one of his few complete failures. Instead, Lang prefers the lowered profiles of less mythic actors. His most congenial performer was Edward G. Robinson, whom Lang directed in two masterpieces of the 40s,

The Woman in the Window and *Scarlet Street*. Lang is more interested in the fringes of society than in its leaders; the left-behinds, the outcasts, and the losers that lie at the center of his best American films command his profound sympathy, while the conventional heroics of power seem to lie beyond his experience and comprehension.

It wasn't always so. Lang's German films display an almost slavish devotion to the spectacular exploits of their aristocratic heroes, whether their talents are in the service of society (*Die Nibelungen*) or set against it (*Dr. Mabuse*). The shift from superhero to common man, accompanied by a corresponding stylistic shift from Expressionism to naturalism, is the main development in Lang's American career, and it makes all the difference. For all their pictorial splendor, Lang's German films are crippled by their naive subscription to the Expressionist's notion of fate—a faintly bogus metaphysical concept inherited from the Romantics and forced to operate in a technological age that seemed increasingly inhospitable to the supernatural. Like the Romantic poets, Lang's protagonists struggled with destiny, and if they invariably lost, the struggle, at least, was glorious. The notion of fate lingers on in Lang's American films, but it loses most of its awkward trappings. No longer a mysterious, otherworldly force, fate begins to operate on the level of emotion and morality, most effectively through the revenge plots that figure in many of Lang's films from *Fury* onward. The protagonists of *Man Hunt*, *Rancho Notorious*, and *The Big Heat* are driven not by the hooded figures of Doom, but by psychological forces that lie, unsuspected, within them. Character thus becomes destiny, as the avenging heroes set out on monomaniacal missions that ultimately overrun the bounds of their conscious control.

The key moment in most of Lang's American films arrives in the split second when the hero realizes that he has lost control—the point at which, in the classical sense, he ceases to be a hero at all. He is swept up in the action, carried along and finally destroyed by it. On those occasions when Lang (or his studio) felt obligated to insert a happy ending, the resolution of the revenge plot seems glaringly unsatisfactory. The hero has lost his humanity and discovered something darker.

Lang, no less than Hitchcock, carries his Catholic background into the structure of the films. The loss of control is often motivated by a sudden powerful pang of guilt, the recognition of a personal transgression. In *Man Hunt*, Walter Pidgeon finds himself flung into the nightmare world of the Gestapo at the precise moment when he discovers he has the capacity to kill: a British big game hunter stalking Adolph Hitler for "the sport of it," he unthinkingly places a bullet in his unloaded rifle as soon as he achieves his professional goal of simply getting Hitler between the crosshairs of his telescopic sight. Similarily, Glenn Ford begins his war on the corrupt city government of *The Big Heat* when his wife is killed by a bomb that was meant for him; somehow, Ford feels that something he has done led directly to her death. In other films, the transgression is sexual: *Scarlet Street*, *Clash by Night*, and *Human Desire* all begin when the characters step outside the narrow bounds of sexuality that society has set for them. Salvation comes only through suffering, and sometimes it never comes at all.

At their best, Lang's films are wonderfully pure and elemental, an aspect of his work that Andrew Sarris has described as "the cinema of the fable and the philosophical dissertation." The desperate journeys that form many of Lang's narratives sometimes operate on a disarmingly clear allegorical level, profane parallels to a Divine Comedy. Lang tends to linger on the circles of Hell as his characters work their way toward spiritual redemption. Through their suffering—at the hands of the law, the underworld, or their own consciences—Lang's characters are forced to confront and acknowledge their own corruption. The trappings of normality established in the opening scenes of *You Only Live Once* and *The Big Heat* are stripped away, exposing a moral chaos. For a lucky few, the end of the road brings absolution: Henry Fonda is literally transfigured at the climax of *You Only Live Once*; Walter Pidgeon undergoes a symbolic beatification as he bails out from an airplane at the end of *Man Hunt*. In the early American films, the agent of redemption is often a woman—Sylvia Sidney in *Fury* and *You Only Live Once*, Joan Bennett in *Man Hunt*—who saves her guilt-ridden partner through love and personal sacrifice. But, just as most modern audiences have trouble with the apparent sentimentality of the romantic theme, Lang himself seems to sour on it in his later work. By the time of *Beyond a Reasonable Doubt*, his last American film, the moral purity of the heroine is the direct cause of her lover's damnation.

Lang never loses his absolute faith in the eternal pattern of guilt, suffering, and redemption, but as his work develops, he increasingly questions its justice. His sympathy always lies implicitly with his accursed protagonists, no matter what their sin. But by the time the sympathetic child-murderer of *M* reappears in a different incarnation in *While the City Sleeps*, the psychotic killer has become a modern Job, begging his pursuers to capture him because he can no longer bear the ravages of his conscience. The implicit question of Lang's late films is, "How much more?" The characters suffer endlessly, but the heavens are never satisfied. In his last, German-made film, *The Thousand Eyes of Dr. Mabuse*, the moral order of Lang's allegorical universe has been completely inverted. Mabuse, the diabolical tempter of the Expressionist films, now occupies a throne of omniscience and omnipotence, keeping watch over the transgressions of his subjects, the residents of a luxury hotel, by means of TV cameras connected to a subterranean control room.

When Lang abandons the Expressionist style of German films for the greater naturalism of his American work, his films don't necessarily become more "realistic"—at least in the usual sense we give to that painfully imprecise term. His characters and situations remain reasonably abstract: he has no interest in the tics and stutters, confusions and contradictions, that are generally the hallmarks of screen realism. Lang's world is stylized and studio-bound, smoothly engineered for the greatest clarity of expression. But when he casts off the more extreme stylistic effects of the German films—the wild shadows, the grotesque distortion of space—Lang restores the integrity of the frame. The image is no longer violated by obtrusive stylistic overlays; instead, Lang simply positions his camera where it will give the best, most revealing view of the action. Directed by the camera angle, meaning flows from the images, rather than being imposed upon it by its various tricks of montage, lighting, or camera movement. Lang does move his camera, probably more in his American films than in his German work, but his tracks and cranes have little of the metaphysical implications of similar shots in the work of Ophuls and Murnau. When Lang dollies into a scene, he does it to give us a better sense of its physical layout, to bring out the implications of the particular arrangement of actors and objects within it.

Lang studied architecture before he became a filmmaker, and the most important feature of his style remains his use of space. His images have a remarkable compositional depth, but, more importantly, they also have a psychological depth: the actors express themselves most clearly through the positions they occupy relative to the other players and to the set. In *Man Hunt*, for example, a tentative romantic scene between the upper-class hero and the prostitute who has given him refuge in her apartment is played out in almost balletic terms: the characters' initial fear of their social differences, their gradual appreciation of each other's qualities, and their final coming together are eloquently dramatized in their movement through the set, their approaches and retreats, and the emphases offered by Lang's camera angles. Where a less talented director would have simply shot the scene as a series of alternating close-ups, Lang is able to preserve the wholeness of the space, its "reality," at the same time he uses it expressively, dynamically. In *Man Hunt*, space is also used as a structuring device: as the plot progresses and the chaos becomes more intense, Lang gradually reduces the scope of the settings, increasing the sense of physical and moral entrapment. The film opens on a mountaintop and climaxes in a small, dark cave, where a man, sealed inside, finally comes face to face with himself.

The Facets retrospective of Lang's American films begins this week with *While the City Sleeps*, *The Big Heat*, *You Only Live Once*, *The Return of Frank James*, *Man Hunt*, and *Western Union*: it continues for two more weeks with screenings of *Hangmen Also Die*, *Ministry of Fear*, *Scarlet Street*, *The Secret Beyond the Door*, *American Guerrilla in the Philippines*, *Clash by Night*, *Rancho Notorious*, *Human Desire*, *Moonfleet*, *Beyond a*

Reasonable Doubt, and *Fury*. Seeing these films together is the best way—they gain resonance when they're experienced as a continuous body of work—but I still feel obligated to offer the traditional Facets caveat: their projection can sometimes be very poor. Don't hesitate to scream and yell when the film slips out of focus or out of frame—Fritz Lang's work is worth the indignity.

Record of a Tenement Gentleman

Directed by YASUJIRO OZU {May 4, 1979}

"Japan Today," the traveling cultural circus sponsored by the Japan Society, will be bringing a number of film events to Chicago in the next few weeks. Chief among them are "Three Decades: Postwar Japanese Society Through Film," a 13-feature series at the Midwest Film Center, and the less distinctively titled "Japanese Film Festival" at Facets Multimedia. The Facets program consists in the main of firmly established classics—Kurosawa's *Seven Samurai*, Mizoguchi's *Ugetsu*, Ozu's *Tokyo Story*, and so on. All that needs to be said about them is that they should be seen, again and again. On a less exalted plain, this weekend will bring a rare screening of Masaki Kobayashi's three-part, nine-hour *The Human Condition*, and the series will end with a few unknown titles drawn from the Audio Brandon collection, including Tadashi Imai's *Muddy Waters* (which is not a rock film) and Susumu Hani's *Bwana Toshi*. All in all, it looks like two glorious weeks of art for art's sake.

The Film Center program, on the other hand, seems to have been organized less as a film series than a social studies course. Assembled for a nationwide tour by film scholars Donald Richie and Audie Bock, "Three Decades" attempts to trace the waning of tradition and the rise of western ways in Japanese culture through representative "problem" films drawn from 30 years of postwar production. "Representative" is a hard rap for any film to beat, particularly in this context of detached anthropological inquiry: movies tend to lose their animating individuality when they're held up as examples of abstract social forces. It's the one approach to film that I never could stomach—it's bad sociology and worse criticism. Still, several of the titles on the program promise some aesthetic value in and of themselves. The most reliable entries, those by name directors, are clustered near the beginning: the first two films were contributed by Kurosawa (*No Regrets for My Youth*) and Ozu (*Record of a Tenement Gentleman*), but from there the program offers only Kon Ichikawa's *A Full-Up Train* and Nagisa Oshima's *The Ceremony* as sops to celebrity value.

Obscurity, though, is certainly no drawback in a Japanese film series. For most filmgoers, myself included, the Japanese cinema remains a dim, vaguely threatening cloud on the horizon line—a distant mass of directors and genres, styles and themes, that we see through a haze when we see it at all. The accumulated evidence seems to suggest that the Japanese film is surpassed in depth and range only by Hollywood output, but the evidence is spotty and incomplete. For every Ozu or Kurosawa who has managed to achieve some measure of American exposure, there are a dozen Heinosuke Goshos or Teinosuke Kinugasas who remain completely unknown. It may be a case of the survival of the fittest; only the best producers of the Japanese cinema, perhaps, have passed the cut for American distribution. But even if that's true (and I'm not sure it is), the cutoff line leaves us without the strong supporting talents that ultimately determine the mettle of a national cinema. Hollywood's classic era depended as much on second-stringers like Minnelli, Mann, and Boetticher as it did on Hawks, Hitchcock, and Ford; the same would seem to be true of Japan. The great seldom exist without the firm backing of the good. And, in the case of a cinema that depends strongly on genre tradition, as do both the American and Japanese, the great may rely equally on the mediocre—the vast number of routine, unambitious films that do nothing more than define the archetypes of plot and character. *The Searchers* is unthinkable without 50 years of B Westerns behind it; *Yojimbo* inconceivable without another half century of samurai films. We have the Westerns, but we don't have the samurai sagas, and so we see *Yojimbo* in eerie isolation, unaware of the generic rules that determine it and that it reacts against.

It's hard to say how much a film like *Record of a Tenement Gentleman* (which the Film Center will show on Tuesday, May 8) might owe to its missing context. Its director, Yasujiro Ozu, was an undoubted *auteur*. His visual style—with the camera almost always fixed at the perspective of a contemporary onlooker sitting on a *tatami* mat—was personal to the point of idiosyncrasy, and he seldom wandered far from his favorite subject, the relations of parents and children. Ozu's career—from the few of his silent films that are available in the U.S. to his last films in the early 60s—reflects a single-mindedness that bordered on oblivion: even the coming of sound and color, even the Second World War, did little to change his style or his focus. The world seemed to have truly passed him by, as he sat spinning his small fables, working only minute variations from film to film.

But *Record of a Tenement Gentleman*, the story of an (apparent) war orphan and the woman who reluctantly takes him in, still seems to owe something to wider tradition, be it Japanese or American, as the program book hints with its derisive reference to the film's "upbeat Frank Capra-like ending." There is much traditional material here, perfectly recognizable to western eyes. Otane, the widow woman struggling to maintain her cynicism and self-interest, is a figure made famous by Marie Dressler; the foundling boy, following his unwilling keeper with the blind compliance of a puppy dog, dates back through Chaplin's *The Kid* to Victorian literature. No doubt, similar parallels could be drawn from the Japanese background—the material belongs to everyone and no one.

And so, interest settles on the ways in which Ozu has made it his own. Thanks to our limited exposure to Japanese film, most of those ways will be unintelligible—how could one tell the difference between a Hawks screwball comedy and a Capra screwball comedy, unless one knew both Capra and Hawks, and the tradition that they came from? The difference is crucial, for it is there that lies the heart of the piece, the individuality that makes the film worth considering as a work of art.

Record of a Tenement Gentleman is unusual for Ozu in that it takes place beyond the confines of a formalized family. Where the majority of Ozu's movies are set in comfortable middle-class homes, often with three generations of the family on hand, *Record* takes place in a postwar shanty town, among people who are not only unrelated, but seem determined to keep it that way. In the aftermath of the war, it is hard enough to take care of yourself. Still, when the boy arrives, small units begin to form among the tenement dwellers, small families of affection and concern that gradually supersede the selfishness imposed by hard times. Characteristically, Ozu doesn't underline the growing bonds with overt displays of emotion. Only small acts speak, as when one man, an unemployed craftsman, does some repair work for the widow, or when a professional fortune teller offers a bit of free advice. The fondness between the widow and the boy likewise grows almost imperceptibly—Ozu's art is above all a matter of nuance, of small details closely observed.

The film is warm and funny and touching in a way that only Ozu's distant, formal camera style can be. At first, the geometric precision of his composition, the unvarying angle of his shots, and the even, measured pace of his editing seem to deny the content of his scenes—nothing in his technique serves to punctuate or comment on the action; events simply pass by, all regarded with the same dispassion. Ozu's sublime passivity is vividly illustrated by one remarkable sequence, set at a seashore: Sitting down after a day's walking, the woman tells the boy to go and gather some shells. As he trots obediently down to the shore, she picks up her things and rises, walking off toward the dunes in the background. Not until the scene is partly over does the realization dawn that the woman is running away from the child. Instead of concentrating on her face—her anguish, her desperation—Ozu quietly records the rolling lines of the dunes, rising to meet the sky; she is only a passing figure in an eternal landscape.

Ozu's coldness, I think, is a vehicle for a humanism of the most profound sort—a humanism that refuses to aggrandize or belittle its objects, but seeks to see people in balance with their surroundings and with each other: as parts of a whole, and not always the determining parts. Ozu's careful, present style couldn't be further removed from the panning epiphanies of Renoir or the open nonstyle of Rossellini, but the end result of all three approaches is much the same. Each grants a special kind of freedom to actors and characters. They stand or fall on their own, unaided—or unhindered—by the director's divine intervention. The greatest virtue in Ozu's films is acceptance: acceptance of one's place in the family, of one's place in society, and of one's place in the ultimate scheme of things. His camera style, too, is founded on acceptance. Every person, every thing embraced by his image is given the same weight and importance. For all its artificiality, it is a style that is strikingly *there*, planted in the present moment.

[Discussion of *Where Chimneys Are Seen* (Heinosuke Gosho) is omitted.]

Peeping Tom

Directed by MICHAEL POWELL {December 7, 1979}

Made in 1960, Michael Powell's *Peeping Tom* will be seen in Chicago for the first time this week, thanks to the daredevil booking policy of the Sandburg Theater. The film has been the victim of a de facto ban for the last 20 years, and holds no reputation beyond the small circle of hardcore cineastes. This is revival programming of a much riskier sort than shuffling out the old Marx Brothers–Humphrey Bogart festivals, and I hope Chicago's filmgoers will, for once, honor the Sandburg's initiative with their attendance. The Sandburg people, in any case, have decided to hedge their bet by doubling Powell's film with two known quantities—Alfred Hitchcock's *Psycho* for the first half of the week, and Charles Laughton's *Night of the Hunter* for the second. These are three great films, all masterpieces from the primal fringe of cinema where movies merge with nightmares.

The link with *Psycho* is particularly appropriate. After Hitchcock, Powell is the most compelling of British directors, perhaps because, after Hitchcock, Powell is the least British of British directors. His voluptuous, highly charged films challenge the British tradition on the two fronts of literary value and realism—qualities that Powell discarded in favor of the Hollywood virtues of movement and visual stylization. Hitchcock, similarly inclined, eventually left England to practice his art in a more hospitable climate, but Powell chose to remain behind, a stranger in his native land. Despite a string of popular successes, Powell's critical reputation became increasingly shaky through the 50s, as Britain's Angry Young Men rose to create the "kitchen sink" school of anguished social realism. Released the same year as Karel Reisz's *Saturday Night and Sunday Morning*, the definitive study in proletarian plumbing, *Peeping Tom* proved to be the last straw. The film's extreme stylization, its apparent garishness, and its focus on a subject widely held to be in "bad taste"—sex—brought down a storm of hostility from London critics. This quote from *The Daily Worker* (unearthed by Elliot Stein for a *Film Comment* article) appears to be typical: "It wallows in the diseased urges of a homicidal pervert. . . . It uses phony cinema artifice and heavy orchestral music to whip up a debased atmosphere. . . . From its lumbering, mildly salacious beginning to its appallingly masochistic and depraved climax, it is wholly evil." In short, a must-see. Meanwhile, on the other side of the pond, *Psycho* was provoking a similar scandal—but where Hitchcock was able to weather the storm (*Psycho*, after all, was a very big hit), Powell's career was left in ruins. He made one other film in England (an upright, patriotic saga, staunchly titled *The Queen's Guards*), and thereafter found work only in Australia—where he's made two films in 20 years.

Peeping Tom is a violent film, but it isn't a particularly graphic one—even by the standards of 1960. And certainly, any random scene in Britain's "Carry On" series exposed more female flesh—and much more "salaciously"—than *Peeping Tom* does in its wholly evil entirety. The British reviewers weren't responding to the bugaboos of sex and violence, but to something else. Powell had broken a more serious taboo, a taboo so powerful that it still goes largely unspoken. *Peeping Tom* violates the sacred pact between the audience and the filmmaker, whereby each agrees to ignore the other's existence. The film refuses to remain on the screen; it isn't the passive, vicarious experience that movies are supposed to be. Instead, *Peeping Tom* ranges into the audience, drawing us into the action, implicating us in the protagonist's guilt. *Peeping Tom* is a movie about movies, making them and watching them. It looks at the process of filming and finds that it's something close to murder. It looks at the process of viewing and finds that it's something close to rape. Powell never lets us forget those processes and the psychological impulses they serve: his highly artificial visual style serves both to keep the director's work in the foreground (to let us know he's there) and to continually remind us that we're watching a movie (to let us know we're there).

Peeping Tom is a shattering experience—it wakes us up from the movie-dream, forces us to take part in its own making. It's an aggressive film, a threat—and that threat, no doubt, is what provoked the film's first reviewers. Powell takes away the protective darkness of the movie theater and leaves us face to face with our own dark motives for movie-going—our desire to see and not be seen, and the unnatural power that that position gives us. He exposes us as voyeurs. That would be outrageous enough, but Powell doesn't stop there. After the initial shock of exposure has passed, *Peeping Tom* becomes, disturbingly, a very compassionate film. It doesn't lay down a moral dictum against movies (that, in any case, would be grotesquely hypocritical—making a film that condemns films). Instead, it draws us into a sense of complicity, of shared pleasures—sweeter, perhaps, because they are forbidden.

Director and viewer are joined in the figure of Powell's protagonist, Mark Lewis (Carl Boehm)—a shy, sensitive young man obsessed with murdering beautiful women as he films their horror in choker close-up. Since Mark makes his movies for his own enjoyment, he is both audience and filmmaker, voyeur and exhibitionist. He is Powell; he is us. And thus, Mark is not, cannot be, a monster—we can't be allowed to push him away. Powell's narrative construction conspires to draw him closer and closer, working in three stages. First, Powell exploits the automatic identification of any movie audience with the movie hero, filming the first murder from Mark's point of view (and through the lens of his own camera), and delaying the first shot of the actor's face until the film is well under way. We see through his eyes; we become Mark before we know him. Secondly, Powell grants us an understanding of Mark through a nice, neat psychological explanation of his obsession (Mark's father, a clinical psychologist, used his child as a subject for his researches into fear—waking the boy up in the middle of the night and watching his reactions to shock). The Freudianism may be facile, but it gives us a rational grip on the problem. The "explanation" demystifies Mark's motives: once we know why he acts, he becomes less demonic and more human; he engages our sympathy as a victim (even as Powell denies our sympathy for Mark's victims). The third movement is the most audacious, bringing us to see Mark as a genuine hero. The action of *Peeping Tom* consists of Mark's efforts to finish his film before the police catch him, or before his newly acquired girlfriend, Helen (Anna Massey), discovers his secret. We come to view him as an artist, struggling against all odds to complete his work. His complete and selfless dedication to his "art" gives him a nobility, a grandeur—he becomes the perfect image of the romantic poet, defying man and God in the name of genius. When, in the end, Mark sacrifices his life to his art, one doesn't know whether to shudder or to cheer. This is the same extravagant view of artistic sacrifice that underlies Powell's famous ballet film, *The Red Shoes*. But what seems dreamy and romantic in the earlier film becomes, in *Peeping Tom*, something horrible—though no less beautiful.

Powell's films have a distinctive rhythm. Instead of following the logic of the overall plot, they seem to fall into discrete, autonomous segments, each with a rhythm and logic of its own. His movies are less single stories, continuously told, than they are a series of reveries, each inspired in turn by some central image contained in the plot. The link between segments is not causal, but associative—the films move according to an intellectual drift, rather than adhering to the strict chain of events directed by narrative. For many critics, Powell's method amounts to nothing more than jerkiness and discontinuity—a flaw. But it seems to me that Powell is after something else: a way, perhaps, of organizing films on a uniquely cinematic basis (that is, centered on the image) rather than following the traditional models of drama and literature, which are organized according to action and character. With Powell, the image precedes the film, and takes an appropriate precedence over the story. *The Red Shoes*, for example, is spun entirely from the image of the magic ballet slippers named in the title. The film examines the meaning of the image—as metaphor, as emblem—tracking down its different senses and implications in different contexts, ranging from myth to psychology, from abstract relations to concrete characters. In *A Matter of Life and Death* (1946), the central image is fantastic: a stairway connecting heaven and earth. In *I Know Where I'm Going*, the image is geographic: an inaccessible island, cut off from the mainland by a raging storm.

The central image of *Peeping Tom* is mechanical: Mark's movie camera, to which he has attached a highly phallic accessory—a tripod leg that springs up and becomes a knife. The associations Powell spins around the image seem endless: it is a symbol of the father's dominance over the son, and the means of the filmmaker's dominance over his subject. It is a sexual weapon and a sexual object (in one remarkable scene, Mark kisses Helen for the first time and then turns and kisses the camera—as if he were afraid it felt neglected). It is a way of seeing and a way of hiding, a source of power and a powerful curse. Above all, it is cinema.

Powell constructs other, subsidiary images around the central one. Movies are the art of light and darkness—the projected image—and so light and dark become a main visual motif. Helen's brightly lit apartment is played against Mark's private sanctuary—his pitch-black darkroom. Darkened sound stages (Mark works as a focus-puller at a movie studio) are suddenly flooded by light; one of Mark's victims is momentarily blinded by a spotlight. A red light adorns a photographer's set of a bordello; it reappears as a flashing warning light over a sound stage door, and, of course, Mark works in red light in his darkroom.

Parents and children make up another motif. Mark shows a film of himself, as a boy, with his father—and the flashback man and child are played by director Powell and his son. Helen lives with her mother, a domineering blind woman. She controls Helen with her lack of sight, playing on her guilt, much as Mark's father controlled his son by keeping him under constant surveillance. Like most blind people in fiction, Helen's mother has a sixth sense; she "sees" Mark better than anyone else (as she runs her hands over his face, Mark asks, "Are you taking my picture?"). Equipped with a pointedly phallic cane, she becomes bisexual—as was the blind seer Tiresias in the original Oedipus myth, which closes the circle on Mark's Oedipal complex. Helen herself is played by Anna Massey, the daughter of one of Powell's favorite actors, Raymond Massey.

One could go on and on. There's another motif centered on movies, embracing everything from the film's score (contrary to *The Daily Worker*'s impression, it's played entirely on a single piano—a reference to silent films) to a detective's impression of Tweety Pie. And there are rhyming motifs: a movie director is played by a blind actor; one of his assistants leafs through a copy of *Sight and Sound*.

Powell plainly enjoys his puns and paradoxes. A list of the variations on "I see" could alone take up the length of this review, and there is one deliriously comic movement in which Powell films a detective watching Mark watch Helen—while we, of course, watch it all from the audience.

It's this sense of playfulness, the undercurrent of wit, that saves *Peeping Tom* from being a hopelessly dark, unbearable film. If making movies is indeed an act of sadism—of aggression and exploitation—and the pleasure of watching them is no less perverse, it is a truth that can only be accepted as a joke. For we are all involved in the process, every day of our lives.

Othello

Directed by ORSON WELLES {May 16, 1980}

Thanks to Perrier and *The Tonight Show*, Orson Welles is with us more than ever. With us, that is, in his monumental, institutional mode: the Great Man, the Presence, reading ad copy with more careful elocution and tricky inflection than Laurence Olivier has brought to his last half dozen screen roles. Welles is everywhere, in magazines, in billboards, on celebrity roasts. But as Welles the actor has parlayed his personality into the supreme late 70s symbol of sophistication and conspicuous consumption, Welles the artist has slowly been slipping away. If he has become a cultural monument, he's the Sphinx, issuing occasional cryptograms such as *F for Fake* and *Filming Othello*, but otherwise keeping his secrets to himself. Welles has been working on a narrative film, *The Other Side of the Wind*, since the early 70s, but now there is a new crop of rumors holding that the picture will never be released—that it will join *It's All True*, *The Deep*, *Don Quixote*, and the other unfinished projects that occupy Welles's ample bedroom closet. As if that weren't enough, there is the news that three of Welles's past films, *The Trial*, *Mr. Arkadin*, and *Chimes at Midnight*, have been withdrawn from distribution because of legal problems. Not only are there no new Welles films, but the old ones have begun to disappear.

In compensation, the rights have finally been cleared to Welles's 1952 film of *Othello*, which hasn't been legally available in over a decade. The Sandburg Theater, in another of their admirable kamikaze runs into certain commercial disaster, will be playing the film for the next week, paired with Welles's own paradoxical exegesis, *Filming Othello*. It isn't often that I urge my readers to lay their cash on the line, but this is one double bill that deserves your support.

Any amateur analyst can explain Welles's silence, as Charles Higham (of *Errol Flynn* fame) did in his *Films of Orson Welles*. Welles, plainly, is gripped by completion anxiety, the Freudian fear of letting go. Disaster befalls Welles with eerie regularity, as financial problems, logistical confusions, and authorial uncertainty delay film after film (and at least part of the point of *Filming Othello* is to celebrate those disasters). It's been his pattern throughout his career: Orson Welles is his own worst enemy. But once Welles's self-destructiveness has been diagnosed, it's pointless to beat him with it, as Higham does. Welles without his demons would not be Orson Welles, and *Citizen Kane* would be just another newspaper movie. It may be maddening that Welles doesn't produce more, but it's not a simple case of a great talent gone to waste—it's a case of a talent that nurtures itself on waste, that thrives on disaster. Failure, frustration, impotence, irrelevance—these are the subjects of Welles's films, and, to judge from the public outline of his career, these are the subjects he has learned a lot about.

Just as his protagonists are divided into public and private selves, there have long been two Orson Welleses: the actor—imposing, powerful, confident—and the director, who sees a fragmented world of frightened people, lost in shadows, dominated by décor, fighting their way through a treacherous, unpredictable screen space. Welles's assertive, conspicuous visual style (invariably, he is the filmmaker who first makes young viewers aware of the presence and work of the director) functions as a block between actors and audience; it makes us know that there's someone else around, a Welles behind the camera as well as a Welles in front of it. If his movies tend toward madness, it's because of a stylistic schizophrenia, a double vision implicit in every frame. Social and subjective viewpoints exist side by side: the actor looks out, the director looks in.

Welles's method finds its perfect metaphor in the fun house ending of his own *Lady from Shanghai*. As Welles the actor stares into distorting mirrors, falls through trapdoors, and slides down curling ramps into the mouths of papier-mâché demons, the director tortures a character who is, at least partly, himself. In the hall of mirrors, Welles multiplies his own image into infinity—but it is a shallow, false infinity, a trick of ego, and it is shattered by a blaze of guns. The director seems to punish the actor, destroying his complacency, undermining his hubristic assumption that he is of some power and consequence in the world.

The quintessential Welles plot leads up to the revelation of a private tragedy masked by public success. Welles suggests that every advance in the world at large is checked by a failure inside—that every successful action is matched by a blocked emotion. It's a romantic notion, almost a Faustian one, but it is played out in purely personal terms. There's no thundering God in Welles's work, only a gnawing self-doubt. As Welles's career progresses, as the tag of genius weighs more heavily on him, the parts he gives himself become increasingly grotesque, increasingly pathetic. From the empire builder of *Citizen Kane*, he turns into the grizzled, drunken Falstaff of *Chimes at Midnight*, tossed away like a used toy by Prince Hal, who will go on to build an empire for himself.

Othello, made in 1952, marked the last time Welles cast himself as a leading man, and the last time he allowed himself a love interest (the single, glorious exception is the past affair and present nostalgic regard implied between Welles and Marlene Dietrich in *Touch of Evil*). Welles here is still a young man, his girth in check, his baby face glowing beneath black makeup. His Othello, likewise, hangs on a boyish naivety, miles removed from the grinning lasciviousness of the Olivier interpretation. His love for Desdemona is uncomplicated: she is a pretty little thing, and she listens sympathetically to him. They also have, by the movie standards of 1952, an unusually healthy interest in sex (this is Shakespeare, after all, and classics are only marginally censorable). This is a brash, freshly hatched Othello, sure of his abilities, secure in society, and confident in his value to it.

But from the first image, Welles subverts his hero—inverts him, in fact: his face, upside down, fills the frame. Like *Kane*, *Othello* begins at the end. The inverted face belongs to a corpse; we look down on the body, as it is raised nearer to us by the bearers who will take it to the funeral procession. The sequence that follows—a parade of icons, black-robed figures, and mourners, moving across the sun-beaten battlements of the fort while a chant booms on the sound track—approaches the formal abstraction of Eisenstein's *Ivan the Terrible*, black masses blotting out white fields. The sequence (it comes before the credits) establishes the harsh black-white polarity of the images that follow, but there is something in the ferocity of its abstraction that gives it an independent life. This isn't simple "foreshadowing," but an outpouring of universal grief, a cry that pierces the film—a cry that serves as its premise.

When the action begins, it burns. Welles has no time for leisurely examination of character—Iago is evil, Desdemona is good, Othello is in between—and he hardly has any use for his actors. By and large, the supporting performances in *Othello* are second rate, flat and uninflected, more declamatory than exploratory. Still, the deficiencies aren't necessarily a fault. The Welles *Othello* is an express train; psychological details are excess baggage. (Michael MacLiammoir, as Iago, proves the point: he gives the "best" performance, but his carefulness breaks up the rhythm.) The action seems to take place in the space of a single afternoon, with incidents fighting each other for screen time. Once Iago awakes the green-eyed monster, the plot is virtually complete; Welles rips through to the climax, as if the slightest glimmer of doubt were enough to bring down a tragedy. At the precise moment when Othello finds himself half a step out of sync with the rhythm of his world, his world collapses around him, with something like literal force.

The key images of *Othello* seem to have been composed with Welles's long-take, deep-focus technique in mind. Clean lines, of walls, railings, and columns, trail off into the background; the actors occupy the full space, arranged into allegorical tableaux of moral and physical power. But, as Welles explains in *Filming Othello*, the long, dragged-out circumstances of the frequently interrupted production sometimes made it impossible to hold the cast together. To cover for missing members, Welles was forced to bring his camera in closer: a two-shot within a group generally means that the other players weren't there. It's typical of Welles to pull a triumph out of such a disaster: the crazy patchwork editing pattern, dictated by necessity, gives *Othello* the maddest swirl of any of Welles's films. By repeatedly cutting on movement, a trick that Nicholas Ray used to famous advantage, Welles creates a mise-en-scène in constant turmoil, in which actions have no beginnings or ends, only ineffectual middles. The image jumps and spins (Welles seldom returns to the same point of view for a second shot), as if the laws of gravity had gone on strike in sympathy with the hero's emotions. The stable, integrated screen space of *The Magnificent Ambersons*, which André Bazin praised as the epitome of movie realism, here suffers an annihilating attack, further cut to ribbons with every swing of Welles's splicer. There is violence within the frame, too: one constant motif is of the cross-hatching, small forests of tense, conflicting lines that appear in wall designs, window frames, hair nets. With the images filled to overflowing with Welles's baroque, dense patterns of dark shadows and bright light, the speed with which the frames flash by creates another subtext of confusion, frustration, waste—you want to stop and enjoy the images, read them and savor them, but they vanish before they can be touched. The director tears them from the screen.

Othello gives Shakespeare his due, though just barely. In the 16mm print on view at the Sandburg (alas, it's the only one available; the sole existing 35mm print is in the clutching hands of the American Film Institute), the dialogue is often muddy and occasionally impenetrable, the result of the cheap-jack recording equipment that Welles was forced to use. The language, more or less, is lost; the words that survive serve mainly as captions, while the rest of the dialogue merges with the symphonic cacophony of the sound track (in this context, Iago's "I hate the Moor" jumps out with startling clarity). Welles has asked that his *Othello* not be understood as a mounting of Shakespeare, but rather, like Verdi's opera *Othello*, as a creation in its own right. The request hardly needs to be voiced. Welles's *Othello* is a shatteringly personal work, not least because its subject, at the deepest level, is the person of Orson Welles. As actor and director work out the vagaries of their love-hate relationship, Welles teases the sense of Robert Burns's famous wish, "to see ourselves as others see us." Welles sees himself, but only as he can—with a mixture of awe and disgust, supplying the secret subtext to a public life.

Crisis, Compulsion, and Creation: Raoul Walsh's Cinema of the Individual

{January 23, 1981}

Writing last week of Martin Scorsese's *Raging Bull*, I wanted to slip in a few paragraphs about Raoul Walsh, the great genre director who is probably Scorsese's single most important influence, but somehow they didn't fit. Walsh, who died a few weeks ago at the age of 88, deserves more than an aside, though that has been his fate in most of the standard film histories. He made well over a hundred movies in a career that began with D. W. Griffith in the teens (he played John Wilkes Booth in *The Birth of a Nation*)—and ended at Warner Bros. in the early 60s, and among them are some of the most energetic, personal, and technically proficient films to come out of Hollywood. Yet, apart from a small, strange cult that crystallized in Paris in the 50s, Walsh was never championed by the critics. His name was always mentioned alongside Hawks and Ford, but somehow his standing never seemed secure: too often, his work was paid lip service—appropriate effusions over its clear, surface virtues—without any further attempt to come to grips with what it was, how it worked, what it meant. I can think of no other case of a filmmaker whose work was so widely, and rightly, perceived as important, but yet received so little intelligent attention.

Perhaps part of the problem with Walsh is that his style and values are bound up so tightly with the genre—action-adventure—in which he worked that it is difficult to tell where the form leaves off and the filmmaker begins. To talk of a Walsh war film is, in a way, to talk of all war films, to talk of a Walsh western of all westerns—in the sense that the main thematic thrust of his films, the redemptive power of action, is also the thematic thrust of his genres in their purest states. But there are important differences between the broad archetypes and their particular embodiments in Walsh's work, differences of character quirks, patterns of action, and internal dynamics that define a personal point of view. Andrew Sarris, in his short notes on Walsh in *The American Cinema*, speaks of an emotional vulnerability peculiar to Walsh's heroes—he cites James Cagney huddled in his mother's lap in *White Heat*—but the rare capacity to show pain, dependence, and uncertainty is only the tip of the iceberg. The Walsh hero, much more than those of Ford or Hawks, is a hero in personal crisis. Ford's heroes define themselves by accepting their friends and professional skills, but the Walsh hero has nothing to hang on to. He is a blank page, either without a past or running away from one. His task—it can take the form of a quest or mission, a rise in business or the making of a reputation—is to invent himself. If he is vulnerable, it is because there is something raw, unformed, brash about him. His personality is still fluid, still open to change and influence.

Walsh was famous for his speed: the initial montage of *White Heat*, which compresses James Cagney's career as a psychotic gangster into a single, slashingly violent train robbery, is perhaps the fastest, poundingest opening in film history, and many of Walsh's movies open *in medias res*, the exposition deftly dropped among the flurries of action. That same demon speed is shared by many of Walsh's heroes, who often seem driven by the unknown, unholy forces—some, like *White Heat*'s Cody Jarrett, over the edge; others, like *Gentleman Jim*'s James J. Corbett, into personal success and prestige. James Cagney gave his best performances in Walsh films—*The Roaring Twenties*, *Strawberry Blonde*, *White Heat*, *A Lion Is in the Streets*—where his spring-wound, simmering physicality found its finest visual presentation and most expressive use. Errol Flynn was another Walsh regular (*They Died with Their Boots On*, *Desperate Journey*, *Gentleman Jim*, *Northern Pursuit*, *Uncertain Glory*, *Objective Burma*, *Silver River*); although his personality was much less complex than Cagney's (in the hands of other directors, he could go unforgivably slack), Flynn still found a striking presence in Walsh's work, where his innate cockiness, his narcissism, could become a part of his character. His drive was different from Cagney's: where Cagney, the rough, slum kid, fought for material success, the smoother, silkier Flynn had more abstract goals in mind: social standing (*Gentleman Jim*), military glory (*They Died with Their Boots On*), political success (*Silver River*). Flynn was the social climber, Cagney was the social scrabbler—but both acted from the same inner compulsion, a compulsion to create themselves through their actions, to wrest an identity from the world. In Walsh, the American myths of success and mobility find a deep psychological, and perhaps existential, resonance: in making it, the Walsh hero is making himself.

If Walsh's films take their tempo, their dynamism, from the inner drives of their central characters, they also allow the hero to dictate their shape and structure. By and large, Walsh is attracted to two types of organization: the "rise and fall of . . ." biographical plot (as in *The Roaring Twenties*, *They Died with Their Boots On*, *Gentleman Jim*, *A Lion Is in the Streets*), and an even looser, more anecdotal structure that might be called the "map movie"—the kind of film that opens with a big black X on a map and follows the characters' progress from point A to point B through a gradually growing dotted line. Walsh's map movies—the best of them are *Objective Burma*, *Along the Great Divide*, *Distant Drums*, and *Saskatchewan*—are tales of neither picaresque adventure nor heroic quest: often, as in *Burma* and the latter half of *Distant Drums*, the characters are in retreat, running from an enemy through a hostile, primal landscape. They meet, in nature, the same kind of challenges that the heroes of the biographical films confront in social terms: it is always a question of a will imposed on the world, of an environment—urban or wilderness—conquered. The heroes of the biographical films move through time, of the map movies through space, but both are running the same sort of gauntlet—not one of punishment or purgation, but of learning and testing. The characters take something from their confrontations: they grow in strength and identity.

For Ford, the ultimate focus is society, for Hawks it is the group; Walsh's focus, uniquely, is the individual—his experience, his progress, his evolution. (The masculine pronoun doesn't always apply: one of Walsh's most striking protagonists, Jane Russell in *The Revolt of Mamie Stover*, is very much a woman.) Walsh's casual, discursive plots create a sense of freedom around the hero, as if his actions alone were determining the direction of the film. Suggestively, Walsh's weakest films, such as the 1943 Eric Ambler adaptation, *Background to Danger*, are generally those with rigid, well-defined plots; he doesn't seem able to deal with elaborate narrative machinations and the limitations of his heroes that they imply, the sense that the character's fate is not always in his own hands. Walsh is the exact philosophical opposite of Fritz Lang, a "happy pagan," as a French critic called him, to Lang's brooding Catholic, innocent of any sense of doom or foreboding, of any power beyond that of man. Some of Walsh's most entertaining films (though they are far from his best) belong to the series of quick musicals he made for Paramount in the 30s—*Going Hollywood*, *Every Night at Eight*, *Artists and Models*, *College Swing*, *St. Louis Blues*. Most are designed as simple showcases for popular entertainers or radio stars; if they have a plot, it exists only to be ignored, and they play out as refreshingly free and easy assemblies of songs, comedy sketches, and character turns, unified only by a pleasant, generous sense of anything goes. Only a director like Walsh, serenely attuned to the rhythms of personality and spirit over those of plot and structure, could have brought them off with such a sense of integrity: they are free without being sloppy, open without being ungainly.

But Walsh's celebration of freedom only goes so far: there is a dark side there too, a sense of anarchy, and many of his best films are concerned with finding the line—the point at which freedom becomes chaos, when the hero's inner drive turns destructive, mad. Often, Walsh gives his heroes a double, an opposite number possessed of the same manic drive but lifted to excess. In the face-offs between James Cagney and Humphrey Bogart in *The Roaring Twenties*, John Wayne and Walter Pidgeon in *Dark Command*, and Robert Mitchum and Dean Jagger in *Pursued*, the only difference between hero and heavy is one of relative restraint, the degree to which the character is willing to ride out his inner energy. (Martin Scorsese appropriated this structure, with some suggestive variations, for *Mean Streets*.) The most remarkable film in this group is *They Drive by Night* (1940), a movie that begins as a growly social drama about the rise of an independent trucker (George Raft) to the head of a company, but breaks cleanly in the middle to become a courtroom melodrama about a woman (Ida Lupino) who has murdered her husband in order to clear the way for her lover. The transference—between personal energy used for positive ends and sexual energy used for destructive ends—doesn't emerge with enough clarity to work for the audience (as does, say, the similar gambit in *Psycho*), but it stands as one of Walsh's most audacious moments.

Most of Walsh's early films are lost or unavailable; those few from the 20s that can be seen—*The Thief of Baghdad*, *The Lucky Lady*, *What Price Glory*—are largely in the standard style of the period, dependent on cutting and broad movements within the frame for their sense of tempo. In the early 30s, Walsh can be seen experimenting with deep focus and panning shots (*The Bowery*, *Me and My Gal*), though it isn't until 1939, with the beginning of his tenure at Warner Bros., that his visual style reaches its full maturity, with extended compositions in depth and a complete sympathy between the movement of the camera and the movement of the actors. Walsh would have made a much better case for André Bazin's theoretical linkage of deep focus and realism than did his own two chosen examples, William Wyler and Orson Welles. Where Wyler's deep focus tends toward empty, pictorial designs (an extension of lines and angles), and Welles's is concerned with the creative re-creation of theatrical space, Walsh's is aimed at placing his characters in a definite physical world. The depth of focus suggests the extension of the world beyond the camera's range, and even behind it: space is captured whole, unsectioned by planes of focus or composition restrictions. There is seldom a sense of "background" in a Walsh shot: the lines of perspective are almost always allowed to extend, explicitly or implicitly, to the horizon line. Space is continuous, solid: it's never the gauzy, transcendent space of a Borzage or the hallucinatory, convoluted space of a Sirk. But still, as in Sirk and Borzage, there is a suggestion of tension between the character and the world he inhabits. Walsh's favorite shot is medium-long, with the actors cut off between waist and knees. Though compositionally the actors are made part of the continuous space, their own hold on it seems tenuous. They are seldom firmly planted, fully there; instead, they inhabit an indefinite foreground, suspended queasily, unsteadily, before the world behind them. When Walsh pans, he is indicating the existence of a world beyond the frame-line—outside the bounds of a single, simple composition—but he is also extending the tension between actor and setting into dynamic terms. He pans with the movement of the hero, giving the actor the apparent power to determine the composition and point of view—again, the sense of freedom—but by panning rather than tracking, he keeps the setting still, static, separate from the actor. In a tracking shot, the décor "moves" with the actor; the space is fluid, changing in response to the actor's movement. In a panning shot, the space retains its integrity: our perspective on it remains constant at the pivot point. Walsh's characters move with freedom through the world, but the world doesn't yield to them: it remains a constant challenge, solid and slightly apart.

Walsh's heroes do battle with the world, defining themselves through the fight. At the climax of his films, the height of the battle, Walsh often shifts literally to a higher plane: the Cagney-Bogart apartment shoot-out in *The Roaring Twenties* (Scorsese duplicates the spatial plan at the climax of *Taxi Driver*), Bogart's last battle with the law in (and on) *High Sierra*, and, most famous, Cagney's mad epiphany atop the flaming gas tank that is about to explode and destroy him, resonate through Walsh's work. "Top of the world, ma! Top of the world!" he screams, posed in short-lived symbolic dominance—the Walsh hero in his moment of ultimate challenge and ultimate danger.

A few years ago, the Museum of Modern Art held an extensive Walsh retrospective; there has never, as far as I know, been an extensive Walsh program in Chicago. Even the individual films seldom play the local societies. Walsh's curse, perhaps, is his prolificity: apart from the handful of famous titles, most of which suffer the contempt of familiarity, who is to choose among the dozens and dozens of films that he made? Like any artist, Walsh was uneven, but I've yet to see a Walsh film, no matter how obscure, that didn't have some of his flair, some of his infectious spirit. Walsh's cinematheque, ultimately, is late-night television. Hardly a week passes without one of his films; at times there are two or three. His work is worth watching for, and worth working with.

A Love That Caresses the Soul: Films by Carl Theodor Dreyer

{October 9, 1981}

Too often, film history comes to us backwards, inasmuch as we usually see a director's late, major works before we know the early efforts that brought them into being. (The exception who proves the rule is Orson Welles, who is still known almost exclusively through his debut films.) We see careers upside down, and then only in fragments—which is partly the fault of a culture that values the masterpiece, the massive achievement, to the exclusion of everything else, and partly the fault of a hopelessly inadequate archive system, which has allowed many (if not most) formative films to disappear, and makes those that do exist almost impossible to see. A program such as the current Dreyer retrospective at the Art Institute's Film Center is invaluable in this context: for those of us without unlimited access to the Library of Congress or the Museum of Modern Art, it provides an almost unique opportunity to view a film artist's entire output in continuity. (The only feature missing from the Film Center's retrospective is the 1944 *Two People*, which Dreyer disowned.) The series has been running for only a week, and yet my image of Dreyer has already changed completely, expanded and shaded by such early works as *The President*, *The Parson's Widow*, *Mikael*, and *The Bride of Glomdale*. The maker of *Ordet*, *Day of Wrath*, *Vampyr*, and *Gertrude* now seems a much more complex individual with his humor and vivacity restored, his roots in the popular cinema revealed.

Carl Theodor Dreyer was, of course, a special case. He was lucky enough to be recognized as an artist during his lifetime, which ensured the careful preservation of his early work (prints in the Film Center program come from the Museum of Modern Art, Svensk Filmindustri, the Danish Film Museum, and the Anthology Film Archives). He was also considerate enough to make relatively few films (15 features in all), which makes a complete retrospective of his work marginally practical in a way retrospectives of Ford or Walsh or Dwan would not be (even if the early films existed). Dreyer also appears to have been one of the first filmmakers to receive a government subsidy—in the form of a license for a theater in downtown Copenhagen, where he supposedly showed only the films he liked—which makes him indeed unique, a director largely liberated from commercial restraints.

Still, one of the most intriguing aspects of Dreyer's early work is the degree to which it is commercial. It's hard to imagine the author of *Ordet* directing broad social farce or thrilling last-minute rescues, but it is all there (in *The Parson's Widow* and *The Bride of Glomdale*, respectively), and there is even what French critic Jean-Louis Comolli described as a “perfect western” (“but for the Finnish snows and forests in which its chases take place”) in the closing episode of *Leaves from Satan’s Book*. Dreyer almost seems to be shuffling through all of the genres available to him as a European filmmaker in the 20s, trying on each format in turn to see which would give him the best fit. With *The President* (1919), his first film, he tries a dense generational melodrama; in *Leaves from Satan’s Book* (1919), a parable form adapted from Griffith’s *Intolerance*. For *The Parson’s Widow* (1920) he has a bawdy folktale; for *Love One Another* (1921), historical melodrama; for *Once upon a Time* (1922), fairy-tale romance. Only with *Mikael* (1924) does he leave well-established forms, here to invent the intimate, psychological drama later known as *Kammerspiel* (“chamber music”) film, but his sudden innovation doesn’t prevent him from returning to domestic comedy (*Master of the House*, 1925) and pastoral romance (*The Bride of Glomdale*, 1925). The stubborn integrity that would later be his chief characteristic as a filmmaker is reflected in this early period mainly through his evident impatience: in his search for his own voice, the form that would free him most completely, he never repeats himself. He seems to exhaust each genre as he comes to it, using up all its opportunities for personal expression. By the time he truly comes into his own, with the 1928 *Passion of Joan of Arc*, he has, in something of a literal sense, left commercial cinema behind: he has passed through it, used it up, and is now left to journey alone, without the companionship of proven forms. Projects become increasingly hard to find: after making eight films in the first six years of his career, he completes only seven more in the next 35.

The path of Dreyer’s career—a thicket at the beginning, a clearing at the end—is also the path of his mise-en-scène: his images become more pure, more sparse, more ascetic as his work progresses. Still, his predilections are evident in the first sequence of his first film, *The President*, in which a dark figure stands against a blank white wall—a shot that wouldn’t seem out of place in *Ordet*. The play of black and white, light and darkness, remains a key element in Dreyer’s work throughout his career; it is one of the ways (though not the only way, as too many critics suggest) in which Dreyer invests the immediate human dramas of his film with timeless metaphysical values. The classical identification of light with divine grace and darkness with the fallen human condition is present in Dreyer’s use of light and shade, but only as a background to the more complex, ambiguous effects he creates from their intermingling. The play of light upon an object is, for Dreyer, an endlessly miraculous moment: it is a bringing to life, a stirring, just as the life of a movie is contained in the play of light upon an empty screen. Very often, Dreyer’s most striking lighting effects are designed not only to lift the object into some transcendent, heavenly sphere, but equally to emphasize its physicality, to give it weight, texture, solidity. In *Mikael* (to be shown this Saturday at the Film Center), light becomes a caressing thing, sensate and sensual, when Mikael plays a spotlight along the body of a woman he is attracted to; in a later shot, after the attraction has been consummated, sunlight pours down upon Mikael's figure as he stands near a window in his master's study, producing an effect of such fierce, vibrating aliveness that the master, horrified, immediately orders that the window be closed. The spiritual, in Dreyer's films, is reached through the physical: through sexuality as well as prayer, through physical intensity as well as emotional abstraction.

The same shot in *The President* that introduces Dreyer's light and darkness also inaugurates another of his formal strategies, less well noted than his lighting but perhaps even more expressive and original—his highly charged representation of space. The dark figure moves along the white wall (which, placed flat to the gaze of the camera, is indistinguishable from the surface of the screen itself) and opens a door set into it, revealing another room beyond, where another dark figure stands. Dreyer carefully establishes a back limit, a flatness, to his images, only to undercut the flatness by opening into a deep-focus space beyond. Shallowness is succeeded by a depth, which—as the repetition of the depth implies—is itself a shallowness for another depth beyond it. As a filmmaker, Dreyer is concerned with photographing the unphotographable, showing the unshowable—the fluctuations of a heart, a soul, a spirit. If he cannot directly depict his unshowable subjects, he will foreground their unshowability, emphasizing the limitations of the image, the narrowness of the photographic point of view. Out of this impulse comes a profound appreciation of "behindness" as a cinematic quality—and, by extension, as a spiritual metaphor. The device isn't always as "dramatic" as it is in the shot from *The President*, with its explicit opening out: more often, it is latent in the image in the form of frames-within-frames—doorways, arches, prosceniums (*Mikael* is especially rich in them) that divide the composition into areas of shallowness and depth, concealment and revelation. Dreyer's famous taste for photographing his actors' backs during their most emotional scenes is another manifestation of "behindness"—it points our attention to the invisible, demonstrates the presence and importance of what cannot be seen. And as the critic Noel Burch has noted, Dreyer's last and possibly greatest film, *Gertrud*, is constructed almost entirely of straight-on, frontal shots. We're never given the reverse angles, the alternating over-the-shoulder shots, that *Gertrud*'s dialogue confrontations call for: we're restricted to one point of view—the frontal. What's behind the characters—behind their homes, their lives, their faces—remains mysterious. Dreyer invokes its presence, but he cannot, will not show it.

Dreyer's manipulation of space hardly stops there. Even when space is fully exposed in his shots, it takes on a strange elasticity, expanding and contracting according to the pattern of Dreyer's montage. In *The Parson's Widow*, Dreyer is already delaying the long, "establishing" shots that allow us to make spatial sense of a setting before it is divided into close-ups of the characters within it. In *The Parson's Widow*, Dreyer often begins a scene close-up, putting off the establishing shot until the middle or end of the scene, at which point it may not correspond to the images we've formed in our minds. The room is larger or smaller, the characters closer together or further apart, than we would have guessed from the close-ups. At other times, Dreyer will begin with an establishing shot and then go on to undermine it: an example from *The Parson's Widow* finds the three main characters sitting loosely around a fireplace, a scene that becomes much more intimate in the shot breakdown when the warmth and tightness of the close-ups seem to draw the characters close together. And in *The Passion of Joan of Arc*, there are, famously, no true establishing shots at all; its space is wholly subjective, wholly plastic.

In his details, Dreyer is a very physical, tactile filmmaker, but his sense of overall space is psychological and spiritual. It reflects the inner reality of his scenes, not exclusively their external arrangement. *The Bride of Glomdale* finds its ruling metaphor in two farmsteads separated by a river (just as the two families are divided on the marriage of their children). Dreyer begins the film by insisting on the strict physicality of the separation, but as the narrative brings the two families together, so does Dreyer's elliptical cutting plan work to collapse the space. The two farms are finally contiguous, linked rather than separated by the river. The elasticity of Dreyer's space is an effect of his editing; it comes from outside the image, in the particular arrangement and rearrangement of shots. His lighting effects are a matter of mise-en-scène, located inside the image. A sense of Dreyer's singular completeness as a filmmaker can be gained by seeing how the two contradictory methods, montage and mise-en-scène, ultimately feed into each other—for what are his white walls but a way of dissolving space within the frame, of creating a montage effect through visual style? The white walls both limit and liberate the space of Dreyer's images, simultaneously collapsing space into the flatness of the movie screen itself, and extending space infinitely by denying the clear black lines of perspective.

Dreyer is, of course, famous for his close-ups (*The Passion of Joan of Arc* consists of little else), but he should also be famous for his long shots, whose eloquence (through perhaps more subtle and diffused) makes the expressiveness of the close-ups possible. A Dreyer close-up is not just the intensification of an emotion, the foregrounding of an actor: it is also an elimination, an isolation. In some ways, *Mikael* seems to me a much richer film than *Joan* (though it is much less well known), because its alternation of long and close shots makes their nature more clear, more dramatically functional. The long shots in *Mikael* seem deliberately theatrical, taken straight into the scene (from the point of view of the spectator in the theater) and frequently framed by proscenium arches in the form of doorways and low ceilings. The compositions are recessive, leading us into the frame and away from the surface of the screen (a surface marked by the flat frame-within-the-frame of the arch). Dreyer's close-ups, on the other hand, are generally taken from a slightly elevated angle, one that grants a degree of depth to the arrangement of head and shoulders. These compositions are (for the want of a better word) "egressive"—they extend toward us from the surface of the screen, escaping the flatness. Thus the alternation of long shot and close-up produces a rhythm of containment and release—a containment within a social, material setting (the theatrical) and a release into individuality, isolation, transcendence (the cinematic).

The division of the mise-en-scène into close-up and long shot is a representation of the conflict of spirit and body that defines Dreyer's profoundly Protestant view of the world. Protestant, that is, but not puritanical: Dreyer cannot support a strict division, just as his most "spiritual" close-ups contain, in their highlighted textures, an element of physicality, of sexuality. For Dreyer, the crisis of Protestantism is centered on the question of love, which can be both a sexual and a spiritual quantity. For Dreyer, both kinds of love contain the possibility of the sacred: he does not rule out one kind in favor of the other, but looks instead for a resolution, a new quantity that might contain them both. *Mikael*, through its use of long and close shots, becomes the most successful of Dreyer's silents in portraying that quantity, which might be described (very inadequately) as a kind of spiritual sexuality, a love that caresses the soul.

In *Mikael*, the spiritual love of a painter (Zoret, played by the Danish director Benjamin Christensen) for his model and substitute son (Mikael, played by an impossibly young and handsome Walter Slezak) is played against the sexual love of Mikael for a fallen noblewoman, the Princess Zamikow (Nora Gregor). It's far too facile to say that the first affair is played in close-up, the second in long shot; rather, these are the extreme poles of the exquisite variations Dreyer introduces. Zoret, as he feels Mikael moving away from him, comes to occupy a close-up space even within the long shots, by means of a black costuming that envelops and dissolves his body, leaving only his face (its whiteness accentuated by makeup) to be clearly defined against the (for once) dark backgrounds. Zoret is incomplete without Mikael, just as Mikael has lost something in his relationship with Zamikow. The final resolution, the discovery of a spiritual sexuality, is achieved through a remarkable confluence of cinematic and psychological themes. Zoret, on his deathbed (and now little more than a head on a pillow) imaginatively projects himself to the distant apartment where Mikael and Zamikow are making love—a projection represented by an abrupt cutaway from death room close-up to boudoir long shot, a cutaway that has no narrative motivation. Dreyer's montage has, again, unified two distinct spaces, and in this exalted metaspace, Zoret seems to participate in the lovemaking. Zoret makes love to Mikael through Zamikow; the terms—body/spirit, long shot/close-up—are united in a single figure. "Now I can die in peace," says Zoret's intertitle, "having known great love." "Don't worry," says Zamikow to a suddenly troubled Mikael, "stay with me."

When a Woman Ascends the Stairs

Directed by MIKIO NARUSE {May 28, 1982}

I've only seen three films by Mikio Naruse—*Wife! Be Like a Rose!* (1935), *Floating Clouds* (1955), and now, *When a Woman Ascends the Stairs* (1960), which the Art Institute's Film Center will be showing this weekend. It's a tiny sample of the 88 features Naruse directed between 1930 and 1967 (only half of which survive), but with the personality, assurance, and range of styles those three films show, it's enough to convince me that Naruse belongs with the greatest Japanese directors—with Mizoguchi and Ozu. If Naruse remains unknown here, it may be because he did his best to remain unknown in Japan. According to Audie Bock, in her indispensable *Japanese Film Directors*, Naruse was a pathologically shy man who did his work and disappeared, never putting himself forward to protest the many routine scripts he was assigned to, barely able to speak to the actors and technicians on his set. Bock quotes the actor Tatsuya Nakadai, who appeared in *When a Woman Ascends the Stairs* and several other Naruse films: "He was the most difficult director I ever worked with. He never said a word." But somehow—perhaps by telepathy—Naruse drew astonishing effects from his actors; short of the utter blankness of Bresson's actors, there are no other performances in film that express so much with so little—with the slightest turn of a head, a world crumbles.

In his late films, Naruse's circumspection became the basis of his style. He was the least intrusive of directors, the least visible. In a film like *When a Woman*, the camera placement seems stripped of every inflection, every imposed attitude. The director withdraws from the spectacle; his presence is all but impalpable. But as the stylistic exuberance of the early *Wife! Be Like a Rose!* demonstrates—with its swinging, undisguised camera movement and aggressively mismatched edits—Naruse's anonymity was something he worked toward, a style consciously developed and constantly refined. It's an irony of the art of movies that, while middle-range directors begin anonymously and develop their expressive quirks over the course of their careers, the greatest filmmakers—Ford, Renoir, Lang, Hawks—begin in a burst of baroque expressionism and gradually narrow their stylistic choices, moving toward simplicity and plainness. Naruse went further than any of them; only time—and the hoped-for reissue of his backlog of work—will tell whether he achieved as much.

When a Woman Ascends the Stairs belongs to Naruse's favorite genre, the woman's melodrama, and stars his favorite actress, Hideko Takamine (who appeared in 17 of his films, including *Floating Clouds*). Takamine, a soft, recessive presence with bright, Mary Steenburgen eyes and a Margaret Sullavan vulnerability, plays Keiko, a professional bar hostess who works in one of the tiny establishments beehived through Tokyo's Ginza district. Though she is not a prostitute, the owners expect her to play up to her customers; a bar's success or failure depends on the popularity of the hostess, and there is a continuous battle among the hundred different bars for the loyalties of the regulars—the high-spending businessmen who pick one bar as their home away from home, their office away from the office. Keiko, who wears kimonos rather than evening gowns, flirts with discretion, and remains faithful to the memory of her late husband, has a small, faithful following, but her manager (Tatsuya Nakadai) believes she is too conservative to attract new business. She should be more accommodating to her customers, Nakadai tells her, particularly to the wealthy provincial businessman who repeatedly offers to set her up in her own shop if only she will be kinder to him on his trips to Tokyo. Keiko resolves to open a place of her own without a "sponsor" and asks her regular clients to contribute to a subscription list, but the plan fails when she falls ill with an ulcer and is unable to work. The last of her savings go to her brother, who faces a jail sentence if Keiko does not pay for his lawyer. Desperate to find some security in her life—and sure that the man she really loves, a handsome banker, will not divorce his wife for her—Keiko agrees to marry Fujisaka (Masayuki Mori, the pudgy potter of Mizoguchi's *Ugetsu*), a kind-faced client who at least promises dim happiness. But then Keiko discovers that Fujisaka has deceived her, a discovery that unleashes a string of betrayals.

At first it seems odd that this least assertive of directors would be attracted to this most extravagant and emotional of genres. But of course, there is nothing better suited than the melodrama, with its manic highs and lows, its outpourings and abrupt reversals, to set off the straight, even line that is Naruse's direction. Naruse gives the most prosaic passages of his story—the bar girls gossiping before work, Keiko chatting with a colleague in a coffee shop—the same weight he gives to his big dramatic moments; there is no acceleration of the editing, no up-scaling of the acting, no dramatization of the camera placement in the transition between the grayly quotidian and the intensely climactic. But Naruse doesn't even out his line simply to neutralize the emotional moments; there's no hint of irony or coldheartedness in his technique. He isn't stepping back from high emotion, but rather struggling to keep it in context—to spin the texture of a life that includes both ordinary moments and extraordinary ones, and suggest that the ordinary may weigh just as heavily. In both *Floating Clouds* and *When a Woman*, Naruse's heroines become weirdly accustomed to tragedy, almost comfortable with it. The ordinary merges with the apocalyptic, and terror suspended, spread out, becomes a pervasive, familiar anxiety. The moments of high emotion come almost as a relief; at last, the issues have become clear and focused, feelings concrete and expressible. With his evenness, Naruse erases the line between the banal and the tragic: there is no variation in the quality of experience, but only a continuity of pain, rising and falling in subtle degrees of intensity.

Naruse's title refers to a repeated image of Keiko climbing the flight of stairs that leads from the street to her second-story establishment. With variations in camera angle and dramatic emphasis, it recurs throughout the film with the regularity of an inner pulse—the metronome that marks the evenness of Naruse's rhythm, and serves as an index to the rolling sameness of Keiko's life. No matter what may happen, this familiar event must always be returned to, like the trope that punctuates the movements of a dance. But the significance of the stairway figure isn't entirely formal: as she ascends the stairs, Keiko feels herself in transition, changing from the complexly human individual who exists on the streets and at home into the smiling, constantly accommodating bar hostess. As she climbs, Keiko becomes "Mama-san," the name applied generally to members of her profession. Her identity is consumed.

Naruse, with his focus on the position of women in Japanese society, shares some of Mizoguchi's proto-feminist themes. Neither director is a simple ideologue, but where Mizoguchi's feminism is emotional and mystical, Naruse's is more pointedly political. Mizoguchi's female characters are genuinely stronger, wiser, more mature than his men; Naruse's are simply expected to be so, because that is the role that has been thrust upon them—every woman must be a Mama-san, whether she has the emotional resources or not. The crucial moment in *When a Woman* comes with Keiko's discovery that she has no right to happiness—no right, even, to her personal wants and personal needs. The men around her will not allow her to be human. When she ascends the stairs for the last time in the film, she will not come down—she will remain Mama-san forever. The role is the only refuge open to her, but to adopt it she must destroy herself as a person, resign her hopes.

Naruse's visual style also makes an interesting contrast to Mizoguchi's method. The hard, clean lines of Japanese architecture, which Mizoguchi employs so brilliantly to cast tense lines of force across his frame, are used by Naruse to balance his compositions. Instead of positioning his camera against the angles of the architecture as Mizoguchi does, creating lines that run diagonally through the image and beyond it, Naruse often squares his frame lines with the lines of the set, as if it were not the camera, but the environment itself, that is holding the characters in frame. Mizoguchi's compositions strain against the frame line, as if the image itself were yearning for something higher, pushing toward the transcendent. Naruse's balanced images embody a world where such transcendence is impossible, where space is packaged, concrete, oppressive. When he works in the wide-screen format, as he does in *When a Woman*, he emphasizes horizontal lines—tabletops, bars, window frames—in a way that seems to make the image even wider. His actors are suspended in a burgeoning emptiness, addressing each other from opposite sides of the frame across an unbridgeable gulf. Space unfolds as something solid between them. Milton has his darkness visible; Naruse has his emptiness palpable.

Naruse uses close-ups sparingly but brilliantly. It suggests something of Naruse's perversity that he uses more close-ups in the wide-screen *When a Woman* than in the standard ratio *Floating Clouds*, when the conventional wisdom dictates that close-ups look awkward and out of place in scope films. But Naruse doesn't put his close-ups to the conventional use, as a way of embracing and intensifying emotion (his actors invariably play their most dramatic scenes in medium shot, generally with their backs turned to the camera). Instead, they represent a momentary reprieve from the prison of space—moments when the characters are taken out of the emptiness and allowed to fill the screen with their own individuality. The expressions in these shots are generally blank or ambiguous; they seem meant less to express emotion than to assert a sense of privacy—the close-ups are occasionally reminders of the thoughts and feelings the characters are keeping back. In the end, this private space will be Keiko's salvation—it's the only place she's free from the demands of others. What is Keiko thinking in these enigmatic close-ups? We can guess, but Naruse will not spell it out. The most private of filmmakers, he will not think of violating the privacy of his characters.

Le Silence de la mer and *Bob le Flambeur*

Directed by JEAN-PIERRE MELVILLE {December 3, 1982}

Jean-Pierre Melville is one of the great unclassifiables of the cinema. Working in France, from his debut in 1947 to his death in 1973, he made 13 films that ran the course from Jean Cocteau to Richard Crenna, melding European high art to American low in a way that confounded both critics and audiences. Melville was a maniacal *cinephile* before the word was invented: he spent the 30s and 40s absorbing American films at a fantastic rate, and by the time he made his first feature—*Le Silence de la mer*—he was almost mystically in tune with the nuances of camera movement and framing. Melville was, perhaps, the first thoroughly self-conscious filmmaker—the first to enter the medium with a detailed, critical knowledge of its history. It was this self-consciousness that made him the spiritual godfather of the New Wave directors—this, and his fierce, almost paranoid insistence on total independence from the established production system. Melville made his most personal films by imitating the most regimented, industrial era in American filmmaking—a paradox that must have appealed to the paradoxically minded Godard, who cast him reverentially as a famous novelist in *Breathless*. But Melville, who seemingly couldn't tolerate being identified with any group, quickly repudiated the New Wave he had helped to create; for him, jump cuts, hand-held cameras, and casual lighting were simply signs of directors who didn't "understand anything about film." He sat out the French boom of the 60s in stony isolation, turning out his rigorously classical gangster films solely for the domestic market. During Melville's lifetime, his only film to play commercially in Chicago was the 1967 *Le Samouraï* which—cut, dubbed, and retitled *The Godson*—played the downtown grind houses in the wake of a certain major motion picture by Francis Ford Coppola.

This weekend and next, the Film Center of the Art Institute is playing host to a series of six Melville films, made available in new 35mm prints by the French Cultural Service. A few of them—the Cocteau adaptation *Les Enfants terribles*, the two late gangster films *Second Breath* and *Le Samouraï*—have been through town before in 16mm, but they should well be worth seeing in their full glory; the other three—*Le Silence de la mer*, *Bob le Flambeur*, and the final, rather disappointing *Dirty Money* (with Richard Crenna) are here in their premieres. (*Without Apparent Motive* and *The Inheritor*, two films by Melville's longtime assistant Philippe Labro, will conclude the series on December 17.)

The story behind *Le Silence de la mer* is almost as good as the film: a novel published clandestinely during the Nazi occupation, *Le Silence* had become a kind of anthem for the members of the French resistance; Melville wasn't able to convince its author, Vercors, that the book could be filmed without betraying its spirit. Production began with the understanding that the finished film would be shown to a jury of former resistance fighters, who would then vote on whether or not the film should be released. In the meantime, Melville's application to the French film union had been turned down, which meant that he wouldn't be able to buy his film stock (still scarce and tightly controlled in the postwar years) legally. Melville and his first-time cameraman, the soon-to-be-legendary Henri Decaë, managed to scrape together a collection of leftover footage—of different brands and different speeds—and shot the film at Vercors's own house, where the events that had inspired the original story had taken place. Melville's principal cast included two amateurs—one family friend (Nicole Stéphane) and one resistance comrade (Jean-Marie Robain). When the resistance jury finally saw the film one year later, they voted unanimous approval—and for his resourcefulness, Melville was fined 50,000 francs by the government film office.

Le Silence de la mer isn't a natural film subject: it consists mainly of long monologues delivered by a German officer (Howard Vernon) to the two French civilians, an old man and his niece, with whom he has been billeted in the provinces. Out of nationalistic pride, the old man refuses to speak to the German, and his stern looks prevent his niece from doing so either, but as the German speaks, pacing their sitting room in his civilian clothes, they are drawn into a kind of sympathy. He speaks of his love for France and French culture, his dissatisfaction with his own country, and his hope that the occupation will represent a healing "marriage" between France and Germany—a union of strengths that will enrich both partners. But a leave spent in Paris among his highly placed friends in the occupation forces shows the German that his dream is a naive one; the Nazis mean to crush France forever. Returning to the old man and the girl, he tells them of his discovery and his decision to transfer to the Eastern Front; the long silence is broken by two words and the German departs—leaving behind the girl who now loves him.

The allegory of broken romance—between France and Germany, the niece and the soldier—is developed with more taste and grace than a synopsis might suggest, but essentially this is still propagandistic material: words like "tradition," "culture," and "national soul" float through the air without being dramatically defined, depending on the atmosphere of the times for their substantive and emotional charge. Yet beneath the jingoistic theme there is something more personal to Melville, a sense of silence and isolation that would take on profound contours in his later work. Where the novel uses interpersonal relations as a metaphor for international politics, Melville's direction—by seizing on human looks and gestures—brings the metaphor back around. In *Le Silence de la mer*, it is politics that holds the characters apart, where in the later films it will be a personal sense of ethics or an attitude toward fate; the motives don't matter as much as the image of stasis, of frozen relationships, that they produce. During the German officer's monologues, the old man and the girl sit motionless in their chairs by the fire; the few movements they do make—the uncle draws on his pipe, the niece attends to her knitting—are self-absorbed, self-contained. But the German is in constant movement, circling the room to inspect the fire, the books, the prints on the walls as he speaks—his gestures are those of reaching out, taking in. And where Melville's camera generally assumes down angles on the old man and the girl, observing them from above and somehow pinning them down, the camera is more likely to look up at the German, giving him grandeur and respect. (The exaggerated perspective of these shots frequently suggests *Citizen Kane*, which was then first being shown in France.) The mise-en-scène makes the German the active, heroic figure, yet dramatically he is still the destroyer. Much of Melville's work hangs on this paradox: in silent self-containment there is certainty, strength, and integrity, but also a kind of death; when the silence is broken—and it must be broken—life and emotion enter, only to destroy completely. Melville's films are about the violation of closed worlds, a violation both necessary and fatal.

Bob (Roger Duchesne), the elegant, aging gambler of Melville's 1955 *Bob le Flambeur*, lives in a closed world, too—the Montmartre district of Paris, with its girlie shows, smoky bars, floating card games, and population of crooks, prostitutes, and tolerant policemen. This is *le milieu*—the Parisian underworld—and Melville made it the setting of most of his late films, though it never again looked quite as cozy and romantic as it did in the lyrical predawn light of *Bob*. The film, with its casual, comic tone, its talky sound track, and its numerous and expressive supporting characters, isn't at all typical of Melville's severe late style, yet it's steeped in his personality—the movie is like Melville on a vacation, relaxed, but still himself.

Within his closed world, Bob is also a character in suspension; once a professional burglar, he's retired on his profits, but a bad run of luck at the gambling tables is chipping away at his resources. He's a prisoner to gambling, to chance, just as he seems a prisoner to his elaborate personal style: every time he enters his favorite nightclub, he's compelled to take a roll of the bar dice; every time he comes to his apartment, he drops a franc in the slot machine he keeps in a closet. Bob has a protégé, Paulo (Daniel Cauchy), who imitates his distinctive dress and gallant manners down to the last detail; every time Bob looks at him, he sees his own mannerisms reflected back. Bob's passivity and isolation are so well ingrained that when he undertakes the "rescue" of a young would-be hooker (Isabelle Corey), he doesn't even think of acting on his attraction for her. Eventually, she falls in with Paulo: Bob, coming home late one night, finds the two of them asleep in his bed; he looks for a moment—enjoying the pain, perhaps—and quietly moves away.

Bob's decision to change his luck—to get back into harness and attempt the robbery of the Deauville casino—has the same value as the two worlds that break *Le Silence de la mer*. The closed world is broken open, and for a while it looks as if the same devastation will result: as Bob goes about planning the robbery, rounding up his team and working out his strategy, word of his activities is slowly making its way to Bob's old friend and nemesis, the Inspector (Guy Decomble). In its close, workmanly concentration on the details of planning and executing a crime, *Bob le Flambeur* strongly suggests John Huston's *The Asphalt Jungle*, but Melville—who altered his screenplay after seeing Huston's film—pulls a sly reverse on the plot. For once, here is a caper film in which the suspense is on the side of law and order: we want the crooks to abandon their plan rather than to follow it through.

The ending is too much of a charming surprise to be spelled out in print; suffice it to say that Bob's luck returns, stronger than ever. Melville is often described as an existentialist, but to execute a scene like the finish of *Bob le Flambeur*, even in jest, you need to have some faith in the basic benevolence of the world—some faith even in a higher, protective power, such as the "luck" that Bob turns his back on and that then returns, in the end, to save and reward him after all. Melville's characters don't feel the existentialist urge to test and define themselves—or when they do, they end by annihilating the self they've tried to discover. There is a drive for safety and stability in Melville—a search for sanctuaries—that lies under his taste for closed worlds, his nostalgia for the studio system, his love for *le milieu*. It's curious that no true family setting, as far as I know, appears in any of his films—there is only the pain of the family's loss.

The Leopard

Directed by LUCHINO VISCONTI {November 25, 1983}

At this point, it seems likely that the best American films of 1983 will be the best American films of 1954: Alfred Hitchcock's *Rear Window* and George Cukor's *A Star Is Born*. It's good to see older films getting a commercial reissue in new or restored prints (as has long been the practice in Europe), but it's depressing to realize how poorly our own films compete with them. It feels like cheating to compare *Rear Window* with *The Right Stuff*, and in a sense it is: the rules of the game have changed so radically since Hitchcock made his film—with the collapse of the studio system, the decay of genre structures, and the disappearance of the adult audience—that *The Right Stuff* appears to be playing in an entirely different (and definitely minor) league. Now you can add to the list the best Italian film of 1962—Luchino Visconti's *The Leopard*, a movie that attracted very little attention when it was first released here 20 years ago (though in a badly mangled version). In the current context, it seems clearly a masterpiece, a film with all the density, sensitivity, scale, and seriousness of purpose that seem to have fled the contemporary American cinema.

The Leopard is, in part, an American film: some of the financing came from Twentieth Century-Fox, based on the reputation of the source novel (by Giuseppe Tomasi di Lampedusa) as an Italian *Gone With the Wind* and the star presence of Burt Lancaster. When the completed film turned out to differ in several important respects from *GWTW*, Fox reduced the running time from Visconti's 205 minutes to 161, printed Visconti's Technicolor images in the far inferior DeLuxe Color process, and released the film in an imperfectly dubbed English language version. The print being shown at the Fine Arts Theater is a product of Fox's newly formed classics division, and it appears to be the 185-minute intermediate version approved by Visconti for international release. The Italian sound track has been restored, and the color freshened to an approximation of the original (and now technically unreproducible) Technicolor hues.

The restored *Leopard* is not only Visconti's greatest film but a far greater film than I would have thought him capable of making. It represents one of those rare occasions in the cinema when a minor artist is able to produce a major work through his intense rapport with given material, a miracle of creative synthesis that seems unique to the movies. It's said that Visconti was assigned the novel because he, like the protagonist, was a member of the Italian aristocracy (Visconti was a count, his hero a prince). The identification was certainly deep, and much of the movie's power comes from the way in which the sensibilities of filmmaker and character complement each other, the dignity, the discretion, and serenity of Lancaster's prince matching the qualities of Visconti's direction step for step. And the film's strong sense of authenticity in its insider's view of the aristocracy could only come from someone familiar enough with the manners and customs of the class to be able to accept them as natural. Visconti doesn't call attention to the elegant habits of his characters, but presents them as simply a part of the daily routine—a perspective always missing from his portraits of lower-class life (*La terra trema*, *Rocco and His Brothers*), in which Visconti underlined every torn T-shirt as a sign of unspeakable exoticism. A social portrait is only successful when it ceases to be strange—when we have the sense of sharing the characters' world, of seeing it as they do. If the world of *The Leopard* seems extraordinarily real, it is because Visconti sees it as ordinary.

Visconti was a count, but he was also a member of the Italian Communist party. The period of *The Leopard*—the Risorgimento of the 1860s, when the divided Italian states were united by Garibaldi's revolutionary peasant army and then taken over by the emerging middle class, which succeeded in imposing its own king—is a ripe one for Marxist analysis, and the film is one of the few historical epics in which economic forces can be seen at work. (Imagine *Gone With the Wind* identifying Rhett Butler as a venture capitalist.) On one level, there is no contradiction between Visconti the count and Visconti the communist: both can agree on their hatred of the greedy, grubby bourgeoisie, though one despises them as oppressors and the other as ill-mannered louts whose evening clothes don't fit. Unfortunately, this unanimity of opinion doesn't make for particularly good filmmaking: from both perspectives, the bourgeois remain incomprehensible objects of contempt and are subjected—mainly through the figure of Don Caloqero, the businessman-mayor of the Sicilian town where the prince has his country estate—to a kind of gross caricature that is out of keeping with the complexities of the rest of the film.

Visconti's contradictions are more fertile. If the prince is a hero to the aristocrat, he is a villain to the Marxist, and out of this struggle of extremes emerges a character of remarkable depth and persuasiveness. Prince Fabrizio de Salina is a man who acts nobly, wisely, and altruistically in the name of his own self-interest. Approaching his 50th year, he is facing the loss of his power, his fortune, his class, and his health; the film is concerned with his efforts to preserve what he can. It is the prince who perverts the revolution Visconti presumably endorses: playing history as if it were a chess opponent, he makes his moves swiftly and well, turning disaster to his advantage, offering strategic sacrifices, and finally achieving stalemate if not checkmate. His is a lean, shrewd, almost invisible style of play, and Visconti brings us to admire his technique, if not his motives. There is something almost lunar, abstract, about the prince in action that ennobles his efforts to save his fading class; he seems so little involved with the life of his family (his wife is a shrewish, small person, and his children have been disappointments to him) that he appears to be acting not for emotional, self-protective reasons, but out of sheer inbred gallantry, as if he were fighting on behalf of strangers. Lancaster's natural detachment, his sense of self-containment, serves him brilliantly here: his prince exists on a plane apart, acting from a moral certainty that the other characters cannot share, cannot penetrate. Despite his vitality, there is something already dead, sepulchral about him—a ghostly, ancient quality that Visconti pinpoints in a striking shot in which the prince and his family, freshly arrived from a long and difficult journey, are seen sitting silently in the family pew of their chapel, their rigid bodies and frozen faces still covered with the white dust of the road. They have become their own tomb sculptures, godlike in their silence and stillness, irretrievably old.

It's difficult to dramatize a figure as private and mysterious as the prince: something of him must always be held back, which means that he can never fully expose himself in dramatic confrontations, never face the other characters as an equal in conversation. To solve this problem, Visconti has surrounded the prince with a series of interlocutors, characters—such as the family priest, the gamekeeper, or the representative from the newly formed government—whose function it is to question and consult him. The prince speaks to his questioners, but never engages them; they are like an audience within the film, and we approach the prince through them. The view of character is entirely an exterior one, and Visconti maintains it rigorously through the first two-thirds of his film. The prince acts, but he does not interact; he remains ultimately inaccessible.

Inaccessible, that is, to all but one character. The prince's single strong emotional bond is not with his wife or his children, but with his nephew Tancredi (Alain Delon), an impoverished nobleman who, as the film begins, has joined Garibaldi's redshirts. Tancredi is clearly the son the prince wishes he had had: Tancredi represents both his past (as a young version of himself) and his hope for the future, the perpetuation of the princely line. But there is an extra, unspoken element in the relationship, an emanation, perhaps, of Visconti's homosexuality. Tancredi, especially as played by the young and beautiful Delon, is also a lover, real or potential, for the prince; their bond represents the kind of ultimate aristocratic refinement, the purely aesthetic passion, that Visconti would later examine much more openly (and much less successfully) in *Ludwig*. It is this element, unacknowledged in the scenario but explicit in Visconti's mise-en-scène, that is the film's hidden motor, the secret source of its grandeur and tragedy. The prince's final move in this game with history is to arrange the marriage of Tancredi to the ravishing daughter (Claudia Cardinale) of the wealthy, vulgar mayor. This alliance with the middle class will mean new money and new blood for the exhausted aristocracy, but at the cost of something sublime.

The story is over with Tancredi's engagement, but the film continues for another hour—an hour that makes the difference between a good film and a great one. First Visconti films the plot, and then he films what's left: the meaning and emotions, the shifts in perception and philosophy, that the plot has released. The ballroom sequence that concludes *The Leopard* is one of the loveliest and most arbitrary sequences in film history, lovely largely because it is arbitrary. Wholly unmotivated by the dictates of the action, it detaches itself from the body of the film, which comes to seem simply a prelude. Visconti has here achieved a remarkable freedom. Liberated from narrative demands, his camera is able to wander at will, engaging the looks, the gestures, and the patterns of movement that elude the narrow focus of a plot, but which provide the purest kind of cinematic expression. Naturally, it was this freedom that Fox couldn't tolerate: most of the cuts in the shortened version of the film were made in this section.

The setting is a gigantic society ball, at which Tancredi and his fiancée will first be introduced to the gentry. The prince dances one waltz with his niece-to-be, thus confirming her acceptance by the nobility, and spends the rest of the ball by himself, moving from room to room, looking and reflecting. Visconti's most crippling limitation as a filmmaker was his theatricality, his tendency to anchor his action in a few restricted settings, and his complementary tendency to attempt to escape those restrictions by pushing his performers to the hollow exaggeration that is the most offensive form of melodrama. But in the ballroom sequence, the basis of his mise-en-scène changes completely, shifting from the static theatricality that was his habit to the fluid cinema that is his ultimate glory. The camera is no longer anchored, but free to move with the character—free to move from room to room, impression to impression, feeling to feeling. With this new discovery of space, the subject of the movie changes, from the theatrical theme of a character's relationship to other characters to the filmic theme of a character's relationship to his world.

What these gliding camera movements, mutations of space, fleeting observations, and moments of solitude tell the prince is that he and his world are dying. The film began with the discovery of a corpse in a garden (the body of a Garibaldi soldier); at the end, death has spread throughout the prince's paradise. The exterior view—of the prince as a remote, superior being, locked in a superhuman struggle with history—has given way to an interior, personal one. The prince realizes that he has engineered his own extinction, but he no longer tries to resist the notion. It is time for his world to fade away. In passing Tancredi from his own sterile embrace to the fertility of a bourgeois marriage, he has ensured that something will survive, that a new order will replace the old. Visconti devoted much of his late career—*The Damned, Death in Venice, Ludwig, Conversation Piece*—to attempting to recapture this twilight ambience. Though his version became more baroque, he never surpassed the simple image with which *The Leopard* concludes: the prince standing alone in a cobbled street at dawn, the past meeting the future.

Hitch's Riddle: On Five Rereleased Films

Film Comment {May–June, 1984}

Is Alfred Hitchcock an artist? The number of books, articles, and doctoral dissertations devoted to answering that question, one way or another, easily accounts for a forest or two. It can even be seen as the fundamental question of film criticism in this half of the century—the question that, when it was first raised by a group of young French critics in the early Fifties, touched off a revolution in the way movies were watched, discussed, and eventually (when those critics became directors) made. It is still the question that divides film aesthetics, separating critics who believe in the expressive power of popular filmmaking from those who see art only in the highbrow asceticism of a Bergman or an Antonioni, separating those who believe that film has its own artistic properties and potentials from those who measure achievement only by older, more established values. Despite all the arguments offered from both sides, the Hitchcock question and the questions it generates are, clearly, still open.

But if the Hitchcock question has proven to be difficult to answer definitively, isn't it in part because Hitchcock himself either couldn't answer it or wouldn't? Reading his interviews, one may find it hard to believe he was anything other than what he claimed to be: a resourceful technician and an accomplished entertainer. The front, if it was a front, was impeccably maintained. Alfred Hitchcock has not left a single word that suggested he saw himself as a serious artist. And yet in watching the films, with their supreme formal inventiveness, their incredibly dense networks of themes and motifs, and their still undiminished power to grip an audience, it is impossible to think that he did not know what he was doing. Hitchcock's art is too elaborately detailed to be instinctive, too self-critical and too self-referential to be subconscious. The public persona—or, for that matter, the private one outlined by Donald Spoto in his Hitchcock biography *The Dark Side of Genius*—seems irreconcilable with the authorial voice of the films. Hitchcock was either a great liar or the most mystically inspired practitioner of automatic film directing in the history of cinema.

Perhaps there is another explanation. The five "lost" Hitchcock films—*Rope*, *Rear Window*, *The Trouble with Harry*, *The Man Who Knew Too Much*, and *Vertigo*—that have recently been returned to circulation by Universal Classics span a crucial period in Hitchcock's career. *Rope*, in 1948, marked Hitchcock's first independent production. With his creative freedom came a steady deepening of themes, an increasing complexity of development, and a soaring mastery of cinematic expression. It is during this period that Hitchcock came into his own. It climaxes, in 1958, with *Vertigo*, perhaps his single greatest achievement.

This extraordinary rush of creative power is not only reflected *by* these films, but *in* them as well—through the appearance, in *Rope*, of a new thematic cluster centered on art and art-making. Whatever else these films contain (and they contain a great deal), they also embody Hitchcock's reflections on himself as an artist. In these films, Hitchcock can be seen doing what he refused to do in life: acknowledging his status as a creator and struggling to come to grips with that status. Though art isn't always the primary theme, it is always closely related to the perennial thematic center of Hitchcock's work: the problem of guilt. If Hitchcock always refused to confess his artistry—and went to maniacal lengths to protect himself from the accusation—it's because art was Alfred Hitchcock's dirty secret, his original sin.

*

"I undertook *Rope* as a stunt," Hitchcock contritely told François Truffaut. "That's the only way I can describe it. I really don't know how I came to indulge in it." Hitchcock goes on to dismiss the film's notorious continuous-shot technique as "a crazy idea" and "nonsensical" before allowing himself to be sidetracked into a safely academic discussion of lighting methods for color films. Most of Hitchcock's critics have been content to second this judgment, but even if *Rope* is a failure (it is, I think, though for different reasons), it's worth pausing to consider what was, in 1948, a remarkably radical way of approaching the medium. At a moment when the social content of neo-realism was the critical rage, Hitchcock was posing a formal question at least 20 years ahead of its time; it would have to wait for the structuralist filmmakers of the late 60s, and in particular, the 45-minute zoom of Michael Show's *Wavelength* (which also has a thriller "plot"), to be further developed.

The continuous takes of *Rope*—there are ten or twelve shots in a film that runs 80 minutes—represent a complete rejection of cutting, a technique then considered the essence of cinema. In its place, Hitchcock erects a new notion of screen space, a space designed not to contain the drama (as was the deep focus of Orson Welles and William Wyler) but to contain the audience. By eliminating cross-cutting, Hitchcock forestalls our identification with the characters. We are no longer caught up in the play of conflicting points of view that normally binds us to the drama, but left outside, tied to a single, remote perspective. We are trapped in the director's point of view, forced to follow the line of his attention, forced to accept his judgments on the characters. But this free-floating consciousness is a cold, empty one: the only identification figure *Rope* gives us is the mechanical one of the camera. For that reason, it's the least suspenseful of Hitchcock's suspense films.

The technique of *Rope* seems designed to underline the primacy of the director, just as standard Hollywood technique is designed to efface it. It's easy to understand why Hitchcock wanted to assert himself: He had just broken free from a long and frequently frustrating association with David O. Selznick, Hollywood's most "creative" producer—had, in fact, just left a film that Selznick produced to death, *The Paradine Case*. For his first independent production, he wanted the world to know that he was in charge at last. And yet, it's just this kind of assertion of power that *Rope* attacks.

In his interviews, Hitchcock gave the impression that just about any piece of material would have served the purposes of his formal experiment. But the text of *Rope*, based on a 1929 play by Patrick Hamilton, turns out to reflect in dramatic terms the main issues raised by Hitchcock's stylistic choices. Within minutes of committing the arbitrary murder that will be his "perfect crime," Brandon (John Dall) observes, "I always wished I had more artistic talent. But murder can be an art, too. The power to kill can be as great as the power to create." Brandon has invited the murdered man's friends, father, and fiancée for a party to be held in his apartment, the scene of the crime; the body will be placed in a massive hardwood chest in the living room. The party, Brandon says, will be "the signature of the artist." His partner, Philip (Farley Granger) concurs: the murder without the party would be like "painting a picture and not hanging it."

Brandon and Philip are old prep school friends, and now, apparently, lovers. (Though their sexuality isn't dramatized, it's indicative of Hitchcock's squeamishness over such matters that the apartment they share, which we otherwise see in meticulous detail, doesn't seem to contain a bedroom.) They have strangled their victim (another school friend) to prove to themselves the Nietzschean doctrine they learned at the knees of their old house master, Rupert Cadell (James Stewart): Superior people have the right to eliminate their inferiors, the people who "merely occupy space." Rupert has been invited to the party, too. As soon as he arrives, he launches into a well-rehearsed routine on the usefulness of murder—"Murder should be an art, not one of the seven lively, perhaps, but an art"—that anticipates the grisly humor of Hitchcock's introductions to his television series.

Though Brandon is a collector of paintings and Philip is an accomplished pianist, the art foregrounded in *Rope* is literature. Rupert is a publisher; Jan, the murdered man's fiancée (Joan Chandler), is a writer; Mr. Kentley, the victim's father (Sir Cedric Hardwicke), is a collector of fine editions. The party is being held, ostensibly, so that Mr. Kentley can examine some rare volumes from Brandon's collection, books that were packed in the chest that now contains his son's body. When Brandon makes a present of a few books to Mr. Kentley, he ties them up with the length of rope used in the strangulation. Books are the means by which the "superior people" define their superiority, define their lives. (Rupert interrupts a conversation about movie stars to announce that "I once went to the movies. I saw Mary Pickford.") But through their insistent association with the crime, books become agents of death. The printed word is a murder weapon.

In *Rope*, art is power, and power kills. Brandon grants himself divine status: By setting up a pair of candelabra and spreading out the party food on the chest that contains the victim's body, he is erecting an altar to himself. He gives himself the power to intervene in the lives of his subjects, to remake fate. He has invited not only his victim's fiancée to the party, but also her old boyfriend, hoping that, in the absence of the dead man, they will get back together (they do). In killing his victim, he revives their romance—the power to kill is also the power to create. He also dominates his lover, who in turn worships him.

All of these images of superiority and dominance (Brandon towers over the other characters, standing while they are sitting, and for the first half of the film his movements dictate the movements of the camera) are undercut by images of childishness. Brandon's altar is grandiose, but it is also the gesture of a child's make-believe. The characters make constant references to their childhoods: Mrs. Atwater (Constance Collier) allows how she "read a book when I was a girl"; we hear how much Brandon enjoyed ghost stories when he was a boy (particularly one about a woman locked in a trunk) and how much Philip enjoyed strangling chickens (until one rebelled).

The domineering mother who appears in virtually all of Hitchcock's films is doubled here. Brandon's mother lives on a farm in Connecticut where he and Philip will go to establish their alibi; the victim's mother, a bed-ridden hypochondriac, keeps telephoning to find out what has happened to her "only son." And she is doubled again: Mrs. Kentley has her earthly representative in Mrs. Atwater, the aunt who has come to the party in the ailing mother's place; Brandon's mother has her emissary in Mrs. Wilson (Edith Evanson), the maid who cares for him and Philip. We learn that at one point Brandon went out with Jan and that she threw him over, raising the possibility that Brandon's perfect crime isn't the immaculately arbitrary act he believes it to be, but the revenge of a jealous adolescent (though Hitchcock doesn't attempt to reconcile this suggestion with Brandon's evident feelings for Philip).

Relationships defined by intellectual superiority are paralleled by relationships based on emotional dependence. The two lines cross only in the figure of Rupert, who at the boarding school had been both the boys' teacher and their substitute father. Brandon has thought of telling Rupert about their plan—"he'd be able to appreciate the artistic angle"—but has decided not to, perhaps because on some level he realizes that Rupert is his intended victim, too. Only in killing the father (which he does, symbolically, by daring to do what Rupert only speaks of doing) can he become fully powerful, fully free.

It's with the character of Rupert that *Rope* falls apart. Though he's clearly the character closest to Hitchcock (at one point, Hitchcock's camera adopts Rupert's point of view, following his gaze as he imagines how Brandon and Philip committed their crime), he is never placed at any moral risk. All of the negative aspects of the "artist"—his assumption of power, his manipulativeness, his murderousness—are laid off on Brandon, leaving Rupert to brush off his responsibilities with a single accusation ("Did you think you were God?") and a flat denial ("You're giving my words a meaning I never dreamed of").

And yet Hitchcock's camera, all this while, has been behaving exactly like Brandon: passing judgment on the characters, manipulating our responses to the material, in a sense assassinating the audience by depriving us of our freedom to look and think for ourselves. The spatial set-up of *Rope* is one of Chinese-box confinement: We are obviously in a sound studio, inside of which is a gigantic, beautiful, and blatantly artificial cyclorama of the New York skyline, inside of which is an oppressively close apartment set, inside of which is a wooden chest, inside of which is a corpse. Hitchcock's camera makes us that corpse; it holds us just as tightly as the packing crate.

There's a tremendous rush of release at the climax of the film, when Rupert flings open the chest, knocking the books piled atop it directly into the camera lens, and then flings open a window to fire the shots to attract the police. The camera seems stunned by Rupert's assault; it retires quickly to the very edge of the set, taking up a neutral, proscenium-arch position. Rupert has banished the director and liberated the audience, freeing us from the work of art that is *Rope*. And yet the struggle has been too easy, the freedom too cheaply bought. Hitchcock would go on to put the stylistic discoveries of *Rope* to more complex, expressive, and responsible use in his next film, *Under Capricorn* (which remains the most seriously underrated of his movies). But he would not return to the thematic tangle raised by *Rope* until six years later, in *Rear Window*.

*

Rear Window seems to pick up immediately where *Rope* left off. Stewart is back, of course, but his broken leg is also an expansion of a curious reference in *Rope*—to a "bad leg" that Rupert "got in the war for his courage." The set of *Rear Window* duplicates the progressive confinements of *Rope*, with an added flourish; now the cyclorama is large enough to contain confinements of its own, the apartments of Stewart's neighbors. Most important, the roving camera of *Rope*, with its impersonal, inhuman point of view, has been humanized in the figure of the crippled Stewart confined to his wheelchair, holding his camera lens up to his eye. This strange, hybrid creature, half-man and half-machine (he even comes with his own tracking apparatus) becomes the audience's identification figure; we stay with him in his apartment, seeing what he sees and feeling what he feels. But he is also an identification figure for Hitchcock, the projection of the director's point of view into the fiction. L. B. Jeffries (Stewart) stands at the center of a three-way relationship: He is the meeting point of creator, creation, and consumer, a paradigm of the power relations in art.

"Tell me everything you saw, and what you think it means." So says Lisa Fremont (Grace Kelly) when she is finally—and rapturously—taken by the idea that Jeffries may really have witnessed a murder in the apartment across the courtyard. But this is also the demand that an audience makes on an artist: to relate an experience and then to interpret it, to draw sense and substance from a jumble of impressions. In the case of a film, those impressions consist of fragmentary sounds and images. It's the job of the filmmaker to find an order for those fragments, an arrangement—a montage—that makes them coherent. Just as *Rope* was predicated on continuous space (on mise-en-scène), so is *Rear Window* based on editing; in his interview book with Truffaut, Hitchcock even cites the famous Kuleshov experiment. The center of the film is the process of ordering and interpreting. It is supposed to be a creative process, positive, constructive, fulfilling. But in *Rear Window*, it becomes an object of horror—a perverse, criminal, even blasphemous act.

Most criticism of *Rear Window* has focused on Jeffries' voyeurism, but he's much more than a passive receptor of stimuli. By profession, Jeffries is a world-hopping photojournalist, with a specialty in war and disaster. His job requires him to be a witness, a walking camera, but it also demands that he call on his artistry to make the events he witnesses seem alive, to give them color and drama. As a photographer, Stewart is caught between two different conceptions of the image. His work isn't quite captured reality, but neither is it wholly manufactured artifice. The contradiction has crippled him. His broken leg is the result of an artistic intervention—an attempt to get a "dramatic," low-angle shot of a crashing race car. The photograph, which we see hanging on the wall above Jeffries' smashed camera, is certainly dramatic. It is also clearly fake, a composite of the kind that Hitchcock, with his love of impossible angles and exaggerated depth of field, frequently fabricated for his own films. Jeffries has done violence to reality to get this image; reality, in turn, has done violence to him.

Like many Hitchcock characters, Jeffries is a man in love with death. He enjoys his job because it means constant risk, and he dreads his impending marriage to Lisa because it means a sunny, perpetual security. Hitchcock implies that Jeffries travels to avoid settling his relationship with Lisa. The broken leg means no more travel, and so the arguments have started: Jeffries feels that he has to defend himself against Lisa's elegance, urbanity, and stability. He needs danger to escape from Lisa and the life she represents. If the broken leg means danger is no longer available in immediate, physical form, Jeffries will have to discover a new kind: intellectual danger, artistic risk.

The shot that follows the credits is one of Hitchcock's most original creations. It begins with the crane-mounted camera moving through the free space of the courtyard, passing from window to window and catching glimpses of the inhabitants; there is a sudden, violent whip pan, and the camera pulls back into Jeffries' apartment, where it catches him in a huge close-up, sound asleep in his wheelchair. The camera movement is so sudden and the focus change is so smooth that we don't have a chance to adjust to the change in scale—Jeffries' head looms up with the same proportions as the apartment building, the head of a sleeping giant. There's a delicate ambiguity at work in the shot: We see the neighbors first, which suggests that they have lives and realities of their own, but the movement into the apartment seems to place them as fantasies in Jeffries' imagination, as if they were characters in the dream he is dreaming. Hitchcock repeats the shot three more times in the film, in different dramatic contexts. Jeffries' relationship with the outside world shifts each time in subtle ways, sometimes giving primacy to the neighbors, sometimes to Jeffries. It is impossible to know who is dreaming whom, who comes first in this mental universe.

If Jeffries hasn't dreamed his neighbors, he has, for all practical purposes, created them. He has given them names ("Miss Torso" for a chorus girl, "Miss Lonelyhearts" for a spinster), and he has invented stories for them. When he tells his stories to Lisa or his visiting nurse (Thelma Ritter), he believes he's telling the truth, acting like a photojournalist, simply reporting the evidence. Strange, then, that five of the seven stories he tells are projections of his personal crisis. Everywhere he looks, he sees predatory women entrapping (or, in the case of Miss Lonelyhearts, trying to entrap) helpless men. Jeffries is sure that he isn't inventing anything, but the other two stories he "sees"—a middle-aged woman working on an abstract sculpture and a composer struggling with a popular song—are both stories of artistic creation, as if Jeffries also needed to project (and in so doing, reject) his self-consciousness as a creator.

Fears are mixed up with desires in these stories, as they are in dreams. Like dreams, they seem to be harmless fantasies, ways of letting off steam. But the fantasies don't stay harmless for long. Having invented his characters, the artist assumes the power to manipulate them, and the fantasy turns dark, malignant, controlling. The fatal moment comes when the camera, following Jeffries' gaze, pans from the voyeuristic spectacle of Miss Torso's dance rehearsals to the neighboring apartment of a costume jewelry salesman (Raymond Burr) and his shrewish, bed-ridden wife. The wife has vanished, and Thorwald, the salesman, is acting suspiciously. Jeffries' fantasies—the interpretation he makes from the fractured reality on view—have shifted from the sexual to the violent. In Miss Torso, he has invented a fantasy lover to ward off his commitment to Lisa; in Thorwald, he has invented a murderer, a projection of his darkest feeling, to eliminate her.

Like any good artist, Jeffries has taken fragments of reality and put them in an order that tells a story and gives them a meaning. But in reordering reality, in making his observations and inferences from his hopelessly limited point of view, he has killed it, turning something complex and ambiguous into a tidy narrative pattern, appropriating real people as the characters of the melodrama he has fantasized. He has created a world in his own image, and, like a hypocritical god (like Brandon in *Rope*), he promptly sits in judgment on it, persecuting Thorwald for the crime that is, at least metaphorically, really his own.

When Thorwald finally breaks into Jeffries' apartment, confronting his tormentor at last, he doesn't look at all like the monster we saw across the courtyard. Thorwald has broken through to Jeffries' side of the building, to Hitchcock's side of the camera, and to our side of the screen. What we see is a frightened, pathetic man who can only ask of his creator, in honest confusion and agony, "What do you want of me?" Only silence follows this supplication, as Jeffries hides in the darkness of his haven and refuses to speak. When Thorwald approaches him, the photojournalist fires the feeble thunderbolts of his flashgun, blinding Thorwald for a moment with his borrowed glory. But Thorwald pushes on, finally reaching Jeffries and forcing him to the window. Dethroned, he falls to the earth.

In *Rear Window*, Hitchcock collapses the sterile opposition of *Rope*: Jeffries is both Brandon and Rupert, both monstrous and benign. He invites our sympathy while he commands our horror because the crimes he commits are our crimes, each time we tell a story or listen to one. The attack on the audience that *Rope* represented has ceased. Now artist and audience are united in an unspoken complicity, all of us sharing the phantom space on the "other side" of the fiction, the space behind the camera or in front of the screen that is also the space of Jeffries' apartment. When Thorwald breaks through that space, we are all vulnerable, and none of us can answer his question.

*

Hitchcock had never pushed himself as far as he did in *Rear Window*. His next film, *To Catch a Thief*, would be largely a diversion; his two after that, *The Trouble with Harry* and *The Man Who Knew Too Much*, would both return to his beginnings in British cinema, though in different ways. *The Trouble with Harry* (1955) is an attempt to make a "typically British" comedy in the United States, drawing on the combination of macabre plotting and understated humor that the Ealing comedies had made popular in America after World War II. The setting for this transatlantic exercise is, appropriately, New England.

Hitchcock doesn't make his customary cameo appearance in *The Trouble with Harry*, and it's the one film in which his presence behind the camera can barely be felt. The stylistic experiments are gone; apart from the low-angle shots of Harry's stiff stockinged feet, the film is shot in clean, classical style that could almost belong to Howard Hawks. But if Hitchcock isn't palpable behind the camera, there is a rotund, dark-suited Englishman in front of it: Edmund Gwenn as Captain Wiles, the retired seafarer who discovers Harry's corpse set out in a clearing in the woods on a lovely autumn day. Gwenn had appeared in an early Hitchcock film (the 1933 *Waltzes from Vienna*) and again in Hitchcock's second American movie (*Foreign Correspondent*, 1940). Hitchcock must have seen much of himself in his fellow emigrant, and in some of the long shots of Gwenn, it is difficult to tell them apart. Like Hitchcock (in his films and in his life), Captain Wiles enjoys telling tales of violence and death, all supposedly drawn from his real-life adventures.

Captain Wiles' dilemma is a parody of the archetypal Hitchcock plot. He's been hunting rabbits on forbidden ground, and for this one misstep his world immediately collapses around him. Finding the stranger's body, he believes he's killed him: "One potshot at a rabbit and I'm a murderer." The fearless sea dog becomes a terrorized child. "Mother always said I'd come to a bad end," he whines, looking desperately for a place to hide the corpse.

Wiles is the Hitchcock of the famous childhood anecdotes—the frightened little boy whose father had him locked in a jail cell for a minor infraction. But there is another Hitchcock in the film: the grown-up, self-confident, and creative Hitchcock represented by Sam Marlowe, the painter played by John Forsythe. The contrast between Gwenn and Forsythe is the same contrast Hitchcock employed in his alternate casting of James Stewart and Cary Grant, with Stewart playing the guilt-ridden, insecure, morbidly romantic persona and Grant representing the polished, confident, often cruel seducer. But in *The Trouble with Harry*, the contrast is pushed to comic extremes. Gwenn is wholly ineffectual, smothered in doom and remorse. Forsythe sees no barriers anywhere; he does what he wants.

Sam Marlowe's art is an idealized image of Hitchcock's own. In the 50s, Hitchcock's work had begun to move toward a greater abstraction, leaving behind the bothersome details of plot construction and character psychology. Sam Marlowe's work (he's an abstract expressionist) has already achieved a perfect freedom. He's discarded narrative entirely, and he expresses himself directly. Marlowe isn't bound by the commercial considerations that haunted Hitchcock; he hangs his paintings at the local produce stand and isn't much bothered or surprised when nobody buys them. He doesn't care about money (when a deus-ex-machina millionaire arrives to buy a few canvases, he tells him "You can't afford them") and he doesn't care about reviews (when a curator from "the Modern Museum" starts to offer his opinion, Marlowe cuts him off—"I know they're good").

Marlowe is free in his work and he's free in his life. As the plot progresses, all the major characters come to believe that they've killed Harry: Captain Wiles because he shot him, Jennifer Rogers (Shirley MacLaine) because she hit him with a milk bottle when he came to her door, Miss Gravely (Mildred Natwick) because she hit him with the heel of her shoe when he dragged her into the bushes. Only Marlowe remains outside the widening circle of guilt; he is, somehow, above such feelings. He begins to acquire the godlike status of Brandon and Jeffries (he describes one of his paintings as "symbolic of the beginnings of the world"), but this artist is a benign deity. When the other characters come to him to confess their guilt, Marlowe forgives instead of judging them; he counsels them to hide the corpse and forget about it. Like Brandon, he allows himself to intervene in other people's lives by arranging a love match, but instead of killing to achieve his ends, he presides over the rebirth of Miss Gravely—a new hairdo that makes her feel years younger and helps her win the heart of Captain Wiles.

When the millionaire arrives, Marlowe declines his offer of cash. He uses his newfound power, instead, to grant the other characters their fondest wishes (a monthly shipment of blueberries for Miss Gravely in or out of season, a new hunting rifle for Captain Wiles). The atmosphere of this scene—warm, fanciful, glowing—is unique in Hitchcock's work; it radiates hope like the loveliest of fairy tales. Marlowe seizes the magic moment to propose to Jennifer, and the words he uses are extraordinary. He loves freedom, he tells her, and promises to respect and honor hers: "We'll be the only free couple in the world." His words seem to echo throughout Hitchcock's work, a promise of salvation for all the unhappy, unequal couples from *Rich and Strange* to *Marnie*.

But there's another deity working this neck of the universe, a dark, unyielding one. The local sheriff (his name is Calvin and he's played by Royal Dano, an actor noted for his religious fanatics from *The Red Badge of Courage* to *The Right Stuff*) gets paid by the arrest. He travels the countryside in his fiery chariot, a hulking antique car he's restored, looking for piecework. It's he who set up the arbitrary no-hunting laws that Captain Wiles violated, and now he's heard something about a mysterious corpse in the woods, but he can't seem to find it. He appears just as Marlowe is finishing his proposal. When everyone leaves, he finds a sketch pad that Marlowe has left behind, open to a pastel drawing of an unmistakably dead Harry. Art is treacherous: The self-expression that has made

Marlowe's magic possible has also, inadvertently but inevitably, revealed his guilt.

But art, blessedly, is so ambiguous. When Calvin confronts the artist with his work, Marlowe tells him that it isn't a portrait of a real person, but an image "drawn from my vast subconscious." Furthermore, the man isn't dead, but only sleeping, and with a few strokes of a crayon, Marlowe wakes him up, bringing Harry back to life. Calvin complains that he's ruined the drawing, but Marlowe says, "I just wanted to show you how you misinterpreted my art." Drawing the mantle of mysticism and obscurity around him, the artist is once again safe.

In most Hitchcock films, guilt destroys; in *The Trouble with Harry*, it brings people together. (Hitchcock could almost be anticipating Eric Rohmer's and Claude Chabrol's "transference of guilt" analysis when he has Captain Wiles gallantly accept the responsibility for Miss Gravely's crime. "It would be an honor," he says.) Harry's death has created two couples: Marlowe and Jennifer, Captain Wiles and Miss Gravely (Alma?).

The ending finds the harmony of a Shakespearean comedy. Captain Wiles feels comfortable enough with his new fiancée to confess to her his darkest, dirtiest secret—that he had never been more than a mile out to sea—and Harry's body will be placed back in the woods where it was found. The two couples conspire to have Jennifer's son Arnie (Jerry Mathers) discover the body, just as he did on the first day; because Arnie is too young to have a sense of time, he'll forget that 24 hours have passed. The day, and the film, begin again, with the same sequence of shots of the little boy wandering through the enchanted forest. As if in a fairy tale, the magic day—the day of Harry's death and the unification of the couples—is a day out of time. It has disappeared from the calendar.

*

If *The Trouble with Harry* has the softness of a fairy tale, *The Man Who Knew Too Much* has the bluntness of a religious tract—a sort of "Handbook of Christian Marriage." Ben MacKenna (James Stewart) is an American doctor on vacation in exotic Morocco with his wife Jo (Doris Day) and 10-year-old son Hank (Christopher Olsen). Theirs seems to be the perfect Eisenhower-era marriage, but beneath the placid exterior, Ben and Jo (Benjamin and Joseph: Biblical names) are another tortured Hitchcock couple.

The immediate cause of their tension is Jo's career. She was a musical comedy star on the London stage before she married Ben and moved to Indianapolis (where he works at the "Good Samaritan" hospital). She misses her work, but Ben has forbidden her to perform; he even feels resentful she's recognized. But more deeply, they are divided by a clash of temperaments. She is emotional, impulsive, and open; he is dispassionate, methodical, distant. When Ben tells Jo that a mysterious "they" have kidnapped their son, Jo cries, "Oh, my God!"—and she is right. Providence will not return their child until they have re-conceived their relationship, until they are really married.

Ben gives Jo a tranquilizer before telling her of the kidnapping; her hysterics give way to sleep, and when she awakes, Ben is standing near her bed, packing their suitcases. Ben tells her of the steps he has taken to find Hank while she slept. It is probably the most graceful and acute scene in a film otherwise marked by harshness and linearity, subtly drawing out the contrast in the MacKennas' characters by framing Ben's precise, efficient movements against Jo's helpless sprawl. As Ben speaks, the sound of a Moslem chant can be heard through the open hotel windows, a sound that suggests where Jo's strength lies—a song that is also a prayer. The emblem of Jo's emotionality is her art, her singing. We have seen her perform a duet with Hank: her singing is an open display of affection, the sign of her bond with her son (while Ben, feeling left out, tells a visitor that "Hank will make a fine doctor someday"). By forbidding Jo to perform, Ben is forbidding her to feel. He feels threatened by the force of her emotions, a spiritual, transcendent force that he cannot share.

When the MacKennas arrive in London, Ben immediately sets out in pursuit of the only clue he has: the name "Ambrose Chapel." But the man Ben tracks down, still working on his own, turns out to be an innocent taxidermist; it's Jo who realizes, in a burst of inspiration, that "Ambrose Chapel" isn't a name but a place. The message would seem right at home in a medieval allegory: Ben has erred in looking to man instead of church. The MacKennas go to Ambrose Chapel together but are forced to separate. Ben discovers that his son is in the church, being held prisoner by an English couple, the Draytons (Bernard Miles and Brenda De Banzie), disguised as a vicar and his wife. The Draytons have taken Hank ostensibly to prevent Ben from telling what he knows about an assassination plot they are hatching against a prime minister. But it's also clear—he is cold and calculating, she's a frustrated mother who's never had children of her own—that the Draytons are the MacKennas' monster twins, the dramatic projection of the tensions Ben and Jo keep inside.

Alone in the chapel, Ben calls out to Hank, and his disembodied voice answers somewhere from above the altar. But Ben is too cautious, allowing Drayton to knock him out and escape with his wife and the boy. (Ben escapes the locked church by climbing the bell tower, an eerie anticipation of *Vertigo*.) Meanwhile, Jo has rushed off to the famous Albert Hall sequence, where her impulsive scream spoils the aim of the assassin and saves the prime minister's life. Ben and Jo have accomplished something separately, but now they must work together to regain their child.

The final sequence, set in the foreign embassy where Hank is being held, tidily unites the film's issues. The plan the MacKennas conceive—she will sing at an embassy reception, to let Hank know they're in the building, while Ben slips off to look for him—represents the exchange of traits the couple needs to reestablish their marriage. Ben will finally allow Jo to perform in public, resolving their surface conflict. But more important, Jo must take some of Ben's detachment in order to bring off her performance—she can't break down again, even though she's singing for her son's life—and Ben must find some of Jo's spiritual force in himself, in order to divine which room in the mansion contains his son. The film ends with the fall of another Hitchcock manipulator. This time it is Drayton who tumbles down the embassy's grand staircase, as the MacKennas, reunited and reborn, sweep out the front door.

The Man Who Knew Too Much seems to conclude a series: two films about the monstrousness of art followed by two films in which art is life-giving, redemptive. What remains is for Hitchcock to move beyond pro and con, to confront the issue of full complexity. What remains is *Vertigo.*

*

Rope took literature as a metaphor, *Rear Window* photography, *The Trouble with Harry* painting, and *The Man Who Knew Too Much* music. With *Vertigo*, the metaphorical distance is dropped. The art at issue is Hitchcock's own: the cinema.

The dream of *Vertigo*—the dream of a love that leads to death, of a beautiful illusion that gives way to nothingness—is also a dream of the movies. Which is why, perhaps, *Vertigo* has always meant more to filmmakers and film critics than to the general public. More so than any other of Hitchcock's works (more so, I would say, than any other movie), *Vertigo* speaks of a passion for film, a passion that isn't always a healthy one. It's a love for the illusory and the ineffable that is also a love for the false, the bloodless, the empty.

Because recorded sound and the photographic image are direct impressions of reality, film is the most immediate and sensually enrapturing. But because those sounds and images are ultimately only a field of light and shadow, the movies are also the least material of art forms. You can't touch a movie in the way you can touch a book or painting: a reel of film is a mute, meaningless thing, articulate only when light and motion make it speak. In *Vertigo*, Hitchcock dramatizes the duality of the material and the intangible that is the inner mystery of the movies. It becomes a tale of sexuality and death, and the tragedy of the story springs directly from the tragic nature of the medium. On film, presence and absence, sex and death, are inseparable. Universal's new prints of *Vertigo* now end with a plug for their studio tour ("when in Southern California . . ."), which is an act of vandalism. Hitchcock put no titles at the end of *Vertigo*, and for good reason. The film is meant to end as harshly as possible, with the dark, seductive images flashing abruptly to a white, empty screen. The physical ending of *Vertigo* is the last of the film's climaxes, and perhaps the most devastating. The dream should end for the spectator just as it ends for James Stewart's Scotty, with a violent return to a diminished reality.

Vertigo is, of course, an intensely personal film, but it is also—uniquely for Hitchcock, the master orchestrator of audience response—a fiercely private one. Private, not in the sense that it's meaningful only for the author, but because it assumes an isolated viewer, a spectator alone with the screen. Unlike Hitchcock's other films, *Vertigo* is not a social event; it gains nothing from the mass choruses of laughs and screams that usually accompany a Hitchcock film (and Hitchcock does nothing to encourage them), and may even lose a little. The film's address is so intimate, so hushed, that it barely seems possible that the film was made for commercial exhibition. Hitchcock's ideal audience seems to have been a spectator sitting alone in a screening room—in short, himself, but also everyone who has ever understood movies as sufficient company. Only an isolated viewer can fully experience the isolation of the Stewart character, and only a viewer on intimate terms with film can understand the strength of the illusion—of ghostly companionship—that Kim Novak's Madeleine represents.

With *Vertigo*, Hitchcock's art achieved the freedom embodied by Sam Marlowe's paintings. In an unusually frank moment, Hitchcock described his creative process to Claude Chabrol: "You understand that, for me, the scenario is almost secondary. I make the film before I know the story. It appears to me as a form, a general impression. I only look for the scenario afterward, and I shape it to what I have in mind." The scenario Hitchcock found for *Vertigo* was derived from a novel by the French thriller writers Pierre Boileau and Thomas Narcejac (*Les Diaboliques*), and it is a contrived, trivial thing, a flimsy network of unlikely coincidences and preposterous motivations. Hitchcock eliminated the mystery element that served as the structuring principle of the Boileau-Narcejac story and fitted what was left to the form he had envisioned—a form that consists of a gradually accelerating push toward abstraction and emotional intensity, set in counterpoint with a diminishing, prosaic reality. The subjectivity of the abstract sequences eventually acquires an edge over the objectivity of the naturalistic scenes, until the startling moment when the rationalist, common-sense point of view (as embodied by Barbara Bel Geddes' Midge) literally walks out of the film, leaving only romantic delirium.

Scotty is clearly an extension of the L. B. Jeffries character in *Rear Window*. *Vertigo* begins by quoting the earlier film, with a dramatic fall, a crippled Stewart (broken ribs this time), and an apartment (Midge's) that features Jeffries' bamboo-curtained rear window as part of the décor. Midge is Scotty's on-again, off-again girlfriend, just as Lisa was in *Rear Window*; whereas Lisa was a fashion plate, Midge is a fashion artist (pointedly, a *commercial* artist). Jeffries was a news photographer, Scotty is a detective. Both men have spent their careers as collectors of facts, but accidents (facts biting back) have shaken them loose. Both men will have to acknowledge that their fascination with death and disaster, as expressed in their choice of work, isn't a detached, rational interest, but a deep and dark component of their personalities. But Jeffries' death fantasies were outer-directed, focused on his neighbors and, through them, his fiancée. Scotty's are internal, the expression of a romantic longing for oblivion. Dreamy and withdrawn, a bachelor with no significant social ties, Scotty has spent his life in search of something he can't define. He is hired by Gavin Elster (Tom Helmore), an old school friend, to follow his wife, whom he suspects of suicidal tendencies. When he first sees Madeleine, Scotty knows that he has found a companion for his inchoate search, and possibly its object.

The first and longest section of *Vertigo* alternates dialogue scenes with Midge (Hitchcock emphasizes Bel Geddes' rich, expressive voice to the point where she seems to disincorporate—she's all words, no body) with extended passages, silent except for Bernard Herrmann's haunting score, in which Scotty follows Madeleine on her mysterious rounds. The spatial organization of these sequences, with the observer and the observed isolated in separate shots, duplicates the spectator's position before the screen: We watch Madeleine as we watch *Vertigo*.

Then slowly, through a complex arrangement of editing and compositional techniques, Hitchcock dissolves the spatial separation, drawing the audience into the screen just as Scotty, step by step, draws closer to Madeleine. Deep-focus compositions, with the perspective clearly marked by the décor and the movement of the actors, create a vivid sense of space opening behind the surface of the screen (its borders become a proscenium, as in the final image of *Rope*). Slow, forward tracking shots, matched to Scotty's movement as he pursues Madeleine, pull the spectator into the newly opened space, as if an irresistible magnetic force were drawing us along. Supremely, there is the film's visual rhetoric of high and low—shots of the San Francisco cityscape, of multi-level sets (Elster's office, Midge's apartment), and the standing figures looking down at characters sitting in a chair or reclining on the floor (first Elster looks down at Scotty, then Scotty looks down at Madeleine). Heights, such as the view from the rooftop in the opening chase, or the famous zoom-forward, track-back combination that presents Scotty's view from the bell tower, are always presented horizontally, with the camera held on a perfectly centered perpendicular in a way that shows a fall *down* as a fall *into*. This is the "vertigo" of the title—a fear and desire of falling into death, into sexuality, but also a fear and desire of falling into the image, into the screen.

Madeleine is an image—the consuming, transcendent, fatal image for which Scotty has been searching. But an image isn't, can't be real; its status as something made is both its glory and its limitation. An image isn't autonomous; someone, somewhere has created it, and perhaps it is Scotty who has invented Madeleine as a projection of his longing, just as the murder of *Rear Window* is the projection of Jeffries'. It is Scotty's look—which is to say, the look of the camera—that gives Madeleine her extraordinary qualities. Scotty watches her, and, in watching her, brings her alive. It is not until midway through the film that she has become real enough, under the generative power of Scotty's look, to be touched. Only after he has saved her from drowning can they share the same frame, the same reality. By pulling her up from the water of San Francisco Bay, Scotty has given birth to her; when he puts her to bed in his apartment, she is as naked as a baby. The process is natural and affirmative, just as it was in Sam Marlowe's rejuvenation of Miss Gravely. At this point, Scotty is still the benign creator, the artist who gives life.

But Madeleine has another author: Gavin Elster, the smooth-talking heavy who has constructed Madeleine from scratch as a lure for Scotty. Speaking of his affection for San Francisco's wide-open past, Elster tells Scotty that he envies the "freedom and power" men had in those days. The phrase (which is repeated later in the film, in the story of Madeleine's great-grandmother and the man who stole her child) suggests the "freedom" that Marlowe promised Jennifer in *The Trouble with Harry*, but also the "power" that Brandon pursued in *Rope*. In the scene in Elster's shipyard office, Elster looms over Scotty as he speaks, commanding just as Brandon did. But through Elster's office window, we see a vista—the massive structure of the ship coming into being under Elster's command—that recalls Marlowe's painting "symbolic of the beginnings of the world." Elster is the artist as manipulator, as self-made God, but he can't be dismissed as easily as Brandon was. Brandon was only a killer; Elster has created (Madeleine) in order to kill (his actual wife).

More than the contrast between Brandon and Rupert, the contrast of Elster and Scotty reveals the Cary Grant–James Stewart division that operates over the body of Hitchcock's work. Elster is part of Hitchcock (he has a British accent; his last name is a near-anagram of "Elstree," the name of the British studio where Hitchcock made his first films; Hitchcock makes his cameo appearance strolling past the gates of Elster's yard), just as he is a latent part of Scotty. When Elster disappears from the film, after the inquest that rules his wife's death an accident, Scotty slips into his role.

Scotty has fallen in love with Madeleine. After she dies, he finds that he loves her all the more—and he must acknowledge that he is in love with death, in love with an image. But a dead thing cannot die, and so Scotty sets about the re-creation of the image, remaking a shop girl, Judy, to resemble his dead lover (without realizing, of course, that it was Judy who played Madeleine for Elster). But this time the birth process is more painful, violent, and artificial: Scotty forces Judy to wear Madeleine's color, taking no notice of the death of personality he is inflicting on Judy in the process. She is only the raw material from which he will wrest his art, just as Hitchcock wrests his art from Kim Novak, a mediocre actress who gives, in *Vertigo*, a performance of genuine greatness.

Once Scotty has transformed Judy into Madeleine, he can no longer be an innocent spectator. He has visited the other side of the camera, and he knows, inescapably, that he has only fashioned an illusion. The reborn Madeleine is both real (she's exactly the same as before) and not real (she never existed), both present and absent, alive and dead. She is the movie on the screen before us. Like Scotty, and like Hitchcock, we accept the illusion of film because of its beauty; art allows us to experience an exaltation and a transcendence that reality does not.

When Judy returns from the beauty parlor, her hair now dyed to match Madeleine's, she walks straight toward Scotty—straight toward the camera and us—and it is the first time in the film that a figure has emerged from the depths of the image to come to us, the first time we are met on the surface of the screen rather than drawn into it. Scotty takes her in his arms, and Hitchcock's camera goes into a circular movement around their embrace, sealing the lovers into a dimension of their own, blurring the background until it finally melts away into a blaze of green light. The lovers are visible only in silhouette. They are dematerialized, made perfect, lifted above time and space. It is one of the most emotionally intense moments on film, and one of the most deathly.

*

By choosing to work in the least respectable of mediums (the movies), and in the least respectable of genres (the thriller), Alfred Hitchcock was hiding. He hid for the same reason his characters did: because he was guilty. Guilty not of committing a crime, but of committing art—of taking upon himself the "freedom and power" of the creator because he was dissatisfied with the things life had provided. Worse, he was guilty of falling in love with his creation, when he knew that what he had made was false. At the end of *Vertigo*, another creator appears, and he punishes Scotty's transgression with a terrible force. The last words of the film are "God have mercy," but God doesn't hear. Hitchcock leaves his artist standing atop the mission bell tower, raised high but looking down, exalted but horribly alone. He will never appear in another Hitchcock film, never climb down.

Once Upon a Time in the West

Directed by SERGIO LEONE {September 14, 1984}

1969 wasn't a good year for the western. Between John Wayne's self-parodying performance as an aging sheriff in *True Grit* and the new definition of the outlaw provided by Peter Fonda and Dennis Hopper in *Easy Rider*, the noble old genre seemed just about exhausted. All that remained was for Sam Peckinpah's *The Wild Bunch* to come along and—after one last spasm of apocalyptic action—give it a proper burial. This wasn't the time for an ambitious Italian filmmaker to be setting out on an epic that would be at once the grandest tribute the genre had ever received and a penetrating criticism of it. When Sergio Leone's *Once Upon a Time in the West* was released, it was an instant failure and just as instantly was cut by 24 minutes. But despite the fact that the crippled American version no longer made even rudimentary narrative sense, the film's reputation has grown steadily in the last 15 years. Various "restored" versions have surfaced at the film societies and revival houses over the years, but none until now has been definitive. The Wilmette-based distributor Films Incorporated has just issued a superb new 35-millimeter print of the 168-minute European cut; though stories persist in buff circles of even more "complete" versions, this is likely to be as close as we will ever come to *Once Upon a Time in the West* as Leone intended it.

And it is a masterpiece, a film that springs entirely from other films—from American westerns as seen by Europeans—and yet assumes an emotional texture every bit as varied and full-bodied as a film taken from lived experience. There's nothing secondhand in it: it's as if Leone had been able to inhabit this landscape that never existed, as if for him the movie west were a place as real as Athens or Rome. Christopher Frayling, in his excellent study *Spaghetti Westerns*, demonstrates how the Italian westerns of the 60s grew out of the mythological epics that had been an integral part of the Italian industry since its beginnings in the 1900s—for Leone, the idea of a western "myth" isn't just a critical construction, but something with a literal force, something that shares the same imaginative dimension with the myth of Hercules. Most of the American anti-westerns that followed in the wake of *The Wild Bunch* were concerned with debunking the myth of the west—with demonstrating how far the movie west departed from the sordid, brutal, and crushingly dull reality documented in the historical records. But all of these films—among them *Soldier Blue*, *Dirty Little Billy*, the absurdist variation of *Little Big Man*—seemed profoundly beside the point; myth can't be attacked by reality, because our belief in myth is very different from our belief in facts—it's a belief in something we already know to be untrue. Leone is the only western director to have realized that myth must be attacked from within—attacked in mythic terms. And because, as a European—an outsider—he can accept the myth untroubled by its problematic links to historical reality, he is uniquely qualified to bring it closer to reality—to restore those elements, chiefly the hard face of capitalism, that the other versions of the myth have left out. In Leone's hands, capitalism itself becomes a mythic force, as much a part of the landscape (it's embodied here by the building of a railroad across the desert) as the horses or mountain ranges. In criticizing the myth—in filling in the economic relationships American westerns have skipped over—Leone expands and enriches it, which is what the best criticism does.

For his framework, Leone chose the western's foundation plot, the most grandiose of the genre's variations and the one upon which John Ford built his masterworks. A corner of the wilderness is turned into a city, a civilization is created—but by whom and at what cost? For Ford, the founder was often a lone hero (Henry Fonda in *My Darling Clementine*, John Wayne in *The Man Who Shot Liberty Valance*); Leone imagines four founders, no one of whom could have done the job alone, but who, bound together in the mysterious relationships that are the film's true subject, succeed in bringing something forth. All four are stock figures, characters distilled from a thousand half-remembered movies: Jill McBain (Claudia Cardinale) is a New Orleans whore who has come out west in hopes of beginning a new life as a wife to a widowed rancher; but when she arrives at Sweetwater farm, she finds that her husband and his three children have been murdered by bandits. Cheyenne (Jason Robards) is the local outlaw, seemingly as much an institution around the town of Flagstone as the mayor; he has his own sense of decency, and when he's accused of killing, he rides out to Sweetwater to tell Jill it wasn't him. The real killer is Frank (Henry Fonda), a sadistic gunslinger who works removing "small obstacles" for the railroad, whose silver path is heading straight toward Sweetwater. Frank is being pursued by an enigmatic figure known only by a nickname, Harmonica (Charles Bronson); to find Frank and exact his vengeance, Harmonica must pass through Sweetwater, too.

The four characters are arranged in an increasingly strained relationship to society: at the center is Jill, associated with the family and sexuality (a mother and a whore, she is a synthesis of the roles the western allots to women). Cheyenne is outside the law, but defined by his relationship to it; as a professional bandit, he has his own role to play in the primitive western economy. Frank, though an outlaw, has been adopted by a society that has a temporary need for his services; his methods are savage, but he is working for the spread of civilization. At the furthest remove is Harmonica, a man whose only social tie is his hatred for Frank. Leone treats him as a ghostly figure—when Frank asks him who he is, he answers with the names of men Frank has killed—who lives not only beyond the law, but seemingly beyond the laws of time and space. Harmonica is never seen entering a set: he is always already present, hiding in the shadows or standing just beyond the frame line, waiting to enter the action at its crucial point. Ennio Morricone's score (itself a masterpiece of movie music) assigns a different theme to each of the four main characters. The music defines and, in some way, idealizes them, freezing each character in his essential traits and rhythms (reportedly, Leone played the music on the set, asking his actors to mold their performances to it; the relationship of music and character is certainly unusually tight, almost operatic). No longer stock figures, they are archetypes, each identified with a distinct moral stance, and each linked to the others because of that distinction: together, they form a closed set, a mythological universe. Standing apart, and perhaps above them, is Morton (Gabriele Ferzetti), the crippled boss of the railroad who directs its construction from within his private parlor car. Morton is the prime mover who brings the static relationships to life, forcing the four main characters to come together and to break apart, to form alliances and enmities in response to his actions. Though he himself has lost the use of his legs, Morton is Leone's embodiment of motion in all of its senses—as narrative impetus, as social progress, as rampaging capitalism. He is not a simple heavy, in the western tradition of the slimy eastern banker; he knows that he will die before his railroad reaches the Pacific, but he presses on, possessed by his dream. It is Morton's itch—an inseparable blend of profit motive and pure idealism—that underlies all the action of *Once Upon a Time in the West*; he is the element of change introduced into the static mythological system, the element that will both animate it and bring it to its end.

The body of the film follows the relationships among the four main characters through nearly all of their possible permutations. Cheyenne throws in with Jill because she's a whore and makes good coffee (two qualities that remind him of his mother); Harmonica joins Jill when he finds out why her husband was killed—his farm sits on the only water supply within a hundred miles of desert, and the railroad needs water for its engines. By staying with Jill, Harmonica knows that he'll draw Frank out. But this configuration doesn't hold. Kidnapped by Frank, Jill offers to ally herself with him in exchange for her life. Frank arranges a rigged auction that will give him Sweetwater at an absurdly low price, but at the last minute, Harmonica enters with a bid of $5,000—money he's raised turning in Cheyenne for a reward. In the film's most perverse twist, Harmonica joins up with Frank to save him from an ambush prepared by Frank's own men (who have been paid off by Morton to get rid of him); Harmonica, after all, wants the pleasure of killing Frank himself—at the right moment and in the right way.

Leone's style, both narrative and visual, is built on bold contrasts. Extreme long shots, often marked by an exaggerated depth of field (at one point, Leone holds in perfect focus both a single bolt on the roof of a train car and a mountain range 30 or 40 miles in the distance), are abruptly broken by the massive close-ups—two gigantic eyes that fill the wide Panavision frame—that were the trademark of his Clint Eastwood films. In much the same way, Leone uses trivial details (Jill making coffee) to lead into epic panoramas (Jill serving coffee to members of the construction crew that has just brought the railroad to the threshold of her house), or align lowbrow burlesque with the loftiest tragic sentiments. Space, time, scale, and tone are all fluid elements, which can be expanded or contracted at will. And yet these transformations aren't arbitrary, decorative touches; they are closely tied to the central themes of change and movement. The film opens with a celebrated sequence in which three gunmen (Jack Elam, Woody Strode, and Al Mulock) wait in a broken-down frontier train station for the arrival of Harmonica, whom they have been assigned to kill. The train is late, and the minutes stretch out: Elam keeps himself entertained by trapping a fly in the barrel of his gun; Strode stands under a leaky water tower letting the slow drips accumulate in the brim of his hat until he has enough to take a drink. The sequence goes on and on (it must occupy nearly two reels of screen time) until the train arrives and it ends in a brief flurry of action. The aesthetic of the opening sequence is one of absolute realism—an insistence on showing everything—but as the film progresses, the action becomes more and more elliptic; by the end, entire scenes—as crucial to the plot as Cheyenne's escape from jail and his brush with Morton's men—are skipped over with the barest acknowledgment. It's as if time has contracted as the film has gone on, growing smaller and less commodious, and indeed it has: the arrival of the train has changed the relationship of time and space, turning the far into the near, turning a day's ride into an hour's. Morton's train devours time, collapses space; the coordinates of the old west no longer hold, and the frozen time of myth gives way to the bustling time of machines.

As the train approaches Sweetwater, Harmonica at last approaches his goal. Frank can no longer ignore the mysterious stranger who has shattered all his plans; in the end, nothing matters to him but finding out what he wants. They meet for a duel in the shadow of Sweetwater; the train crews are just over the hill. As they prepare to draw, there is one final expansion of time—one final burst of the "old" time. The sequence is extraordinary: Harmonica stares into Frank's eyes, and with the force of his stare, he seems to project the memory that is filling in his mind—the memory of his first meeting with Frank, when he was a boy. Frank receives the images, seeing them as Harmonica sees them—it's a dual flashback, a fused memory. A shot is fired, and it's over.

With this killing, the central relationship is broken: the main characters are now free to move away, as if the mythic time that bound them together had been shattered, and they could now move into Morton's time, the new time. The train begins to move, pulling up to the open ground in front of Sweetwater, which has now become a station and soon will become a town. The Panavision frame, so achingly empty at the beginning of the film, is now full to bursting with men, machinery, buildings. It's Jill's city—Jill's civilization—and the camera follows her as she moves into the crowd of men, carrying a pot of the coffee that first endeared her to Cheyenne. There isn't any room for the survivor of a gunfight in this image of teeming domesticity, and as the camera continues to move—past the chugging locomotive and down to the end of the tracks, where the wilderness takes over again—it catches the figure of a lone rider, moving away. In the continuity of this final sequence, Leone balances a beginning and an ending, a setting and an escape, a celebration and a profound mourning. It is one of the most complex images in the history of the western, and certainly one of the most beautiful.

French Cancan

Directed by JEAN RENOIR {June 14, 1985}

Of all Jean Renoir's late films, *French Cancan* (1955) has always been the easiest to like, which is probably why Renoir's most serious critics have tended to underrate it. It's a film packed with immediate pleasures—music, color, movement, beautiful women and handsome men—as Chicago audiences will be able to see when it returns this week to the Fine Arts, in a newly struck Technicolor print that incorporates ten minutes of previously unseen footage. François Truffaut once observed that *French Cancan* was the only time Renoir set out, self-consciously, to make a "Renoir," and it's true that it's his only film that seems to look back, recapitulating old themes and old techniques, rather than to thrust forward into unknown terrain. *French Cancan* represents a pause in Renoir's career, yet it seems a necessary, revitalizing pause. It was the first film Renoir had made in France after a long period of exile—first in Hollywood during the war, then in India (*The River*) and Italy (*The Golden Coach*)—his first French film, in fact, since *Rules of the Game* in 1939. That Renoir would want to reorient himself, to renew old acquaintances (with Jean Gabin, his star through much of the 30s) and revisit old haunts (the streets of Montmartre) isn't surprising. If *French Cancan* seems to spill over with an immoderate, almost indulgent pleasure, it's largely the pleasure of coming home, of burrowing into the familiar.

Indeed, Renoir seems determined to gorge himself on images of "Frenchness"—images that flirt with cliché. The *belle époque* setting evokes the widely reproduced Paris of the Impressionists (though the colors and iconography belong much more to Toulouse-Lautrec and Manet than to Renoir *père*); the character types—top-hatted roués, lusty cabaret dancers, street urchins—spring straight from conventions of boulevard farce. There is a heavy dose of "ooh-la-la" in *French Cancan* (especially now that the film's brief flashes of nudity have been restored) that has also hurt its reputation. At times, Renoir seems to be peddling a tourist's fantasy of gay Paree: the sets have an exaggerated, artificially "picturesque" quality that suggests a Disneyland re-creation more than the palpably real locations of Renoir's prewar films. When *French Cancan* was first released, one French critic complained that the spectator "cannot believe for one second that he has been taken into an actual Paris street." Renoir appears to have turned his back on the immediacy and authenticity of *Boudu Saved from Drowning* and *Toni*; in place of the weight and texture of the real world, he seems to be offering secondhand, commercialized images—postcards from a France that never existed.

And yet this transformation of reality into a commercial commodity, of life into spectacle, is one of the film's principal themes. Renoir's protagonist, Danglard (Gabin) is a nightclub impresario who has decided to take a hopelessly old-fashioned folk dance and transform it into the rage of Paris. He rebaptizes the old dance, in English, the "French Cancan," because everything in English is the fad of the moment. He buys a broken-down dance hall in a working-class neighborhood, tears it down, and builds a fresh new structure topped by a red windmill—the "Moulin Rouge." And he takes Nini (Françoise Arnoul), a laundress who lives up the hill, and sends her to dancing school to relearn the steps of the folk dance she has been doing half her life. Authentic traditions are gradually changed into flashy illusions, and with each step in the transformation they acquire a monetary value: the traditions become products, sold for the price of a ticket.

Like many of Renoir's protagonists (and like Renoir himself, in *Rules of the Game* and *Grand Illusion*), Danglard is intensely class conscious, and his plans for the Moulin Rouge rest on a shrewd manipulation of class envies. By building his club in disreputable Montmartre, he hopes to appeal to the aristocrats, who enjoy the thrill of slumming among the workers (and criminals) of the capital. But by building a large, gaudily appointed hall, he hopes also to attract the masses, who will be able to enjoy the illusion of living the high life of the boulevards for a fraction of the price. The Moulin Rouge is to be a world unto itself, intermingling the common and elevated, the genuine and the factitious. And the means of this magical intermingling is to be the spectacle that Danglard will create. The dash and swirl of color of the "French Cancan" will break down all the barriers, both social and artistic: the world will become a show.

Danglard's project might seem cynical, yet Renoir was fascinated by actors, often using them as main characters or finding excuses to slip theatrical performances into the plots of his films. *French Cancan* is the only Renoir film to take a director as its subject. There is, obviously, a lot of Renoir in Danglard—Danglard's work in creating his show exactly parallels Renoir's work in creating his film, and Danglard's revisionist cancan finds its aesthetic equivalent in the artificial Paris Renoir has fashioned to contain it. And we can assume that there is a lot of Danglard in Renoir, particularly in his fashion of handling his performers, accepting their eccentricities along with their talents, and trying to bring out their most profoundly individual abilities. But direction is the most mysterious of creative processes, and Renoir knows to respect the mystery. What does Danglard do, exactly? Not much that we can really see. For the most part, he is simply there, observing intently and saying nothing. And yet the vision that emerges is Danglard's vision, developed through an almost imperceptible series of choices and inflections. It is Danglard's sublime passivity that makes *French Cancan* Renoir's most direct and most penetrating statement of the art of the movies. The director is the medium between the world and the image: he takes from people the reality that belongs to them and then sells it back in a heightened form. If Danglard is an artist, he is also a bit of a con man. For Renoir, the two are inseparable. The artificiality of *French Cancan* is a way of making the director appear, both in his glory and in his guilt.

One of the clear sources of *French Cancan* is the American backstage musical (some of Renoir's set designs, in fact, owe an obvious debt to Vincente Minnelli's back-lot constructions in *An American in Paris*). The formula is a simple, time-honored one: the process of mounting the show is played in parallel to a developing romance between a boy and a girl from the cast, and opening night coincides with the sealing of their relationship. In the old formula—it worked all the way from *42nd Street* to *The Band Wagon*, with a modernist hangover in *All That Jazz*—the two levels of the plot are allowed to cross-pollinate: courtship becomes a kind of rehearsal for the marriage that is to follow; the production of the show becomes a kind of romantic ritual, climaxing with the seduction of the audience. The backstage musical is about the creation of two fixed entities: the show (which attains a state of absolute perfection on opening night, evolving no further) and the couple (the movie ends with a marriage or a promise of marriage, the lovers frozen in a state of eternal bliss).

Renoir clearly has a great affection for the old formula (it becomes one of the many elements of *French Cancan*'s deliberate, proudly worn artificiality), yet he makes some significant and very characteristic changes in it. For Renoir, motion pictures are above all a matter of motion: no director has ever filmed movement more beautifully, graciously, and joyfully; no director has ever incorporated movement—in the sense of constant change and evolution—into the shape of his narratives. The usual symbol of this principle in his work is water, from the dirty Seine that disgorges Michel Simon's anarchic hobo in *Boudu Saved from Drowning* to the rolling Ganges that invests almost every shot of *The River* with a mystical sense of eternal destruction and eternal renewal. If there is no water imagery in *French Cancan*, it's because the dance itself embodies movement—flashing, leaping, sparkling, in perpetual transition. Accomplished camera work is often described as "fluid," but the word has a special appropriateness when applied to the dance sequences in *French Cancan*: Renoir consistently finds the single angle that plunges us most fully in the swirl of the motion, or finds the one camera movement that most effectively accentuates the waves of color. When Renoir moves back from the center of the dance to give us an encompassing overview, it isn't to emphasize the order of symmetry of the choreography (as Busby Berkeley did in his films), but to show us how the movement overspills the fixed pattern, finding its own life and logic. His framing always leaves enough room to capture the unforeseen—the chance flash of a brilliant blue skirt, the spontaneous grace of an improvised kick. For Renoir, the show is not a fixed, final thing, but an event that will be different every night, an organism that will continue to evolve.

The romantic plot, too, refuses to be fixed. The film is not the story of one couple's formation, but of the coming together and falling apart of many couples—a network of relationships in continual flux. Where the backstage musical would perhaps interpolate a single rival to add suspense to the central love story, Renoir surrounds his central couple—Danglard and Nini, the laundress he has made a dancer—with half a dozen potential lovers. Though Nini believes herself in love with Danglard, she can't bear breaking off with the neighborhood boy, a baker's assistant, she once promised to marry, and neither can she wholly resist the blandishments of a sad young prince who has fallen in love with her dancing. Though, as usual, there are no overt villains in Renoir's film (16 years after *The Rules of the Game*, everyone still has his reasons, and Renoir gives those reasons a full and fair hearing), there are characters who play a negative role—a role defined by their determination to stop the movement, to fix a relationship permanently. One of Danglard's lovers is a fiery Spanish dancer who goes under the name of "la Belle Abbesse" (Maria Felix); jealous of Nini's closeness to Danglard, she gives her rival a vicious, crippling kick to the shin and arranges to have Danglard's financing for the Moulin Rouge withdrawn. But because she acts wholly on emotion and impulse (by the end of the film, she has embraced Nini as a sister in show business), la Belle Abbesse is less of a threat than the more superficially sympathetic prince (Gianni Esposito), whose gentility masks a deathlike stillness (he is the most restricted in his movements of all the characters, and Renoir at one point shows him sitting motionless in a chair for hours, as he waits for Nini's return).

On the evening the Moulin Rouge opens, Nini discovers, from the rapture with which Danglard watches the new singer he has discovered, that she has a new rival. She locks herself in her dressing room, announcing that she will come out to perform the cancan finale on one condition only—that "Danglard must be mine alone." Danglard is able to coax her out, with a speech that convinces her that her loyalty is to the show, not to him. Renoir suggests that only now, with her emergence from the dressing room and her implicit acceptance of the philosophy of freedom and change, is she fully prepared to join the dance—her life and her art must be one. And this final dance sequence—a cancan that occupies a full 15 minutes of screen time—becomes a celebration of unity in difference: not only the newfound unity of Nini's life, but also, as the dance unfolds and Renoir cuts between the spectacle and the spectators, of reality and artifice, of aristocrat and worker, of planning (the overall form of the dance) and improvisation (the spontaneous contributions of the individual dancers), of a joyous beginning (Nini's entry into a new world) and a melancholy conclusion (Danglard's realization that his project is finished and that he must move on to something else). But above all, the sequence is a celebration of the movies, the one medium that is able to form a unity of permanence and change, the one medium that is able to preserve movement, in all its freedom and freshness, forever.

APPENDIX: Top Ten Lists, 1974–86

1974

1. *Le Petit théâtre de Jean Renoir* (Jean Renoir)
2. *Fear Eats the Soul* (Rainer Werner Fassbinder)
3. *The Tamarind Seed* (Blake Edwards)
4. *Wedding in Blood* (Claude Chabrol)
5. *The Three Musketeers* (Richard Lester)
6. *Chinatown* (Roman Polanski)
7. *The Phantom of Liberty* (Luis Buñuel)
8. *Lacombe, Lucien* (Louis Malle)
9. *The Godfather, Part II* (Francis Ford Coppola)
10. *Juggernaut* (Richard Lester)

1975

1. *Lancelot du Lac* (Robert Bresson)
2. *The Middle of the World* (Alain Tanner)
3. *A Woman Under the Influence* (John Cassavetes)
4. *The Passenger* (Michelangelo Antonioni)
5. *La Rupture* (Claude Chabrol)
6. *Love Among the Ruins* (George Cukor)
7. *Fox and His Friends* (Rainer Werner Fassbinder)
8. *The Romantic Englishwoman* (Joseph Losey)
9. *Hard Times* (Walter Hill)
10. *Supervixens* (Russ Meyer)

1976

1. *Family Plot* (Alfred Hitchcock)
2. *The Age of Medici* and *Blaise Pascal* (Roberto Rossellini)
3. *Robin and Marian* (Richard Lester)
4. *Jonah Who Will Be 25 in the Year 2000* (Alain Tanner)
5. *The Man Who Would Be King* (John Huston)
6. *The Shootist* (Don Siegel)
7. *Just Before Nightfall* (Claude Chabrol)
8. *Mother Kuster's Trip to Heaven* (Rainer Werner Fassbinder)
9. *French Provincial* (André Techiné)
10. *Allegro non troppo* (Bruno Bozzetto)

1977

1. *F for Fake* (Orson Welles)
2. *The Memory of Justice* (Marcel Ophuls)
3. *The Marquise of O* (Eric Rohmer)
4. *A Piece of Pleasure* (Claude Chabrol)
5. *Numéro Deux* (Jean-Luc Godard)
6. *Moses und Aron* (Jean-Marie Straub/Daniele Huillet)
7. *Islands in the Stream* (Franklin Schaffner)
8. *The Gauntlet* (Clint Eastwood)
9. *Padre, Padrone* (Paolo and Vittorio Taviani)
10. *The Rescuers* (Wolfgang Reitherman/John Lounsbery/Art Stevens)

1978

1. *Days of Heaven* (Terrence Malick)
2. *That Obscure Object of Desire* (Luis Buñuel)
3. *The American Friend* (Wim Wenders)
4. *Meetings with Anna* (Chantal Akerman)
5. *The Messiah* (Roberto Rossellini)
6. *The Driver* (Walter Hill)
7. *Halloween* (John Carpenter)
8. *Big Wednesday* (John Milius)
9. *Blue Collar* (Paul Schrader)
10. *Filming Othello* (Orson Welles)

1979

1. *10* (Blake Edwards)
2. *The Left-Handed Woman* (Peter Handke)
3. *Dawn of the Dead* (George A. Romero)
4. *Perceval* (Eric Rohmer)
5. *The Warriors* (Walter Hill)
6. *Luna* (Bernardo Bertolucci)
7. *Escape From Alcatraz* (Don Siegel)
8. *In a Year with Thirteen Moons* (Rainer Werner Fassbinder)
9. *Fedora* (Billy Wilder)
10. *Angi, Vera* (Pal Gabor)

1980

1. *The Devil, Probably* (Robert Bresson)
2. *The Human Factor* (Otto Preminger)
3. *The Constant Factor* (Krzysztof Zanussi)
4. *The Big Red One* (Samuel Fuller)
5. *Used Cars* (Robert Zemeckis)
6. *Quadrophenia* (Franc Roddam)
7. *The Black Stallion* (Carroll Ballard)
8. *Gloria* (John Cassavetes)
9. *Mad Max* (George Miller)
10. *The Long Riders* (Walter Hill)

1981

1. *Melvin and Howard* (Jonathan Demme)
2. *Loulou* (Maurice Pialat)
3. *The Chant of Jimmie Blacksmith* (Fred Schepisi)
4. *Ici et ailleurs* (Jean-Luc Godard)
5. *Every Man for Himself* (Jean-Luc Godard)
6. *Confidence* (Istvan Szabo)
7. *From the Clouds to Resistance* (Jean-Marie Straub/Daniele Huillet)
8. *Modern Romance* (Albert Brooks)
9. *Atlantic City* (Louis Malle)
10. *Reds* (Warren Beatty)

1982

1. *The Aviator's Wife* (Eric Rohmer)
2. *Barbarosa* (Fred Schepisi)
3. *Coup de torchon* (Bertrand Tavernier)
4. *Eijanaika* (Shohei Imamura)
5. *Mes petites amoureuses* (Jean Eustache)
6. *Moonlighting* (Jerzy Skolimowski)
7. *Le Pont du nord* (Jacques Rivette)
8. *Smash Palace* (Roger Donaldson)
9. *Too Early, Too Late* (Jean-Marie Straub/Daniele Huillet)
10. *Victor/Victoria* (Blake Edwards)

1983

1. *Francisca* (Manoel de Oliveira)
2. *A Room in Town* (Jacques Demy)
3. *Berlin Alexanderplatz* (Rainer Werner Fassbinder)
4. *Ana* (Antonio Reis/Margarida Cordeiro)
5. *The Golden Eighties* (Chantal Akerman)
6. *The State of Things* (Wim Wenders)
7. *Exposed* (James Toback)
8. *Risky Business* (Paul Brickman)
9. *Sudden Impact* (Clint Eastwood)
10. *Fanny and Alexander* (Ingmar Bergman)

1984

1. *L'Argent* (Robert Bresson)
2. *Love Streams* (John Cassavetes)
3. *Once Upon a Time in America* (Sergio Leone)
4. *Passion* (Jean-Luc Godard)
5. *A Sunday in the Country* (Bertrand Tavernier)
6. *The Three Crowns of the Sailor* (Raul Ruiz)
7. *A nos amours* (Maurice Pialat)
8. *In the White City* (Alain Tanner)
9. *Boy Meets Girl* (Leos Carax)
10. *My Brother's Wedding* (Charles Burnett)

1985

1. *Ran* (Akira Kurosawa)
2. *Lost in America* (Albert Brooks)
3. *Mikey and Nicky* (Elaine May)
4. *After Hours* (Martin Scorsese)
5. *Les Enfants* (Marguerite Duras)
6. *Day of the Dead* (George A. Romero)
7. *Pale Rider* (Clint Eastwood)
8. *City of Pirates* (Raul Ruiz)
9. *Maria's Lovers* (Andrei Konchalovsky)
10. *The Legend of Tianyun Mountain* (Xie Jin)

1986 Ten Best List (prepared for the *Chicago Tribune*)

1. *Shoah* (Claude Lanzmann)
2. *The Sacrifice* (Andrei Tarkovsky)
3. *Something Wild* (Jonathan Demme)
4. *Vagabond* (Agnes Varda)
5. *The Fly* (David Cronenberg)
6. *Trouble in Mind* (Alan Rudolph)
7. *Himatsuri* (Mitsuo Yanagimachi)
8. *Heartbreak Ridge* (Clint Eastwood)
9. *Peggy Sue Got Married* (Francis Ford Coppola)
10. *Blue Velvet* (David Lynch)

INDEX OF NAMES

Abbott, Diahnne, 117
Adams, Brooke, 25
Adjani, Isabelle, 68
Aldrich, Robert, 7
Allan, Ted, 119
Allen, Sally Coryn, 124
Allen, Tom, 108
Allen, Woody, 7, 28, 33, 95, 96, 144, 151
Almendros, Nestor, 24, 139
Altman, Robert, 6, 7, 16, 72, 79, 139
Alvaro, Anna, 191
Andrews, Julie, 28, 31, 32, 86
Arnoul, Françoise, 270
Arquette, Rosanna, 100
Arriagada, Jorge, 193
Ashby, Hal, 7
Attenborough, Richard, 62, 167
Audran, Stéphane, 115, 187

Bakshi, Ralph, 171
Baldwin, Roger, 76
Banzie, Brenda De, 258
Barroso, Mário, 45
Bartel, Paul, 8, 111
Baye, Nathalie, 151, 158, 159, 160
Bazin, André, 21, 22, 72, 222
Beatty, Warren, 75–78
Becker, Jacques, 186
Belmondo, Jean-Paul, 158
Bendix, William, 145
Bennett, Joan, 207
Bergman, Ingmar, 17, 131, 132, 174, 247
Black, Karen, 16–18
Blain, Gérard, 175
Bloom, Verna, 100, 104
Bock, Audie, 210
Boehm, Carl, 215
Boetticher, Budd, 71, 211
Bogart, Humphrey, 158, 214, 225, 227
Bogdanovich, Peter, 8, 71, 72
Borzage, Frank, 32, 44, 81, 164, 226
Bouquet, Carole, 136
Bozzetto, Bruno, 171–73
Brahm, John, 56
Brasseur, Claude, 158, 159
Brazin, André, 226
Brecht, Bertolt, 139, 141, 164, 165
Bresson, Robert, 59, 69, 70, 71, 79, 95, 116, 137, 197, 201, 202, 234
Brickman, Paul, 91–94
Bronson, Charles, 59, 69, 265
Brooks, Albert, 7, 95–99
Brooks, Mel, 186
Bujold, Geneviève, 122
Buñuel, Luis, 135–38, 153
Burch, Noel, 230
Burr, Raymond, 253
Busby, Berkeley, 108

Cagney, James, 223, 224, 225, 227
Caine, Michael, 53
Capra, Frank, 35
Cardinale, Claudia, 32, 244, 265
Carlino, Lewis John, 91
Carpenter, John, 8, 58, 72–74, 106
Carradine, Keith, 122
Carrière, Jean-Claude, 153
Carriere, Mathieu, 41
Cassavetes, John, 7, 116–21
Cassel, Seymour, 117
Cauchy, Daniel, 240
Chabrol, Claude, 72, 132–34, 257, 260
Chandler, Joan, 249
Chaplin, Charlie, 3, 33, 56, 77, 95, 96, 201, 211
Cheech and Chong, 103, 104
Christensen, Benjamin, 232
Cirincione, Richard, 78
Clement, Dick, 186
Coburn, James, 69
Cocteau, Jean, 238
Collier, Constance, 250
Comolli, Jean-Louis, 229
Connery, Sean, 53

Coppola, Francis Ford, 6, 8, 16, 98, 131, 238
Corbett, James J., 224
Corey, Isabelle, 240
Corman, Roger, 8
Coscarelli, Don, 106
Costa, Pedro, 2
Coutard, Raoul, 155
Crenna, Richard, 238
Cruise, Tom, 92
Cukor, George, 242
Cuny, Alain, 158, 159
Curtis, Jamie Lee, 73
Curtiz, Michael, 56

Dali, Salvador, 135
Dall, John, 249
Dano, Royal, 256
Dante, Joe, 8
Day, Doris, 257
Decaë, Henri, 239
Decomble, Guy, 241
Delon, Alain, 244
Demme, Jonathan, 7, 35–39
De Mornay, Rebecca, 93
De Palma, Brian, 6, 7, 73, 97, 174
Depardieu, Gérard, 179
Derek, Bo, 29, 30, 85, 86, 89
Dern, Bruce, 16–17, 67, 68, 69, 70
Devane, William, 16–17
Dietrich, Marlene, 220
Disney, Walt, 171–72
Doazan, Aurele, 159, 160, 161
Dória, Diego, 45
Dressler, Marie, 211
Dreyer, Carl Theodor, 228–33
Duchesne, Roger, 240
Dunne, Griffin, 100
Durant, Will, 76
Duras, Marguerite, 153
Dutronc, Jacques, 151, 154

Eastwood, Clint, 8, 59, 60, 79–83, 267
Edwards, Blake, 7, 28–34, 85–90, 108
Eisenstein, Sergei, 21, 22, 25, 136, 164, 221
Elam, Jack, 267
Esposito, Gianni, 272
Evanson, Edith, 250

Fassbinder, Rainer Werner, 174, 177
Felix, Maria, 272
Ferzetti, Gabriele, 266
Fiorentino, Linda, 102
Fish, Hamilton, 76
Flynn, Errol, 224
Fonda, Henry, 205, 207, 265
Fonda, Jane, 144, 150
Fonda, Peter, 264
Ford, Glenn, 205, 206
Ford, John, 3, 4, 5, 6, 44, 61, 72, 73, 146, 167, 201, 205, 211, 223, 225, 228, 234, 265
Forsythe, John, 255
Fosse, Bob, 7, 151
Frayling, Christopher, 264
Fuller, Samuel, 112–15, 174

Gabin, Jean, 269
Ganz, Bruno, 175
Garner, James, 86
Garr, Teri, 100
Geddes, Barbara Gel, 260
Gegauff, Paul and Danielle, 132
Gere, Richard, 25
Glenn, Pierre William, 188
Godard, Jean-Luc, 19, 44, 77, 95, 112, 131, 144–48, 149–53, 154–57, 158–61, 163, 164, 165, 166, 178, 197, 238
Goldman, Bo, 36
Gosha, Hideo, 183
Goshos, Heinosuke, 211
Granger, Farley, 249
Grant, Cary, 101, 108, 205, 255, 262
Greene, Graham, 62, 63, 64, 65
Gregor, Nora, 232
Griffith, D. W., 5, 140, 169, 223
Gwenn, Edmund, 255

Hagerty, Julie, 96–98
Hallyday, Johnny, 158, 159, 160
Hani, Susumu, 210
Hardwicke, Sir Cedric, 249
Harris, Barbara, 16–17
Hawks, Howard, 31, 56, 70, 71, 72, 73, 74, 120, 201, 205, 211, 212, 223, 225, 234, 255
Hecht, Ben, 67
Hellman, Monte, 7
Helmore, Tom, 261
Hemingway, Mariel, 32
Hepburn, Audrey, 32
Herrmann, Bernard, 70, 261
Herzog, Werner, 174, 177

Higham, Charles, 219
Hill, Walter, 8, 67–71
Hingle, Pat, 82
Hitchcock, Alfred, 3, 5, 6, 7, 9, 16–18, 58, 92, 94, 101, 108, 132, 134, 137, 174, 201, 205, 206, 211, 214, 242, 247–63
Holden, William, 56
Hopper, Dennis, 175, 264
Hudson, Rock, 32
Hughes, Howard, 20, 36–38
Huillet, Danielle, 95
Huppert, Isabelle, 152, 156, 179, 187
Huston, John, 8, 52–54, 241

Ichikawa, Kon, 210
Imai, Tadashi, 210
Imamura Shohei, 182–85
Izumiya, Shigeru, 184

Jacobi, Derek, 63
Jagger, Dean, 225
Jarrett, Cody, 224
Jessel, George, 76

Kael, Pauline, 2, 6, 19
Karina, Anna, 159
Karras, Alex, 90
Kasdan, Lawrence, 122
Kaufman, Philip, 6
Keaton, Buster, 3, 79, 81, 95, 97, 139, 141, 183, 184
Keaton, Diane, 28, 76
Keller, Marthe, 56
Kelly, Grace, 101, 252
Kinugasas, Teinosuke, 211
Kluge, Alexander, 163, 164
Kobayashi, Masaki, 210
Kosinski, Jerzy, 78
Kristofferson, Kris, 122
Kubrick, Stanley, 40
Kurosawa, Akira, 182, 210

Lancaster, Burt, 242
Lang, Fritz, 3, 146, 175, 183, 204–9, 225, 234
Langlois, Henri, 174
Laughton, Charles, 214
Lean, David, 23
Léaud, Jean-Pierre, 158, 159, 160
Lehman, Peter, 87
Le Mat, Paul, 35
Leone, Sergio, 60, 79, 80, 265–68
Lewis, Jerry, 77
Lewis, Joseph H., 4, 5
Lewton, Val, 73
Locke, Sondra, 80, 81, 82, 83
Lucas, George, 7, 8, 71, 193
Luchini, Fabrice, 141
Luhr, William, 87
Lupino, Ida, 226

MacLaine, Shirley, 256
MacLiammoir, Michael, 221
Macready, George, 123
Malick, Terrence, 23–27
Mankiewicz, Joseph, 67
Mann, Michael, 7
Manz, Linda, 24
Marchand, Guy, 179, 187
Marielle, Jean-Pierre, 187
Marlaud, Philippe, 40
Martin, Ross, 87
Marvin, Lee, 113
Marx brothers, 214
Massey, Anna, 216, 217
Massey, Raymond, 217
Masson, Alain, 192
Mathers, Jerry, 257
McGoohan, Patrick, 59
Melendez, Bill, 171
Méliès, Georges, 190
Melville, Jean-Pierre, 71, 238–41
Menezes, Teresa, 45
Meury, Anne-Laure, 41
Miéville, Anne-Marie, 146
Miles, Bernard, 258
Milius, John, 71
Miller, Henry, 76
Miller, Michael, 8
Minnelli, Vincente, 271
Mitchell, Eddy, 187
Mitchum, Robert, 225
Mizoguchi, Kenji, 197–200, 201, 210, 234, 235, 236
Molina, Angela, 136
Momoi, Kaori, 184
Montand, Yves, 144, 150
Moore, Dudley, 28, 32, 33, 85, 86, 89, 96
Moreau, Jeanne, 13
Mori, Masayuki, 235
Morley, Robert, 63, 64

Morricone, Ennio, 266
Morton, Joe, 122
Mulock, Al, 267
Mulvey, Laura, 20
Muret, Paule, 151
Murnau, F. W., 204, 208
Murray, Bill, 103

Nabokov, Vladimir, 20
Nakadai, Tatsuya, 234, 235
Naruse, Mikio, 234–37
Natwick, Mildred, 256
Neenan, Audrie J., 82
Nichols, Mike, 8, 79
Nicholson, Jack, 77
Noiret, Philippe, 186
Novak, Kim, 260, 263

O'Hara, Catherine, 100
Oliveira, Manoel de, 44–48
Olivier, Laurence, 219, 220
Olsen, Christopher, 257
O'Neal, Ryan, 67, 68, 69, 70, 71
Ophuls, Marcel, 167–70
Ophuls, Max, 45, 169
Oshima, Nagisa, 210
Ozu, Yasujiro, 197, 210–13, 234

Peckinpah, Sam, 71, 264
Penn, Arthur, 6
Peppard, George, 32
Pialat, Maurice, 85, 178–81
Piccoli, Michel, 154
Pidgeon, Walter, 205, 206, 207, 225
Pleasence, Donald, 74
Ponti, Carlo, 154
Poupaud, Melvil, 192
Powell, Michael, 214–18
Power, Tyrone, 205
Preminger, Otto, 7, 61–65
Preston, Robert, 86, 90

Quester, Hugues, 192

Radziwilowicz, Jerzy, 154–57
Rafelson, Bob, 7
Raft, George, 226
Ray, Nicholas, 174, 176, 222
Reichenbach, François, 19, 20
Reisz, Karel, 214
Renoir, Jean, 13–15, 56, 61, 88, 164, 166, 201, 212, 234, 269–73
Rey, Fernando, 135
Richards, Dick, 122
Ritter, Thelma, 253
Riviere, Marie, 40
Robain, Jean-Marie, 239
Robards, Jason, 36, 265
Robinson, Edward G., 205
Rohmer, Eric, 40–43, 139–42, 257
Romero, George, 8, 106–11, 186
Rosenberg, Stuart, 59
Rossellini, Roberto, 63, 98, 130–31, 197, 201–3, 203
Rothman, Stephanie, 8
Rowlands, Gena, 116, 117, 119, 120
Rudolph, Alan, 122–25
Ruiz, Raul, 190–93
Russell, Jane, 225

Sarde, Alain, 158
Sarris, Andrew, 4, 5, 6, 56, 108, 207, 223
Sautet, Claude, 146
Schatzberg, Jerry, 6
Schrader, Paul, 7, 71
Schygulla, Hanna, 154, 156
Scorsese, Martin, 6, 7, 8, 16, 71, 79, 100–104, 223, 225, 227
Scott, Randolph, 71
Sears, Fred F., 19
Sellers, Peter, 30
Selznick, David O., 249
Sennett, Mack, 201
Sharif, Omar, 32
Shephard, Sam, 24, 25
Show, Michael, 248
Sidney, Sylvia, 207
Siegel, Don, 8, 58–60, 79, 80
Simon, Michel, 271
Singer, Lori, 122
Slezak, Walter, 232
Spielberg, Steven, 6, 7, 8, 190, 193
Spoto, Donald, 247
Spottiswoode, Roger, 79
Steenburgen, Mary, 37, 38, 234
Stéphane, Nicole, 187
Stevens, Craig, 31
Stewart, James, 249, 251, 252, 255, 257, 260, 262
St. Johns, Adela Rogers, 76

Storaro, Vittorio, 76
Straub, Jean-Marie, 44, 45, 95, 163, 178
Strode, Woody, 267
Sturges, Preston, 67
Sullavan, Margaret, 44, 235
Surtees, Bruce, 59

Takamine, Hideko, 234
Tanner, Alain, 163–66
Tanner, Cécile, 151
Tanney, Sherloque, 89
Tashlin, Frank, 95
Tati, Jacques, 95, 116
Tavernier, Bertrand, 8, 186–89
Terzieff, Laurent, 158, 159, 160
Tracy, Spencer, 205
Trauner, Alexandre, 188
Truffaut, François, 68, 71, 197, 248, 252, 269
Tryon, Thomas, 55
Tsuyuguchi, Shigeru, 183
Tuggle, Richard, 60

Ulmer, Edgar G., 4, 5

Vernon, Howard, 239
Vidor, Charles, 122
Visconti, Luchino, 242–46

Wajda, Andrzej, 154, 156
Walsh, Raoul, 223–27
Warren, Lesley Ann, 89
Wayne, John, 60, 225, 264, 265
Welles, Orson, 3, 19–22, 77, 191, 193, 201, 219–22, 226, 228
Wenders, Wim, 174–77
West, Rebecca, 76
Wilder, Billy, 7, 55–57, 67, 112
William, Richard, 171
Williamson, Nicol, 63
Winner, Michael, 59
Wollen, Peter, 20
Wyler, William, 226, 248

Yared, Gabriel, 152
Young, Freddie, 23

Zeiff, Howard, 96
Zhang-ke, Jia, 2

INDEX OF TITLES

Acts of the Apostles, The (Rossellini), 130
After Hours (Scorsese), 100–104
Age d'or, L' (Buñuel), 192
Age of the Medici, The (Rossellini), 130
Alice in the Cities (Wenders), 175
Alien, 58
Allegro non troppo (Bozzetto), 171–73
All That Jazz (Fosse), 7, 271
Along the Great Divide (Walsh), 224
American Family, An, 99
American Friend, The (Wenders), 174–77
American Guerrilla in the Philippines (Lang), 205, 208
American in Paris, An, 271
Annie Hall (Allen), 7, 144
Artists and Models (Walsh), 225
Asphalt Jungle, The (Huston), 52, 241
Assault on Precinct 13 (Carpenter), 73
Augustine of Hippo (Rossellini), 130
Aviator's Wife, The (Rohmer), 40–43
avventura, L', 116

Babes in Bagdad (Ulmer), 5
Background to Danger (Walsh), 225
Band Wagon, The, 271
Beguiled, The, 80
"Belle Epoque, La" (Renoir), 13–14
Beyond a Reasonable Doubt (Lang), 207, 208
Big Heat, The (Lang), 205, 206, 207, 208
Big Red One, The (Fuller), 112–15
Birds, The (Hitchcock), 3, 16, 70
Birth of a Nation, The, 223
Blaise Pascal (Rossellini), 130–31
Bob le Flambeur (Melville), 238, 240–41
Body Heat (Kasdan), 122
Bonnie and Clyde (Penn), 6
Boudu Saved from Drowning (Renoir), 269, 271
Bowery, The (Walsh), 226
Breakfast at Tiffany's (Edwards), 31, 32
Breathless (Godard), 144, 149, 155, 158, 238
Bride of Glomdale, The (Dreyer), 228, 229, 231
Bridge Too Far, A (Attenborough), 167
Bringing Up Baby (Hawks), 205
British Sounds (See You at Mao) (Godard), 144
Bronco Billy (Eastwood), 79
Bwana Toshi (Hani), 210

Cabinet of Dr. Caligari, The (Lang), 204
Carey Treatment, The (Edwards), 31
"Carry On," 215
Ceremony, The (Oshima), 210
"Chastity" (Rossellini), 130
chien andalou, Un (Buñuel), 135
Chikamatsu Monogatari (Mizoguchi), 199
Children of Paradise, The, 188
Chimes at Midnight (Welles), 219, 220
Chloe in the Afternoon (Rohmer), 40
Choose Me (Rudolph), 123
Chronicle of Anna Magdalena Bach, The, 163
Cinétracts (Godard), 144
Citizen Kane (Welles), 3, 19, 21, 197, 219, 220, 240
Citizen's Band (Handle With Care) (Demme), 38
City of Pirates (Ruiz), 1, 190–93
Clash by Night (Lang), 207, 208
Class (Carlino), 91
Class Relations (Huillet and Straub), 95
Clockmaker, The (Tavernier), 187
Close Encounters, 138, 190
College Swing (Walsh), 225
"Comedies and Proverbs" (Rohmer), 40
Coming Home (Ashby), 7
Comment ça va? (Godard), 148
Contempt, 154
Conversation Piece (Visconti), 246
Coogan's Bluff (Siegel), 59
Coup de torchon (Tavernier), 186–89
Cousin, Cousine, 163

Crazy Mama (Demme), 38
Cries and Whispers (Bergman), 17

Damned, The (Visconti), 246
Dark Command (Walsh), 225
Dark Star (Carpenter), 73
Darling Lili (Edwards), 7, 30, 31, 32
Dawn of the Dead (Romero), 106–11, 186
Day of Wrath (Dreyer), 186
Days of Heaven (Malick), 23–27
Days of Wine and Roses, The (Edwards), 31
Deadly Trackers, The, 112
Dead Pigeon on Beethoven Street, 112
Death in Venice (Visconti), 246
Death Race 2000 (Bartel), 8, 111
Death Watch (Tavernier), 186, 187
Deep, The (Welles), 219
Desperate Journey (Walsh), 224
Detective (Godard), 9, 158–61
Devil Is a Woman, The (Sternberg), 4
Die Nibelungen (Lang), 204, 206
Dirty Harry, 59
Dirty Little Billy, 264
Dirty Money (Melville), 238
Discreet Charm of the Bourgeoisie, The (Buñuel), 135, 138
Distant Drums (Walsh), 224
Donovan's Reef (Ford), 44
Don Quixote (Welles), 219
Doomed Love (Oliveira), 44
Doulos, Le (Melville), 71
Driver, The (Hill), 8, 67–71
Dr. Mabuse the Gambler (Lang), 204, 206
Dr. Zhivago, 23

Earth vs. the Flying Saucers (Sears), 19
Easy Rider, 97, 264
8½ (Fellini), 32
Eijanaika (Imamura), 182–85
El Dorado (Hawks), 56
Elena et les hommes (Renoir), 14, 61
Enfants terribles, Les (Melville), 238
Escape From Alcatraz (Siegal), 58–60
Every Man for Himself (Sauve qui peut (la vie)) (Godard), 149–53, 154
Every Night at Eight (Walsh), 225
Exorcist, The, 191
Experiment in Terror (Edwards), 31, 87

False Movement (Wenders), 175
Family Plot (Hitchcock), 7, 16–18
Fantasia (Disney), 171
Fantôme de la liberté, La (Buñuel), 135
Farewell, My Lovely (Richards), 122
Fedora (Wilder), 7, 55–57, 112
F for Fake (Welles), 19–22, 219
Fighting Mad (Demme), 38
Filming Othello (Welles), 219, 221
Films of Orson Welles (Higham), 219
Firefox (Eastwood), 79
First Name: Carmen (Godard), 160
Fixed Bayonets (Fuller), 112
Floating Clouds (Naruse), 234, 235, 237
Flowers of St. Francis, The (Rossellini), 201–3
Foreign Correspondent (Hitchcock), 255
Forty Guns (Fuller), 113
42nd Street, 271
Francisca (Oliveira), 9, 44–48
French Cancan (Renoir), 269–73
Frenzy (Hitchcock), 17
Front Page, The (Wilder), 57
Full-Up Train, A (Ichikawa), 210
Fury (Lang), 73, 204, 206, 207, 209

Gai savoir, Le (Godard), 144
Gauntlet, The (Eastwood), 60, 80, 81
Gentleman Jim (Walsh), 224
Gertrude (Dreyer), 228
Getaway, The (Peckinpah), 71
Ghostbusters, 103, 116
Gilda (Vidor), 122
Goalie's Anxiety at the Penalty Kick, The (Wenders), 175
Godfather, The (Coppola), 6
Going Hollywood (Walsh), 225
Golden Coach, The (Renoir), 88, 90, 269
Gone With the Wind, 242, 243
Goupi mains rouges (Becker), 186
Grande illusion, La (Renoir), 14, 61, 270
Great Race, The (Edwards), 29, 108
Gun Crazy (Lewis), 5
Gunn (Edwards), 31, 85, 87

Hail Mary (Godard), 158, 159, 160
Halloween (Carpenter), 58, 72–74, 106
Hangmen Also Die (Lang), 208
Hard Times (Hill), 69, 71

Hey, Good Lookin' (Bakshi), 171
High Sierra (Walsh), 53, 227
Honkytonk Man (Eastwood), 79
House of Bamboo (Fuller), 113
Human Condition, The (Kobayashi), 210
Human Desire (Lang), 205, 207, 208
Human Factor, The (Preminger), 7, 61–65
Husbands (Cassavetes), 116
Hypothesis of the Stolen Painting, The (Ruiz), 191

I Know Where I'm Going, 217
I've Always Loved You (Borzage), 81
Ici et ailleurs (Godard), 148
India (Rossellini), 131
Informer, The (Ford), 61
Inheritor, The (Labro), 238
Intolerance (Griffith), 169
Iron Age, The (Rossellini), 130
It's All True (Welles), 219
Ivan the Terrible (Eisenstein), 221

Jackson County Jail (Miller), 8
Jaws (Spielberg), 7, 106
Jonah Who Will Be 25 in the Year 2000 (Tanner), 163–66
Judge and the Assassin, The (Tavernier), 186, 187

Kagemusha (Kurosawa), 182
Kid, The (Chaplin), 211
King of Comedy (Scorsese), 103
Kings of the Road (Wenders), 174, 175
Klansman, The, 112
Kramer vs. Kramer, 116

Lady from Shanghai (Welles), 220
Lancelot du Lac (Bresson), 155
Last Embrace, The (Demme), 38
Laura (Preminger), 61
Lawrence of Arabia, 23
Leaves from Satan's Book (Dreyer), 229
Leopard, The (Visconti), 242–46
Let Joy Reign Supreme (Tavernier), 187
Limelight (Chaplin), 56
Lion Is in the Streets, A (Walsh), 224
Little Big Man, 264
Locket, The (Brahm), 56
Lost in America (Brooks), 95–99
lotta del l'uomo per la sua sopravvivenza, La ("Man's Struggle for Survival") (Rossellini), 130
Loulou (Pialat), 85, 178–81
Love One Another (Dreyer), 229
Love Streams (Cassavetes), 116–21
Lucky Lady, The (Walsh), 226
Ludwig (Visconti), 244, 246

M (Lang), 204, 207
Magnificent Ambersons, The (Welles), 21, 222
Main Event, The, 58
Maltese Falcon, The (Huston), 52
Man Escaped, A (Bresson), 59
Manhattan (Allen), 28, 33
Man Hunt (Lang), 205, 206, 207, 208
Man of Iron (Wajda), 154
Man Who Knew Too Much, The (Hitchcock), 58, 247, 254, 257–59
Man Who Shot Liberty Valance, The, 265
Man Who Would Be King, The (Huston), 8, 52–54
Marnie (Hitchcock), 3, 256
Masculine Feminine (Godard), 112
Master of the House (Dreyer), 229
Matter of Life and Death, A, 216
Me and My Gal (Walsh), 226
Mean Streets (Scorsese), 225
Melvin and Howard (Demme), 35–39
Memory of Justice, The (Ophuls), 167–70
Merrill's Marauders (Fuller), 113
Messiah, The (Rossellini), 130
Metropolis (Lang), 204, 205
Middle of the World, The (Tanner), 165
Mikael (Dreyer), 228, 229, 230, 231
Milky Way, The (Buñuel), 135
Ministry of Fear (Lang), 208
Modern Romance (Brooks), 96, 99
Moonfleet (Lang), 208
Mr. Arkadin (Welles), 219
Mr. Cory (Edwards), 31
Muddy Waters (Imai), 210
My Darling Clementine, 265

Naked Kiss, The (Fuller), 112
Nashville (Altman), 18, 131
New York, New York, 71
Night of the Hunter (Laughton), 214

Night of the Living Dead (Romero), 106, 108
Night Shift, 94
No Regrets for My Youth (Kurosawa), 210
North by Northwest (Hitchcock), 16, 108
Northern Pursuit (Walsh), 224
Numéro deux (Godard), 144–48, 149

Objective Burma (Walsh), 224
Once Upon a Time (Dreyer), 229
Once Upon a Time in the West (Leone), 264–68
One Plus One (Godard), 144
Only Angels Have Wings (Hawks), 74
Open City (Rossellini), 130
Operation Petticoat (Edwards), 31
Ordet (Dreyer), 228, 229
Othello (Welles), 201, 219–22
Other Side of the Wind, The (Welles), 219
Outlaw Josey Wales, The (Eastwood), 8, 60, 80

Paisan (Rossellini), 130
Paradine Case, The (Selznick), 249
Parson's Widow, The (Dreyer), 228, 229, 231
Part Time Work of a Domestic Slave, The (Kluge), 164
Party, The (Edwards), 29, 87
Passage to Marseille (Curtiz), 56
Passion (Godard), 154–57, 160
Passion of Joan of Arc (Dreyer), 229, 231
Peeping Tom (Powell), 8, 214–18
Penthiselea (Wollen and Mulvey), 20
Perceval (Rohmer), 139–42
Perfect Furlough, The (Edwards), 31
Peter Pan (Barrie), 192
Petit théâtre de Jean Renoir, Le (Renoir), 13–15, 56
Phantasm (Coscarelli), 106
Picnic on the Grass (Renoir), 61
Piece of Pleasure, A (Chabrol), 132–34
Pink Panther, The (Edwards), 31, 85
Pinocchio (Disney), 171
Play Misty for Me (Eastwood), 79
Porky's, 92, 94
Pravda (Godard), 144, 145
President, The (Dreyer), 228, 229, 230
Private Lessons, 91
Private Life of Sherlock Holmes, The (Wilder), 57
Prophecy, 58
Psycho (Hitchcock), 3, 16, 134, 192, 205, 214, 226
Pursued (Walsh), 225

Queen's Guards, The (Powell), 215

Race for Your Life, Charlie Brown (Melendez), 171
Raggedy Ann and Andy (William), 171
Raging Bull (Scorsese), 100, 103, 104, 223
Raiders of the Lost Ark, 178
Rain People, The (Coppola), 131
Rancho Notorious (Lang), 206, 208
Real Life (Brooks), 96, 98, 99
Rear Window (Hitchcock), 16, 242, 247, 251–54, 259, 260, 262
Record of a Tenement Gentleman (Ozu), 210–13
Red Badge of Courage, The, 256
Reds (Beatty), 75–78
Red Shoes, The (Powell), 216
Remember My Name (Rudolph), 123
Rescuers (Disney), 171
Return of Frank James, The (Lang), 208
Return of the Pink Panther, The (Edwards), 87
Revolt of Mamie Stover, The (Walsh), 225
Rich and Strange (Hitchcock), 256
Right Stuff, The, 242, 256
Rio Bravo (Hawks), 74
Rio Lobo (Hawks), 56
Riot in Cell Block 11 (Siegel), 58, 59
Rise of Louis XIV, The (Rossellini), 130
Risky Business (Brickman), 91–94
River, The (Renoir), 269, 271
rivoluzione industrial, La (Rossellini), 130
Roaring Twenties, The (Walsh), 224, 225, 227
Robinson Crusoe (Buñuel), 135
Rocco and His Brothers (Visconti), 243
Rogopag (Rossellini), 130
Rope (Hitchcock), 247, 248–51, 252, 254, 259, 261, 262
Rules of the Game (Renoir), 269, 270, 272

Samourai, Le (*The Godson*) (Melville), 71, 238

Saskatchewan (Walsh), 224
Saturday Night and Sunday Morning (Reisz), 214
Scarface (Hawks), 186
Scarlet Letter, The (Wenders), 176
Scarlet Street (Lang), 205, 206, 207, 208
Scenes from a Marriage (Bergman), 131, 132
Searchers, The, 5, 211
Seashell and the Clergyman, The (Dulac), 192
Second Breath (Melville), 238
Secret Beyond the Door, The (Lang), 208
Seven Samurai (Kurosawa), 210
7 Women (Ford), 146
Severed Head, A (Clement), 186
Sgt. Pepper, 67
Shadow of a Doubt (Hitchcock), 16
Shark, 112
Shock Corridor (Fuller), 113
Shootist, The (Siegel), 8
Sierra Madre (Huston), 52
Silence de la mer, Le (Melville), 238–39, 241
Silkwood (Nichols), 79
Silver River (Walsh), 224
"Six Moral Tales" (Rohmer), 40, 139
Small Change, 163
S.O.B. (Edwards), 85, 87
Socrates (Rossellini), 130
Soldier Blue, 264
Sorrow and the Pity, The (Ophuls), 167
Spoiled Children (Tavernier), 186, 187, 189
Star Is Born, A (Cukor), 242
Star Wars (Lucas), 7, 71, 190
Steamboat Bill Jr., 81
Steamboat 'Round the Bend (Ford), 61
St. Louis Blues (Walsh), 225
Story of the Last Chrysanthemums, The (Mizoguchi), 197–200
Strawberry Blonde (Walsh), 224
Stromboli (Rossellini), 202
Struggle in Italy (Godard), 144
Sudden Impact (Eastwood), 79–83
Summer in the City (Wenders), 176
Sunset Boulevard (Wilder), 56, 57
Sur et sous la communication (Godard), 148

Tales of the Taira Clan (Mizoguchi), 199
Tamarind Seed, The (Edwards), 31, 32
Taxi Driver (Scorsese), 227
10 (Edwards), 28–34, 85, 88, 89
terra trema, La (Visconti), 243
Terror Train (Spottiswoode), 79
Testament of Dr. Mabuse, The (Lang), 204
Texas Chainsaw Massacre, 186
That Obscure Object of Desire (Buñuel), 135–38
They Died with Their Boots On (Walsh), 224
They Drive by Night (Walsh), 225
Thief (Mann), 7
Thief of Baghdad, The (Walsh), 226
Thing, The (Hawks), 74
This Land Is Mine (Renoir), 14
Thousand Eyes of Dr. Mabuse, The (Lang), 146, 207
Three Crowns of the Sailor, The (Ruiz), 191
To Catch a Thief (Hitchcock), 101, 254
To Have and Have Not (Hawks), 120
Tokyo Story (Ozu), 210
Toni (Renoir), 269
Too Early, Too Late (Straub), 44
Topaz (Hitchcock), 16
Touch of Evil, 220
Tout va bien (Godard), 144, 150
Treasure of the Sierra Madre, The (Huston), 52
Trial, The (Welles), 219
Tristana (Buñuel), 138
Trouble in Mind (Rudolph), 122–25
Trouble with Harry, The (Hitchcock), 247, 254–57, 259, 262
True Grit, 264
Twilight's Last Gleaming (Aldrich), 7
Two-Lane Blacktop (Hellman), 7
Two People (Dreyer), 228
2001, 63

Ugetsu (Mizoguchi), 197, 210, 235
Uncertain Glory (Walsh), 224
Under Capricorn (Hitchcock), 251
Under Fire (Spottiswoode), 79
Une film comme les autres (Godard), 144
Unfaithfully Yours (Zeiff), 96
Unmarried Woman, An, 138
Utamaro and His Five Women (Mizoguchi), 199

Vampyr (Dreyer), 228
Velvet Vampire, The (Rothman), 8
Vengeance Is Mine (Imamura), 182
Vertigo (Hitchcock), 5, 16, 92, 247, 248, 258, 259–63
Victor/Victoria (Edwards), 85–90
Vincent, Paul, Francois, and the Others (Sautet), 146
Violette (Chabrol), 72
Vladimir and Rosa (Godard), 144
Voyage to Italy (Rossellini), 98, 130, 201

Waltzes from Vienna (Hitchcock), 255
War of the Worlds (Welles's radio broadcast), 19
Warriors, The, 107
Wavelength (Show), 248
Week's Vacation, A (Tavernier), 187, 189
Welcome to L.A. (Rudolph), 123
Western Union (Lang), 208
What Did You Do in the War, Daddy? (Edwards), 87
What Price Glory (Walsh), 226
When a Woman Ascends the Stairs (Naruse), 234–37
While the City Sleeps (Lang), 205, 207, 208
White Heat (Walsh), 223, 224
Wife! Be Like a Rose! (Naruse), 234
Wild Bunch, The (Peckinpah), 264
Wild Rovers (Edwards), 31
Wind From the East (Godard), 144
Without Apparent Motive (Labro), 238
Wizards (Bakshi), 171
Woman in the Window, The (Lang), 206
Woman of Paris, A (Chaplin), 201
Woman Under the Influence, A (Cassavetes), 116

Yojimbo, 211
Yolanda and the Thief (Minnelli), 58
You Only Live Once (Lang), 205, 207, 208
You're a Big Boy Now (Coppola), 6

CPSIA information can be obtained at www.ICGtesting.com
Printed in the USA
LVOW12s1506220814

400465LV00002B/549/P

9 780226 429410